The Celebrated
GEORGE BARRINGTON

1800.

Sketch of George Barrington in the guise of author, 1800. This design was used for the engraved portrait that accompanied 'Barrington's' *An Account of a Voyage to New South Wales.* Courtesy of National Library of Australia.

The Celebrated

GEORGE BARRINGTON

A Spurious Author, the Book Trade, and Botany Bay

NATHAN GARVEY

HORDERN HOUSE

Literature of travel and discovery

First published in 2008 by
Hordern House Rare Books Pty Ltd
77 Victoria Street
Potts Point NSW 2011 Australia

www.hordern.com

Design: Natalie Bowra
Editorial and production: Bridging the Gap
Typesetter: Initial Typesetting Services
Printed in China by Everbest Printing Company

National Library of Australia
Cataloguing-in-Publication Data

Author: Garvey, Nathan.

Title: The celebrated George Barrington : a spurious author,
             the book trade, and Botany Bay / Nathan Garvey.

ISBN: 9781875567546 (hbk.)

Notes: Bibliography.

Subjects: Barrington, George, 1755-1804.
             Book industries and trade–England–History–18th century
             Book industries and trade–England–History–19th century.
             Books and reading–History–18th century.
             Books and reading–History–19th century.
             Popular culture.
             Australia–History–1788-1851.

Dewey Number: 070.50994

CONTENTS

PUBLISHER'S NOTE

The Bibliography presented with this book is the most comprehensive work on the 'Barrington' books assembled to date. However, in recognition of the probability that subsequent variants and new examples of these works will be discovered, Hordern House intends to maintain a digital addenda and corrigenda as a companion to this work, to ensure that bibliographical research into the 'Barrington' books remains as up-to-date as possible.

Please visit the Hordern House website <www.hordern.com> for more information.

ACKNOWLEDGEMENTS

This book began life as a doctoral dissertation undertaken at the University of Sydney. I thank the staff and students of the English department for providing such a stimulating working environment, even during difficult years for Australian universities. In particular, I would like to thank Deirdre Coleman, Helen Hewson and Robert Dixon, who all provided kind support and expert advice at various stages in this project. This book owes a special debt of gratitude to Elizabeth Webby, for her wisdom and encouragement throughout a long and difficult research process; I have benefited tremendously from her generosity and guidance, as well as from her vast store of knowledge on early Australian literature and history. All flaws in this work, of course, are my own.

Thanks are due to Derek McDonnell and Anne McCormick, and everyone at Hordern House. In the midst of panic about the future of scholarly book publishing, it has been a great pleasure to work with a publisher prepared to take the time and trouble to ensure this would be a publication of very high standard. I am deeply grateful to Natalie Bowra, for her wonderful work on the design of this book, to Carolann Martin, for typesetting and corrections, and especially to Kathryn Lamberton, for her careful editing and dedicated efforts to keep the project on track. Special thanks are also due to Matthew Fishburn, who carries off the role of publisher with some style. I thank Hordern House, too, for permission to reproduce images from their excellent collection of 'Barrington' books.

Researching this book has required a great deal of help from the staff of libraries throughout Australia and the United Kingdom. The staff of Fisher Library, University of Sydney, deserve special thanks, and I would also like to acknowledge the assistance of the staff of the State Libraries of Victoria, Queensland and Tasmania, the British Library, the Bodleian Library, the University of Glasgow Library, the Archives Office of New South Wales, and the Public Records Office [now National Archives of the United Kingdom]. I am particularly indebted to the staff of the State Library of New South Wales, and the staff of the National Library of Australia, who have contributed greatly to this project with much valuable assistance over a number of years. Thanks are also due to these two libraries for permission to reproduce images from their extensive collections of 'Barringtonia'.

In the hectic final stages of writing this book, a number of people gave up their valuable time to assist me, often at lamentably short notice. I thank especially Eldar Aliev, Paul Brunton, Gayle Cooper, Ann Morgan Dodge, Paul Eggert, Stephen Ferguson, Ebony Gulliver, Mark Hildebrand, Wallace Kirsop, Leanne McCredden, Andrew Sergeant and Patrick Spedding, for the provision of various kinds of advice, information and generous help.

It would be impossible to list all the people who have given me their love and support over the course of this project; my heartfelt thanks, then, are collectively extended to all my family and friends, who make it all worthwhile. I must, however, acknowledge the immense contribution of my parents, Ian and Janet Garvey, and thank them for all they have done for me, and the consistently good humour with which they have done it.

Last but never least, I offer this book to Tara Johnson, with love, and eternal gratitude for her endless kindness, wit, patience, and proofreading.

INTRODUCTION

*I*n 1807, an English newspaper warned its readers about a man 'who said his name was Bond', who was travelling through small towns in Middlesex and Essex 'endeavouring to obtain subscriptions for a new History of Botany Bay, price 10s. 6d. of which he pretended to be the author'. This Bond apparently had promised to deliver his work to the Post Office of each town 'within three weeks at the longest':

> He might, however, have said within three hours; for those persons with whom he succeeded in obtaining the half-guineas, received each a little trumpery pamphlet, not worth a shilling, almost immediately, sent by the first hand he met when he had left the town scarcely half a mile.[1]

Not all the deceptions in the selling of books about the peculiar new British colony on the other side of the world were so swiftly revealed, however. In the same period, one might have purchased an even more expensive *History of New South Wales*, full of plagiarised material and spuriously attributed to a famous pickpocket and transported convict named George Barrington. For a handful of pennies, you might also have secured one of the many pamphlets or chapbooks that purported to tell the story of Barrington's life. This book examines the many works produced in England, and indeed throughout the Western world, which exploited the Barrington name, and explores the curious circumstances under which they were published.

An international celebrity in his own day, and a famous name through most of the nineteenth and early twentieth centuries, George Barrington (c. 1758–1804) has been all but forgotten in recent years. An apparently genteel young Irishman known for his sartorial elegance, his command of the etiquette of romantic sensibility, and for his prowess at picking pockets, Barrington lived under the constant scrutiny of a public fascinated by the incongruity between his fashionable appearance and his tawdry 'profession'. After his transportation to New South Wales in 1791, Barrington found some measure of grace in a pardon and subsequent career as a police constable in the settlement at Parramatta. The two-hundredth anniversary of Barrington's death in New South Wales passed without notice in 2004 – yet this anonymity is a fate Barrington himself might have preferred. In the period in which he was active in his apparent criminal career, Barrington constantly and strenuously denied allegations levelled against him, and represented himself as the victim of a dedicated press campaign to besmirch his character. While there is little doubt that his protestations of innocence were often disingenuous, it is also certain that the legend – the growth of a reputation as 'the Prince of Pickpockets' – considerably outgrew Barrington's actual achievements as a thief. Long after the cessation of his criminal career, long after his transportation and his death, references to Barrington's prodigious abilities were still current, growing only more implausible with time. The strength of the legend was such that some forty years after Barrington's transportation to New South Wales, Edgar Allan Poe would cite him as a definitive example of the fundamental amorality of genius, in the process comparing Wordsworth's skills as a poet unfavourably to Barrington's as a pickpocket.[2]

The dubious nature of much of the contemporary material on Barrington makes his life something of a historical enigma, as his most recent biographer points out.[3] Yet in itself the legend of 'the celebrated Barrington', master thief of the late Georgian age, is more readily recoverable, and potentially constitutes a more important subject of inquiry, than a speculation on the details of the real George Barrington's life. For it is this figure, forged initially in the crucible of a scandal-hungry newspaper press, and broadening into a phenomenon of eighteenth- and nineteenth-century popular publishing, that has the capacity to teach us much about the print culture of the age, and how that culture shaped history.

English popular culture, of course, has a long history of celebrating notable outlaws in print.[4] But if there was nothing unusual in 'the celebrated Barrington' being made the subject of popular biographies and, in later years, novels and plays, there was a unique twist in the Barrington story in the form of the spurious authorial career concocted for the famed thief. While Barrington spent his latter years quietly in the antipodes, in Europe and America he would become still more celebrated as the author of a number of popular books – works which in actuality he had nothing whatsoever to do with. The books attributed to Barrington constituted a far more elaborate and extensive body of work than the usual run of chapbook memoirs and 'gallows speeches' which astute booksellers and printers sometimes produced to capitalise on the fame of notorious criminals in the eighteenth century. The original allonymous Barrington text – a narrative first published in 1795 as *A Voyage to New South Wales*, which subsequently appeared in a dizzying number of republications, translations and adaptations – was a cleverly structured mix of plagiarism and fiction that represented the supposed author in the guise of an authoritative travel writer and historian of the infant colony. The formula of *A Voyage to New South Wales* was followed, more or less successfully, in a number of further publications, and eventually the Barrington name became so well known as a brand in popular publishing that it was appropriated for texts with little or no relevance to the supposed author's life experience. The 'Barrington' books never created the kind of controversy associated with other eighteenth-century literary frauds[5], and the booksellers responsible continued using his name with impunity for years. In far-sundered New South Wales, the ex-convict was hardly in a position to prevent these publications. Barrington did become aware of the misuse of his name, however, and was said to have

> expressed a very considerable degree of displeasure ... at his name being affixed to a narrative, which he knew only by report, as being about to be published, and which subsequently did appear, under a deceptious mask.[6]

While certainly 'deceptious', Barrington's putative authorial career was significant in that it helped introduce the English colony in New South Wales to a readership which had little access to the original sources from which the 'Barrington' books had been plagiarised. The Botany Bay scheme – a colony founded by and for transported British convicts – was the somewhat controversial initiative of the conservative government of William Pitt.[7] Once news reached Britain (in 1789) that the colony had been established, risible public comment on the kind of nation likely to be formed by these anti-social rejects quickly gave way to curiosity about the natural and cultural topographies of the land and its Indigenous peoples, and to a genuine interest in the progress of the colony. Narrative accounts from the colony were thus in high demand in the early years of its existence. Much of the material that was published, however, took the form of expensive works aimed at an exclusive market – a genteel readership for whom a well-stocked library of recent exploration literature was a solid signifier of their position in enlightenment society.[8] Yet as William St Clair and others have shown, the shape of the English 'reading nation' was changing in the late eighteenth century, with a rapid expansion in literacy among the middling and lower classes of society being matched by a more commercially focused, entrepreneurial brand of bookselling and publishing.[9] The books published in Barrington's name were products of this changing market, and the 'Barrington' brand provided an innovative way to rehash second-hand material for the burgeoning readership among the lower orders of British society.

The recognition that the 'Barrington' books were in fact counterfeit productions is not new. A review in the *Gentleman's Magazine* evinced a healthy scepticism about *A Voyage to New South Wales* on its first appearance in 1795[10], and John West's *History of Tasmania* (1852) correctly identified a later 'Barrington' work as a plagiarism concocted by 'ingenious booksellers'.[11] At the end of the nineteenth century, the bookseller and scholar E. A. Petherick wrote a number of articles pointing out the dubious nature and origins of the books[12], and in the early twentieth century, the book collector and bibliographer J. A. Ferguson showed the extent of the fraud with his survey of the many different works produced under the Barrington name.[13] A more recent work on early Australian books concludes emphatically that 'there is no question that all the books ascribed to Barrington are completely fraudulent and that he had no share in them'[14], and in her edited version of one 'Barrington' text, Suzanne Rickard has presented an account of the 'publishing forgery' which was perpetrated under this name.[15]

Yet the myth of the pickpocket–author has proved a difficult one to completely dispel. A rash of press articles on Barrington which appeared in the later nineteenth and early twentieth centuries found the story of the 'convict historian' an irresistible one, especially as it coexisted with a wealth of historical fiction romanticising Barrington's life.[16] Thus the first quasi-scholarly biography of Barrington, R. S. Lambert's *The Prince of Pickpockets*, accepted the books written under Barrington's name as the genuine testimony of its subject[17], and even Ferguson was prepared to leave the door at least a fraction ajar on the question of Barrington's literary career.[18] With scholarly equivocation and credulity on the one hand, and a tradition of romantic embroidery on the other, it is scarcely surprising that the myth of Barrington the author survives to this day.[19] On the Internet, that superhighway of information of all degrees of reliability, one still finds numerous attributions to Barrington of the celebrated 'Prologue' which poked fun at the reformed pickpocket and his fellow involuntary colonists:

> From distant climes, o'er wide-spread seas we come,
> Though not with much éclat or beat of drum;
> True Patriots all; for be it understood
> We left our country for our country's good.[20]

The persistent confusion and uncertainty about the works attributed to Barrington at least partly stems from the fact that little scholarly work has previously been done on the history of the books themselves. This book seeks to address this deficiency, to contribute to a greater understanding of the significance of the 'Barrington' books by means of a careful study of their publishing history. A wider assumption of this book is that George Barrington – the attributed author and/or subject of these books – needs to be understood not only as a historical personage, but as a figure generated within the print cultures of the late eighteenth and early nineteenth centuries. For the capital that the printers and booksellers of the period traded on with their appropriation of 'the celebrated Barrington' had clearly been produced through the press's earlier transformation of Barrington into a larger-than-life notorious celebrity. The history of the 'Barrington' books, then, is seen here as a single development beginning with Barrington's first arrival on the public stage in 1775, progressing through the early fascination of the newspaper press and the public, into mythologising with the biographical narratives, and culminating in the spurious authorial career.

The first chapter of this book, 'The Prince of Pickpockets', traces Barrington's rise to fame and notoriety in the late eighteenth century. From his spectacular debut in 1775, Barrington represented a figure of great interest to the British public, later growing into international fame, and the nature and course of this fascination is examined here through a range of contemporary sources. While structured as an account of Barrington's criminal career and his time in the public spotlight, this chapter focuses particularly on the role of the newspaper press in creating and defining the Barrington phenomenon, though Barrington's spirited attempts to reclaim his reputation are also detailed. The chapter closes with Barrington's final trial and conviction in 1790, an event that was to signal his departure from the public stage and prove the cue for the book trade to assume control over his 'life' and legacy.

The second chapter, 'The *Lives* of George Barrington', outlines the publishing history of the biographies of Barrington that appeared after his sentence of transportation in 1790. While Barrington's background and criminal activities had often been the subject of press speculation over the course of his career, these works purported to establish the facts of Barrington's life and, while clearly unreliable, they have often served as the basis for modern historians' attempts to retell the Barrington story. While numerous biographies were published up until the late 1820s, these works were all derived from two prototypes, both published as *Memoirs of George Barrington*, which were speedily concocted by London booksellers and published immediately after Barrington's final trial and conviction in 1790. Particular attention is given, in this chapter, to the different ways in which these two prototype texts constructed the Barrington story, how each related to the conventions of eighteenth-century criminal biography, and how the booksellers who originally published them attempted to gain ascendancy in the market for their respective texts. This chapter then goes on to chart the process by which these texts were appropriated by other publishers, showing how they were reshaped as chapbooks and in other forms, and suggesting reasons why the same biographical texts on Barrington were republished over a period of nearly forty years.

The third chapter, 'Under a Deceptious Mask: Barrington as Author', examines the fraudulent use of Barrington's name in the publication of a number of works from 1795. The story of the original 'Barrington' publication, A Voyage to New South Wales, is given prominence, and the nature of this text and the circumstances of its publication are examined in some detail. The chapter also explores how the original 'Barrington' text was appropriated by a number of different publishers and adapted into different forms, and how the success of the text resulted in the Barrington name being applied to a number of further narratives. As will become clear, Barrington's spurious authorial career was a phenomenon that needs to be understood in the context of the trade practices of marginal publishers struggling to carve out a niche for themselves in the changing world of bookselling at the turn of the nineteenth century. Special attention is therefore given in this chapter to identifying the personnel involved in the production of the 'Barrington' books, and elucidating their histories in the book trade.

The work concludes with a comprehensive bibliography of the 'Barrington' books published in the period 1790–1840, which both supports and draws on the publishing history outlined in the previous chapters. Particular attention is paid to establishing the chronology of the 'Barrington' works, identifying the various states of the texts and discerning the textual relationships between different publications. The bibliographic data presented here should prove a useful resource for those interested in early Australian books and late Georgian popular literature alike.

This is a book about the 'Barrington' books, the main aim of which is to describe, understand and clarify a body of work that has long been regarded as a curiosity of early Australian literature. But in a broader sense it is also an inquiry into the print cultures of the late eighteenth and early nineteenth centuries and, more particularly, the somewhat shadowy world of popular publishing in this period. It is hoped, then, that this book will prove useful not only to book collectors and scholars of Australian history, but also to those interested in the history of the book in the Romantic period more generally. It is also hoped that through an exploration of how this particular figure – the 'celebrated George Barrington' – was created and commodified by the press, it may be possible to gain some new insights into the broader processes by which the culture of celebrity is produced and consumed. The impact of celebrity in defining or redefining the cultural artefact, of course, is a theme that resonates as powerfully through our own time as it did in the age of George Barrington.

CHAPTER ONE

The Prince of
PICKPOCKETS

*I*n late eighteenth-century Britain, the name Barrington was a famous one. An Irish comic actor, John Barrington, had developed a reputation as 'the pre-eminent stage Irishman of his day' over an almost forty-year career in the theatres of Dublin, London, and most of the stages in between.[1] An Irish barrister, parliamentarian and author named Jonah Barrington was just rising to prominence.[2] There was also an English baronet family of Barringtons – whose seat was Barrington Hall in Essex – who maintained an interest in the House of Commons in this period.[3] Above all, there was the family of John Shute Barrington, a theological writer and MP who was elevated to the Irish peerage in 1720.[4] The children of this first Lord Barrington included four sons remarkable for the range of their worldly success – a politician who held high positions in government for over thirty years, a bishop, an admiral, and a judge who was also a noted antiquarian and Fellow of the Royal Society.[5] In short, this was an extraordinary aristocratic family, 'eminently distinguished for Rank of Talents', as one contemporary newspaper put it.[6] Yet when late eighteenth-century Britain read about a man often described as 'the celebrated Barrington', 'the noted Barrington' or 'the ingenious Mr. Barrington', it was reading about a differ-ent man from any of the above – a man whose claim to fame, as

GEORGE BARRINGTON.

Published Feb. 1. 1810. by ...

Portrait of Barrington, published in 1810. Hordern House Rare Books.

much as he sought to avoid it, was as the greatest thief of his generation.

An early critical work on popular culture, Charles Mackay's *Memoirs of Extraordinary Public Delusions and the Madness of Crowds*, reflected on the curious 'popular admiration for great thieves' in English history:

> [whether] it be that the multitude, feeling the pangs of poverty, sympathise with the daring and ingenious depredators who take away the rich man's superfluity, or whether it be the interest that mankind in general feel for the records of perilous adventures, it is certain that the populace ... look with admiration upon great and successful thieves.[7]

More recent scholars, while allowing the antiquity of the English cultural tradition of popular veneration of robbers, have seen the eighteenth century as a critical period in the development of the 'cult of crime'.[8] Christopher Hibbert's influential study, *The Roots of Evil*, argues that English culture of this time indulged, as no era before, in the 'romance of crime'.[9] This romanticisation appears to have been made possible by a progressive decline in violence and violent crime in England through the eighteenth century, a trend Robert Shoemaker attributes to changing attitudes, particularly amongst the gentry, towards the social (un)acceptability of violent actions.[10] Perhaps it is symptomatic of this growing repugnance for antisocial violence that the most famous thief of the late eighteenth century was not a bold, macho highwayman, but a sophisticated, elegant pickpocket who went by the aristocratic name George Barrington. That this may have been something of an epochal shift is worth considering; though the pickpocket would seem to have little of the refractory glamour attached to the highwayman, this figure was perhaps more attuned to the spirit of the age. At least one contemporary writer was prepared to risk charges of foppery by announcing his preference toward 'being genteely eased of my purse by the accomplished Barrington, to being knocked down and robbed by a villainous footpad'.[11]

Yet while the pickpocket Barrington followed a criminal course fundamentally dissimilar to the bold robbers 'whose peculiar chivalry formed at once the dread and delight of England'[12], he can nonetheless be placed in the tradition of quasi-heroic popular thieves stretching back to Robin Hood and beyond. Comments made by foreign visitors surprised by Barrington's 'great reputation' echo the bemusement of earlier visitors in the popular reception of British criminals of previous eras.[13] But it was the magnitude of the reputation itself, rather than the man behind it, which was the most salient point of comparison between Barrington and earlier criminals who had captured the

public imagination. If Barrington was able to maintain somewhat
more control over his 'public image' than, for example, Jack
Sheppard – whose feats of escape became so exaggerated that
Defoe was able to represent him as 'a Creature something more
than Man, a Protœus, Supernatural'[14] – all his considerable skills
at self-representation could not prevent the growth of a reputation as a super-thief, the 'Prince of Pickpockets'.[15]

The apocryphal nature of much that was written about the famed
pickpocket leaves the details of his life, particularly his early years,
shrouded in obscurity. Barrington made repeated claims to being
by profession a surgeon[16], and it does seem likely that he had
some medical training. The philosopher and prison reformer
Jeremy Bentham found Barrington acting as a medical officer
while on the prison hulks in Woolwich in the late 1770s, a version
of events supported by the fact that Barrington was once
identified in court by a man 'who had been in the care of him at
the hulks'.[17] This in itself does little to clarify Barrington's background, however. While arguing that eighteenth-century medical
practitioners should not be automatically caricatured as quacks,
Irvine Loudon has emphasised the profound diversity among
those who identified themselves as medical practitioners, noting
'the absence of a clear distinction between the orthodox or regular
practitioner and the unorthodox irregular or quack'.[18] Moreover,
as medicine had not yet become a clearly defined profession, it
was not uncommon that 'educated men … "took up" medicine as
a hobby or as a means of helping their less fortunate neighbours'.[19] Barrington, whose articulate speeches in court suggest
that he was well educated, may have fallen into this latter category
as easily as into the former.

Of course, the post-1790 biographies of Barrington, which
sensationalised his 'life', assumed criminal activity was his main
livelihood before and after leaving Ireland. The version of the

Memoirs of George Barrington that would become the most influential account of Barrington's life casts its protagonist in a particularly incorrigible light, representing his claims to being a surgeon as nothing more than a ruse, just another in the series of impostures which, for that text, defined Barrington's identity.[20] In this version of his 'life', Barrington runs away from a grammar school in Dublin and joins a company of travelling players, where he receives his training both in dissimulation and in crime.[21] While this would seem a very convenient way of constructing Barrington's background to fit his later life, it is not out of the question that he had become a professional thief and gentlemanly impostor very early on. The *Morning Post* of Friday, 27 October 1775, reported that on the previous day, 'a young man with the appearance and dress of a gentleman, was detected picking a gentleman's pocket in the park'. On that occasion, the ignominy of a trial was spared the genteel pickpocket, but a traditional form of rough justice was meted out: the alleged offender 'was delivered to the mob, by whom he was conducted to the canal'.[22]

If the subject of this report was in fact Barrington, he was apparently undeterred from the practice of picking pockets, and was quickly to become familiar with more formal legal proceedings. Barrington's arrival in the public sphere was, moreover, a truly sensational event. The London papers had been carefully detailing the movements of one Count Orlov, a visiting Russian nobleman known for ostentatious displays of wealth.[23] On Friday, 27 October 1775, Orlov attended Covent Garden theatre. As the papers the following week had it, while the nobleman was putting on his coat in the lobby after the performance,

> he felt a man's hand in his pocket, and instantly missed his snuff-box; he seized the person directly, and received his box; the man was taken into custody, and carried before the Magistrates in Bow-street

on Saturday morning. He denied taking the box, but said he received it from another. He said he was a surgeon, and a native of the city of Cork in Ireland. He was committed for further examination on Wednesday. The box is valued at about 30,000l. there being two pictures set with large brilliants.[24]

This famous incident, aside from its importance as Barrington's debut, is a useful illustration of the kind of reportage that prevailed in the late eighteenth century. Newspaper reports were not considered to be literary property, and they were plagiarised in wholesale fashion, or else traded in an *ad hoc* manner – depending on the current state of the ever fluid politics of press ownership and editorial policy. The above report, which appeared in the *Gazetteer and New Daily Advertiser*, also appeared word for word in the *London Chronicle*. The *Morning Chronicle* printed the same paragraph, adding some intelligence about the place of residence and movements of Orlov in the theatre district – and an identical version to this also appeared in the *Middlesex Journal*. By the time the report got to the weekly papers, the editors needed only to abbreviate the report a little and append the conclusion: 'on further examination he was acquitted'.[25]

At Bow Street Public Office, just a few doors down from the Theatre Royal, Covent Garden, Barrington was to begin his career in providing the public with a different kind of theatre. When his hearing resumed on 1 November, Barrington's cause was aided immensely by the non-appearance of Orlov, or any other material witness. The two constables at the theatre testified, but as they could only produce hearsay evidence Barrington was bound to be released. Nevertheless, he treated the audience on hand at the Public Office to a convincing performance of innocence that the newspapers related to the public at large. The *Gazetteer and New Daily Advertiser* of Thursday, 2 November, described a 'genteel looking young man ... of a fashionable appearance' who 'seemed greatly distressed, and sensible of the disagreeable predicament he stood in'. On acquittal, and after a lecture from the magistrate Sir John Fielding, Barrington 'burst out into a flood of tears', insisted on his innocence and, as if to acknowledge the theatricality of the whole proceeding, 'made a low obeisance to the Bench'.[26] The press was fascinated and, on this occasion, overwhelmingly sympathetic to Barrington. The *London Chronicle* described in some detail the appearance of this 'young gentleman', and further related the gossip that Barrington was 'said to be heir to a good fortune'.[27] Indeed, the young man so neatly resembled the fashionable 'man of feeling', the idealised hero of sentimental novels[28], that he was generally presumed to be innocent as he claimed. Ironically, it was the archetypal muck-raking scandal sheet, the *Morning Post*, which reacted most approvingly to the 'well applied humanity of the bench' in releasing Barrington, and echoed the 'momentary noise of approbation at his release' by commenting that

> If external attestations, and a most pleading and affecting sense of his unfortunate situation, may be at all allowed to govern our opinion, we may with reason conclude that this young fellow had been made a tool of by some experienced villain, who, after committing the felony, transferred his custody [of Orlov's snuff-box].[29]

It was no mean feat to get a sympathetic reception from the scandal-hungry London press, and the credence given to Barrington's profession of his innocence is best testified to by the fact that his name was not given in any of the newspaper reports of the incident. The tears, in particular, seem to have been an inspired act on Barrington's part – though how far they were a calculated gambit remains to be seen, given that he was still a very young man and probably terrified by the potential consequences of the crime he was charged with. In conjunction with his fashionable appearance, Barrington's tears differentiated him from the brute criminal underclass paraded daily before the magistrates at Bow Street. They showed him to be possessed of the cherished virtue of a heightened sensibility, and what is more, seemed to provide unconscious testimony to his innocence. Describing France in the 1770s and 80s, Simon Schama has pointed out that in 'this first hot eruption of the Romantic sensibility',

> tears were especially prized as evidence not of weakness but of sublimity. They were cherished precisely because (it was assumed) they were unstoppable: the soul directly irrigating the countenance. Tears were the enemy of cosmetics and the saboteur of polite disguise.[30]

Contemporary newspaper reports show that tears remained a standard part of Barrington's repertoire throughout his early years in the public eye, and it was only much later – when the 'cult of sensibility' had ebbed – that they were denounced as 'tears perhaps that could start on all suitable occasions'.[31]

Barrington's period of anonymous grace would not last, however, and the *Morning Post* was to play a significant role in his downfall. The *Post* had been started in 1772, but it was the commencement as editor of the Reverend Henry Bate in 1775 that transformed it into 'a notorious success'.[32] Initiating what Lucyle Werkmeister has described as 'the age of the scandal sheet', Bate's *Morning Post* introduced a style of journalism geared toward entertainment rather than information, with a particular specialisation in 'gossip and abuse'.[33] This material was designed to be scurrilous and vitriolic enough so that Bate and the other proprietors of the *Post* could supplement the revenue from advertisements with a sideline in extortion and blackmail, euphemistically described as 'suppression fees'.[34] The *Morning Post*'s 'anecdotes' almost invariably centred on the fashionable world, and the potentially lucrative peccadillos of the upper ranks of society, but it was evidently thought worthwhile to expose a pretender to these circles. On 4 December 1776, a paragraph appeared in the *Post*, and also in the *Public Ledger*, naming Barrington as the man who had been tried for the theft of Prince Orlov's snuff-box.[35] The paragraph labelled him an infamous impostor who had infiltrated fashionable circles by claiming that he was a relative of Lord Barrington. The *Post* also stated that the Saturday previous, this same man had been 'detected picking pockets' in the House of Lords. The author of the paragraph could well have been the Reverend William Jackson, editor of the *Public Ledger* at the time, who had earned the nickname 'Doctor Viper' for his unrivalled expertise in defamatory personal attacks.[36] Impostor or not, Barrington joined battle as any late eighteenth-century gentleman concerned to protect his reputation might: he wrote a letter to the editor.

Robert Shoemaker has shown that as violence became increasingly scandalous and unacceptable in genteel circles through the eighteenth century, print media became a more and more common site of conflict.[37] Always concerned to represent himself as a natural inhabitant of the polite world, Barrington was aware of the power of words to build or to destroy reputations, and over the course of his career he published a number of letters in London newspapers, attempting to defend himself from various imputations.[38] Barrington's first letter to the papers, dated the same day the defamatory paragraph appeared in the *Morning Post* and the *Public Ledger* and published the following day in the *Morning Chronicle*[39], shows the lengths to which he was prepared to go to protect his character. While nominally a letter 'To the Printer of the Morning Chronicle', Barrington's letter, printed on the front page amidst other advertisements, was certainly a paid insertion – for that matter, the paragraph Barrington protested against may also have been financed by some party with a grievance against the young man.[40] In his letter, Barrington makes the imputation that he was the victim of a libellous assertion on the part of a mercenary gossip-writer. One wonders whether he had been given an opportunity to pay 'suppression fees', and was unwilling or unable to do so.

In his fascinating case study of one famous scandal of the late 1770s, John Brewer argues that eighteenth-century newspapers provided a site

> where public rumour, news, and intelligence could circulate as if it were printed conversation. Freedom of the press in this period meant not only freedom from government control but freedom of access – not just to information, but to the pages of the press itself in order to transmute opinions into news. The producer of a paper was not so much an editor, shaping its opinions, as a technician, making available a new means of transmitting the disparate opinions of the public at large. The press was thus very open to manipulation.[41]

While apparently not able to prevent his denouncement as an impostor and a pickpocket, Barrington attempted to refute the offending paragraph and rescue his reputation with his own pen. Supposedly written by a third party and signed 'A Foe to Detraction', Barrington's letter to the *Morning Chronicle* appealed to that paper's status as a reputable publication standing against the sleazy muckraking of papers like the *Morning Post* and the *Public Ledger*. The letter admitted that Barrington was indeed the person who had been examined over the Orlov theft – but pointed out that that allegation 'appearing groundless ... was dismissed, to the satisfaction of a crouded audience, and in no sense to the discredit of the person accused'.[42] The letter also admitted that Barrington had recently been in the gallery of the House of Lords, where he was recognised by 'a news-collector or paragraph-monger' – in other words, a hack who made his living by spreading gossip and blackmailing society figures in his 'paragraphs'. As Barrington tells it, that 'paragraph-monger' informed the usher about Barrington's examination in relation to the Orlov theft. Barrington claimed that he was 'thereupon courteously desired to withdraw', which, owing to 'the respect he entertained for the noble assembly convened', and notwithstanding his avowed innocence in the Orlov affair, he did.

Both versions of the *Memoirs of George Barrington*, the 1790 biographies which were subsequently pirated and adapted into numerous different forms[43], state that after this incident Barrington was arrested and confined in Tothill Fields Bridewell for uttering 'menaces' against a 'Mr G——', supposedly the same 'paragraph-monger' who had started all the trouble in the House of Lords.[44] This version of events seems to be largely fictional, however. For the 'menaces', Barrington is said to have been detained in Tothill Fields Bridewell for 'a considerable time', but in fact it was less than a fortnight between the letter Barrington wrote to the *Morning Chronicle* and his next arrest, for picking the pocket of Ann Dudman at Drury-Lane on Wednesday, 18 December 1776.[45] Certainly, the 'menaces' story scarcely tallies with the usual accounts of the fashionable, slender, foppish George Barrington. In the letter to the *Morning Chronicle* of 5 December 1776, he threatens his detractors with only 'the full redress offered by the law'.

If Barrington was concerned enough with the protection of his reputation to advertise in newspapers, and make threats (if only with legal action) towards those who had exposed or defamed him, it is somewhat surprising that he should have been arrested for picking pockets again so shortly afterwards. While it is not the purpose of the present study to surmise about the motivations behind Barrington's criminal career, it is worth pointing out the explanation put forward in one version of the *Memoirs of George Barrington*, that the fallout from the House of Lords affair and subsequent public exposure had left Barrington with a reputation 'completely blasted':

> ... entry to all decent company was absolutely shut against him, and
> he was set down as a professed impostor, and a common pick-pocket
> ... From this time forward, being precluded from all intercourse with
> polished or respectable society, he was, by inevitable necessity,
> obliged to descend to all the mean practices and arts of a common
> and professed pilferer ...[46]

But if Barrington was a pickpocket by profession from late 1776 onwards, he certainly never made any admission to that effect. On the contrary, he continued to cultivate the appearance of victim; his was always a character unfairly injured, with a sensibility far too refined for the trials fate was forcing him to endure. Indeed, this was a hand Barrington would sometimes overplay. In a letter written to Ann Dudman in January 1777, pleading with her to stop the prosecution, Barrington melo-dramatically illustrated the 'unhappy situation':

> [from which] you have it in your power to extricate me without
> sustaining the smallest injury ... innocent or guilty I have suffered
> severely, suffered more than you can think or suppose; my character,
> if not totally lost, is injured in the highest degree; my confinement
> and the manner in which I have been exposed I shall not mention,
> though I am certain they must have the greatest weight in an humane
> and feeling mind, and by such would be considered as a sufficient
> punishment even for a guilty person; may this consideration animate
> your heart ...[47]

On this occasion, Barrington's audience was evidently not sufficiently swayed by his suffering sensibility, and the trial went ahead at the Old Bailey. The letter, which was admitted as evidence for the prosecution, probably did little to help Barrington's cause as it remained ambiguous, to say the least, on the question of his culpability for the crime.

With this new trial so soon after the House of Lords affair, Barrington's 'character' received predictable treatment in the press. The *Morning Post* advertised the trial of 'the famous George Barrington' on the morning of 16 January, and several newspapers carried gloating reports of Barrington's spiral into criminal status. A particularly prosaic newspaper report on Barrington's first appearance at the Old Bailey described him decked out in the full sartorial swagger of a fashionable man-about-town:

> [Barrington] is a very genteel man, about twenty-one, and very far from athletic; his hair dressed a-la-mode; cloaths quite in the taste; a fine gold-headed taper cane, with suitable tassels, and elegant Artois buckles. In short, (says our correspondent) he is the *genteelest* thief ever remembered to have been seen at the Old-Bailey, and it is a *great pity* he should be condemned to so *vulgar* an employment as ballast-heaving.[48]

The editors of the London dailies were perhaps compensating for their credulity in their treatment of Barrington after the Orlov affair, but there were other subtexts to their celebration of his disgrace. While a romantic notion of the importance of sensibility and the idealisation of the 'man of feeling' was an important emerging discourse, there was still a strong current of thinking which saw such displays as unmanly, and somehow threatening to the social order.[49] In the press reports of Barrington's conviction and punishment, it is possible to read not only righteous contentment that a thief and impostor was getting his just rewards, but *schadenfreude* about the public punishment of a young man of fashion.

Barrington's famed fashion sense, so often commented on in the contemporary press, recalled the much caricatured 'macaroni' subculture of the early 1770s.[50] Though Barrington was never known to dress in quite the extreme fashion associated with the macaroni, his always elegant and up-to-date deportment was enough to justify such an identification for the *Morning Post*, who referred to him as 'the Macaroni pickpocket'.[51] In terms of public perception, there were perhaps more important points of connection between Barrington and the macaroni. Amelia Rauser has argued that the reaction to the extravagance of macaroni fashion represented a fundamental change in social attitudes, where 'the old acceptance of social artifice as a necessary part of public life was giving way to a new fear of the deceptiveness, corruption, and arbitrariness of manners'.[52] Barrington's dress and manners could be seen to mask an even more sinister threat to society than that of effeminacy – a direct threat to property and to the stability of the system of ranks and degrees which maintained the social order – and the slippage of this fashionable criminal figure seemed to provide confirmation of the implicit dangers of social mobility and 'self-fashioning'.[53] And yet, just as Rauser has shown in relation to the macaroni, the careful newspaper descriptions of Barrington's public appearances betrayed an ambivalence about this curious figure. Like the macaroni, 'the celebrated Barrington' was to provide both a 'cautionary tale and a secret exemplar for the rising middle class[54], and remained a source of intense fascination for a society increasingly anxious about its traditional class hierarchies.

Barrington's punishment for the Dudman theft was at the time still a recent innovation: he was sentenced to three years hard labour 'on the river', that is, ballast-heaving (dredging), and confinement on the prison hulks at Woolwich.[55] The hulks, which would remain a feature of the British convict system for the best part of a century, had been instituted by Act of Parliament in May 1776, and began operation in August that year, just six months previous to Barrington's sentence there. If it was the disruption to Britain's policy of transporting convicts abroad brought about by the American revolutionary war that provided the exigent circumstances behind the founding of the hulk system, there was also a body of thought supporting the enterprise as a permanent solution to the crime problem. In essence, the hulk system brought together two of the eighteenth century's most cherished ideological threads – the purifying value of hard work, and the power of public shaming. Administration of the hulks was entrusted to the Justices of Middlesex, who in turn outsourced it to a 'merchant', Duncan Campbell, who had formerly been a transportation contractor and thus knew something about how to turn a profit from convict management.[56] While convict labour was directed towards improving the quality of the bed and foreshore of the Thames at Woolwich and constructing shipping facilities for the Royal Arsenal, there is a sense in which what Campbell was really asked to provide, especially at the outset of the scheme, was the spectacle of public punishment. This was quickly accomplished, and the convicts working on the Thames 'became recognised as among the sights of the capital'.[57] There was, however, a tremendous cost for the convicts embarked upon the scheme in its early stage; the notoriously unsanitary conditions of the hulks caused a shocking mortality rate – of the 632 convicts embarked between August 1776 and March 1778, 176 died, mainly from 'gaol fever' (typhus).[58]

While Barrington languished in the hulks, the press ensured that the public was not likely to forget him, and curiosity about this new form of punishment was also fed by a media always ready, for a price, to oblige. Barrington's ignominious new situation 'on the river' was appropriated in an apparent bid to 'sell' the Hulk system. The *London Magazine* for May 1777 carried as its lead article a piece on 'the two noted criminals' – Barrington and David Brown Dignam.[59] The article dwelt on how the Woolwich scheme upset the pretensions to gentility of offenders like Barrington and Dignam, treating them on a level with common criminals and thereby making them suffer the proper consequences of their dissolute courses and criminal actions. Dignam was supposed to have arrived at Woolwich with 'a servant in livery', expecting some concessions to his genteel status:

> but the overseer at his coming on board presented him with the felon's apparel, and told him, that notwithstanding his gold laced waistcoat he must wear it, and also shewed him his lodgings in the midst of the other convicts, and pointed him to one of the miserable wretches for his bed-fellow.

Barrington was similarly represented as having been humbled by the hulks, and was said to have

> intreated the judge and court to preserve him from the ignominious slavish punishment of working on the Thames, and pleaded his utter inability for such a service, from the delicacy of his frame and constitution. All pleas were fruitless. The law knows no distinction—he was sentenced to the ballast lighter, and it is evident from his appearance when at work, and by his being often on the *sick list*, that the labour is both extremely difficult and disgustful to him.[60]

In other words, the hulk scheme was providing an ideal and exemplary punishment for these effeminate and fraudulent young men of fashion. Given the mores of the eighteenth-century press, it is quite likely that Campbell or someone in his clique had in fact paid for this 'profile', among other pieces.[61] Campbell's contract for the charge of the prisoners was to be renewed annually, so a measure of public support for the scheme would no doubt have been useful to him – even prisons could be 'puffed'.

The accounts of visitors to the hulks agree that there was a marked improvement in conditions through the year 1777, and all were prepared to speak in reasonably positive terms of the scheme, albeit each with their own caveats and proposals for improving the system.[62] Yet it would not be long before the hulks were generally reviled as a catalyst both for crime – for which they received the nickname 'Campbell's Academy' – and for the spread of disease. The role of the press in forming this body of opinion was crucial, but the process was gradual. Initially, the harshness of the system was sensationalised. Wilfrid Oldham, in his excellent thesis on the English convict system in the latter years of the eighteenth century, has suggested that Campbell *had* to begin issuing pardons for good behaviour because of the 'astonishing depression' which press reports of life on the hulks inspired in convicts arriving there.[63] Yet for some publications, too much violence directed at criminals was not enough. In a later article on the hulk system, the *London Magazine* shifted its editorial policy, suggesting that the conditions on the *Justitia* hulk were in fact not dire enough to terrify prospective criminals into following lawful courses. It also suggested that the 'sick list' – that is, exemption from physical labour and admission to the ship's hospital – was open to corruption, a view that may have had some truth to it, but still displayed a callous indifference to the extremely high rate of illness and death which prevailed in the early stages of the scheme. Rather than being the malingerer that the *London Magazine* insinuated, Barrington in fact played an active part in combating this mortality rate, supervising the hospital on board the *Censor* hulk.[64] As Campbell was well aware, this employment was fraught with danger. On his tour of the *Censor* in January 1778, Bentham noted that Campbell 'declined going down with us into the hospital and soon called us out'.[65] But if unwilling to see for himself, it seems that Campbell was sufficiently grateful for Barrington's efforts to recommend him for a pardon, and Barrington duly received a remission of his sentence in February 1778.[66]

Barrington's period of respite from life 'on the river' was all too brief. Less than a month after his remission of sentence was made official, Barrington was again arrested for picking pockets. The occasion was a service benefiting the Humane Society at St Sepulchre's Church, Holborn, on Sunday, 15 March 1778.

According to one source, Barrington's arrest took place after a chain of events that would seem to indicate that for a police force essentially comprised of bounty hunters, Barrington was now something of a marked man:

> [two] gentlemen going to St. Sepulchre's church, one of them, who had some slight knowledge of Barrington, pointed him out to his friend previous to their entering the church; a short time after the other gentleman seeing Payne, the city constable, informed him that Barrington was there, at the same time describing his dress, &c. This put the Little Carpenter on the search; he found him, pursued him out of church, and then seized him, and he will now probably suffer severely for misapplying the lenity which he has recently experienced.[67]

The constable Payne, who had earned the nickname 'the Little Carpenter' for his assiduity in nabbing criminals who ended up on the scaffold, was said to have found on Barrington bank notes, coin, and three watches 'concealed under his hair'.[68]

It was easy to condemn Barrington for his foolhardiness in offending again so soon after his release from the hulks. Certainly, the *Morning Post* had no qualms about doing so the day after his arrest – even though the matter was still sub judice – when it labelled Barrington's behaviour the apotheosis of 'human depravity'.[69] A compendium of criminal biographies published about 1779, entitled *The Malefactor's Register, or New Newgate and Tyburn Calendar*, also expressed shock that Barrington should return to crime 'after having experienced the intolerable severities to which offenders sentenced to labour on the Thames are exposed'.[70] But the fact that Barrington was now a candidate for inclusion in such a publication would doubtlessly have eased his passage back to picking pockets. With his notorious profile, Barrington would surely have had trouble earning a living as a surgeon: regular or irregular, the business of an eighteenth-century medical practitioner would have required a degree of public trust and confidence. On the whole, it seems unlikely that Barrington, who continually returned to crime, was ever seriously established in medicine or indeed in any other profession or trade.

Unfortunately for Barrington's future prospects, *The Malefactor's Register* was not the only publication of ill-repute that he was listed in about this time. He was also mentioned in another work published by Alexander Hogg (the publisher of the *The Malefactor's Register*), issued variously as *The Frauds of London Detected ...* and *The New Cheats of London Exposed.*[71] These publications were among a substantial number of similar titles published in the eighteenth and early nineteenth centuries, forming a particular species of London guide book, purportedly designed to alert country folk to the nefarious practices of the London underworld. This genre of voyeuristic guide to the lowlife of the metropolis was initially popularised by Ned Ward with his *London Spy* at the turn of the eighteenth century.[72] Alexander Hogg's former master, John Cooke, had revived the genre with such publications as *The Midnight Spy: or, a View of the Transactions of London and Westminster* (1766), *The Cheats of London Exposed* (c. 1770), *The New London Spy* (c. 1771) and *The Countryman's Guide to London; or, Villainy Detected* (c. 1775). The authorship of Cooke's *The New London Spy* was also ascribed to 'Richard King, *Esq.*' – and this name was used by Hogg for his *The Frauds of London Detected* and *The New Cheats of London Exposed*, probably to help ease the transition between Cooke's publications and his own. One thing seems certain: neither Barrington, nor 'Richard King, *Esq.*', would have suspected that, in little more than twenty years time, Barrington himself would become the attributed author of a version of *The Frauds of London Detected*.

The Alexander Hogg publications detailing Barrington's apparent criminal activities all claim Barrington was an associate of another infamous pickpocket, Elizabeth West.[73] It is certainly possible that there was some truth in this: the *Gazetteer and New Daily Advertiser*'s report on Barrington's arrest on 15 March 1778 claimed that Barrington had been in West's company when arrested.[74] The question of Barrington's criminal acquaintances as a whole should probably be addressed here. If we assume that, discounting lengthy periods in gaols and on the hulks, Barrington was active as a pickpocket from late 1775 to 1790, he is certain in that time to have established a fairly extensive network of contacts in the criminal underworld, particularly in London. The press often published alarmist gossip about criminals becoming organised, but it is difficult to gauge the truth of these statements. Many reports on Barrington, as with the paragraph in the *Daily Universal Register* in 1786, which mockingly claimed he had established a 'club' with other 'noted pickpockets ... where all business in their trade is scientifically transacted'[75], were apocryphal, and intended only to play with the ironies present in the figure of the gentleman thief. For obvious reasons, the denizens of the eighteenth-century London underworld resisted close scrutiny, and consequently little reliable evidence survives about the criminal networks that undoubtedly existed. One observer with considerable experience dealing with the underworld, the Bow Street magistrate Sir John Fielding, observed in his own London guide-book that

> [there] are harboured in London a considerable gang of rogues, who for ingenuity and dexterity exceed all in the world of their fraternity. These are the pickpockets of the place, who have made their occupation a science, of which they are exquisite professors. They look upon themselves as a sort of incorporated body, and seem to have a regular correspondence amongst themselves. For, as many of these are always under confinement in the public prisons, there is scarce any thing of extraordinary value lost, but what may, upon proper application to them, be effectually recovered in a short time.[76]

Beyond such general statements on the character of the criminal underworld in London, however, there is little evidence through which to establish Barrington's relationship, if any, with Elizabeth West and other pickpockets. All that is certain is that Barrington and West were linked in a number of sources from the end of the 1770s. The *London Magazine* was among the first to declare a connection between Barrington and West, describing the former as the 'accomplice and paramour of the noted pickpocket Miss West', and two years later *The Malefactor's Register* concurred on the former charge, at least, that Barrington was 'long an accomplice of the famous Miss West'.[77] A publication of 1778 included a passing reference to the '*Gangs of W-st*', claiming in a footnote that 'the notorious Barrington' was a salaried employee in these 'gangs', paid 'no less than 10 guineas a week ... for *picking pockets*'.[78] No doubt there were a good many such tales about Barrington and West circulating in the taverns and coffee houses of London.

The post-1790 biographies of Barrington treated the supposed partnership of Barrington and West very differently. The biography first published as *The Memoirs of George Barrington* by 'J. Bird' and H. D. Symonds dramatises the relationship with innuendo and anecdotes of joint criminal endeavours, while the biography originally published by George Kearsley ignores West altogether.[79] In the Bird and Symonds *Memoirs*, Barrington meets West when he happens to sit close to her one night at Covent Garden, and the latter picks his pocket of a handkerchief containing his pickpocketing implements. West then 'called the owner aside',

> and giving him a *Masonic* hint, an explanation ensued: after the play, the lady took her new-found brother home to her lodging; and before they parted—which was not till the next morning—many tender civilities passed, and many were the *lessons* which Miss West bestowed on the hero of these Memoirs ...[80]

It would seem to be a predictable enough literary trope to make Barrington and West lovers, and to cast the latter as the former's instructor in criminal practices, concomitant with a sexual initiation. This can be seen as something of a development on the typical trajectory of the eighteenth-century criminal biography, where, as Phillip Rawlings points out, criminal careers generally followed from a collapse of the master–apprentice relationship, with this collapse often attributed to the pernicious influence of a lascivious woman.[81] According to the Bird and Symonds *Memoirs*, Barrington's criminality was instead the result of a successful, if perverse, master–apprentice relationship with West. But while there is no evidence to show that Barrington and West were not linked, either criminally or romantically or both, it would be very unwise to take the stories derived from the Barrington biographies at face value. The Bird and Symonds *Memoirs*, for example, contain an episode where West robs David Brown Dignam on a visit to see Barrington on the hulks. As R. S. Lambert points out, this could not possibly have occurred, as West was imprisoned in Newgate by the time Dignam was sent to the hulks.[82]

The same caution is necessary when approaching reports of Barrington as the leader of his own gang of thieves. Although there were a number of contemporary references to Barrington's 'crew', and 'the boys of Barrington'[83], from the late 1770s on Barrington's name was used emblematically as often as literally; 'Barrington' became a ready reference point or shorthand to employ when speaking about pickpockets and thieves.[84] The most detailed contemporary account of Barrington's criminal 'associates' appeared in a piece in the *Daily Universal Register* profiling Barrington in the wake of his arrest – and subsequent escape from custody – on 19 January 1787.[85] It stated that Barrington, 'Sovereign of his profession ... never goes unattended, but has a constant private guard to aid in the execution of his depredations, and in protecting his person'. According to the article,

> On [Barrington] being recognised, his partizans commenced hostilities, and a general battle ensued, in which hard blows were given and received, the gentleman [who had been robbed] having been assisted by a large party, which however would have failed in securing the culprit, but for the intervention of the military.

> On being brought out, a fellow with a loaded stick struck several gentlemen repeatedly. Lord Tyrconnel and Captain Hanger did good execution. At the Rose tavern, the battle raged; a sergeant was robbed of his sword, and a soldier of his hat, and many persons had their pockets rifled.

> Barrington being brought to the Brown Bear, a new riot was commenced, and he had the good fortune to escape.

> His associates were all fashionably dressed, and, what is more remarkable, spoke like gentlemen.

Some details in this account can be confirmed by other sources. Barrington's identification by the constables and the mob had taken some time, and had caused a tumultuous public spectacle.[86] Upon confirmation of the notorious identity, 'someone immediately struck Barrington a violent blow on the head with a stick', and he was taken to the Brown Bear tavern, 'where there was a great uproar and disturbance'.[87] The fact that a riot occurred on Barrington's arrest, however, hardly supports in itself the supposition that Barrington was a kind of proto-Fagin, leading a small army of gentleman pickpockets. It is more likely that the fighting on the night of his arrest in 1787 arose out of the disputes between 'gentlemen' with different opinions about Barrington's identity and what to do with him. Given the mores of the Georgian fashionable world, it is certainly plausible that a proportion of Barrington's associates actually were gentlemen.

The eighteenth-century justice system was overtly theatrical, and deliberately so. Just as exposure to the public gaze was part of the punishment of the criminal, the public spectacle of retributive justice was intended to function as a cautionary tale for the general populace. As Michael Harris has put it, '[the] machinery of justice defined and reinforced economic, social and political distinctions through a sort of ritual drama, whose effectiveness depended on a high degree of visibility'.[88] Barrington, whose genteel appearance and eloquent professions of injured sensibility clashed ludicrously with the base crime of picking pockets, was destined to become one of the great stars of this drama. By 1778, moreover, Barrington's status as a national celebrity was clear. According to the *Gazetteer and New Daily Advertiser*, the initial examination by the magistrates the day after Barrington's arrest for the alleged theft at St Supulchre church caused a huge sensation. Payne, the constable, had brought Barrington, 'amidst an astonishing concourse of people', to Guildhall – where they could not find a sitting magistrate and were obliged to go on 'with great difficulty' through the crowds to Mansion-house.[89] There again they found 'the gates surrounded by a prodigious concourse of people', so many that

> Even Common-Councilmen lost their consequence for a day, and could not gain admittance into the chamber of justice, but were obliged to content themselves with a few exclamations without doors against the rudeness of the officers.[90]

Another report states that Barrington was taken by coach from Guildhall to Mansion-house

> through a great concourse of the people, who thronged about the coach to such a degree, that it was stopped several times on its way, that the populace might have a full view of him. At the Mansion House the mob was increased so much, that the prosecutrix [the alleged victim] was obliged to be handed through the windows.[91]

Clearly, these were incredible scenes to greet the committal proceedings of a pickpocket, and they say much about the intense public interest in 'the celebrated Barrington'.

Those privileged few able to penetrate to the inner sanctum of 'the chamber of justice' were disappointed on this occasion, as Barrington reserved his defence for trial. Barrington did, however, make a bid to avoid the inconvenience of such a proceeding altogether, as he 'begged permission to enlist in the East-India Company's service', an indulgence he was denied. In a final, richly performative exchange, the magistrate lectured Barrington:

> 'Young man, I am exceedingly sorry to be under the necessity of sending a person so capable of getting his own living by honest means to jail.' To which Barrington replied, 'Sir, you have shewn yourself a man of feeling; Sir, I am'—and then out his hat to hide his tears.[92]

The *Gazetteer and New Daily Advertiser* commented that Barrington's 'behaviour throughout was very decent and shewed not the hardened pickpocket'.[93] This, of course, was Barrington's forte: though his frequent brushes with the law left little doubt about his criminal activities, time and again he managed to give a plausible impression of a victim rather than culprit, and as a public performer he was skilled enough to wring sympathetic responses even from cynical audiences. The reporter for the *Gazetteer and New Daily Advertiser*, for example, was willing to see Barrington in much the way he represented himself, as an unfortunate exemplar of the individual romantic sensibility under threat from an unfeeling mob:

> He cried very much on his way to Newgate [...] The mob was extremely violent and had nearly dragged him out of the coach to gratify their curiosity. The answer he gave in the watchhouse might very suitably have been applied to this uncharitable multitude, 'Do not reflect upon me, I am sufficiently troubled with my own unhappy feelings'.[94]

It is likely that another large crowd was on hand to see Barrington go to trial in May 1778. The *Morning Post*, which like many other papers often placed sections of 'Old Bailey Intelligence' and 'Bow Street Intelligence' side by side with 'Theatrical Intelligence' and 'Opera Intelligence' (and sometimes reviewed the main performers of each sphere in much the same way), promoted the prospect of an appealing double bill when it announced on the morning of 4 May that '[this] day, Barrington, the Macaroni pickpocket, and Williams, the famous Swindler, are to be tried'.[95] Those who attended the Old Bailey to see 'the celebrated Barrington' in action were treated to an eloquent defence from the prisoner. Barrington claimed to have found Elizabeth Ironmonger's watch on leaving the church and to have taken it, 'intending to advertise it'. It was only the persecution he had suffered – in general through the prejudice of the press, and in particular through the actions of Payne the constable (whom Barrington painted as an unscrupulous and unprincipled informer with 'a black and cruel imagination: he thinks that the reputation of the Little English Carpenter, as he is pleased to stile himself, will not be complete, without he follows it with my conviction') – which had brought him to his present predicament. Barrington, moreover, attempted to turn the traducing of his name in the press to his advantage. He noted that '[the] daily papers have been filled with paragraphs against me ... loaded me with a liberality bordering on profusion, with the epithets of notorious, infamous, abandoned', but expressed a confidence that the jury was above such vile trumpery: 'nor would I think, even for a moment, that my life will be paragraphed away, or that my jury would cast me before I came into court'.[96] Barrington's use of the term 'paragraphs' here was clearly meant to implant in the minds of the jury the belief that he was the victim of a calculated persecution campaign. This was no doubt a clever tactic on the part of one whose name was so thoroughly blackened in the press, and it was continually employed by Barrington in his future court appearances.

On this occasion, Barrington had good reason to complain about the reputation that the press had built for him. The evidence against him was not the strongest: the victim, Elizabeth Iron-monger, had not seen Barrington in the church and stated that she did not know how she came to lose her watch.[97] Without Barrington's reputation, it is unlikely that the case would have made it to court. In the event, however, he was found guilty, and once again sentenced to hard labour on the hulks, this time for five years. Barrington again pleaded with the court to allow him 'to enter into his majesty's service', bitterly asking the jury to second his petition with the emotional exhortation: 'and may your children, and your children's children, never experience the misery I now suffer'.[98] Such favourable treatment was certainly not unknown in the eighteenth century, when the influence of a powerful patron could easily circumvent the principles of the justice system. In the same sessions as Barrington's conviction, another 'noted playhouse pickpocket' managed to obtain 'leave to serve on board one of the King's ships of war' *after* his con-viction.[99] A similar example was to be found in the pardoning of another of Barrington's contemporaries, D'Arcy Wentworth, in 1788. Wentworth, the black sheep of an ancient aristocratic family, was certainly well connected enough to receive such favour.[100] Ultimately, Barrington's polite manners and appear-ance of gentility were apparently no substitute for these family ties, and it seems none of the fashionable acquaintances that Barrington may or may not have had were prepared to intercede on his behalf.

So once again Barrington was sent down to 'Campbell's Academy' at Woolwich. A newspaper report stated that, while in Newgate awaiting transportation to the hulks, Barrington attempted suicide by 'stabbing himself in the breast'.[101] The Kearsley *Memoirs of George Barrington* would later elaborate on his motives for this attempt, and the text amplified Barrington's suffering by moving the scene of the suicide attempt to the hulks themselves.[102] The prospect of spending five long years on the hulks may well have driven Barrington to desperation. Yet despite the many trials of life at Woolwich, Barrington endured; indeed he remained active in promoting his own cause through correspondence. Two letters by Barrington, addressed to 'a very worthy and well known clergyman of the church of England', dated 4 January 1781 and 16 February 1781 respectively, are included in the Bird and Symonds *Memoirs*.[103] In the second of these letters, Barrington expressed the kind of contrition that would certainly please the audience he was addressing:

> I view with the deepest compunction the errors of my past life; errors which have drawn upon me the displeasure of God, and the displeasure of good men; blasted me in fame and fortune, and plunged me into inexpressible misery without leaving me a single advantage in return. Painful as these reflections are, I endeavour to keep despondency at a distance; resolved patiently to abide the determination of that Supreme Being, who has mercifully preserved my life even amidst the greatest dangers [...] I cannot sufficiently thank you for your excellent advice and charitable wishes; they will not, I hope be thrown away upon me, but that my future conduct will strongly demonstrate my gratitude to God by real reformation.[104]

Whatever Barrington's gratitude towards God, he could only be thankful for a very small mercy on the part of the King. After nearly four years on the hulks, and with his health (as he would testify later in court) 'ruined', Barrington was pardoned on condition that he leave the country.[105] Barrington's movements after his release are uncertain; the Kearsley *Memoirs* give various tales of criminal activity in Ireland, Scotland and England, but this account should not be relied upon as accurate, even if Barrington's

modern biographers have accepted it more or less uncritically.[106]
All that is known for sure is that Barrington was once more at the
bar of the Old Bailey in January 1783, charged with not fulfilling
the conditions of the pardon by remaining in the Kingdom. In
court, Barrington spoke of his suffering on the hulks:

> after four years was past, colds that I had repeatedly caught had
> ulcerated my lungs, and labour often exceeding my strength by day,
> and putrefied air by night, had greatly reduced, and wasted my
> frame: the surgeons [...] obtained a milk and vegetable diet for me;
> this was a regime never allowed there, but like extreme unction to
> those that were at the point of death ...[107]

Claiming to have done nothing wrong since his release – '[but] I
have learned that a man whose character has been once
blemished, will always be suspected: I was merely for a name
apprehended' – Barrington also claimed to have been unaware of
the conditions of pardon. He asked the court, quite reasonably,
what was the justice of a *pardon* which would 'saddle [him] with
the condition of being transported for ever', after he had already
been incarcerated for four years. He also expressed his view that
'certain death must be the consequence' of his return to the
hulks.[108] Once again, however, he received no favour, and was
remanded to his former sentence. The *Morning Herald* reported
on what looked to be the sorry, though apparently morally
appropriate, end to the melodrama of Barrington's life:

> The celebrated Mr George Barrington made a stout defence at the
> Old Bailey on Saturday evening in order to prevent another visit to
> the floating academy at Woolwich. He was released from that
> seminary of vice on condition of going out of the realm in ten days.
>
> By the ingenuity of some reputable twig of the Law an affidavit was
> prepared denying the acceptance of a pardon and a stipulation of
> that kind. Barrington arraigned the pardon to be rather an act of
> cruelty than of mercy for he had suffered the sentence of five years

hard labour within eleven months when it came to liberate him, and if he had understood he was to be banished from all his relations and friends, durante vitae, he certainly should have refused it and remained on board until April next when the time expired; the treatment he had met with had injured his health and unless he had been set at liberty perhaps he might have died, which was preferable to being exiled from his native country. The Recorder said His Majesty thought it unsafe to suffer so hardened a character to remain amongst his subjects, and therefore wished effectually to get rid of him; the prisoner had not complied with the condition of his pardon and on that account stood exactly in the same situation as when the pardon was granted which was that there remained eleven months of the five years to serve on board the Hulk. He was taken from the bar and appeared in a deep decline, so that in all probability this young man to whom nature Nature has been so liberal and whose education is a reproach to his morals, will die a wretched example of the certain consequences of abilities misapplied being inevitable ruin and disgrace.[109]

In the event, Barrington, ever one to frustrate the 'master narrative' of eighteenth-century criminal life, lived, and was allowed to serve out the rest of his sentence in Newgate.

While Barrington languished in gaol, his legend continued to grow apace. After years of newspaper notoriety, 'the celebrated Barrington' was beginning to leave tracks through a broader range of cultural artefacts. A 'novel of circulation'[110], which first appeared about 1781, includes a fictional encounter with a handsome young man who turns out to be a pickpocket:

> I could not help admiring the exterior of this youth: he had all that refined elegance in his person and manner my reader would expect from the finest mould of nature, and the tuition of the Graces:—and can this man be a pickpocket, thought I.—'You look very well to-day, George,' says his companion; 'the K— would as soon be suspected of your intention this morning.'—'Tis a cursed life,' says he, 'but I must feed my ambition'.[111]

The figure of Barrington would be appropriated in several further novels published up to the turn of the nineteenth century. Sometimes only the name 'Barrington' was used, in a context clearly meant to convey associations of criminality or disreputability[112], and in others passing reference was made to 'the famous Barrington' as a cultural reference point.[113] This fame was also beginning to spread to other parts of the Western world. The travel journal of Johann Willhelm von Archenholz, published in Germany as *England und Italien* in 1785, described an unusual species of London pickpocket

> who, by means of fashionable clothes, insinuate themselves into the first company, and their impudence is often crowned with success. A fellow of this kind, called Barrington, renowned in London, on account of his great dexterity, elegant manners, and boldness unparalleled, still carries on his trade with great reputation.[114]

Yet while Barrington and his 'great reputation' were already becoming world famous, all this predates his most successful period. But if Barrington now managed to escape further convictions for almost seven years, he would live out this time under the constant scrutiny of the law, and the more invasive and unscrupulous gaze of the press.

Once released from Newgate towards the end of 1783, Barrington's period of anonymity was characteristically short. On 31 January 1784, at the Opera House, Covent Garden, the theatre was 'very crowded' with both patrons of the opera and theatregoers who were entertained by not only Mrs Crawford's Alicia in *Jane Shore* – a performance which excited 'the enthusiastic admiration of the whole house' – but also the pantomime afterpiece, *Harlequin Rambler, or The Convent in Uproar*, which the theatrical critic for the *Public Advertiser* considered to be 'on the high Road to popular Favour'.[115] After the opera, Sir Godfrey Webster, a member of the House of Commons, attempted to make his way to the tearoom but was frustrated by the crowd. According to the testimony Webster would tender later at the Old Bailey, as he leaned against the doorway a man leaned against his right shoulder, and while he looked at this stranger he perceived 'a gentle pulsation just above my right cuff'; this, Webster alleged, was the 'touch' of the noted Barrington.[116] Shortly thereafter Webster noticed his purse was missing:

> had I known his name and his former character I should without the least hesitation have seized him on the spot, but his dress and his appearance put him externally so much above committing a crime of that sort, and not wishing to make a riot and bustle in a publick place, I resolved not to disturb the society at that instant, but to follow him […][117]

Webster's decision to follow Barrington and observe his behaviour rather than apprehending him on the spot, though ruinous to his case in the long run, may provide a valuable insight into how Barrington operated as a pickpocket.[118] After the alleged theft, Webster followed Barrington to the inner lobby, where he observed that Barrington 'made a semblance of joining some ladies':

> he proceeded with them till he came to a flight of seven or eight steps which were very much crouded with servants who wait there, he rather raised himself as if looking for his domesticks, and cried, are my servants there … he went through the line of servants, but instead of proceeding strait forwards which he should have done, he deviated to the right and went out of the centre arcade … the moment he put his foot on the kirb stone of the pavement he set off … I pursued him down the middle of the street through the carriages …[119]

According to Webster's testimony, after such a breathless chase sequence, a ludicrously polite exchange took place:

> finding I laid hold of him I believe he said … what do you mean, I am a gentleman … I said to him, Sir, it is an awkward thing to mention, but I think you have robbed me of my purse …

Following this, there was another long and convoluted public scene, involving constables, soldiers, theatregoers, and genteel passers-by. According to Webster, Barrington kept saying

> Sir, have a care, you will get yourself into a scrape, I am not the person you take me for; [Webster] was rather irritated, and said at last, if you have any friends that can speak for you I do not wish to expose you, I will take you to a tavern or coffee- house, and you may send for your friends, but I will never quit you ...

The implication here, that Webster might have excused Barrington if he was in fact a gentleman and had connections willing to answer for his conduct, shows how much the justice system of the eighteenth century depended on class divisions: a dispute in the genteel sphere might be resolved in a much different way to an attack which crossed class boundaries. It also shows that Barrington once again lacked such connections at the crucial moment.

When searched, Barrington was found to be wearing 'a kind of bandage' underneath his fashionable attire, but none of Webster's property was found on his person.[120] This certainly helped Barrington's cause when he was tried at the Old Bailey on 26 February 1784. Since Webster had accused Barrington of stealing the property from his person, the judge instructed the jury that 'it is either a capital offence or no offence at all', and went on to advise the jury that in view of the fact that the case for the prosecution rested solely on Webster's testimony – 'whatever your suspicions are, there does not appear to me sufficient grounds to convict him of a capital offence'.[121] Thus Barrington left the Old Bailey as a free man – that is to say, he had his liberty. For the press, although acquitted, he was still 'that well-noted *and genteel* pickpocket, George Barrington'.[122] The *Morning Post* and the *Morning Herald* printed the same report on Barrington's acquittal, noting that this 'celebrated' personage had escaped death only because no stolen property had been found on his person.[123]

Barrington on this occasion fared a little better at the hands of the press – relative to the sensations he had caused in the late 1770s – perhaps because the newspapers were preoccupied with politics on account of the impending general election of 1784.

Even amidst eighteenth-century London's famous panoply, one wonders how Barrington could have managed to ply his trade as a pickpocket, given all the attention surrounding him. In the theatre district – which with its bustling crowds and intermingling of all ranks and classes was the traditional haunt of London pickpockets – the infamous Barrington name was reportedly bawled out 'every night' by one of the theatre constables as a caution to the general public.[124] Moreover, Barrington's fame by now was such that he was even mentioned on stage. A reference to Barrington occurs in the comic opera *Fontainbleau: or, Our Way in France*, by the popular dramatist John O'Keeffe. In a libretto trading on national stereotypes, the protagonist 'Sir John Bull' explains his snub of a French colonel on the grounds that he was unaware of his rank – 'why, they dress and scrape and shrug so much alike, that there's no knowing a prince from a pickpocket'. Later, when John Bull is fuming on discovering that his daughter has married a penniless, dissipated English émigré, Lady Bull reproaches him: 'Ay, you would have an English husband! She may have married Barrington for aught you know.'[125] *Fontainbleau*, which premiered in November 1784, became a popular addition to the Covent Garden repertory, and was given every season until 1799–1800.[126]

At about the same time as this 'appearance' in *Fontainbleau*, the figure of Barrington was appropriated for his first foray into political satire. He was alluded to as 'a noted pickpocket' in *The Oriental Chronicles of the Times*[127], a work in a voguish style of mock-heroic satire which parodied 'prophetic' or 'oriental' writing in delineating current events, generally with a heavy political bias. *The Oriental Chronicles of the Times* was written in support of Charles James Fox, the charismatic 'radical Whig' politician who had been soundly defeated in the general elections of 1784 by the Tories under William Pitt.[128] Barrington's part in the text was small, a comic diversion – just another example of the use of Barrington's name as a topical reference point – but the publication made more capital from this reference by depicting Barrington as part of its frontispiece illustration. Barrington is depicted as the train-bearer of a judge in a burlesque scene set in the Court of King's Bench, Westminster (where Barrington would later appear as a defendant), and one of the assembled legal notables exclaims, in a speech bubble, 'Barrington in Court!'.[129] The figure of the notorious Barrington is probably used here to impute vice upon the assembly; the author elsewhere attacks the legal 'Sages' for their part in the Westminster Scrutiny (that is, recount), which temporarily denied Fox his place in parliament after the 1784 Westminster election.

From 1784, it would become increasingly common to see 'the notorious Barrington' deployed in the press as a figure with which to stain prominent politicians, a symptom both of Barrington's ever-growing fame and of the intensification of party politics. The Westminster election of 1784 became notorious as 'the most conspicuous example of all the abuses of which the old electoral system was capable'.[130] Since the electorate had the widest constituency in the country, with something approaching universal male suffrage, it was considered a barometer of popular opinion, and was further talismanic as the district of the seat of government. Both the adherents of Fox and those of Pitt coveted the constituency, and accordingly the 1784 election was bitterly fought. Both sides splashed money around, hiring shady characters to further their ends, and the whole process was 'disgraced throughout by scenes of drunkenness, tumult, and violence,— and by the coarsest libels and lampoons'.[131] A fairly high proportion of the latter were aimed at the fashionable aristocrat,

Georgiana, Duchess of Devonshire, who campaigned vigorously for Fox, and was duly accused of trading sexual favours for votes by the Pittites.[132] It is unsurprising then that a paragraph in the *Morning Post* (which was then partly financed by the Treasury)[133] should marry two popular targets of ridicule with the claim that 'the noted Barrington voted for Mr. Fox ... at the earnest solicitation of her Grace of D——.'[134] This was to be the first in a series of associations of Barrington and Fox, though it is likely that this connection was in reality nothing more than the scurrilous concoction of the conservative press. Fox's orbit was among the hard-drinking, high-stakes gamblers of the exclusive world of genteel club life, and it is difficult to imagine that even this charismatic 'man of the people' could justify having such a notorious acquaintance.[135] Fox's companions had earned an altogether more elevated kind of disreputability; there was a world of difference between those dissipated gentry who drank and gambled their money away and those who would become petty thieves to get cash. Although it would turn out that Barrington actually was a supporter of Fox[136], there is no evidence, aside from newspaper squibs and calumnies, that this high opinion was reciprocated.

Before the matter of the Westminster Scrutiny was settled, Barrington was in trouble of his own once again. Exactly a year and a day after his acquittal over the Webster theft, Barrington spent another Saturday night in the crowded theatre district. This time he was at Drury Lane, where *Macbeth* was being staged, with the greatest actress of the day, Sarah Siddons, playing Lady Macbeth.[137] It was Siddons who attracted John Bagshaw, Esq., to the theatre that night, but he was not to see the play. Between the box office and the door to the pit section of the theatre, he thought he detected someone rifling his pocket:

> I found my watch was taken; on turning my head, [Barrington] was then standing with his back to me, endeavouring to make his way out through the persons that were collected together; I said nothing, but

immediately followed him; as soon as we had cleared the persons who were behind us ... I immediately laid hold of him, and said, Sir, you have got my watch; his answer was, have I, Sir, got your watch?[138]

Although still very much preoccupied with politics, the newspapers did not fail to report the latest scandal of 'Barrington, the famous pickpocket'.[139] The *Gazetteer and New Daily Advertiser* went so far as to express the hope that 'the notorious Barrington ... will meet the punishment due to his deserts [*sic*], and society will be rid of an offender who has so long subsisted in splendour by such nefarious practices'.[140] Clearly, the editors of this paper had assumed that public sympathy for Barrington had run its course, and now advocated a far harsher treatment for the man they had supported in 1778. It was of course not unusual for those in the public eye to face such reversals of policy at the hands of the press, and fortunately for Barrington, the legal system prided itself on its independence from such sources of comment. Again, the evidence against Barrington here was not the strongest; the judge on this occasion described it as 'circumstantial' in his charge to the jury.[141] On being challenged by Bagshaw, Barrington had apparently dropped the watch, and since Bagshaw did not detect Barrington in the act of the crime, the case failed. Once again, Barrington gave the court an eloquent, if slightly superfluous, speech in his own defence, representing himself as the victim of 'ill-natured report, and ... wanton invention', and he also spoke of 'a gentleman in whose employment I have been in for some time, but who is now absent on his affairs in Ireland'.[142] According to the *London Chronicle*, Barrington's speech was delivered with 'the greatest propriety, and [was] much admired by every person present; indeed, the like has not been heard since he was tried last'.[143] In summing up, the judge offered the forlorn hope that

a man possessed of such talents as [Barrington] is possessed of, and having, as he says, friends which may assist him, and by which those talents may be made of advantage; that he will turn them to that

advantage, and will make good use of them; and that this will be the
last time that we shall see him in this place.[144]

Even while the newspapers praised the quality of Barrington's
defence and reprinted his speech at length[145], they still treated
him as a guilty man – the *London Chronicle* describing him as one
of the 'felons acquitted' by the court.[146] The *Morning Post*, returning to politics, proceeded to use 'the notorious Barrington' as a
device with which to attack the Foxite Whigs. The *Post* had
become the Pitt government's most important organ through the
election and subsequent events of 1784 and 1785.[147] Since March
1784, the editorship of the paper had been entrusted to William
Jackson – that same 'Doctor Viper' who had previously been the
editor of the *Public Ledger* and whose '*forte* [was] that species of
writing known by the name of Paragraphs, which he has the
happy knack of giving more *point* to, than any of his contemporaries'.[148] Even though the *Post* had lost ground in terms of
influence and circulation to Henry Bate Dudley's new paper, the
pro-Fox *Morning Herald*[149], it retained the *Post*'s old specialisation
in gossip and invective, which, thanks to the ministerial bank-
rolling, now had an overwhelmingly political emphasis. Fox and
his associates were constantly lampooned and abused in the
Morning Post, and virtually every possible opportunity was pressed
into this service. With the topicality of Barrington's recent trial, it
should not be surprising that the following squib appeared in the
Post of 13 April:

> The [Fox-North] Coalition have the merit of being assiduous to enlist
> men of abilities from every quarter. Principle they know to be rather
> an impediment to genius; therefore they are not very sollicitous [*sic*]
> about it;—hence we need not wonder at their anxiety to get Mr.
> *Barrington* over to their party.[150]

The figure of Barrington was in all probability used here for no
other reason than his continuing infamy. Nonetheless, this

paragraph encapsulates a pervasive sentiment on Barrington: that he was a man of great talent who, for variously ascribed reasons, lacked a proper moral facility. The next day the *Post* printed a specious 'retraction' of its paragraph:

> It is not true that *Barrington* stands proposed for a member of the Whig Club; that gentleman's abilities and character are certainly respectable enough to qualify him for a seat there; but some of the company making a little objection to his introduction on account of *the look of the thing*, the motion was over-ruled.[151]

Eventually the *Morning Post* grew tired of Barrington, and moved on to other topical metaphors for their attacks on the Foxites. But after Barrington's second successive acquittal in as many years at the Old Bailey, other London dailies began to take a greater interest in his movements. Two months after his trial in April 1785, the newly instituted *Daily Universal Register* reported on the progress of 'the celebrated Mr. Barrington, of *nimble fingered* memory'. In the sarcastic, innuendo-laden tone that would become increasingly familiar, the paper claimed that 'the illustrious hero' had fractured his skull 'on a late nightly expedition', and as a consequence was 'obliged to submit to the operation of *trepanning his penecranium!*'.[152] Over the next few years, the *Daily Universal Register* was particularly assiduous in reporting on Barrington's movements – although there is more than a suspicion that many of these reports were little more than excuses to exercise a slender wit at Barrington's expense.[153] How Barrington reacted to his increasing fame and notoriety during these years is not clear. There is a possibility that his movements were not always as surreptitious and wary as might be expected, however. An oil portrait by the prominent artist William Beechey, thought to be of Barrington *circa* 1785, is in the collection of the National Library of Australia.[154]

Barrington's next confirmed public appearance was the

sensational night of 19 January 1787. Barrington's victim on this occasion was Havilland Le Mesurier, a well-connected merchant[155], who later alleged that, after feeling his purse move, he had seized Barrington's hand 'close to his pocket', and a Mr Adeane 'stept up and said, sir, you are right, I saw him do it'.[156] The subsequent furore culminated in Barrington's escape from the custody of constable Blandy at the Brown Bear tavern. If the newspapers were somewhat confused by the events of that night, they were clear in their desire to sensationalise them. The *Daily Universal Register* introduced its highly spiced report of the event by describing Barrington as 'one of the most extraordinary figures of the age'[157], while *The World* and the *General Evening Post* made their contributions to the legend of Barrington the super-thief by printing the same highly dubious report, which claimed that, while waiting for the constables to arrive, Barrington robbed the 'gentleman' who had 'collared' him.[158] The press also began to hint that other 'solutions' could be found for dealing with the infamous pickpocket and his kind. Each of the newspapers mentioned above included another paragraph in close proximity to their accounts of the latest Barrington escapades. This was a report that the citizenry in Glasgow had recently caught a pickpocket in the act of theft, and immediately mutilated him by cutting off his ear. The report further incited readers with the reflection: 'were the London mobs to make a few such examples, it might thin the numbers of the light-fingered family who infest the metropolis, and daily escape with impunity'.[159] With such prospects, it is scarcely surprising that Barrington chose to flee.

Thereafter, Barrington was on the run, an outlaw, for a period of nearly eighteen months. What he did during this period is speculated on in the post-1790 biographies. According to the Kearsley *Memoirs* – which rather gloss over this period – Barrington

was travelling in various disguises, and in various characters, through
the northern counties of this kingdom. He visited the great towns, in
those parts, as quack doctor, or as a clergyman, sometimes he went
with an E O [gaming] table, and sometimes he pretended to be a
rider to a manufacturing house ...[160]

The scant details provided by the Kearsley *Memoirs* about this
period were probably taken from a variety of newspaper reports.
Accounts of Barrington 'habited as a clergyman' actually predate
the escape from the Brown Bear, and, when he was eventually
apprehended in Newcastle-upon-Tyne, he was reported to have
claimed he was a dentist.[161] The account of Barrington pretend-
ing to be a 'rider' was probably taken from a widely reported
incident where a genteel hunting party stumbled across 'the
noted *Barrington*' in a Lincolnshire Inn, not long after his flight
from London:

> habited in a brown frock, and with his hair cut close in all the stile of
> village simplicity.—He was called to by his proper name by Mr. Oliver
> of Essex, who had been robbed by him some time past of sixteen
> guineas; he at first denied he was the person alluded to—but
> afterwards acquiesced in the fact.—The people of the house asserted,
> that he called himself a rider, and said, he was travelling for orders.—
> He had bags by his side, and was in all respects a type of the character
> he assumed.[162]

The Bird and Symonds *Memoirs* provided a more fanciful
itinerary of Barrington's travels as a fugitive. In this narrative
Barrington flees first to Edinburgh, where he was supposedly
recognised by the influential Scottish politician Sir Henry
Dundas.[163] After Edinburgh, the Bird and Symonds *Memoirs* place
Barrington in Glasgow, 'where he engaged himself as a comedian;
and it is said, shone to great advantage in the Beggar's Opera'. In
all probability, this is one of those witty jokes – that the real
criminal Barrington should play, and of course play brilliantly,
one of the fictional criminals of Gay's opera – favoured by those

who would embellish the history of 'the celebrated Barrington'.[164] From Glasgow, Barrington was supposed to have run off with a Miss 'H——' belonging to the company of players, with whom he returned to Edinburgh and there subsequently abandoned. Barrington then crossed the border back into England and, at Carlisle, 'luckily meets Jack Brown, one of his own acquaintances, who kept an E. O. table'. The story of the E. O. table is thence embellished, with a tale of Barrington picking the pocket of a patron who had won handsomely from him at Derby races. This anecdote served to allow some moralising on the pernicious habits of the 'sportsmen' of the age – for in revenge for the theft,

> the company broke the E. O. table with every mark of indignation and contempt: not once conceiving that themselves, who were in the *illegal* act of robbing each other, had in some sort merited the treatment with which they had been complimented.[165]

From Derby, Barrington is said to have travelled to York, where he picked pockets with great success at 'the Music Meeting of that city'[166], and proceeded to Newcastle, where finally his luck ran out – he was apprehended and brought back to London.

It may well be that certain elements of these stories are true. It seems likely that Barrington would have had to leave London, and that he probably would have had to disguise himself at times. He was apprehended in Newcastle, so presumably he did travel through a number of English counties. But the tendency in both versions of the *Memoirs of George Barrington* to freely embroider their narratives with moralising or humorous anecdotes, or to associate Barrington with well-known names, detracts from their credibility to the point where even the broad outlines they give of Barrington's movements must be regarded as suspect. Certain omissions, moreover, are still more difficult to explain: why, for example, do these accounts ignore the fact that Barrington had a pregnant wife with him when apprehended in Newcastle?[167]

Indeed, Barrington's wife is absent from both versions of the *Memoirs*, probably because the image of Barrington as a family man did not quite fit with the conventions of criminal biography.

The London newspapers gave a different version again of Barrington's time as a fugitive. Again, the reliance on rumour and hearsay leads one to wonder about the factual basis, if any, to their reporting; and, again, it is certain that some incidents were fabricated or exaggerated merely for the purpose of delivering snappy one-liners. In this latter category we can place the report that appeared in the *Daily Universal Register* for 13 April 1787:

> Some days ago Mr Cowper in his road to Lord Orford's was followed and secured by some people at Barton who took him on suspicion he was the notorious Barrington from the extraordinary length of his fingers. Mr Cowper humoured the thing until he was carried to Lord Orford's at which place the matter was put right, and the countryman who had secured him informed he had mistaken his man and that the gentleman was a lawyer. 'A lawyer', said the disappointed rustic, 'Aye. I thought those long fingers weren't given him for nothing'.[168]

Such was the continued level of press interest in Barrington that it should not be surprising if 'rustics' and others all over the kingdom were chasing after Barrington's shadows. A little more than two months after the sighting in Lincolnshire, the *Daily Universal Register* reported on 'a person, supposed to be the famous Barrington', picking pockets at the Cock Tavern in Threadneedle-street [London].[169] In January 1788, the *Morning Post, Public Advertiser* and *St James's Chronicle* reported that '*Barrington* has committed a robbery in Worcestershire', which those journals thought would be his undoing.[170] But he remained free, and by the end of March, even the respectable *Morning Chronicle* announced the gossip that the 'notorious Barrington is at present in Dublin, and has begun to exercise his profession'.[171]

Shortly thereafter, the *Daily Universal Register*, now under its new title, *The Times*, reported at greater and more prosaic length on the activities of '[the] celebrated Barrington—that arch-genius of filching—that prince of pickpockets' in Dublin.[172] Another report claimed that 'the Protean filcher Barrington' had been operating in Dublin cross-dressed as a woman, 'with a large French night cap, which hid the most part of his face, that was well decorated with rouge and pearl powder'.[173] As Sheila Box has observed, the principal value of such a report for modern readers is that 'it shows the fascination with Barrington that held the public and produced such ridiculous accounts'.[174] Certainly, whatever the factual basis of such accounts, the constant press coverage kept Barrington's notorious name firmly before the public eye, and the increasingly incredible feats of dissimulation and criminal prowess ascribed to him all contributed to the growing Barrington legend.

Another sign that Barrington was assuming still greater importance as a cultural icon was the publication, about this time, of the first literary work to bear his name. This was a long satirical poem, entitled 'An Heroic Epistle, from George Barrington, Esq. to Major Semple, On his Sentence of Transportation to the Coast of New South Wales'. The work falls into the category of mock-heroic allonymous satire, a popular eighteenth-century form, where the work is falsely attributed to and narrated by a celebrated personage who is often the main target of the satire itself.[175] The 'Heroic Epistle' was published in February 1790, but it seems to have been written significantly earlier: the event which provided the inspiration for the work (Semple's trial and sentence to transportation) occurred in September 1786, and it would have been highly unusual for a poem satirically commenting on a topical event to have been composed years later.[176] References in the poem to the narrator fleeing from 'the babble of the Bow Street pack'[177] suggest that some time in 1787, when

A DEEP ONE.

Dublin Publiſhd by Walker 79 Dame Street

This caricature, from a print formerly in the Webster collection, has a pencilled note
identifying the figure as 'Barrington the Pickpocket in disguise'. Hordern House Rare
Books.

Barrington was outlawed after his escape from the Brown Bear,
was the most likely time of the writing and first publication of
this piece.

Framed as an 'address' from one celebrity criminal to another, the major subject is the proposed penal settlement of New South Wales, with the ostensible narrator Barrington 'consoling' Semple on his sentence to transportation by praising the prospects of the colony in comparison with England. A self-consciously literary work, the 'Heroic Epistle' contains a number of allusions to and imitations of Juvenal, in particular from the third and seventh Satires; indeed, the third Satire of Juvenal provides the guiding narrative structure for 'An Heroic Epistle', since that work is also presented as a poem inspired by the departure of a friend.[178] But while Juvenal's satires focus on the corruption at the heart of empire, 'An Heroic Epistle' adumbrates a mock-utopian colony; 'Barrington' describes his 'fancy's nobler flights' extending

> O'er half the world's great ball, my exil'd friend.
> She loves, with bold prophetic ken, to soar
> 'Mid the dim wonders of the destined shore;
> To rend the mystic veil of years away,
> And bare the future glories of the *Bay*—
> That *Bay* where now, methinks, at anchor ride
> A mighty nation's bulwark, wealth, and pride—
> That *Bay* round which the prophet's eye descries,
> In cumbrous pomp, a second London rise.
> Fir'd with the thought, I feel my soul dilate,
> Half-doom'd to envy ev'n my Semple's fate.[179]

Along with a slew of other literary references, the writer of 'An Heroic Epistle' displays great familiarity with the decidedly low-brow genre of criminal biography, and a reference to an obscure incident in 1785, when Barrington was reportedly injured by a collapsing wall, shows that the writer was also well versed in the newspaper gossip about Barrington in particular.[180] The author was quite possibly Henry Lemoine, a hack writer and sometime bookseller, who was editor – 'in part with others' – of the *Attic*

Miscellany, the periodical in which the poem was published in 1790.[181] In the third chapter of this book, the possibility that Henry Lemoine may have played a larger role in the Barrington publishing fraud, as the potential author of 'Barrington's' *Voyage to New South Wales*, will be considered. It should be pointed out here, however, that 'An Heroic Epistle' was clearly aimed at urbane reading audiences already well used to allonymous satirical verse, and there is little chance that the attribution to Barrington would have been meant or interpreted as genuine in the same way as the later 'Barrington' books. In this sense, 'An Heroic Epistle' is more of a testament to the broadening significance of the Barrington name than a genuine attempt to impersonate George Barrington.

It was also during the period when Barrington was a fugitive that the first significant biographical account of his life appeared. This was part of a series of gossipy pieces published in *The World* newspaper, which went under the running title of 'The Schools'.[182] *The World* was a comparatively short-lived but highly influential London daily which first appeared on 1 January 1787. Its elegant and innovative layout and typography, the brainchild of the Strand bookseller John Bell, was quickly imitated by the rival dailies, and the paper's writing style, with its mixture of town tattle, theatre criticism and, above all, its devotion to the poetry of the Della Cruscan movement, was similarly influential.[183] The paper's original editor, Edward Topham, a Cambridge graduate and 'gentleman of means', formed around himself a coterie of 'men of high literary character' at his residence in Beaufort-buildings.[184] From the end of 1787, this included particularly the Reverend Charles Este, an experienced newspaperman who assisted Topham in the editorship of *The World*.[185] The idea of 'The Schools' was to survey the more notable British public schools, and reflect on some of their more famous alumni. Some of the material was controversial: a correspondent to the *Morning Chronicle* in January

1788 complained about the liberties taken with the character of Richard Brinsley Sheridan in 'an essay called The Schools [in] a daily print of yesterday'.[186] In May 1788, *The Times* criticised 'the Reverend biographer of the Schools' for his choice of biographical subjects, among whom Barrington had recently featured: 'surely, the events of such a notorious thief, were not proper company for some very honourable characters which he has unfortunately lugged into his elaborate primmer of puerility'.[187] *The Times* damned the series, which apparently also detailed the background of other noted criminals, for the 'great pains' taken in detailing such notorious figures, and the 'disgrace' of associating them in the same series with more respectable subjects. Yet despite these moral scruples, *The Times* knew what interested the public, and at the same time as criticising 'The Schools' for its subjects, it printed a lengthy summary of its biography of Barrington.

According to the biographical account in 'The Schools'[188], Barrington had attended the Blue Coat School in Dublin, before being bound as an apprentice to a leather breeches maker, and his real name was said to be Waldron. This last detail was one of the few 'facts' about Barrington generally agreed upon in the contemporary biographies.[189] In her recent biography of Barrington, Sheila Box includes a copy of her correspondence with the archivist of the Blue Coat School, which reveals that a 'John Waldron' attended the school from 1762 to 1769 – so perhaps there was an element of truth in this story. Neither of the two versions of the *Memoirs of George Barrington* slavishly follows the biography from 'The Schools', but both may have been influenced by it. The Kearsley *Memoirs* have Barrington attending the Free Grammar School in Dublin, before he stabs a fellow pupil and subsequently runs away, while the Bird and Symonds *Memoirs* place Barrington as an apprentice to an apothecary and surgical instrument maker in Dublin. Another claim apparently made in 'The Schools' was that Barrington's mother was 'cook to the late Lord Barrington'. It is possible this detail was muddled between *The World* and *The Times*, but it is very unlikely that Barrington's mother could have been cook to the 'late Lord Barrington' – who had died in 1734, at least twenty years before Barrington was born. The rest of the biography was the standard one: after some initial attempts at picking pockets in Ireland, he journeyed to London, changed his name to Barrington, and 'became an adept in the science of pocket picking'.[190]

Barrington was reportedly engaged in practising his 'science' at the Theatre Royal in Newcastle when finally apprehended at the end of June 1788. The way the Bird and Symonds *Memoirs* tell it, Barrington was about to be released over the charges in Newcastle when a visitor from London informed the magistrate of the identity of the prisoner, who was then arrested as an outlaw.[191] It is not clear that this was in fact what took place, or whether the outlawry simply took precedence over any charges arising from Barrington's activities at Newcastle; at any rate a messenger arrived at Bow Street on 1 July informing the magistrates that Barrington was in custody at Newcastle. By 3 July, the London papers were reporting the story, stating that Barrington had been living incognito when caught, masquerading as a dentist from North Wales, and picking pockets, and that he would soon be brought back to London to face the charge of outlawry over the Le Mesurier theft eighteen months earlier.[192] The *St James's Chronicle* published a slightly different report from Newcastle, which stated that Barrington 'had a Lady with him, who, upon his being taken in Custody, decamped, an Officer is in Pursuit of her'.[193] This pursuit was apparently successful: according to the *Newcastle Chronicle*, 'the lady who travels with [Barrington] and calls herself his wife' was caught shortly afterwards and examined by the magistrate:

> She said her name was Johnson (Barrington had at first said his name was Jones) and that her father was a waiter at a tavern in York. No information could be gained from her that could lead to a discovery

of any malpractice by herself or her husband. She still remains in [custody], but, being far advanced in pregnancy, if no hope remain [*sic*] of gaining any criminating matter from her evidence, humanity would seem to plead much for her enlargement.[194]

Barrington's wife, whose Christian name was Mary, was subsequently released and bore the couple's child.[195] Barrington was not to enjoy any happy domestic scenes for some time, however. After a short period in Newcastle gaol, where he provided an object of curiosity for the local gentry – whom he received 'in the politest manner', earning the sympathy and approbation of the *Newcastle Chronicle* in the process[196] – Barrington was escorted back to the capital.

Barrington arrived in London on Friday, 24 July 1788, and was taken to Newgate. The papers, though thoroughly preoccupied with paid invective in the midst of another bitterly fought Westminster election, did not neglect to notice his return to the metropolis. The ongoing melodrama of Barrington's life remained irresistible copy; from the lecture he received from Sir Sampson Wright at Bow Street (at which Barrington 'bowed, and thanked the Magistrate') to his arrival at Newgate (where 'he gave a deep sigh, and said "He hoped should be as well treated there as he had been in the prison of Newcastle"'), Barrington's return to London was reported with voyeuristic avidity.[197] But in spite of all efforts to transform Barrington's story into the sort of cautionary tale typical of eighteenth-century criminal narratives, the Barrington saga resisted the necessary closure. Barrington had clearly not given up on his own cause: he maintained that, though 'he had been guilty of a few *foibles*, he had never committed *crimes*'[198] – and certainly, he had not lost the power to charm his audience into believing him. The Bow Street runner Townsend, who had been sent to collect Barrington from Newcastle, supposedly stated on his return that 'his behaviour was so much that of a gentleman, as to have divested him of every prejudice against him as a pickpocket'.[199]

If Barrington was attracting a degree of sympathy, it was probably because his situation was now parlous in the extreme. Since he had been declared an outlaw after the escape from the Brown Bear, he was technically liable to the death penalty without further trial once his identity had been established in court. Barrington's hopes were therefore pinned on a legal challenge to the writ of outlawry itself. These hopes were regarded as slender by the *Morning Chronicle*, which reported on 30 July 1788 that it was 'generally thought' that Barrington's latest legal difficulties 'would prove fatal to him', an assumption that was apparently shared by the magistrate at his committal.[200] The *Chronicle* even reported that 'some of the lower order of booksellers' were preparing biographies of Barrington, which were to be completed with the 'last dying words' speech Barrington was expected to furnish in due course.[201]

Yet Barrington did not give up hope. On 5 August, *The Times*, still in full election mode – that is to say, determinedly lambasting every prominent Whig it could – published an allonymous squib entitled 'Copy of a Letter from the NOTORIOUS GEORGE BARRINGTON; TO THE CELEBRATED CHARLES FOX'.[202] This piece was an ironic version of a 'last dying words' speech, addressed to Fox and pointing out the supposed similarities between the two public figures:

> … I was King of the Pickpockets, you grasped the purses of the people in a collective capacity—I took their money individually—your expenditure has always exceeded your honest income, and so has mine.—You took much money at the gaming tables—I took not a little at all public places of resort—the only difference was this, you got yours *openly*—I had mine by *stealth*—but a gambler and a pickpocket, I believe are almost synonymous in that merciful court above, where I shall shortly appear …[203]

To his credit, John Walter, the editor of *The Times*, printed a rejoinder written by Barrington himself (dated from Newgate, 6 August), which Walter conceded '[does] *honour* to his judgement and *credit* to his language'.[204] The respect accorded Barrington here is all the more surprising, since his letter took *The Times* to task, drawing parallels between the crime he was accused of ('a charge that remains to be proved', he reminded his audience) and the crimes committed by the press:

> honesty is not confined to a single point;—it exacts truth, candour and benevolence from its votaries. Lies and forgery are as gross violations of it as the charge that is laid against me.[205]

Barrington described the squib of 5 August as 'an attempt to ridicule one of the first men in the kingdom [Fox], and to injure at the same time a man who certainly never injured you', before going on to establish Walter's personal responsibility for the attacks on his character – 'in cases of calumny the publisher is as bad as the inventor, especially if he knows it to be such'. He then returned, in brilliant fashion, to his familiar theme of representing himself as the victim of 'cruelty and injustice' at the hands of a prejudiced press:

> however the charge against me has been magnified or misrepresented, I know I have nothing to fear from it, if you, and some others of the conductors of the daily prints would condescend to desist from poisoning the minds of my judges, and leave the event to a fair and impartial trial.—This, Sir, would be honest and manly on your part, and perhaps afford you as much pleasure on reflection, as exercising your wit, at the expense of your good nature.[206]

Barrington's appeal for discretion from the press was never going to succeed, of course, and *The Times* could not resist picking up on his praise of Fox in a sarcastic comment a few days later.[207] Yet at least the opportunities still existed for Barrington to represent himself, in his own inimitable style, before the public – for the time being, at least.

But it was before the courts that Barrington produced his greatest work. When brought before the Old Bailey for a committal proceeding on 18 September, Barrington delivered a typically eloquent speech. He claimed, rather implausibly, that he was unaware of the outlawry or any charges against him until he was brought to London, and he was ready and confident to face any charges, once the disagreeable matter of the outlawry was dealt with:

> For, my Lord, notwithstanding the confident assertions that have appeared in some erroneous, I will not say malevolent prints, and elsewhere, I am credibly assured, the charge laid against me before the Magistrate was merely on suspicion; and it is very unreasonable to suppose, that a person, under such circumstances, should subject himself to a process so summary as outlawry, knowing any thing about it. Or will the liberal spirit of the laws, justify dooming a man to death, untried and unheard, because it appears he has been negligent.[208]

Barrington's speech on this occasion was widely covered in the press.[209] The reporter for *The Times* noted that the speech was 'most favourably received by the Court, and made a strong impression on every person who heard it', once more lamenting the wasted talents of its author, who could 'have done honour to any honourable profession'.[210] The speech was even printed as a broadside, which appeared under the title: 'The Famous Speech of George Barrington, Esq. before the Judge and Jury at the Old Bailey, together with the learned Recorder's Answer, 18th Sept., 1788'.[211]

By a combination of sympathy for Barrington's talents, and a general feeling that the process of outlawry was a somewhat archaic and illiberal part of the law, public opinion seemed to be turning in the pickpocket's favour. *The Times* opined that 'the system of outlawry is a matter not very agreeable to the constitution of a free state', and argued that Barrington should have the opportunity of the trial he was 'entitled to by the spirit, though not by the express letter of the law'.[212] The *Whitehall Evening Post* supposed that '[the] abilities of Barrington render it impossible for the public to avoid feeling some pity for him, notwithstanding the criminal excesses of his conduct', though it felt duty bound to remind the public that 'we should, at the time we feel compassion for a criminal, remember that there is a community also to be pitied, which his practices may disturb and endanger'. Nevertheless, the editor agreed that Barrington should have the chance of a trial by jury.[213] While Barrington, for once, might have been content to let the opinion of the press prevail, it was of course a matter that would still have to be resolved in court. In early November 1788, Paul Le Mesurier, brother and legal counsel of Barrington's victim, applied for the case to be removed to the Court of King's Bench, the highest court in the land outside the House of Lords.[214] Perhaps he wished to take the proceedings into a realm where Barrington's affecting speeches might have less bearing on the proceedings.

In the event, Barrington's trial at the King's Bench was long delayed – it was more than a year between the writ to remove the proceedings to that court and the actual trial. In the interim, Richard Blandy, the Drury Lane constable who had allowed Barrington to escape, was tried at the King's Bench. Blandy was damned by the testimony of his fellow constable Townsend, who swore that both he and Blandy had 'a perfect knowledge of Barrington', and that he had even 'disputed with [Blandy] as to which of them knew him best'.[215] Townsend's testimony was all the bench needed to judge Blandy guilty. The 'old and infirm' constable was subsequently sentenced to one year's imprisonment in Newgate, which he did not survive.[216] Barrington was clearly unhappy that this trial – which was reminding all and sundry of his notorious reputation, and about the flight from the Brown Bear itself – was taking place so soon before he was due to appear over the outlawry. Again, he wrote to the newspapers, this time to the *Morning Chronicle*, protesting against that paper's coverage of the Blandy trial. Barrington skilfully cast doubt on the motives behind the Le Mesurier brothers' timing of the trials (they were also prosecuting Blandy), and represented the pursuit of the outlawry as a means of denying him a fair trial. Once again, Barrington was reducing the legal process to a gentlemanly dispute, one in which he was being unfairly used. And once again, Barrington urged that the press should refrain from any comment that 'had such a manifest tendency to inflame and mislead the public':

> if cruelty, malice, or wantonness, obtruded anything prejudicial on the subject, the Editor should act like the Recording Angel, and blot it out with a tear. The approbation of his own mind will amply recompense him.[217]

The editor of the *Morning Chronicle*, in a note affixed to Barrington's letter, pointed out that the paper had simply reported on the evidence presented at the trial.[218] An admirably dogged Barrington then sent a follow-up letter, stating that if the reporting on the trial was accurate, then the evidence itself must have been wrong: 'or the expense and trouble I have sustained in trying to reverse the outlawry, must have been very vainly applied'.[219]

If Barrington availed himself of delaying tactics to put more distance between his trial and that of Blandy, he also made good use of the long period of incarceration. By the time the trial commenced in November 1789, Barrington had secured the services of a heavy-hitting barrister, William Garrow, and a solicitor, George Wood. One wonders how Barrington, who had recently complained of his difficulty in supporting himself (by his profession of surgery, he claimed) while imprisoned, and of his heavy expenses in gaol[220], could have afforded such high-quality representation. It is conceivable, of course, that Garrow worked *pro bono*. As an ambitious and still young lawyer, Garrow may have enjoyed having such a high-profile client, and he would represent Barrington at each of his subsequent court appearances. Another possible explanation revolves around Garrow's then deter-minedly Foxite political leanings.[221] There remains a possibility that Barrington had influential, if somewhat fair-weather, friends on this side of politics; conceivably the Foxite Whigs may have enjoyed frustrating the Pittite Le Mesurier brothers (against whom they had old scores to settle[222]) by sponsoring Barrington's cause. A different explanation was subsequently provided by a piece of gossip printed in *The Times*:

> It is said when BARRINGTON was tried, it was known that he had five or six thousand pounds in the funds; formerly it was great enjoyment to the city to see men hung with ruffles, but now ruffles have quite at [*sic*] different effect.[223]

The cause of the outlawry was eventually won by Barrington's counsel; the writ of outlawry was reversed and Barrington was committed to stand trial before a jury. Of the case, the most important thing to observe in the context of the present study is how closely the developments were followed in the press. There were no salacious details here; it was a case purely of legal wrang-ling, which was ultimately decided by minor clerical errors in the writ of outlawry itself.[224] Yet somehow the involvement of Barrington made even this case interesting and newsworthy. The *Morning Post* ignored most of the tedious legal arguments to concentrate on Barrington's 'able and eloquent speech', his 'light green coat with every fashionable appurtenance', his 'extremely well-dressed' hair, and his 'calm and gentlemanly' conduct.[225] There was a perception that Barrington's challenge to the outlawry would be a test case, likely to set a new precedent in a rather outmoded legal process, and indeed the case would be referred to in a variety of legal texts after this time.[226] Yet this in itself does not account for the extraordinary level of interest displayed by the newspaper press in the case: *The Times*, the *Morning Post*, the *Morning Chronicle*, *The World*, the *Whitehall Evening Post*, and the *Universal Magazine* all published detailed accounts of what was essentially an extended legal debate on a fine point of law.[227]

Almost three years after the incident itself, Barrington finally went to trial over the Le Mesurier theft at the Old Bailey in December 1789. Once in court, Barrington immediately challenged the whole of the jury, apologetically explaining that 'I must own, that I am acting under the influence of a report, which is perhaps very untrue'.[228] Whether or not there were any grounds to the insinuation Barrington so tactfully made here, it is impossible to say; but it should be observed that Barrington had previously questioned the motives of the Le Mesurier brothers, and that their prosecution had certainly been pursued with dogged determination over a very long period of time. By the time Barrington's appearance at the Old Bailey was over, however, the Le Mesuriers might have wished they had saved themselves the trouble. Their case was badly damaged by the non-appearance of the only material witness: the Mr Adeane who had helped secure Barrington in the lobby of Drury Lane was apparently in the West Indies at the time. William Garrow, in his cross-examination, was frankly contemptuous of the abilities of his opposing counsel, Paul Le Mesurier – who had also been responsible for the clerical error that spoiled the writ of outlawry. Barrington also delivered a very long speech in his defence, though his trademark eloquence, and protestations of victimisation, had apparently become somewhat tired. The *Public Advertiser* opined that Barrington's speech was 'by no mean delivered with that force and energy in which several of his former speeches have been conceived'[229]; while the *Morning Post*, characteristically more virulent, described Barrington's defence as 'inflated with vanity and marked by audacity'.[230] Nonetheless, after three years as an outlaw, Barrington was acquitted and walked from the Old Bailey a free man.

Although he had won his long, drawn-out cause, the papers did not let up their harangue, and continued to exploit the notorious Barrington name for their own purposes. Jackson's *Morning Post*, which usually led the way with its particularly vicious treatment of Barrington, warned that the pickpocket's acquittal, while granting the incorrigible offender 'temporary freedom',

> will by no means operate favourably to his fraternity; for the Judges are determined, and so is the Crown, that every convicted offender of his class shall feel the utmost rigour of the law.[231]

The above paragraph has the ring of ministerial propaganda, a possibility which is supported by the fact that it was also inserted in two other newspapers, the rigidly pro-government *Times*, and the *London Chronicle*.[232] But if this paragraph was financed by the Treasury, it was now something of an anomaly for the *Morning Post*, which had reinvented itself as an opposition newspaper, possibly after being abandoned by the government.[233] The change in the *Post*'s political principles, however, affected the paper's characteristic use of Barrington's notoriety to make ludicrous jibes at the expense of public figures only in so far as its targets were now drawn from the opposite side of politics. Where the *Post* in 1785 had aligned Barrington with the 'Buff and Blue' (the colours of the Foxite Whigs), it now claimed that Barrington's 'suite' arrived in court in 'blue and orange' (Royalist colours).[234] Where Fox had once been the butt of the *Post*'s scabrous Barrington-themed witticisms, the paper now aimed its paragraphs at Warren Hastings, the former governor-general of India whose trial for corruption was a major embarrassment for the Pitt ministry. The *Post* had Barrington applying to Hastings for recommendation for an appointment to India:

> For, says the ingenious ornament of the *freebooting* fraternity, Englishmen in general are converted into *pickpockets* after they get into the East: but I shall go ready made, and therefore make shorter work of it.[235]

Another jibe, this time aimed at the *ci devant* radical John Wilkes, was considered witty enough to also appear in the ministerial *Times*:

> BARRINGTON's ill success in attempting the pocket of Mr. WILKES, is easily accounted for; the thief made his attempt on the worthy Alderman the day he was reconciled at St. James's, and *turned his coat*.[236]

Along with these petty squibs and jokes, the press displayed a renewed interest in following Barrington's movements. In the week following his acquittal, several papers reported that Barrington had inherited a property in Hampshire on the death of an aunt, and had gone there with his wife and child: 'thus placed above want', the report opined, 'there can be no excuse for further Risques in his former profession'.[237] As with most of the gossip surrounding Barrington's life, it is difficult to know if there was any truth in the rumours of an inheritance. In any case, less than three months later, reports began to surface that Barrington was once again engaged in the profession of picking pockets. A paragraph in *The Times*, which also appeared in the popular *Lady's Magazine*, gave a description of a theft allegedly perpetrated by Barrington while on board a packet boat to Ireland.[238] *The Times* also reported that Barrington was later to be found hobnobbing at the Rotunda Gardens in Dublin, and claimed that 'he mentioned some elevated and respectable characters as his friends, and declared an anxiety to be at the Castle on a particular day to pay his devoirs'.[239] But the press left no room for doubt as to what it considered Barrington's true connections to be. A further *Times* report on Barrington's activities in Ireland spoke of Barrington's 'suite', in which criminals 'of the first capacity are enlisted'.[240] Again, it is difficult to give full credence to such reports, when there is a clear intent to sensationalise Barrington, 'this Prince of Pickpockets', and to exaggerate 'that furtive adroitness in which Barrington and his agents exceed everything recorded of Lacedemonium ingenuity'.[241]

At length, 'the celebrated Barrington' returned to London; *The Times*, 'for the caution of the public', reported his return to the capital on 9 April 1790.[242] Within five months, Barrington was arrested again, for picking the pocket of one Henry Hare Townsend at a race meeting at Enfield on 1 September. This proved to be the final act of Barrington's criminal career. He was convicted of the theft at the Old Bailey later the same month, and sentenced to seven years transportation. To the end Barrington refused to acknowledge his criminality, and his final speech, given after his sentence on 22 September, was a brilliant recapitulation of the theme he had pursued for so many years, that he was a victim of the malignity of an unfeeling world:

> ... I cannot help observing that it is the strange lot of some persons through life, that with the best wishes, the best endeavours, and the best intentions, they are not able to escape the evenomed [*sic*] tooth of calumny; whatever they say or do is so twisted and perverted from the reality, that they will meet with censure and misfortune, where perhaps they were entitled to success and praise. The world, my Lord, has given me credit for much more abilities than I am conscious of possessing; but the world should also consider that the greatest abilities may be so obstructed by the mercenary nature of some unfeeling minds, as to render them entirely useless to the possessor. Where was the generous and powerful man that would come forward and say, you have some abilities which might be of service to yourself and to others, but you have much to struggle with, I feel for your

situation, and will place you in a condition to try the sincerity of your intentions; and as long as you act with diligence and fidelity you shall not want for countenance and protection? But, my Lord, the die is cast! I am prepared to meet the sentence of the Court with respectful resignation, and the painful lot assigned me, I hope, with becoming resolution.[243]

Whatever the nature of Barrington's criminal career, there was certainly an element of truth in his protestations of suffering at the hands of a 'mercenary' press. The press, on the other hand, was losing one of its favourite subjects, and by the time Barrington was embarked for transportation in early 1791 the newspapers were already lamenting the exit of this extraordinary figure. The *Morning Chronicle*, veering between sarcasm and nostalgia, eulogised this 'great man ... now on a voyage of colonization for the good of his country, [who] was not only at the head of his own *profession* ... [but] shewed uncommon talents for public speaking and epistolary composition'. The *Chronicle* went on to opine that

A complete edition of [Barrington's] speeches in Courts of Justice, and his letters from different gaols, revised and corrected by the Author, with notes critical and explanatory, would be a valuable accession to the *law* and *literature* of the country.[244]

Barrington, of course, was never to write any such book. Though he had vigorously fought a losing battle to salvage his reputation over his fifteen years in the public spotlight, his conviction and departure for New South Wales marked the end of his attempts to maintain any semblance of control over his image. The life and trials of George Barrington, however, were henceforth to find even more enthusiastic champions within the British book trade.

CHAPTER TWO

The Lives of George BARRINGTON

*P*redictably, Barrington's final trial and conviction in September 1790 sparked a flurry of press activity. In George Barrington's darkest hour, the 'celebrated Barrington' reached the peak of his fame, and for a time was the most talked about topic of the day, as *The Times* noted:

> During the Parliamentary vacation, the public mind has been tolerably well gratified by variety:–1st, the General Election; which kept on tolerably well, until it was relieved by various new lies respecting the Spanish Negotiation, and an overflow of politics from France. The Coalition between the Duke of Orleans and de la Fayette, was talked of for a day or two, until the peace between the King of Sweden and the Empress kicked that out of memory, and was soon followed up by the Margate Duels, which after boring the public ear for ten days, was trampled into oblivion by the Trial of Barrington.[1]

The London dailies certainly seemed unwilling to give up the subject that had provided a font of copy for so many years. After having printed a very pedestrian anecdote about 'the NOTORIOUS BARRINGTON' three days earlier, *The Times* of 25 September proposed that the gentleman thief might be made an officer and sent as 'Captain to an army of convicts', to fight Britain's enemies abroad.[2] *The World* had used Barrington's arrest at the start of the month to editorialise on the incorrigibility of the criminal mind:

> *Barrington*, again detected in picking pockets, shews the futility of tenderness to established culprits. Were he pardoned to the end of the chapter, would he not sin again to the *end of the chapter* likewise?[3]

Such wickedness clearly remained of interest to the paper's readers, however, and over the next month *The World* would publish a steady stream of court reports, gossip, invective and 'revelations' about Barrington.[4] Barrington's career was also celebrated in popular ballads, printed in broadside form, which used 'flash' – the dialect of the underworld – to heap ironic praise on the celebrated thief.[5] Luckily for the circulation of the press, the capture of Barrington did not bring criminal activity in Britain to a close, as *The World* noted in its characteristic jocular style:

> BARRINGTON being gone—has yet left '*his like behind him.*' His scholars say, 'he certainly was a *Professor*; but yet there are a great many amateurs of the—*fine arts.*'[6]

With the 'celebrated Barrington' generating considerable comment in the press, and no doubt also in the taverns and coffee houses, it was only a matter of time before the book trade obliged the public with more substantial accounts of Barrington's life and trials. The first such publication – *The Trial at Large of George Barrington*, a pamphlet account of Barrington's final trial as recorded by the Old Bailey's shorthand reporter Edmund Hodgson – was advertised in *The Times* just four days after the trial on 15 September – that is, before Barrington had even been sentenced.[7] Speed, of course, was paramount in marketing publications of topical interest such as this, and it is a testament to the public interest in the genteel pickpocket that there was a market for such a production at all. The engraved portrait of Barrington in the dock of the Old Bailey that adorns the work scarcely seems to justify the price of one shilling for the proceedings of a trial that was amply reported in a plethora of magazines and newspapers, and contained no information on Barrington beyond that which had been stated in court.[8] *The Trial at Large of George Barrington* functioned, then, as something like a souvenir edition, commemorating Barrington's final public appearance. The tract was presumably produced under some sort of arrangement between the booksellers and Hodgson, who would also publish the same text in the Old Bailey sessions paper, *The Whole Proceedings*, of which he was the current proprietor.[9] It is worth pointing out that one of the booksellers who so quickly anticipated the public interest in Barrington and published *The Trial at Large* was Henry Delahay Symonds, who over the following decade would make great capital from the Barrington name.[10]

Given the public interest in Barrington, it was inevitable that works giving a fuller biographical account of the celebrated pickpocket would appear following his final trial. Criminal biography was a staple of popular literature throughout the eighteenth century, with the lives and 'last dying speeches' of notable criminals widely published in the form of pamphlets, broadsides and *Newgate Calendar*-style compilations.[11] The factual basis of such works was usually highly questionable, and their narratives generally followed a very similar plan, detailing the subject's descent into vice and crime, and ultimate repentance on the scaffold prior to execution. If Barrington eventually thwarted the master narrative of 'Newgate biography' by avoiding such an ignominious end, for much of his time in the public spotlight it appeared that his story would indeed end in this well-worn manner. When facing execution over the outlawry in 1788, the *Morning Chronicle* reported that 'some of the lower order of booksellers' were so sure of Barrington's impending demise that

[they] have ordered the man's life to be written, though they cannot positively ascertain his fate. The book is to be entitled the Biography of B——n, written by HIMSELF. This title will render the work ludicrous

enough—if any blunder on so serious a subject as death *can* be ludicrous—for his last words are committed to paper, and will be related in the course of his narration.[12]

In the event, Barrington's sentence to transportation sufficed as the cue for the 'lower order of booksellers' to begin exploiting his fame. Two competing biographies were published little more than a fortnight after Barrington's final trial.[13] These were *The Memoirs of George Barrington*, published by 'J. Bird' and H. D. Symonds[14], and *Memoirs of George Barrington*, nominally published by 'M. Smith' – which was in fact a false imprint used by the Fleet Street bookseller George Kearsley.[15] The texts of these two prototype biographies of Barrington were freely plundered by a number of other publishers: while at least nineteen other book-length biographies were published over forty years following Barrington's trial in 1790, every one of these to a greater or lesser extent pirated or plagiarised one or other of these two sources.

The two biographies approach their subject in fundamentally different ways. In the first place, the details they each provide about Barrington's background, and his subsequent descent into a life of crime, are significantly divergent. In the Kearsley *Memoirs*, Barrington learns his criminal trade in a company of strolling players headed by one John Price.[16] In the Bird and Symonds *Memoirs*, he is apprenticed to an apothecary until led astray by 'a female, named Ranby, whose *extravagance* being strictly proportioned to her *chastity*, our hero was led into the greatest pecuniary embarrassments'.[17] The latter narrative then follows what Phillip Rawlings has identified as a common trope of eighteenth-century crime biography, where criminality results from a collapse of the master–apprentice relationship – a rupture which is often represented as brought about by the influence of a libidinous woman.[18] It is significant in this context that a woman, and the 'considerable encrease of expence' she represents, also features in Barrington's downfall in the Kearsley *Memoirs*, though Barrington's 'connexion' with an ill-fated fallen woman named only 'Miss Egerton' in this narrative probably owes more to the sentimental novels of the later eighteenth century than to the traditions of criminal biography.[19] Both narratives show Barrington passing through a phase of criminal apprenticeship, but they locate this phase differently. In the Kearsley *Memoirs*, it takes place in Ireland in the early 1770s with Price and his players, while in the Bird and Symonds *Memoirs* it is under the guidance of the pickpocket Elizabeth West in London, in the late 1770s.[20]

There are even greater differences in terms of structure between the two narratives. The bulk of the Bird and Symonds *Memoirs* is taken up with trial reports, reproduced verbatim from the Old Bailey *Whole Proceedings*.[21] By contrast, the Kearsley biography contains very little on Barrington's public appearances, devoting the greater part of the narrative to elucidating the protagonist's life out of the spotlight. As the reviewer for the *Monthly Review* noted, this allowed the anonymous biographer to approach their subject in a suspiciously novelistic manner[22], and indeed the Kearsley text contained a generous helping of 'filler' material, such as light verse supposed to have been written by Barrington himself.[23] While this space for literary embellishment was no doubt the main reason for concentrating on the lesser known aspects of Barrington's life, it may also have been partly due to the expediency with which the narrative was published. Kearsley may have got wind that a rival *Memoirs of George Barrington* was in the works, and decided to forego any lengthy digressions on Barrington's later career in order to get the book published as quickly as possible, thereby capitalising on the peak of Barrington's fame.

Certainly, the swiftness with which Kearsley published his *Memoirs of George Barrington* suggests that the manuscript was already in a state of advanced preparation by the time Barrington went to trial. An established publisher of criminal biographies, Kearsley

A

NEW EDITION.

MEMOIRS

OF

GEORGE BARRINGTON;

FROM

HIS BIRTH IN MDCCLV,

TO

HIS LAST CONVICTION

AT THE

OLD BAILEY,

ON

FRIDAY, THE 17th OF SEPTEMBER, MDCCXC.

LONDON:

PRINTED FOR M. SMITH,

OPPOSITE FETTER-LANE, IN FLEET-STREET.

MDCCXC.

Title page of the second edition of George Kearsley's *Memoirs of George Barrington*. Hordern House Rare Books.

had recently enjoyed great success with his biographies of the swindlers Charles Price and James Semple.[24] These works were more ambitious than the usual run of eighteenth-century crime biographies, being 'wrought up in the novel style'[25], a formula that proved immensely successful and established a template for the Barrington biography. The attention given to criminal life in Kearsley's novelised biographies left the works open to moral condemnation, and the rapid sale of the books was noted, with disgust, in the newspaper press:

> Since the first appearance of THE MEMOIRS OF CHARLES PRICE, little else has been read or talked of. There have been several thousands already sold, and as many more are now printing! This fact is stated as a proof, that the contemplation of the baseness of human nature is become a more pleasing subject than its virtues.[26]

Apparently the profit motive outweighed the impact of such strictures, however, and Kearsley was certainly savvy enough to anticipate the demand for a Barrington biography and to appreciate the need for speed in publishing it after his trial. Only eight days separated Barrington's final speech at the Old Bailey (which was quoted on the final pages of the *Memoirs*) and Kearsley's attendance at Stationers' Hall, bearing nine copies of his published narrative as the legal deposit required for the granting of copyright.[27] It was fairly unusual to copyright such a work – this was a step Kearsley had not felt compelled to take with the publication of his successful works on Price and Semple. Given the low literary and moral esteem in which 'Newgate biographies' were held, to submit such a work to the perusal of his peers in the conservative setting of the Stationers' Hall must have been something akin to running the gauntlet, particularly as Kearsley was claiming rights to a work on which his name did not even appear.

Whether or not the existence of the Bird and Symonds *Memoirs* helped hasten the publication of Kearsley's *Memoirs*, the converse certainly appears to be true. The Bird and Symonds narrative begins in a similar vein to the Kearsley *Memoirs*, though its anecdotal style is more reminiscent of traditional eighteenth-century crime biography than the novelistic Kearsley text. In the initial section of the work, there are anecdotes, of dubious authority, on Barrington's upbringing, his experiences in Ireland, and his 'apprenticeship' with Elizabeth West. There are no extended poetic interludes as in the Kearsley *Memoirs*, but the Bird and Symonds *Memoirs* do include a similarly Menippean embellishment with a story about Barrington robbing a trades-man with a special pickpocketing tool the latter had designed for him, a tale partly written in dialogue.[28] But following this episode, the narrative form established in the first pages of the text abruptly breaks down. The omniscient third-person narrator who begins the work goes missing, and little effort is made to maintain a continuous narrative, or to disguise the fact that the vast majority of the text from this point on has been simply cut and pasted from the Old Bailey sessions paper. The publishers seem to have had a small pamphlet format in mind for their publication, and the excerpted material has been crammed into the work using a very small type, with the text densely packed on the page. Though in some sense this surfeit of documentary material represented better value for money over the sparse, somewhat pretentious letterpress of the Kearsley *Memoirs*, the varying font sizes and crowded text look untidy, and one assumes that the typography as well as the narrative structure would surely have been improved had the publishers been less concerned with rushing the work onto the market.

A close examination of the six copies of the Bird and Symonds *Memoirs* held by the Mitchell Library supports the theory that production of the work was rushed. While regarded as one edition in the classification of the work in Ferguson's *Bibliography of Australia*[29], only two of the six copies in the Mitchell Library are identical – the other four manifest minor variations consistent with a limited resetting of the type between pressings. One copy, from David Scott Mitchell's collection, contains numerous printing errors and misspellings, and may therefore be assumed to be an early version.[30] The subsequent versions make corrections to the text, as well as various minor changes in typography and presentation. These, however, are only limited cosmetic changes; a question, in printing terms, of substituting a handful of pieces of type here and there. There are some more significant changes between versions where the paragraph alignment of the text has been changed, which would have involved a more substantial resetting of the type. This occurs only towards the end of the narrative, however, which is consistent with the theory that multiple versions of the work were produced within a short space of time, with only minor typographical changes made and no significant changes to the text.

If the publishers of both versions of the *Memoirs of George Barrington* had raced to get their productions completed and onto the market first, this race finished in something like a dead heat. The competing *Memoirs* were advertised, side by side, in the same issue of *The Times*, on 4 October 1790. The advertising used for the different works reflected their divergent characters. Bird and Symonds emphasised the copious details of Barrington's trials and speeches in court included in their publication. Kearsley concentrated on advertising the fact that the 'principal part' of his *Memoirs* was supposedly written by a fellow 'partaker of the guilt of Barrington', who had since repented his former life and gained the superior moral standing that would guarantee an appropriate perspective for the criminal biography genre – an author, in other words, who could offer the reader the best of both worlds. It will not surprise those familiar with the workings of the eighteenth-century book trade to learn that both sets of advertisements make claims which are not fully borne out in the publications themselves. The Symonds and Bird advertisement prominently draws attention to two sets of engravings, where in the actual book the illustrations form two sections of a single frontispiece. The Kearsley advertising is more thorough in its deceptiveness. The author promoted in the advertising – one 'Mr. James', conveniently residing 'in a Convent in Westphalia' – does not in fact function as the narrator of the work, nor is this character as significant in the text as the advertising makes out. What the character 'Mr. James' actually does provide in the text of the Kearsley *Memoirs* is a moral parallel to Barrington's story; the backgrounds of James and Barrington are similar: they both turn to crime and act in cahoots for a brief period, but James eventually finds remorse, repentance and grace, while Barrington spirals further into crime.[31] In the advertising of the Kearsley *Memoirs* it is a different story; here James is claimed to be Barrington's 'constant companion', who knew him 'above twenty years'.[32] The actual narrative is far less convincing than the advertising, however, and one reviewer was decidedly nonplussed by a biography which bore 'no marks of authenticity, nor is it very interesting'.[33]

Both of the two prototype Barrington biographies were emblazoned with frontispiece illustrations of the celebrated pickpocket. Such illustrations were traditionally important in the marketing, sale and reception of eighteenth-century crime biographies. Even more markedly than in the nascent form of the novel, the genre of criminal biography employed illustrations as 'interpretive guides' to the text and, certainly, portraits of criminal figures 'offered a miniature surrogate to the book's absent [subject], a small private fetish that the book buyer could take home with text'.[34] When the *Trial at Large of George Barrington* and the two different *Memoirs* came to be noticed in the leading reviewing periodicals of the day, the *Monthly Review* and the *Critical Review*, five out of six of these notices described or mentioned the illustrations in some way.[35] This was probably partly due to a lack of interest in the narratives themselves on the part of the reviewers, who no doubt thought such works beneath their critical attention. But pictorial depictions of their infamous subjects were clearly an important part of the criminal biography package. In the case of the Barrington books, frontispiece illustrations constituted another site where the publishers could battle for advantage in the market, and underhand tactics were certainly used in terms of pictorial plagiarism – the frontispiece to the Bird and Symonds *Memoirs*, in particular, was imitated in a number of other publications.[36] The engraving issued with the Kearsley *Memoirs*, an appropriately sensational piece of work depicting the famous theft of Count Orlov's snuff box, executed by one of the Barlow family of engravers, was published on 6 October 1790.[37] This date was somewhat later than the actual publication date of his *Memoirs*, raising the possibility that Kearsley issued copies of his biography before the plate was ready so as not to lose ground to the competition. In any case, it is very likely that the illustrations from both versions of the *Memoirs* were also sold independently, providing a further avenue for the booksellers to exploit Barrington's fame. There was even a souvenir Staffordshire earthenware mug produced, emblazoned with the illustration from the Bird and Symonds *Memoirs*.[38]

George Kearsley was a publisher who had gained something of a reputation in the trade for his hardnosed business tactics. One of his neighbours in Fleet Street, John Murray, had broken off their 'modest but lucrative trade' in 1786 after Kearsley insulted him in a newspaper advertisement.[39] The following year, Kearsley was criticised by an anonymous writer in a satirical pamphlet, which lampooned him as 'puffing K——y' for his habit of taking out newspaper advertisements that praised his own publications, and denounced him as 'a fellow of formidable effrontery' who on more than one occasion had declared bankruptcy in order to avoid paying his trade connections.[40] If Kearsley was chastened by

Above and opposite: The frontispiece and title page from *The Memoirs of George Barrington*, published by Bird and Simmonds. Hordern House Rare Books.

THE

M E M O I R S

O F

GEORGE BARRINGTON,

CONTAINING

EVERY REMARKABLE CIRCUMSTANCE,

FROM HIS BIRTH TO THE PRESENT TIME,

INCLUDING THE FOLLOWING TRIALS—

1. For robbing Mrs. Dudman	5. Mr. Bagſhaw
2. Elizabeth Ironmonger	6. Mr. Le Meſurier
3. Returning from Tranſportation	7. For Outlawry
4. Robbing Sir G. Webſter	8. For robbing Mr. Townſend.

WITH THE WHOLE OF HIS

CELEBRATED SPEECHES,

Taken from the Records of the King's Bench, Old Bailey, &c.

L O N D O N,

Printed for J. BIRD, No. 22, Fetter Lane, Fleet Street; and
SIMMONDS, No. 20, Paternoſter Row.

[PRICE ONE SHILLING.]

such criticism, it seems not to have altered his business practices, and in 1790 he responded to the threat posed by a competing Barrington biography using the same strategy he had been lampooned for in 1787; he 'puffed' his publication in the press:

> The MEMOIRS of BARRINGTON, published for M. Smith, at No. 46, in Fleet-street, and written by his quondam friend in iniquity, Mr. James, now resident in Westphalia, is a most extraordinary production.
>
> The pages are rich with the tricks of deception, and form an excellent companion to the Lives of Price and Semple.
>
> It is difficult to say which of the three raise our astonishment most, the Swindler, the Bank-note forger, or the Pick-pocket.
>
> Of Barrington there are now no less than three Lives; that, however, abovementioned, printed for M. Smith, is the only one that is written with a well informed pen.
>
> James knew him above twenty years, as appears by his account; he was his constant companion; and the transactions of every day furnished him with excellent materials for these Memoirs. This caution is become absolutely necessary as a guard against two spurious productions, which are made up of Newspaper matter only.[41]

Kearsley's biographies of Price and Semple were similarly cross-promoted in an advertisement leaf issued with his *Memoirs of George Barrington*.[42] Perhaps because of the lucrative library of criminal biographies he was amassing, Kearsley was determined not to cede any advantage to the 'spurious productions' in the market. Moreover, some effort at strategy was probably necessary, as the Kearsley publication was priced at two shillings – double the price of the Bird and Symonds *Memoirs*.

With competition in the Barrington biographies mounting, Kearsley continued his marketing blitz. In mid-November, a new edition was announced, the advertisement now appearing under the header of 'JAMES'S MEMOIRS OF BARRINGTON'.[43] The public was again warned, in even stronger terms, 'against some vile impositions ... unauthentic, and unentertaining', which had had the audacity to compete with 'James's *Memoirs*'. The new advertising re-emphasised the unique claim to authority of the supposed author:

> As a strong instance of the respectability of James's materials, having retired into a Convent to expiate his crimes, he is not backward in acknowledging himself for upwards of a dozen years a brother depredator with the subject of these Memoirs.

It is worth noting that the duration of James' association with Barrington has now been revised downward by some years, presumably as a concession to verisimilitude. There are new fraudulent claims, however. The advertisement claims that 'a few, and by no means indifferent, poetical effusions, written by Barrington, are added to this Edition'. In fact all 'poetical effusions' in the 'new' edition were also to be found in the original; there were no differences whatsoever between the texts of the two nominal 'editions'. A further 'New Edition, Greatly Improved', subsequently appeared, making some typographical but no textual changes. One wonders how many more twists the marketing of the Barrington *Memoirs* may have taken, had not Kearsley suddenly died, 'of an apoplectic fit', on 6 December 1790.[44]

The other 'spurious production' attacked by Kearsley in his advertisements was likely to have been another publication entitled *The Memoirs of George Barrington*. This work was published under the imprint 'B. Urquhart' – almost certainly a false imprint – and rather audaciously bore the surtitle 'the only Authentic edition'.[45] In reality, this publication was a piracy of the Bird and Symonds *Memoirs*. Some attempt had been made to differentiate the narratives by the provision of a new introduction, which represented the reading of 'Newgate biography' as a social and moral necessity:

The amazing progress of vice in later years renders it a duty incumbent on every individual ... to hold its picture up to mankind, with its striking features of deformity, in order that the rest of his fellow creatures, frightened at the caricature, may refrain from those enormities which have always the most fatal consequences ...

Nothing less than the vigilance of the magistracy, and the presenting to public view, in its most shocking light, the disgraceful consequences of evil courses can effectually stop the foundation of immorality; it is for this purpose that we have undertaken to give a genuine and more ample account of the late unfortunate GEORGE BARRINGTON than any that has hitherto appeared; that from his untimely fate our fellow subjects may take warning and rectify their own conduct.[46]

But this original introduction in the 'Urquhart' *Memoirs* – to the extent that such general reflections on the dire consequences attendant on vice can be called original – serves as a facade for what in reality was the first in a series of piracies from the two prototype versions of the *Memoirs*. The 'genuine and more ample account' that followed was almost wholly taken – though considerably abridged – from the Bird and Symonds text. As is characteristic of the piratical productions which appropriated one or other of the prototype *Memoirs*, there was no attempt (apart from the new introduction) to rewrite the work – sentences, paragraphs, and sometimes whole pages were simply omitted. It was certainly the 'Urquhart' *Memoirs*, and not the Bird and Symonds version, that was the piracy, however. Apart from the early advertisements on the part of the latter publishers, there is a crucial piece of internal evidence in the 'Urquhart' *Memoirs* itself. With the exception of the new introduction, there is only one other occasion where this work uses material not sourced from the Bird and Symonds *Memoirs*. This occurs on pages 17–18, where the 'Urquhart' *Memoirs* suddenly interpolates a three-paragraph passage from the Kearsley *Memoirs*.[47]

At forty pages, the 'Urquhart' *Memoirs of George Barrington* is the same size as Bird and Symonds' pamphlet, making up for the shorter length of its text by using a larger type, uniform throughout the work. Typographically this is a great improvement on the higgledy-piggledy font sizes and densely packed letterpress of the Bird and Symonds *Memoirs*, which give that production the impression of a rushed job. The abridgements to the text also trimmed much of the superfluous detail from the Barrington trial reports. With these changes, the work may be seen as in some regards superior, both in aesthetics and in terms of the flow of the narrative, to its source. Unlike the majority of the works which pirated the original Barrington biographies, the 'Urquhart' *Memoirs* does not use a new title: in fact its title page imitates the wording, and even the typography, of the Bird and Symonds *Memoirs*, and its frontispiece illustration is also an imitation. It may be that what the publisher of the 'B. Urquhart' work had in mind was not only piracy but usurpation: by producing an improved version of the same text, and then labelling it 'the only Authentic edition', he may have sought to displace in the marketplace the original work. This argument is supported by the fact that the 'Urquhart' *Memoirs* carried the same price tag (one shilling) as the work it copied – this was unusual, as pirated publications generally offset their illegitimacy by means of a substantial price reduction. An intriguing footnote to the piracy of the Bird and Symonds *Memoirs* by the 'B. Urquhart' version lies in the possible identity of the publisher behind the latter work. One of the copies of the 'Urquhart' work in the collection of the Mitchell Library has an additional advertisement leaf, which advertises the 'Memoirs of Major Semple'[48] – published by none other than George Kearsley. It is thus quite possible that 'B. Urquhart', like 'M. Smith', was another false imprint for the resourceful and competitive Kearsley, who may have issued the work in a further attempt to corner the market in Barrington biographies.

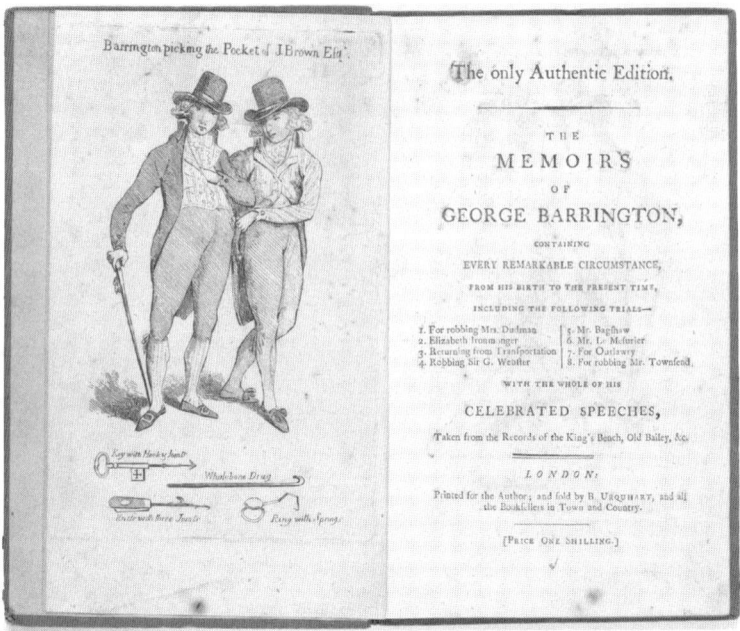

The frontispiece and title page from the surreptitious 'Urquhart' edition of *The Memoirs of George Barrington*. Courtesy of Mitchell Library, State Library of New South Wales.

Several other unauthorised productions stemmed from the Bird and Symonds *Memoirs*. A 1792 *Life of George Barrington*, published under the anonymous imprint 'Printed for the Booksellers', was an outright piracy, without abridgement, of the Bird and Symonds text.[49] This work did, however, append some new textual material, in the shape of 'A Copy of a Letter from [Barrington] at the Cape of Good-Hope, To a Gentleman in the County of York, dated 1st July 1791'. This letter, which appeared in magazines and newspapers at the end of 1791[50], was probably genuine. It contains accurate details of Barrington's experiences during his voyage and, moreover, resembles Barrington's sentimental language, his propensity for exaggeration, and his characteristic care to focus attention on the extent to which he was sinned against rather than sinning:

> If ever there was a man who seemed destined to encounter difficulties, and to struggle with disappointments, that man is myself ... The world imagined I had done it some injury; but however it might have been magnified by the tongue of detraction, the balance between us, in that respect, was more equal than was generally supposed, for I also met some injuries, and those of as harsh a nature as any I ever inflicted.[51]

Another work entitled *The Life of George Barrington*, which also pirated the text of the Bird and Symonds *Memoirs*, was published around the same time (1792). This work was produced under the imprint 'printed and sold by Andrew Hambleton'.[52] Hambleton was a chapbook seller who also published editions of the 'Barrington' *Voyage* after 1795.[53] His *Life of George Barrington* supplements the Bird and Symonds text with an abridged version of the 1791 Cape Town letter and a final paragraph derived from the newspaper reports of Barrington's new situation as a constable at Parramatta.[54] Two extant copies of the Hambleton *Life* carry the edition statement of the 'seventh edition', which may suggest that Hambleton produced a number of other 'editions' in small print runs, and that the work sold well enough to merit reprinting.

Even with the addition of new material, and typographical improvements over the Bird and Symonds *Memoirs*, the 1792 *Life of George Barrington* and the Hambleton *Life* were priced at sixpence – half the cost of the original. To some degree this reflects the fact that Barrington, whose final public appearance was made nearly two years previously, was no longer the focus of such intense topical interest. Yet the life of 'the celebrated Barrington' was obviously still worth something, if only at a discount rate. Another work derived from the Bird and Symonds *Memoirs* was an eight-page chapbook, priced at one penny, produced by the Darlington printer, William Appleton.[55] The text of the Bird and Symonds work was of course drastically cut down to fit into such a small format, and much of the information on Barrington's trials became a summary assemblage of names and dates. The anecdote about the naive Cutler being robbed was considered good enough to retain verbatim, however, and it was also thought advisable to add a concluding paragraph to help the reader draw the appropriate moral from the Barrington story:

> Here endeth the life, for the present, of the noted George Barrington, and however we may admire the greatness of his abilities, we cannot but lament the sad perversion of them—abilities which might have rendered him the ornament of society, he has basely employed to the destruction of it; and is now held out as an example to all men, that neither extensive knowledge, nor crafty ingenuity, are able to avade [*sic*] that justice which every injured fellow-creature has a right to demand.[56]

At least one other *Life* of George Barrington was published in this greatly abbreviated, penny chapbook form[57], and it is certainly possible that further works of this kind were printed and sold in the streets and markets by chapmen and flying stationers.

If the text of the Bird and Symonds *Memoirs* met with reasonable demand, it was the Kearsley *Memoirs* that would be adopted most thoroughly as the definitive Barrington biography; that is to say, it was this text that was most frequently pirated, plagiarised and rehashed in the years to come. The first work in this vein to appear was *The Genuine Life and Trial of George Barrington*, a 48-page sixpenny chapbook abridged from the text of the Kearsley *Memoirs*, originally published by Robert Barker, an itinerant chapbook seller who issued at least four versions of the work between November 1790 and August 1791.[58] As had been the case

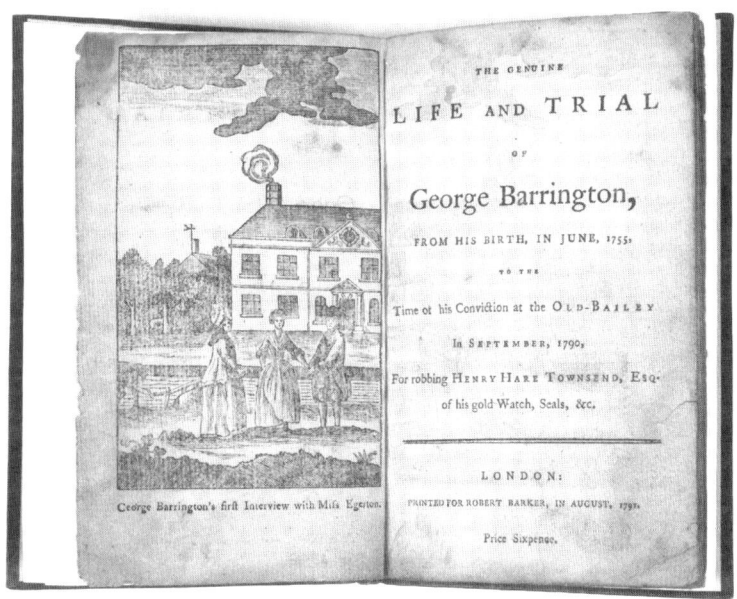

The frontispiece and title page of one of Robert Barker's *Genuine Life and Trial of George Barrington* chapbooks. Hordern House Rare Books.

with the redactions of the Bird and Symonds *Memoirs*, the abridgment was made by omitting sections, large and small, rather than by rewriting. Once the Kearsley *Memoirs* had been successfully translated into chapbook form, there was apparently little need for further change. Apart from the four known editions produced by Barker himself, the text of the *Genuine Life and Trial of George Barrington* was appropriated by a loosely connected group of publishers who produced at least five editions between 1791 and some time in the early nineteenth century.[59] Little is known about these publishers – William Clements, James Sadler, Mary Clements, J. Eves and T. Thomas – but it seems likely that they, like Barker, were itinerant stationers and chapbook sellers, whose publishing activities were limited to the reprinting of popular works which they could readily sell on their travels.[60] The proliferation of chapbook editions of the *Genuine Life and Trial of George Barrington* does not by itself indicate that this was the version of the Barrington biography that was most widely disseminated, however. It is likely that the print runs of these publications were very small, probably limited to the number of copies that itinerant traders like Barker, and Clements and Sadler, et al., could afford to print and were able to carry on their travels. On the other hand, the fact that marginal traders like these – who speculated only in the most liquid commodities – continued to produce editions of the *Genuine Life* over a period of some years provides some indication of the enduring popular appeal of the text.

The five editions of this work published, in various combinations, by William Clements, Mary Clements, Sadler, Thomas, and Eves, all use the title *The Genuine Life and Trial of George Barrington*, which was appropriated from Barker's chapbooks along with the text itself. Barker was not known to publish any other work after his August 1791 version of the *Genuine Life* and, under these circumstances, it again seems possible that Barker traded his chapbook abridgement, or perhaps that William Clements and Sadler, who published an edition in 1791[61], cut a deal with Barker's printer and usurped him. One definite improvement on the Barker editions of the *Genuine Life* was made in the important area of the frontispiece illustration: the Clements and Sadler edition of 1791 (and all those that followed it) abandons the crude, old-fashioned illustration used by Barker in favour of a frontispiece imitating the illustration from the Bird and Symonds *Memoirs*. This frontispiece was produced from the same plate used in the *Life of George Barrington* 'Printed for the Booksellers' in 1792, suggesting that the anonymous 'Booksellers' may have been, or at least may have had some connection with, Clements and Sadler. While the first Clements and Sadler *Genuine Life* edition was claimed to be printed in London, later editions were produced by the Manchester printer Alice Swindells.[62] Internal evidence in the Swindells-printed chapbooks shows that these works were still being printed into the first decade of the nineteenth century.[63]

At least one other version of the biography of Barrington was published in the first flurry of activity in 1790–1791. This was *The Life of George Barrington (King of the Pickpockets)*, published by the Liverpool printer Charles Wosencroft.[64] Again this was not an original work, but it was unique in being the only work to synthesise the texts of both original versions of the *Memoirs of George Barrington* into one narrative. While still a piratical publication, then, it was at least an original pirate, and Wosencroft expended some energy on editorial emendations to make the sections cut and pasted from the different *Memoirs* texts fit together fluently. The narrative, published after Barrington's transportation, also concludes with the new (and erroneous) claim that 'On the 12th of February, 1791, George Barrington accompanied by his Wife and Child, embarked with eighty convicts for Botany Bay, and in all human probability will never more return for England'.[65]

From 1795, the Barrington biographies still on the market had to contend with a popular travel narrative, *A Voyage to New South Wales*, which had the attraction of being (supposedly) written by Barrington himself. While this work was pirated and reworked into chapbook form with similar rapidity to the biographies, the original publisher of the work, H. D. Symonds, made continued efforts to keep ahead of the competition by revamping the work in new editions and repackaged versions, with expansions and changes in presentation. One of these later versions, published in 1800 under the title *A Voyage to Botany Bay*, included as preliminary material a 'Life of George Barrington' and 'Particulars Relating to the Trial and Conviction of George Barrington'.[66] The latter section was abridged from the report of Barrington's final trial that could be found in the Bird and Symonds *Memoirs*, among other sources. The 'Life of George Barrington' that precedes it, however, is a digest of the Kearsley *Memoirs* version of the Barrington story. This was perhaps a tacit acknowledgement on Symonds' part that the novelistic Kearsley *Memoirs* was a more entertaining version of Barrington's life, and that by the turn of the nineteenth century the biography Symonds himself had published in association with 'J. Bird' was no longer a marketable commodity.

After 1802, Symonds ceased publishing Barrington books, and, as will be argued in the following chapter, appears to have handed over his 'rights' to the Barrington works to another Paternoster Row bookseller, Maurice Jones.[67] Jones was no chapbook merchant. From late 1802, he began developing 'Barrington' material into a more elaborate format, publishing an extended version of the *Voyage to New South Wales* that included an expanded 'Life of George Barrington' as preliminary material.[68] Like the biographical introduction in Symonds' 1800 *Voyage to Botany Bay*, this narrative was clearly derived from the Kearsley *Memoirs*. The Jones 'Life of George Barrington' was significant, however, as the first derivative biography of Barrington to substantially rewrite the text it was based on. The revisions to the original text were more concerned with modifying the style and language of the Kearsley *Memoirs* than altering the outlines of the story; Jones' version of the Barrington biography might therefore be described as a creative plagiarism of the Kearsley text, as opposed to the piratical abridgements produced by the chapbook sellers. In addition to including this biography as part of 'Barrington's' *Account of a Voyage to New South Wales*, Jones also issued it as a separate work, entitled *The Life of George Barrington, Officer of the Peace at Parramatta.*[69]

The compilers of biographical anthologies of criminal figures were similarly free with what they took from Kearsley's *Memoirs of*

George Barrington. From the turn of the nineteenth century, one of the leading players in this market was the printer–publisher James Cundee[70], who digested and rehashed the Kearsley *Memoirs* for inclusion in a number of biographical anthologies. The first of these was *The Criminal Recorder; or Biographical Sketches of Notorious Public Characters*, a work featuring brief criminal biographies modelled on the 'Newgate Calendar' plan.[71] A more extensive biographical sketch of Barrington, once again rewritten from the Kearsley *Memoirs*, appears in Cundee's *The Eccentric Mirror* of 1807, an anthology of biographies of persons 'particularly distinguished by extraordinary qualifications, talents, and propensities, natural or acquired', attributed to one G. H. Wilson.[72] These compilations of criminal biographies obviously provided a fruitful avenue of book sales for Cundee. About 1809, he collaborated with the Liverpool firm of Nuttall, Fisher and Dixon[73] in the production of *Criminal Chronology; or, the New Newgate Calendar*, an expansive work which reinvigorated the 'Newgate Calendar' genre[74], and a similarly summarised biography of Barrington appears here. Alexander Hogg, the bookseller who had dominated this genre in the late eighteenth century, responded by republishing his own version – *The New and Complete Newgate Calendar or Malefactor's Universal Register* – in 1818.[75] Hogg, however, did not bother to update the biographical sketch of Barrington he had used when Barrington was sent to the hulks in 1779.[76]

After 1810, the output of Barrington biographies seems to have slowed. The biographical material that prefaced Maurice Jones' elaborate version of the *Voyage*, as well as the 'Newgate Calendar'-style anthologies published in those years, did provide some continued access to the story that first appeared in the Kearsley *Memoirs* of 1790. But compared to the glut of material that had appeared in the fifteen years after Barrington's final trial, the 1810s were quiet years. In the 1820s, however, the Kearsley Barrington biography was revived by at least two London printer–publishers. The *Life, Amours and Wonderful Adventures of George Barrington*, published by William Mason[77], was yet another descendent of the Kearsley *Memoirs* via the abridgement first made in Robert Barker's *Genuine Life and Trial of George Barrington* chapbooks. Once again, the abridged text first published by Barker was accepted as good enough for reissue without significant alteration. Despite a thirty-year gap between the publication of the works, the only changes the Mason *Life, Amours and Wonderful Adventures* makes to the text of Barker's *Genuine Life* are minor amendments to tense and style. For example, where the opening line of the Barker *Genuine Life* reads 'The attention of the public has been, for several years past, fixed, in a particular manner, on George Barrington', the Mason *Life, Amours and Wonderful Adventures* has 'The attention of the public was for several years fixed, in a particular manner, on George Barrington'.[78] Original material is confined to one additional anecdote, given in a concluding paragraph, which follows the narrative taken from the *Genuine Life*. Probably because it appropriates the text of the earlier productions of Barker, and Clements and Sadler et al., the date of publication of the Mason *Life* was badly miscalculated as '[1790]' by Ferguson.[79] A final leaf of the advertisements for Mason's publications includes one for a version of the *Trial of Robert Wedderburn* – a trial that took place in May 1820.

Another later Barrington biography, also issued under the title *Life, Amours and Wonderful Adventures of George Barrington*, was produced by the industrious bluebook publisher John Fairburn.[80] Ferguson dated 'Fairburn's Edition' of the Barrington biography at '1804' but again this is too early – the work certainly dates from the 1820s.[81] While the Mason and Fairburn biographies were both essentially derivatives of the Kearsley *Memoirs*, their paths back to the original text were different. While Mason used the abridged *Genuine Life and Trials of George Barrington* text pioneered by Robert Barker in 1790, Fairburn's text was an abridged version of

Barrington robbing a Nobleman at Court.   Barrington taken prisoner on the Race Course.

The frontispiece of Fairburn's *Life, Amours and Wonderful Adventures of George Barrington*. Courtesy of Mitchell Library, State Library of New Wales.

the Maurice Jones 'Life of George Barrington', almost certainly taken from that publisher's 1810 edition of 'Barrington's' *Account of a Voyage to New South Wales*.[82] While comparatively little advance had been made in terms of textual material between the Barrington chapbooks of the 1790s and the bluebooks of the 1820s, improvements in typography that came with technological developments in printing are certainly evident in the Fairburn biography, and not to be overlooked as a selling point of 'Fairburn's Edition' is the hand-coloured folding frontispiece which graces the work.

The Mason and Fairburn publications dating from the 1820s are the last known examples of Barrington biographies descended in a direct line from the prototype biographies of 1790. From the 1830s, the Barrington story began to be reimagined for new generations. One of the first manifestations of this reinterpreted Barrington was a dramatic work, *Barrington the Pickpocket!, or the Gypsies of Tiverton Glen*, which premiered at the Surrey Theatre on 21 October 1833.[83] This first 'dramatic sketch' on Barrington, advertised as being 'Founded on Facts, poutraying some of the leading features of that celebrated Person's life', was a one-act play presented as an afterpiece, which managed fourteen performances at the Surrey before making way for newer fare in mid-November. As required from drama at the non-patent theatres, it included an obligatory song – 'What a merry life does a Soldier lead' – performed by the Surrey's resident ingénue, Eliza Vincent. The claim that the play was 'founded on facts' should, of course, be taken with a grain of salt: Barrington's criminal acquaintances are dramatised as 'Harry Lowe, *alias* Harry of Hounslow' and 'Young Giles *alias* Young Hop-the-Twig', and Georgian high society is painted in similarly broad strokes, represented by 'Lord Hannibal Poodle', 'Lady Slapdab', and so on. Other characters like 'Ralph Ploughshare', 'Eelskin, a miser', and 'Dolly Rosebud' no doubt had a lot more to do with theatrical clichés than the Barrington story. One contemporary account suggests this 'improving melo-drama' was 'extremely popular' with the raucous audiences of the time[84]; and it was apparently for productions like *Barrington the Pickpocket!* that the Surrey's manager, David Webster Osbaldiston, earned the censure of *Figaro in London* in 1833:

> Mr. Osbaldiston is running an insane career at the Surrey and is overwhelming the bargemen, in the classic neighbourhood of St. George, with the pathos of the hulks and the touching twaddle of the treadmills.[85]

Around 1840, Barrington's life was also reimagined in prose fiction, in the form of a bluebook pamphlet entitled *The Life, Times and Adventures of George Barrington*, published in two editions, nominally by 'John Wilson', who gave his location as

'Oxford Street, London'.[86] This was possibly a false imprint for the printer and bookseller Edward Duncombe, who used the pseudonym 'John Wilson' in an unsuccessful attempt to avoid prosecution over the risqué nature of the works he published and sold.[87] The 'Wilson' work came with several illustrations etched and engraved by George Stiff, whose involvement helps establish the date of the work as late 1830s or early 1840s.[88] Whether the Barrington story from the 1790s biographies was felt to be too dated and over-used, or simply not exciting enough for a generation raised on gothic bluebooks, the Barrington story in the *Life, Times and Adventures* was thoroughly transformed. The most important structural feature of the 'Wilson' *Life* is the addition of large sections of dialogue, which the author uses to dramatise the major incidents of Barrington's life. But these incidents themselves have also undergone a major revision. In the Wilson *Life*, Barrington is given the same geneaology and early life as in the Kearsley *Memoirs*, and he still flees his school to meet up with Price and his travelling players. But here 'Miss Egerton' is not a fallen woman, as in the Kearsley text, but the daughter of a Dublin gentleman, and she and Barrington marry. The sensational twist occurs, however, when 'Mrs Barrington' is subsequently raped by the Duke of Leinster while her husband is away.[89] This sensational event, rather than the humdrum business of pickpocketing, then drives the remainder of the narrative. Barrington's wife dies from shame ('I cannot—I will not survive my dishonour'), and Barrington seeks revenge on the Duke, eventually murdering him.[90] A tangential story of adventuring at sea, narrated by the captain of a boat Barrington travels on, then occupies a large portion of the narrative[91], before the story returns to tie up the loose ends of the Barrington tale. The high-profile crimes and the speeches in court – the real Barrington's reason for being 'celebrated' in the first place – have completely fallen by the wayside in this novelisation of his life.

The texts of the two biographies of George Barrington that appeared with such swiftness after his sentencing in 1790 thus enjoyed a considerable life span in the late eighteenth- and early nineteenth-century market for popular literature, disappearing only after new and more lurid representations of the 'Barrington' story began appearing in the 1830s. Neither of these original Barrington narratives is particularly interesting in itself, much less reliable as a biographical source, and it is testament to the continuing interest in Barrington that both should have been continually revived and republished by a host of publishers looking to sell the texts in their own particular niche markets. From the 1830s on, the life of George Barrington was treated in an even more imaginative manner by new generations of writers and publishers, and the 'facts' of his criminal career, dubiously established through the original biographies, were subsumed by a nostalgic appropriation of Barrington as a rogue-hero from a bygone era. Before this occurred, however, the story of the 'celebrated Barrington' had taken a curious turn in the form of a spurious authorial career, and it is to this aspect of the Barrington legacy that we now turn.

CHAPTER THREE

Under a
DECEPTIOUS
MASK
Barrington as Author

y the mid-1790s, it could have been supposed that the famous transportee George Barrington would have been forgotten by the British public, discarded like yesterday's news. But fate, and the book trade, had different things in store for 'the celebrated Barrington'. By the turn of the century, Barrington was being celebrated as the putative author of a popular travel narrative that had already passed through numerous editions, piracies, and a translation into French. In New South Wales, the real George Barrington had retired from his position as a constable, his health having declined sharply in the late 1790s. In 1801, the merchant John Turnbull – one of a number of visitors to the colony curious to see the famous Barrington – found him 'a meer living skeleton':

> he was emaciated, and apparently in the last stage of human life. Having absolutely lost the use of his intellectual faculties, he had retired on a small pension allowed him for his former services, a melancholy instance of abused talents, and the force of remorse and conscious sensibility operating a mind capable of better things.[1]

The death of 'Mr. George Barrington' was quietly noted on the back page of the colony's fledgling newspaper, *The Sydney Gazette*, on 30 December 1804 – though the front page had already

The frontispiece portrait of Barrington that appeared in *An Account of a Voyage to New South Wales* (1803 and 1811). Hordern House Rare Books.

announced the sale of the '*Estate of Mr.* GEORGE BARRINGTON, *a Lunatic, deceased*'.[2] But even the death of the author was only a minor inconvenience for the publishers of the spurious Barrington books. In 1810, the publishers of the most elaborate 'Barrington' works overcame this difficulty by stating that, although Barrington had died 'within a few months of the publication of the first Edition of this work', they had been 'assisted by a person resident in the colony to whom Barrington bequeathed his papers'.[3] The publishers indignantly denied the report that Barrington had 'died *insane!*', claiming instead that it was his 'unremitting attention to the duties of his office' which had brought about his demise. By this time, the myth of Barrington the author was so well entrenched that such claims were difficult to dispute.

Although Barrington knew little about the successful publishing fraud conducted under his name, events in the colony had played their part in inspiring it. From mid-1792, reports had begun filtering back to England that Barrington had been appointed to an official position in the colony as 'Head Constable' at the settlement at Parramatta. While the idea of a notorious thief administering justice seemed a suitably antipodean transformation and excited some risible comment in the British press, this appointment was actually not all that unusual. In its infant state, the colony of New South Wales had no free settlers and only a bare minimum of civil officers. Consequently, the early colonial governors were always on the lookout for what were later termed 'trusties' – convicts or ex-convicts capable and responsible enough to fill low-ranking positions within the colony's improvised public service. Well-educated convicts, along with experienced tradesmen, were particularly highly valued, and many (like Barrington) received early pardons as a reward for their services.[4] The colony's original police force was formed in 1789 entirely from serving convicts, partly to circumvent the recalcitrance of the Marine corps[5], and Barrington, with his

famed ability to move between polite society and the underworld, must have seemed an ideal candidate for service in this
constabulary.

According to David Collins, judge advocate in New South Wales,
Barrington was sent to the outlying settlement at Toongabbie
shortly after his arrival in the colony, and was 'first placed as a
subordinate and shortly after as a principal watchman'.[6] This
promotion was certainly rapid, and probably involved a move to
the more populous agricultural centre of Parramatta: a letter from
an unnamed convict at Rose Hill (Parramatta) dated November
1791, published in *Ayre's Sunday London Gazette* of 15 July 1792,
states that 'Barrington is made Head Constable here'.[7] It was
through this and similar correspondence published in the British
press that the news of Barrington's metamorphosis from criminal
to authority figure first became known. *The Times* had clearly received this information from an earlier source, for on 22 June 1792
it persevered with its line of dreadful puns by commenting that:

> The notorious convicts BARRINGTON and WENTWORTH, have
> been admirably disposed of at *Botany Bay*—the former will be quite
> at home as High CONSTABLE, having always had a TAKING way with
> him—the latter as an Assistant Surgeon, will no doubt labour well in
> his vocation, by making all his customers BLEED freely.[8]

Further details on Barrington's new role came to light the
following year, apparently from a reputable source. The founding
governor of New South Wales, Arthur Phillip, had returned to
England for health reasons, arriving in late May on the *Atlantic*.[9]
Between official engagements – such as his presentation to the
King on 24 May 1793 – Phillip seems to have made some statements on the colony and its inhabitants which were picked up by
the press. Two 'paragraphs' relating to Barrington were printed
in the newspapers in 1793, both being reprinted in the *Annual
Register* for that year. These pieces illustrate the dichotomous ways

of approaching Barrington. On the one hand, there is the hope-ful picture of a man of abilities finally putting his celebrated talents to good use –

> The celebrated Barrington is likely to become a man of some conse-quence at last. His natural talents entitle him to a more respectable dis-tinction than that which he enjoyed; and we hope he has tasted enough of the bad effects of vicious courses, to abandon them entirely.[10]

– on the other, there is the tendency to approach Barrington's trans-formation with a note of innuendo, as an antipodean absurdity:

> Governor Phillips [*sic*] tells many curious stories of his Majesty's subjects in Botany-Bay. Barrington is high-constable of the settle-ment, and administers justice with a most impartial hand ...[11]

Later in 1793 there was also Watkin Tench's prosaic account of '*Barrington*, of famous memory', in his new environs, published in that author's *Complete Account of the Transactions at Port Jackson*:

> I saw him with curiosity. He is tall, approaching to six feet, slender, and his gait and manner, bespeak liveliness and activity. Of that elegance and fashion, with which my imagination had decked him (I know not why), I could distinguish no trace. Great allowance should, however, be made for depression, and unavoidable deficiency of dress. His face is thoughtful and intelligent; to a strong cast of countenance, he adds a penetrating eye, and a prominent forehead: his whole demeanour is humble, not servile. Both on his passage from England, and since his arrival here, his conduct has been irreproachable. He is appointed high-constable of the settlement at Rose Hill, a post of some respectability, and certainly one of impor-tance to those who live here. His knowledge of men, particularly of that part of them into whose morals, manners, and behaviour, he is ordered especially to inspect, eminently fit him for the office.

> I cannot quit him without bearing my testimony, that his talents promise to be directed in future, to make reparation to society, for the offence he has heretofore committed against it.[12]

The celebrated pickpocket's respectable new role as a colonial
official was seized upon as the premise to further transform
Barrington into an authority on the colony for British readers. In
early 1795, a work entitled *A Voyage to New South Wales*, attributed
to 'George Barrington, now Superintendent of the Convicts at
Paramatta [*sic*]', was published in London.[13] This narrative was
an ingenious mix of plagiarism and fiction in the 'imaginary
voyage' tradition.[14] While the bulk of the text was 'borrowed'
from a First Fleet journal – John Hunter's *An Historical Journal of
the Transactions at Port Jackson and Norfolk Island*[15] – there was just
enough of a fictionalised veneer, and pretence that it was
Barrington's story, to deceive and interest readers. Over the next
forty years, the 'Barrington' *Voyage to New South Wales* spawned
an impressive number of abridgements, enlargements, piracies
and translations, making the text – derivative and partly fictional
though it was – probably the most widely read account of the early
years of European settlement in Australia.

The original *Voyage to New South Wales* was the inspired speculation of the publisher Henry Delahay Symonds. A bookseller best
remembered for his radical publications[16], Symonds was himself a
prisoner of the Crown at the time of the first publication of the
'Barrington' *Voyage*, serving a four-year sentence in Newgate for
publishing Thomas Paine's *The Rights of Man* and Charles Pigott's
anti-aristocratic satire, *The Jockey Club*.[17] In Newgate, Symonds
and a number of other booksellers and radicals imprisoned there
became something of a cause célèbre for gentlemen of liberal
sympathies, and they continued to publish radical works in the
prison and maintain their general bookselling businesses outside
it. Housed – for a fee – on the State Side of the prison (traditionally reserved for political or well-to-do prisoners), Symonds
shared a 'suite of apartments' with his friend and fellow bookseller James Ridgway, the Reverend William Winterbotham, a
Baptist minister convicted of preaching seditious sermons, and

A
VOYAGE

TO

NEW SOUTH WALES;

WITH

A DESCRIPTION OF THE COUNTRY;

THE

MANNERS, CUSTOMS, RELIGION, &c.

OF

THE NATIVES,

In the Vicinity of

BOTANY BAY.

BY GEORGE BARRINGTON,

NOW

SUPERINTENDANT OF THE CONVICTS

AT

PARAMATTA.

PRINTED FOR THE PROPRIETOR;

SOLD BY H. D. SYMONDS, NO. 20, PATERNOSTER-ROW.

[PRICE HALF-A-CROWN.]

1795.

The title page of the original spurious 'Barrington' publication. Hordern House Rare Books.

another bookseller, Daniel Holt.[18] Conscious of the perception
that they were suffering for the cause, the Newgate booksellers
marketed themselves as something like an official source of
radical literature. Shortly after their incarceration in 1793,
Symonds and James Ridgway formed a publishing partnership –
or more accurately, an imprint – based on their profile as suffering 'Newgate booksellers'. Some of the 'Ridgway and Symonds'
publications and advertisements from 1793 are emblazoned with
the legend 'First Year of Our Imprisonment in Newgate'[19], and
the following year, 'Messrs Symonds, Winterbotham, Ridgway and
Holt' even minted a commemorative trade token 'Payable At
[their] Residence' in Newgate.[20] The philanthropic medical doctor John Lettsom, who visited Newgate in 1793, found Symonds
and Ridgway 'very busily employed ... in the sale of books, &c.
which not only diverted the melancholy of confinement, but
afforded continual employment both of body and mind'[21], while
an American publication praised the resilience of the pair, citing
them as evidence that it was 'next to impossible, for despotism to
over-whelm the divine art of printing'.[22]

But the production of radical works represented only one aspect of
Symonds' bookselling activities during his years of incarceration.
Whatever his activities in Newgate, Symonds' shop in Paternoster
Row – the street near St Paul's Cathedral that served as the main
hub of the London book trade – was clearly still a going concern,
with employees handling the trade Symonds had steadily built up
since establishing himself in business in 1783.[23] To a great degree,
Symonds' success in the trade was built on catering to the emerging
markets in newly literate sections of society – especially tradesmen
and middling class professionals – placing him squarely within the
new breed of booksellers whose entrepreneurial innovations and
commercial acumen were helping to reshape the trade at the end
of the eighteenth century.[24] One contemporary remembered Symonds
particularly as an important wholesale buyer and distributor of the

publications of other booksellers[25], though by the early 1790s he had also compiled a fairly extensive list of his own publications.

H. D. Symonds was not, as Jonathan Wantrup asserts, a 'chapbook publisher'[26]; rather, he specialised as a publisher of pamphlet literature – a subtle but important distinction in the late eighteenth-century context. While chapbook printers and sellers were typically marginal traders who rarely produced original works, the market in pamphlet literature was dominated by London booksellers publishing new works of topical interest at a cheaper price and to a broader market than more elaborate bound volumes would allow. A measure of Symonds' standing in the pamphlet trade is evident from the fact that he was the publisher of the cheap edition of Paine's *The Rights of Man*, one of the most widely disseminated pamphlets of the period.[27] The wholesale distribution of cheap radical works to lower class readers was a cause of serious anxiety for the conservative ministry of William Pitt, and in the latter months of 1792 the government moved to prosecute Symonds and a number of other booksellers. There is a distinct suggestion that these prosecutions resulted from the fact that the booksellers deliberately sought to distribute their radical works to the masses, as much as from the content of the works themselves. The indictment against Symonds labelled him 'the Master Mover of all the libellous Matters in Paynes Works'.[28]

Given that Symonds' business depended on high-volume sales of inexpensive works, his imprisonment must have been a serious inconvenience and, moreover, an extreme financial burden. Prior to his trial in 1793, Symonds had written a last ditch letter to the Attorney General, pleading in somewhat Barringtonesque terms – 'I am wretched; ruin and destruction await my wife and family, unless withheld by your clemency'[29] – an appeal which was, predictably, ignored. Aside from the costs of subsisting in Newgate and maintaining a family outside, Symonds' convictions carried large fines (to

the amount of £300), and a further £1000 in security (£500 from
Symonds and £250 each from two friends) had to be paid before
leaving the prison. In a letter dated 2 January 1795, Symonds,
Ridgway and Holt wrote of the 'calamitous pressure of a long,
distant and ruinous separation from our businesses, our families,
and our friends at large', calculating that between them their losses
and liabilities already amounted to £3800.[30] Under these
circumstances, it is hardly surprising that Symonds would have
looked for publications that might realise a large sale with minimal
costs. As we have seen, Symonds had previously been involved in the
publication of one of the original biographies of Barrington, so he
was in a good position to see what profit could be made from the
celebrated pickpocket's name. If the many republications and
adaptations of the text first produced by Symonds are anything to
go by, the idea of a plagiarised narrative with Barrington's name
affixed to it seems to have been one of Symonds' more successful
responses to the financial pressure he was under.

Although the *Voyage to New South Wales* was a spurious work,
falsely attributed and substantially plagiarised from other sources,
there was certainly an amount of creativity and art in the overall
construction of the text. Indeed, the success of the work was
surely due at least in part to the way the plagiarised sections of the
narrative were rewritten within an overarching original story. This
story was essentially a fictionalised account of Barrington's real
life transition from disgraced convict to respectable authority
figure in New South Wales. At the beginning of the narrative, the
character of Barrington is used as a 'hook' to interest the reader.
The introductory letter which serves as the dedication for the
work promises a further narrative containing 'some farther
particulars relative to, Sir, Your most obedient, And obliged,
Humble Servant, G. Barrington'[31], and the first sentences of the
narrative give an almost burlesque imitation of the Barrington
idiom and his supposed history as a genteel thief:

It was with unspeakable satisfaction that I received a summons to be ready early the next morning for my embarkation, agreeably to my sentence. I instantly made the most of my time, and, by the assistance of a friend, procured a few pounds' worth of necessaries for my voyage; government allowance being extremely slender, especially for one like me, who had hitherto been accustomed to most of the luxuries of the table.[32]

The writer certainly had more than a passing familiarity with Barrington and his sentimental mode of address. The first chapter of the *Voyage*, the only one in the work wholly composed of original material, contains several neat imitations of the language of sensibility so skilfully employed by Barrington throughout his public life. The procession of the convicts from Newgate, for example,

made a deep impression on my mind; and the ignominy of being thus mingled with felons of all descriptions, many scarce a degree above the brute creation … inflicted a punishment more severe than the sentence of my country, and fully avenged that society I had so much wronged.[33]

'Barrington' also recalled parting from his unnamed 'benefactor' in similar terms:

my heart swelling with gratitude, was too full, and interdicted all verbal acknowledgements; but the remembrance is too strongly engraven thereon for the most distant time to effect the slightest eradication.[34]

Predictably, 'Barrington' also did a good line on the pathos of transportation, as evidenced when narrating the ship's passage out from the English Channel:

it was delightful weather, and the prospect on each hand must have afforded the most agreeable sensations to every beholder, and is, perhaps, as rich and luxuriant as is any where to be met with; but, alas! it only brought a fresh pang to the bosom of one who in all probability was bidding it adieu for ever.[35]

The parody of 'the celebrated Barrington' so well known from newspaper reports, however, is mostly confined to the opening chapter of the *Voyage to New South Wales*, and there is no attempt to invoke the events of Barrington's criminal career in 'his' narrative. Rather, the parts of the narrative dealing with Barrington himself become in important respects a moral tale; Barrington's voyage from England to Australia is a journey from infamy and dishonest courses to obedience and eventual authority. To some extent, the conventions of the genre demanded this transformation of the narrator's character. Voyage narratives of the eighteenth century were generally quasi-scientific texts focused on providing information for the gentlemanly elite, and the reliability of the author–narrator was a crucial ingredient in their acceptance.[36] The stories of explorers who charted foreign cultures sometimes caused great controversy when it was suspected that their authors had invented or exaggerated details, as was the case with the 'Abyssinian traveller' James Bruce, whose stories of his travels were met with scepticism and ridicule.[37] While the 'Barrington' *Voyage to New South Wales* was aimed at a popular market where such controversies were less likely to occur, the question of credit still remained as a textual problem, and it was evident that the eloquent but untrustworthy persona of 'the celebrated Barrington' was not a suitable vehicle for the narration of the travel descriptions plagiarised from the Hunter *Historical Journal* and other sources. Thus 'Barrington', through the course of the *Voyage* narrative, undergoes a reformation so that he can be accepted as a matter-of-fact, reliable observer, and the supposed path to the colonial authority that underpins this authorial credibility is charted in a series of vignettes which are interwoven through – and tie together – the large swatches of text taken from the Hunter *Historical Journal*.

The most important episode in the textual development of the Barrington character takes place at the start of the second chapter of the *Voyage to New South Wales*, where he foils a mutiny on board his ship. A mutiny did in fact occur on one of the Third Fleet ships (on the *Albemarle* rather than the real Barrington's transport, the *Active*), and the account of the event in the Hunter *Historical Journal* was likely to have been the inspiration for the *Voyage* version.[38] The *Voyage* cleverly parleys the event into an exciting novelised action scene, in which 'Barrington' is the central figure in preventing the mutiny, holding off the mutineers with 'a handpike luckily in my reach' until more substantially armed help arrives.[39] Besides enlivening the narrative with a breathtaking action sequence, this episode fulfils a structural function in providing a concrete, if fictional, foundation for Barrington's favourable treatment in the colony and his transition to respectability. Shortly after the mutiny episode, 'Barrington' relates that the rewards of good courses were now a more effective means of securing 'the luxuries of the table' he had previously acquired by dishonest means:

> seldom a day passed but some fresh meat or poultry was sent me by the captain, which considerably raised me in the estimation of my messmates, who were no ways displeased at the substitution of a sea pie made of fowl or fresh meat, to a dish of Lobscourse, or a piece of salt junk.[40]

When 'Barrington' arrives in New South Wales, his services on board ship are said to occasion 'a most gracious reception from the governor', in which he is told that 'on account of my behaviour on board, he would place me in a situation that should render my exile from England as little irksome as possible'.[41] He is then taken to a soldier's house where he has 'a good fish dinner', later journeying to 'Paramatta' to take up the post of 'superintendant of the convicts'.[42] This position was a considerable elaboration on Barrington's actual post of constable. The 'Barrington' of the *Voyage to New South Wales* states that

> My business was chiefly to report the progress made in the different work carrying on at Paramatta; for which purpose I was furnished

with abstracts from a kind of overseers [*sic*] or head man of the various gangs; and in less than a week I was much at home, and as perfectly master of the business, as though I had been coeval with the colony.[43]

This exaggeration of Barrington's role and responsibilities seems to have been made to extend his claim to authority and, by extension, authorship – a Barrington 'coeval with the colony' was also 'coeval' with the task of narrating the colony's history. In reality, Barrington's role as constable was probably confined to police duties, and though he was often referred to as an exemplary officer[44], it is likely that this role was a good deal more 'irksome' than merely keeping up with the public works at Parramatta.

The novelised sections of the *Voyage*, centred on the character of Barrington and his path to colonial credibility, are an important but minor portion of the overall content of the work, however. The remainder of the narrative is made up of text plagiarised from other travel narratives published in the early 1790s. By far the greatest proportion of this plagiarised text is taken from Hunter's *Historical Journal*; indeed, as far as descriptions of New South Wales are concerned, the *Historical Journal* was to all intents and purposes the exclusive source for the *Voyage*.[45] Other travel narratives were drawn upon, however, to make the *Voyage* a more comprehensive tour of the exotic destinations en route to the antipodes. The fleet's landing at the island of Teneriffe, for example, was enlivened by a passage reworked from Peter Rye's *An Excursion to the Peak of Teneriffe in 1791*.[46] Similarly, the description of the Cape of Good Hope was plagiarised from the English translation of François Le Vaillant's African travel journal.[47]

The parts of the Hunter narrative that were especially favoured for incorporation into the 'Barrington' *Voyage* were those which dealt with descriptions of Aboriginal society and accounts of cross-cultural contact; the majority of the *Historical Journal*'s descriptions of the interaction between the colonists and the Eora peoples of the greater Sydney region, including the lengthy accounts of specific Aboriginal figures like Bennelong and Colbee[48], were transplanted in partially rewritten but still easily recognisable form. Presumably, these depictions of 'the natives' were considered the most interesting – and commercially appealing – aspects of the Hunter work. The *Voyage* took on even more of the complexion of a 'first-contact' narrative in its final chapter, with the addition of a fictional tale in which Barrington and his young companion, Tim (the son of Barrington's 'convict woman servant'), become lost in the bush.[49] While navigating their way back to the settlement, the narrator and his offsider happen upon an exotic sentimental tableau:

> a most interesting scene presented itself to my view: a young creature seated on the jut of a rock, mournfully contemplating the extended body of a man, whose expiring groan had just pierced our ears; all her faculties were so absorbed with grief that we were yet unnoticed: a sympathizing sorrow pervaded all my frame ...[50]

Barrington learns from the young woman – named Yeariana – that the man, who he discovers has 'a deep wound under his left pap, made with a spear', is her brother, Palerino, and Barrington offers to watch the wounded man while she goes for help:

> Her eye glistened with joy as she gathered my meaning, and with an affecting inclination of the head, more eloquent and expressive of her feelings than in the power of the most refined language to convey, she quitted us with a celerity quicked by fraternal love, and in a few moments was out of sight.[51]

This act of generosity on Barrington's part endears him not only to Yeariana, but also the whole family:

> The mother of Yeariana was quite troublesome with her caresses for my services to her son; and I could perceive in the mild eye of her daughter that it anxiously sought a farther acquaintance.[52]

The sentimental episode of the encounter between Barrington and Yeariana and her family introduces the possibility of erotic encounters between Aboriginal women and European men. The image of the South Seas as a sexual utopia had become popular in England following the publication of John Hawkesworth's edition of the voyages of James Cook and others in early 1773.[53] However, the 'coarse features' and dark skin of Eora women, described by colonial journalists such as Hunter, were evidently not to English tastes. Thus Yeariana is described by 'Barrington' as an anomaly; and more a classical beauty transposed to the antipodes than an exotic specimen:

> [Yeariana's] image has made a strong impression on my mind, being the most interesting I ever saw: with a form that might serve as a perfect model for the most scrupulous statuary; her face and hair unlike any thing I had ever seen in this country; the first of a perfect oval, or Grecian shape, with features regularly beautiful, and as fine a pair of eyes as can be imagined; the latter long, and of a shining black; she was likewise of a much lighter colour than any of her countrywomen, and might easily have been taken for a beautiful Oriental Creole.[54]

But the romance theme is not long pursued, and 'Barrington' peremptorily breaks off his fantasies with a risqué allusion to 'certain views just dawning on my mind with respect to Yeariana'.[55]

As a publication, the 'Barrington' *Voyage to New South Wales* would seem to have little resemblance to the radical political works for which H. D. Symonds had been imprisoned. Yet there were perhaps some resonances of the radical agenda in the sub-plot of Barrington as a man who finds respectability and a fitting outlet for his talents when removed from the repressive social structures of the Old World. The authority claimed for Barrington in the *Voyage* was of course taken from another source, but in this appropriation there is an even more marked connection between the *Voyage* and the politics of its publisher. The Hunter *Historical Journal* had been published by John Stockdale, a bookseller with strong connections to the Pitt ministry – indeed Stockdale's 'Botany Bay' works (including the *Historical Journal*) had been published under an arrangement with government agencies.[56] In general, there was considerable enmity between the radical booksellers persecuted by the conservative Pitt government and those who profited from their support of the ministry, and in the case of Stockdale and the Newgate booksellers, this was intensified by personal disputes. Symonds' cell mate and sometime partner James Ridgway was the brother-in-law and also former employee of Stockdale, who appears to have loathed him with a particular passion. In 1784, Ridgway had been responsible for a vituperous biographical sketch which denounced Stockdale in both political and personal terms, as a 'puppet' controlled by those who penned works 'calculated to delude the public' and an 'ignoramous' who could barely read or write, ultimately claiming that he owed his success to dishonest dealings.[57]

There are certainly grounds to argue that the decision to use the *Historical Journal* as the exclusive source for descriptions of New South Wales in the 'Barrington' *Voyage* was a deliberate one. Since the *Voyage* plagiarises the account of Teneriffe written by an officer on the *Gorgon*[58], the same ship on which Watkin Tench returned, the writer of the *Voyage* presumably had access to Tench's *Complete Account of the Transactions at Port Jackson*. Indeed, there are textual indications that Tench's *Complete Account* had been consulted. The *Voyage* uses the name 'Araboo' for the young girl who had been 'adopted' in the colony by the chaplain Richard Johnson and his wife, presumably derived from the name she is given in Tench's *Complete Account* (Abaroo), in preference to the *Historical Journal*, where she is called Boorong.[59] There is also the distinct suggestion, as Suzanne Rickard has argued, that the figure of Yeariana was at least partly derived from Tench's sentimental description of the Eora woman he calls Gooreedeena.[60] Yet if Tench was consulted, his narrative contributed only in an oblique fashion to the *Voyage*, while the *Historical Journal* was comprehensively plagiarised. While the main reason for publishing such a narrative under Barrington's name was surely commercial, the chance to subvert the work of a political and book trade rival may well have governed the choice of its source material. This possibility is strengthened by the fact that about the time the *Voyage to New South Wales* was concocted, Symonds and Ridgway were putting another of their cell mates – William Winterbotham – to work plagiarising a number of Stockdale's books on America, which they subsequently published.[61]

The question of who plagiarised the *Historical Journal* – and penned the original 'Barrington' material – for the *Voyage to New South Wales* bears investigation here. It is certainly of interest that someone so close to Symonds (Winterbotham) was working with the Newgate booksellers in the production of second-hand histories at much the same time as the 'Barrington' *Voyage* was written.[62] But the Winterbotham publications of 1795 were issued under his own name, and though from Newgate he had little opportunity to see first hand the places he was writing about, his method of composition could be defended, however tendentiously, as a style of scholarly compilation, which of course the spurious 'Barrington' work could not. Furthermore, there is no evidence that Winterbotham had any experience or interest in the kind of creative writing that the impersonation of Barrington in the *Voyage to New South Wales* demanded. Ultimately it seems unlikely that Winterbotham was the one to don the 'deceptious mask' of George Barrington.

It is quite possible that the writer who concocted the *Voyage to New South Wales* was also involved in another spurious South Seas work published by Symonds in 1796, *Letters from Mr. Fletcher Christian*.[63] This publication was almost certainly a response to the success of the 'Barrington' *Voyage*, which by then had reached a fourth edition. In Fletcher Christian, leader of the mutiny on board the *Bounty* in 1789, Symonds had appropriated a figure that had already become something of a 'Romantic hero'[64]; it could also be observed that as a symbol of resistance to perceived tyranny Christian was a less compromised figure than the petty thief Barrington. Thus while Wordsworth and Coleridge were toying with this romantic idea of Christian in their poetry[65], Symonds was using it as the capital for another spurious travel narrative. *Letters from Mr. Fletcher Christian* is somewhat more ambitious in its scope than the *Voyage to New South Wales*. It weaves together a narrative based on the accounts of the *Bounty* mutiny, with a 'history' of Christian's supposed travels through South America – plagiarised from a range of late eighteenth-century travel narratives.[66] But the *Letters from Mr. Fletcher Christian* never achieved anything like the success of the 'Barrington' *Voyage*, possibly because, unlike the *Voyage*, it was quickly recognised as a fraud. One reader concerned enough to bring this to the attention of the public was none other than William Wordsworth, who in October 1796 wrote to the *Weekly Entertainer* (which had published an extract from the work) with the comment: 'I think it proper to inform you, that I have the best authority for saying this publication is spurious. Your regard for truth will induce you to apprise your readers of this circumstance'.[67]

One tentative attribution of the real authorship of the *Voyage to New South Wales* was made in 1898 by E. A. Petherick. Petherick, who also noted that the *Voyage* was 'issued from the same manufactory whence came another spurious work, "The Letters of Fletcher Christian"', asserted that the actor and playwright Francis Godolphin Waldron was a possible author of the original 'Barrington' work.[68] Petherick's argument was based on the fact

that Waldron's surname was the same as Barrington's supposed
real name – a very tenuous basis for an attribution – and also on
the fact that Symonds published one of Waldron's plays in 1798.[69]
There is little in Waldron's background to suggest that this
attribution has any merit, however. Apart from dramatic works,
Waldron's publications tended to reflect his 'strong literary and
antiquarian interests'[70], while the spurious fictional sections of
the 'Barrington' *Voyage* suggest a background in modish sentimental fiction and 'Newgate biography' material. Besides, Waldron
was performing with the Drury Lane company in the winter of
1794–1795 and may have had limited time for extracurricular
literary pursuits.[71]

It seems more likely that the 'Barrington' *Voyage* was put together
by a writer with experience in handling a variety of different kinds
of popular narrative, rather than a part-time literary man like
Waldron or Winterbotham. In other words, the best candidate for
the authorship of the *Voyage* would be a hack writer, perhaps
drafted in by Symonds with the idea of the 'Barrington' narrative
in mind, or perhaps proposing the idea to Symonds and taking a
share of the profits. One writer fitting this description is Thomas
Hastings, the author of anonymous satirical works published by
Symonds in the early stages of his career.[72] These satirical works,
with their free, rambling plot structures, were not completely
dissimilar to the fictional sections of the *Voyage* in form and,
moreover, in the central character of 'Barrington' the *Voyage*
employed a persona whose development was mired in the press
gossip and scandal literature to which Hastings' satires were
intimately connected. But perhaps the best candidate for the
authorship of the *Voyage* is another marginal London hack writer,
Henry Lemoine. Like Hastings, Lemoine became known as a
travelling vendor of books and pamphlets, though until 1795 he
operated a bookstall in Bishopsgate churchyard in London's East
End.[73] Lemoine knew Symonds at least as early as 1791, when the

latter was involved in the sale of *The Conjuror's Magazine: or, Magical and Physiognomical Mirror*, of which Lemoine was 'the projector and editor'.[74] *The Conjuror's Magazine* reflected Lemoine's strong and wide-ranging interest in occult and millenarian subjects[75], and both this publication and its successor, *The Astrologer's Magazine, and Philosophical Miscellany*, were filled with essays, stories and letters on a range of mystical, supernatural and alternative theological topics. The early issues of *The Conjuror's Magazine* were said to be vastly popular, no doubt amongst the large and heterogeneous counterculture of 'radical enthusiasts' of the early 1790s.[76] Besides the *Conjuror's Magazine*, Lemoine was quite possibly the author of two works on similar themes published by Symonds: *Le Petit Sorcier, or the Little Wizard*, a fortune-telling book apparently intended for children, and *The Oneirocritic, being a Treatise on the Art of Foretelling Future Events*.[77] As both Symonds and Lemoine had an early and continued interest in catering for the radical dissenting subcultures of the 1780s and 1790s, it is reasonable to suggest that they may also have collaborated on other works that appealed to this emerging readership, such as the spurious 'Barrington' and 'Fletcher Christian' works.

A biographical sketch of Henry Lemoine published in Alexander Hogg's *New, Original and Complete Wonderful Museum and Magazine Extraordinary* of 1806 contains valuable information on the careers of Lemoine and other late eighteenth-century trade writers and booksellers.[78] It emphasises the diverse skills and great flexibility – both intellectual and ethical – which Lemoine possessed. He was said to have 'conceived the idea of producing an Irish edition' [that is, a piracy] of the works of the popular satirist Peter Pindar, but found it more convenient to have them printed in London – 'and whenever he went to the Printing-office in Black Horse Alley in Fleet-Street, he used to call that errand *going to Dublin*'.[79] The biographer somewhat embarrassedly concedes that Lemoine was 'a great dabbler in alchemy, astrology, chiromacy, and the doctrine of sympathies', but notes that anonymous hacks could not always afford to set their own agenda, and that Lemoine was a specialist at working 'to order' for the booksellers:

> ... the mind that gives value to the paper ... is seldom so well rewarded unless he possesses a name; but our subject here follows a different method. Custom has given [Lemoine] facility, and he enquires for work as an artist, of such as propose to publish, and writes up as well as he can to the bookseller's *idea*, it matters not what, cookery, physic, love-letters, any thing, or every thing, for nothing seems amiss, and a guinea is his price for a six-penny pamphlet, and at compilation he is said to be just the "thing".[80]

Lemoine's main literary occupation was said to be in 'the genteel chapbook line' or 'the small pamphlet line', a style of publication that his biographer asserts

> is a great improvement in what was denominated fifty years ago, the *chap-book* line ... in these modern manufactures, great care is taken to make them co-operate with a virtuous education, and they are worthy a place in the best parlour window or dressing room ... as they contain nothing to make young folks more cunning than good.[81]

Since the *Voyage* dramatises the reformation of Barrington, interweaving a fictional story of the celebrity convict's progress towards respectability through its plagiarised account of colonial history, the work could be viewed as similar to the morally focused 'genteel chapbooks' that Lemoine was skilled at producing. There is also evidence in the text of the *Voyage* itself to suggest that its author shared Lemoine's characteristic interest in weird and wonderful phenomena. Two original episodes in the text, both set in the sea voyage section of the narrative, prompt this comparison. The first is the description of a 'crossing the line' or 'ducking and shaving' ceremony, a carnivalesque maritime custom which takes place when crossing the equator.[82] The lurid novelised depiction of the ceremony in the *Voyage*, where sailors dressed as Neptune and other characters extracted 'forfeits' of liquor and sugar from those who had not previously crossed the equator, has no identifiable source in other published travel accounts of the period.[83] The episode is also neatly incorporated into the narrative: 'Barrington' himself pays the forfeit and escapes the indignity of the whole affair; only the ship's cook (to whom 'most of the ship's company owed a grudge') is 'ducked' and the rest of the victims are 'let off with only a shaving'.[84] The other episode in the *Voyage* of 'wonderful' interest is a reputed encounter with the *Flying Dutchman*. This was in fact a very early reference, at least in English literature, to the legendary ghost ship which would come to greater prominence in the nineteenth century as a cultural icon.[85] The encounter with the *Flying Dutchman* in the *Voyage* turns out to be chimerical; the rational 'Barrington' learns that it had been 'very cloudy' at the time of the sighting and thus 'easily divined what kind of phantom had so alarmed my messmate'.[86] But it is of great interest that another very early reference to the *Flying Dutchman* legend was made in what was likely to have been another Lemoine work, *New Lights from the World of Darkness*.[87]

Overall, the evidence is too scanty to make a definitive attribution of the 'Barrington' *Voyage* to Henry Lemoine. But it can certainly be said that Lemoine had the necessary skills to 'compile' the narrative, as well as experience in the production of similar works, and furthermore that the *Voyage* contains distinct traces of an interest in 'wonderful' phenomena, so redolent of Lemoine's writing. There is one further connection that is relevant here. In 1798, two years after Symonds had published his original edition, Lemoine published the only other known version of the *Letters from Mr. Fletcher Christian*, renaming it *Voyages and Travels of Fletcher Christian*[88]; a side-by-side examination of the works shows that Lemoine had simply reissued the sheets of the Symonds edition with a cancel title page. That Symonds had handed over his discredited publication to Lemoine suggests that the latter, who published few works during the 1790s under his own imprint, may have had some prior involvement with the text.

Whoever the real author of the *Voyage to New South Wales* was, the work certainly went before the public as the work of George Barrington, and unlike the later *Letters from Mr. Fletcher Christian*, it was not exposed as a fraud. Some sections of the literary establishment assumed it was beneath them even to care whether the *Voyage* was original or not; hence the cursory notice of the work in the *Gentleman's Magazine*:

> [whether] this be the genuine work of the celebrated convict or not, it contains nothing that has not been seen before on the subject; and if it gives a genuine account of Mr. B's reformation, we are glad to find that his distance from his native country has put him beyond the reach of temptation to violate her laws and the laws of society in general.[89]

But Symonds' enterprise in passing off a large quantity of second-hand material as the work of the celebrity transportee Barrington cannot have been harmed by a credulous notice in the reputable *Monthly Review*. Indeed the *Monthly Review* specifically addressed the question of fraudulent publishing practices, likening them to Barrington's own crimes, and cleared the *Voyage* of such a charge:

> We confess that we took up this performance with prejudice and suspicion, arising from the *name* which appears in the title-page as being that of the author. Not that we supposed the celebrated Mr. George Barrington to be incapable of writing a very readable book; but the well-known character and exploits of the man at once brought to our minds such a recollection of past imposture and depredation on the public, that it was impossible for us to read a line of *such* a production without caution and distrust. Our suspicions, indeed, were not at all placed to the account of the writer ... On perusing, however, a few pages of the work, our suspicions abated:

and before we arrived at its conclusion, not a doubt remained of its authenticity.[90]

It is difficult to understand how a respectable reviewing periodical like the *Monthly Review* could have reached such a judgement, particularly at a time when the reviewers of voyage narratives claimed to be especially wary of 'travels performed *up three flights of stairs*, – so common in this book-making age'.[91] One explanation is that William Wales, the reviewer who had handled the early New South Wales material, including the Hunter *Historical Journal*[92], had been replaced as the *Monthly Review*'s main reviewer of 'voyage and travel' narratives by this time. From mid-1795, the reviewer responsible for most of the *Monthly Review*'s travel reviews was James Burney, a retired naval captain who, like Wales, had accompanied James Cook on his last two Pacific voyages.[93] Like many of the Romantic literati of the 1790s, Burney was sympathetic to the radical cause[94], and it is not outside the realms of possibility that the favourable notice of the 'Barrington' *Voyage* in the *Monthly Review* was in fact a deliberate attempt to secure a favourable reception for this production of one of the suffering Newgate booksellers. On the balance of probabilities, however, it seems more likely that the reviewer of the 'Barrington' work, whether it was Burney or not[95], was simply unfamiliar with the Hunter *Historical Journal*, and thus made a glaring mistake with his opinion on the authenticity of the *Voyage*.

If John Stockdale, publisher and copyright holder of the Hunter work[96], was frustrated by the credulity with which the 'Barrington' *Voyage* was received by the *Monthly Review*, there is no indication that he ever attempted to expose the work as a fraud. Though noted for his litigious disposition, and though he railed privately against another 'villainous Newgate compilation'[97], Stockdale seems to have remained silent on the matter of the plagiaristic *Voyage*. It is certain that Stockdale became aware of the 'Barrington' work at some point, however, and his only known response to the fraud was a very curious one. In 1808, with his Tory patrons out of power and his eminence as a bookseller considerably diminished, Stockdale published his own 'Barrington' book – which was in fact a reissue of a work he had published in 1787 with a new title page claiming Barrington as the author.[98]

While Symonds would certainly have been glad that the *Voyage to New South Wales* was not exposed as a fraud in the reviewing press or elsewhere, it was not the literary establishment that he particularly wished to please. The 'Barrington' *Voyage* was clearly aimed at the popular market. By mining the *Historical Journal* for its descriptions of Aboriginal culture and of early instances of cross-cultural dialogue, extending the work by means of other interesting travel narratives and, last but not least, adding novelistic elements centred around Barrington, the author produced a travel narrative designed to appeal to 'every class of readers'.[99] Symonds' publication was not a chapbook, however. Extending to 136 pages, priced at 'Half-a-Crown' (2s. 6d.) and advertised in the metropolitan daily press[100], the 'Barrington' *Voyage* in the hands of its original publisher was a topical pamphlet marketed towards Symonds' usual clientele of middling classes, artisans, professionals and 'street-wise' gentry.[101] But it wasn't long before pirated versions of the *Voyage* appeared, now abridged and aimed at the chapbook market, but still, of course, trading mainly on the idea of 'the celebrated Barrington' as author.

Probably the first of these redactions of the 'Barrington' *Voyage* was a thirty-two page chapbook published under the imprint 'London: Printed for the Proprietors, 1795'.[102] This anonymous imprint left open the matter of ownership of copyright – echoing the Symonds imprint, which was 'Printed for the Proprietor … and H. D. Symonds' – a ruse probably meant to imply that the 'proprietor' of the copyright was Barrington himself. But complete anonymity was not ideal from a trade point of view, and the printer of the work – Thomas Walker, a bookseller, news-paper proprietor and printer in the market town of Preston, Lancashire[103] – affixed a page of advertisements for his other publications on the last page of the publication. Walker's other advertised productions included chapbook biographies of Robespierre and Marie Antoinette, as well as more extensive works such as Buchan's *Domestic Medicine*, which were said to be 'sold by all the Booksellers who circulate this interesting account of Botany Bay'.[104] This gives a clue to the networks catered for by Walker and other provincial printer–booksellers like him. Larger provincial towns like Preston acted as minor centres of book production, where items of local interest, as well as locally produced versions of popular material, could be produced at a cheaper (or at least competitive) rate to comparable works emanating from London. These works were then distributed through the nearby towns and villages by chapmen and 'flying stationers', travelling hawkers whose traditional method of promoting their wares was the vocal 'crying' of the titles and often the public reading – or in the case of ballads, singing – of their contents. As William St Clair has shown, the late eighteenth century saw a transformation of the chapbook trade, where the traditional corpus of chapbooks and ballads was being replaced by abridgements and adaptations of 'more recently composed texts'.[105] Certainly, one modern text that was embraced by the chapbook trade with great speed and enthusiasm was the *Voyage to New South Wales*.

Few of the abridged chapbook versions of the 'Barrington' *Voyage* carry dates, and none were noticed in the periodical reviews or newspapers, so reconstructing their publishing history is difficult. A survey of the chapbook editions in the Mitchell Library and the National Library of Australia, however, has revealed that all the chapbook versions of the *Voyage* stemmed from a single prototype. It was not the case that a number of booksellers and printers made individual abridgements from the original *Voyage*.

Rather, an abridgement was made and then this text was copied, to a greater or lesser degree verbatim, in a multitude of editions produced by a number of different booksellers.[106] From the early date of publication given on its title page (1795), the Walker redaction of the *Voyage* could well have been the original abridgement, and would thus have served as the 'master' copy from which the other editions descended. Another candidate, however, could be the first edition produced by Andrew Hambleton[107], who had also been involved in producing chapbook biographies of Barrington. The Walker and Hambleton versions of the *Voyage* are textually identical and, moreover, exhibit certain typographical features that reveal one of these versions had served as the model for the other. The same text and typographical idiosyncrasies were also present in the editions produced for the chapbook sellers James Sadler, Mary Clements, T. Thomas, and J. Eves, who were also publishers of the *Genuine Life and Trial of George Barrington*.[108] These editions were produced over what seems to have been a long period of time, and the print runs were probably small, with a new edition being produced whenever demand arose and capital permitted.[109] The text they used was always the same, clearly descended from the original redaction, albeit slightly truncated so that the narrative concluded with the description of Yeariana as 'like a beautiful Oriental Creole'.

The majority of chapbook editions of the *Voyage* were printed in the northern provinces of England. While Andrew Hambleton's editions may have been printed in London, and one or more of the Sadler–Clements–Thomas–Eves versions may also have been printed in London, the latter group of publishers certainly had a number of editions printed in Manchester by Alice Swindells, and in 1801 at least two editions of the same abridged text were produced in Newcastle-upon-Tyne by the printing firm Margaret Angus and Son.[110] Towns like Manchester and Newcastle were traditional centres for the production of inexpensive sub-literary material like chapbooks and ballads, and as the shifting social and economic landscape engendered by the industrial revolution expanded both the size and sophistication of provincial reading audiences, so too did the chapbook form adapt to feed this market. The redaction of the *Voyage* that was produced in so many different editions in these places may be seen as an example of how the late eighteenth-century chapbook trade had come to embrace more recent popular texts, while at the same time adapting them into this traditional format for cheap, entertaining reading material. The fact that the same abridged text of the *Voyage* was reprinted over and over again in these places is not surprising in view of the fact that the chapbook trade was based on the reproduction of proven saleable material, with little time or money wasted on rewriting. Like the abridged biographies of Barrington, this *Voyage* redaction seems to have remained a saleable commodity in the north of England for a considerable period: internal evidence in one of these editions shows they were still being produced by Alice Swindells in Manchester after 1808.[111]

One edition of the abridged *Voyage* text that was produced and sold in London was a work that appeared under the title, *An Impartial and Circumstantial Narrative of the Present State of Botany Bay ... by George Barrington*, published by the East End printers Susan and John Bailey.[112] The date of this publication has been misjudged in various sources, most recently in the work of Suzanne Rickard, who has also erroneously claimed the work as the original incarnation of the *Voyage*.[113] Internal evidence in extant copies of the *Impartial and Circumstantial Narrative*[114], along with the trade histories of the printers, indicates that the work appeared around the turn of the nineteenth century rather than at Rickard's estimated date of 'c. 1793–1794'.[115] Far from being the original version of the *Voyage*, the *Impartial and Circumstantial Narrative* was in fact merely another reprint of the abridged version of the text produced by minor traders hoping to

BARRINGTON's VOYAGE

TO

NEW SOUTH WALES;

WITH A

Description of the Country ;

THE

MANNERS, CUSTOMS, RELIGION, &c.

OF

The Natives

in the

Vicinity of Botany Bay.

A New Edition, by GEORGE BARRINGTON,

Now Superintendant to the Convicts at PARAMATA, and sent to his
FRIEND in England.

Printed by A. Swindells, Hanging-bridge.
Manchester.

AND SOLD BY T. THOMAS, AND J. SADLER.

Price only Nine-pence.

Title page of a later edition of the abridged chapbook version of the *Voyage*. Courtesy
of Mitchell Library, State Library of New South Wales.

capitalise on the popularity of the text generated by the earlier Symonds editions.

It was certainly not the case that all editions of the *Voyage to New South Wales*, apart from those published by Symonds, were chapbook redactions, however. Outside England, booksellers tended to appropriate the *Voyage* text in its original state and, in this way, the work became an international publishing phenomenon. In 1796, shortly after Symonds published his 'Third Edition' of the *Voyage*, a version was published in the United States by the Philadelphia printer and bookseller Thomas Dobson.[116] Dobson's edition was a reprint of the original *Voyage* text, and while it is not out of the question that he paid some sort of consideration to Symonds for de facto American 'rights' to the publication, it seems more likely that the enterprising printer–publisher had simply seen fit to pirate Symonds' first edition of the *Voyage* for distribution in the United States. The fact that the Barrington *Voyage* should have so swiftly made its way across the Atlantic says much about the international reputation of Barrington, and probably also about the popularity of the text; the Dobson edition of the Barrington *Voyage* was one of only two works on New South Wales to be published in America before 1800.[117]

Less than two years later, in what according to the French Revolutionary calendar was the year VI, the Parisian publisher Victor Desenne published the first translation of the *Voyage* as *Voyage a Botany Bay*.[118] The unnamed translator of the work played a significant role in recreating the 'Barrington' narrative for French readers. The work featured a translator's preface that extolled 'Citoyen Barrington' as an example of a reformed character and a positive result of the English transportation system[119], and there are a number of explanatory footnotes through the text, dealing mainly with translation issues, but also comparing

V O Y A G E

A

B O T A N Y - B A Y,

AVEC UNE DESCRIPTION

DU PAYS, DES MOEURS,

DES COUTUMES

ET DE LA RELIGION

DES NATIFS.

PAR le célèbre GEORGE BARRINGTON.

Traduit de l'Anglais, sur la troisième Édition.

A PARIS,

Chez DESENNE, Libraire, Palais-Égalité,
Nᵒˢ 1 et 2.

AN VI.

The title page of the first French edition of the *Voyage*. Courtesy of Mitchell Library, State Library of New South Wales.

the 'new' discoveries of 'Barrington' to the work of the natural historian Georges-Louis Leclerc, Comte de Buffon. In addition to this scholarly apparatus, the translator also participated in the process of furthering Barrington's spurious authorial repertoire; at the conclusion of the text there is a new paragraph not found in the English original, melodramatically expressing 'Barrington's' sentiments on his banishment:

Pour l'Angleterre! pour ce pays que je ne reverrai donc plus! pour ma patrie don't á jamais mes fautes m'ont banni. Ah! vous á qui j'adresse cet ouvrage, ah! monsieur, vous ne pouvez savior quelle force a ce sentiment que chaque homme porte dans son cœur pour le lieu qui l'a vu naître, et tout ce que souffre l'infortuné condamné à ne plus le revoir: il faut l'avoir perdu pour éprouver combine on l'aime! Hélas! Combine de fois le cœur oppressé, et les yeux tournés vers le nord, ne suis-je pas resté immobile, accablé de douleur et de regrets! combien de fois passant des heures entières dans cette situation, mon imagination, franchissant les espaces, ne s'est elle pas transportée près de mes parens, au milieu de mes amis! Rêves trop flatuers! Plaisirs mensongers! Que chèrement vous me faites payer ces courts instants d'un bonheur passager! Réveillé bientôt par l'afreuse vérité, je l'entends qui me crie: home coupable! Ton pays t'a rejeté; il a voulu mettre l'éntendue des mers et leurs profondes abîmes entre lue et toi. Expie tes crimes! non, malheureux! ta tombe ne sera jamais où fut ton berceua! ...[120]

The French translation of the *Voyage* published by Desenne in 1797–1798 seems to have been produced in a fairly large edition, and the work served as the basis for further French editions and for subsequent translations of the *Voyage* into other European languages: the texts of all these include the paragraph quoted above.[121]

With the *Voyage to New South Wales* now making waves around the world, it is hardly surprising that the original publisher, H. D. Symonds, chose to refashion and republish the work. One of Symonds' first strategies for revamping the *Voyage* was to commission an engraved illustrated plate to add pictorial interest. This plate, which consisted of a frontispiece illustration and a pictorial title page, was first used in the 'Fourth Edition' of the *Voyage to New South Wales*, published in 1796. The frontispiece, titled 'An Interesting Discovery in the Woods', depicted the initial

The frontispiece illustration, 'An interesting discovery in the Woods', which accompanied later versions of the *Voyage* published by H. D. Symonds. Hordern House Rare Books.

encounter between Barrington and his companion Tim and the 'natives' Yeariana and Palerino, while the pictorial title page, which used the title *A Voyage to Botany Bay*, included a vignette depicting convicts landing in New South Wales.[122] Shortly after the publication of the 'Fourth Edition', Symonds published a cheaper reprint of the *Voyage*, using the engraved plate from the 'Fourth Edition' as its title, but modifying the plate to revise the price of the work from two shillings and sixpence to one shilling and sixpence.[123] Symonds revived the *Voyage* again about 1800 when he published another edition using the *Voyage to Botany Bay* pictorial title page as its title, adding new material in the form of a brief preliminary section giving a biography of the celebrated author (an epitome of the Kearsley *Memoirs of George Barrington*), and an account of his trial in 1790.[124] This later edition of the *Voyage* was the first to carry the name of a printer, C[harles] Lowndes[125], though a comparison of the earlier *Voyage to New South Wales* editions and the *Voyage to Botany Bay* copies strongly suggests that the Lowndes' press had also produced the earlier editions. Perhaps, seeing the popularity of the work, the Lowndes family no longer minded being associated with a plagiaristic publication, and possibly acquired a stake in the sale of it.

The publication of Symonds and Lowndes' 1800 edition of the *Voyage* seems to have been timed to coincide with the release of a new narrative, published as *A Sequel to Barrington's Voyage* in late 1800.[126] The *Sequel* drew the vast majority of its content from David Collins' *An Account of the English Settlement in New South Wales*, the first part of which had been published in London in 1798.[127] Collins had been meticulously recording events in the colony from its foundation; as early as July 1788 the naval surgeon G. B. Worgan noted the existence of the judge advocate's 'narrative', commenting in a letter to his brother that if Collins

> intends to give it to the Public, I will recommend You & yr friends to his in preference to any other, because from his Genius I am certain it will be the most Entertaining, Animating, Correct and satisfactory of any that may appear.[128]

What Collins eventually did give to the public was an exhaustive catalogue of events in New South Wales from 1788 to 1796, and his published work proved particularly fertile material for the production of plagiarised narratives, beginning with the 'Barrington' *Sequel*.

The *Sequel to Barrington's Voyage* made halting attempts to follow the successful pattern of the original *Voyage* narrative. The first chapter includes a brief continuation of 'Barrington's' adventures with Yeariana and Palerino – the cross-cultural romance hinted at in the final chapter of the *Voyage* has now blossomed into a tableaux of domestic happiness. Yeariana is said to be 'as it were, a part of [Barrington's] family'; this 'lovely girl' approaches 'Barrington' with 'love, satisfaction, and joy' after her brother extricates himself from his latest scrape.[129] There is also some attempt to install 'Barrington' as an active agent in certain episodes taken from Collins' narrative where events at Parramatta are described[130], and in other places there is an attempt to make the material taken from the Collins' narrative more prosaic, as in the narration of an episode where a settler by the name of Charles Williams laments the death of his wife:

> The profligacy of this man indeed manifested itself in a strange manner: a short time after he had thus buried his wife, he was seen sitting at his door, with a bottle of rum in his hand, and actually drinking one glass and pouring another on her grave until it was emptied, prefacing every libation by declaring how well she had loved it during her life.
>
> Collins, *Account*, p. 264

> This mournful event made not the least impression on this hardened character; for a few days after he had thus buried his wife, he was seen sitting at his door, with a bottle of rum in his hand, and actually drinking one glass himself, and pouring the next over her grave, till it was emptied: saying at every glass "there's your share my old girl," concluding with, "the devil's in it if you won't be quiet now."
>
> 'Barrington', *Sequel*, pp. 8–9

For the most part, however, the text of the *Sequel* makes little attempt to disguise its origins, and the arrangement of the Collins *Account* as a diary of events written mostly in the objective third person is generally replicated in the 'Barrington' *Sequel*.

As with the original, the plagiaristic *Sequel to Barrington's Voyage* received a favourable if cursory notice in the *Monthly Review*. This review devoted more attention to the question of Barrington's reformation, deferring its critical opinion of the work – and assertion of its authenticity – back to the earlier review of the original *Voyage*:

> What we then remarked concerning the character of this heteroclite adventurer in the wildest walks of society, and the general merit of his narrative, will circumstantially and strictly apply to this second narrative.[131]

It seems as if the *Monthly Review* wanted the *Voyage* and its *Sequel* to be genuine because it wanted Barrington, and his reformation, to be an antipodean success story. In any case, Symonds would once again have been glad that further attention was not paid to the question of authenticity here.

The 'Barrington' *Sequel* clearly did not enjoy the success of the original *Voyage*. No abridged versions of this work appeared, and soon after its original publication, Symonds and Lowndes reprinted the *Sequel* in a cheaper format.[132] At some point in 1801, the publishers also resorted to the tactic of 'puffing' the work in the press:

> The celebrated George Barrington (whose abilities appear as if they would be of service to his country, and to society at large,) has lately sent to his friend Mr. Wentworth, a *Sequel* to his *Voyage to Botany Bay*; containing an official register of the crimes, sentences, and executions, that have taken place during the first eight years of its establishment; a typographical, physical, and moral account

of the country, manners, customs, &c. of the natives; including anecdotes, &c. &c. of the most distinguished characters transported from this country; a work highly entertaining to every class of readers.[133]

'Mr. Wentworth' here seems to have become conflated with the 'friend in England' to whom Barrington was supposed to have sent the original *Voyage*.[134] In any case, the 'puffing' seems not to have improved the shelf life of the *Sequel* as an independent work. In late 1801, Symonds revamped his 'Barrington' catalogue once again by publishing a combined edition of the *Voyage* and *Sequel*. This was advertised under the heading 'BARRINGTON'S HISTORY OF BOTANY BAY ... A COMPLETE HISTORY OF NEW SOUTH WALES, divided into Two Parts', at the price of 3s. 6d.[135] Initially, this combined edition of the *Voyage* and *Sequel* was not a reprint but rather a reissue of the version of the *Voyage* (including the preliminary biographical and trial material) that had appeared in 1800, along with the *Sequel* of 1801.[136] However, another version of the combined edition was issued, in which the *Voyage* section of the work was reprinted while the *Sequel* section was again a reissue of the sheets of 1801[137] – suggesting that the *Voyage* continued to sell well enough as an independent work to merit reprinting while the *Sequel* did not.

The publication of Symonds' combined edition of the *Voyage* and *Sequel* in 1801 prompted renewed interest in the work of 'Barrington' on the part of overseas publishers. A reprint of the combined *Voyage* and *Sequel* was swiftly published by a conger of Dublin booksellers who specialised in pirating London publications[138]; and this work in turn was reprinted by a printer and circulating library proprietor in Cork.[139] While these Irish reprints no doubt served local markets, their existence also suggests that the 'Barrington' texts enjoyed a continuing popularity across the Atlantic, since the American market was one of the main sites where Irish reprints competed with the London originals.[140]

A VOYAGE

TO

NEW SOUTH WALES,

COMPRISING AN

INTERESTING NARRATIVE

OF THE

TRANSACTIONS AND BEHAVIOUR OF THE CON-
VICTS:

THE PROGRESS OF THE COLONY;

AN OFFICIAL REGISTER

OF THE

CRIMES, TRIALS, SENTENCES, AND EXECUTIONS

THAT HAVE TAKEN PLACE:

*A Topographical, Physical, and Moral Account of the Country,
Manners, Customs, &c. of the Natives.*

AS LIKEWISE

Authentic Anecdotes

OF THE MOST DISTINGUISHED CHARACTERS,

AND

NOTORIOUS CONVICTS THAT HAVE BEEN TRANSPORTED TO

BOTANY BAY.

By George Barrington,

PRINCIPAL SUPERINTENDANT OF THE CONVICTS.

TO WHICH IS ANNEXED

HIS LIFE AND TRIAL.

New-York:

PRINTED BY JOHN SWAIN.

Title page from the New York edition of the combined *Voyage* and *Sequel* printed by
John Swain. Hordern House Rare Books.

There was also interest in the 'Barrington' work on the part of American publishers. In March and April 1802, Benjamin Franklin Timothy, printer of the *South-Carolina State Gazette and Timothy's Daily Advertiser*, attempted to interest readers in a proposed subscription edition of the combined *Voyage* and *Sequel*, though the work appears not to have been published.[141] In July the same year, William Durell in New York did publish an edition of the combined *Voyage* and *Sequel*, advertising it heavily in the local press[142]; Durell's 'Barrington' publication was possibly the work that was issued under the imprint of the New York printer John Swain.[143] It appears that the Barrington books sold well enough in the United States for the famous pickpocket to remain topical. In October 1802, a paragraph appeared in a number of American newspapers denying a supposed rumour that 'an official invitation and a public ship are to be dispatched to *Botany-Bay* for the noted GEORGE BARRINGTON'.[144] This 'report' turned out to be a squib attacking the radical Irish–American journalist William Duane, but it is significant that Barrington's international reputation as an author had advanced to the point that he and the conductor of the influential Philadelphia *Aurora* could be thus lumped together as 'Irish editors'.[145]

At the other extremity of the Western world, Russian readers of the early nineteenth century also had the chance to become familiar with the putative work of the celebrated Barrington after a translation of the *Voyage* was published by the Moscow University printer in 1803.[146] The Russian translation was made from the French edition of the *Voyage* by Prince Alexsei Petrovich Golitsyn, a civil servant and officer in the prestigious Guards corps stationed in St Petersburg.[147] One recent writer has described Golitsyn's translation of the *Voyage* as a 'huge success' which 'provoked a lasting Russian interest in the mechanics of transported convicts' life'; the work was at least popular enough to merit a new edition in 1809.[148]

By the end of 1802, the efforts of publishers in London ensured that 'Barrington' had expanded his oeuvre beyond the *Voyage* and its *Sequel*. In this year two new publications appeared under Barrington's name. One of these, *The Frauds of London Detected*, was virtually a straight reprint of a London underworld 'guide-book' of the same title from the late 1770s[149], published as a shilling pamphlet by the bookseller J. Lee, with woodcut illustrations by Richard Austin and handsome printing by the Covent Garden printer Alexander Macpherson.[150] If the nefarious activities of the underworld of the metropolis had changed by the turn of the nineteenth century, no such development was reflected in 'Barrington's' *Frauds of London Detected*. No effort had been made to reinvent the work, although the dated references to Barrington himself in the original text had been omitted from 'his' version.[151] The republication of this work was not technically a piracy, as the copyright on the 1770s *Frauds of London Detected* had lapsed by 1802.[152] But the decision to claim Barrington as the author of the work was an interesting step, and one wonders how seriously it was taken by contemporary readers: a single sentence at the end of the preface of the Lee publication is the only attempt to make the figure of Barrington a presence in the work.[153]

The other new 'Barrington' book to appear in 1802 was a more ambitious work entitled *The History of New South Wales*.[154] The *History* was published by Maurice Jones[155], a bookseller who had recently established himself in Paternoster Row and had set about developing a specialisation in publishing works in part-issues.[156] Jones evidently had faith that the Barrington name could sell books in a more prestigious market than had hitherto been exploited. The *History* was part of a planned two-volume set, with the companion volume being a greatly expanded version of the *Voyage* published under the title *An Account of a Voyage to New South Wales*.[157] Like the original *Voyage*, the *History* and *Account* were plagiaristic works. The *History* drew the majority of its content from the first volume of Collins' *An Account of the English Colony in New South Wales*, while the *Account* expanded the original *Voyage* by adding a detailed preliminary biography (plagiarised from the Kearsley *Memoirs of George Barrington*), and filling out the rest of the narrative with further reference to the African travels of François Le Vaillant, the seemingly inexhaustible Collins narrative and, somewhat more curiously, Sir George Staunton's account of China.[158] Despite the derivative nature of the texts, the *History* and *Account* were hardly clandestine publications. The works were produced on a lavish scale, with numerous illustrations by the engraver Vivian Woodthorpe (who, like the unknown author, was certainly adept at reworking the material of others[159]) and a wealth of prefatory and supplementary material, including a dedication to no less a personage than the King.[160] In short, the 'Barrington' *History* and *Account* were clearly meant to emulate 'official' voyage narratives, and their elaborate nature represented an intriguing transformation of the spurious work conceived by a publisher detained at His Majesty's pleasure less than a decade earlier.

Maurice Jones' main avenue of sales for the *History* and *Account* was publication in part-issues. In October 1802, a newspaper advertisement announced that 'Barrington's History of New South Wales' would be issued in weekly parts from the end of the month:

> This work will be completed in Twelve Numbers, making Two elegant Volumes in Octavo, illustrated with elegant Engravings of Views and Customs, coloured in exact imitation of nature.

> The Proprietors beg leave to assure the Public, that nothing can impede the regular publication of the work, as the Manuscript has all arrived from the Author, and the Plates are in great forwardness; they trust, therefore, that, as every attention has been paid, to render the work truly valuable, they will ensure the patronage of the public.[161]

In the event, the *History* extended to fourteen numbers, and in a 'Preface to the Reader' included with the final number, Jones directed

> the attention of the Public to a Republication, much enlarged, of *Barrington's Voyage to New South Wales, with his Life, Trials, Speeches,* &c. &c. which will be completed in Twelve Numbers, at One Shilling each, and be enriched with Views, Map, &c. elegantly coloured, and a fine portrait of the Author.[162]

In fact, after the initial part publication of the *History* was completed in February 1803, Jones advertised the publication of the *Account* and *History* as a single series in weekly parts:

> This work will be completed in Twenty-six Numbers, making two large Volumes 8vo. illustrated with elegant Engravings ... also an elegant Portrait of the Author or Map of the Country.

> The Public have now an Opportunity of being in Possession of the COMPLETEST HISTORY of NEW SOUTH WALES ever offered to them.[163]

At the price of one shilling for each number, collecting the full set of both volumes would have been an expensive undertaking, and the works clearly did not sell out at their first publication; Jones reissued the 1802–1803 *Account* and *History* together as a twenty-six part series on at least two other occasions.[164] He also offered bound versions of the works for sale: the new publications catalogue in the *Monthly Magazine* for July 1803 notes the publication of 'Barrington's History of New South Wales' (that is, both the *History* and the *Account*), bound in two octavo volumes, at £1 7s.[165] However, the wide variety of different collations and bindings of extant copies of these works strongly suggests that publication in parts was their main mode of sale[166], and the fact that Jones' advertising often appeared in provincial newspapers may suggest that the publication of his elaborate 'Barrington' works resembled a kind of direct marketing, which may have helped

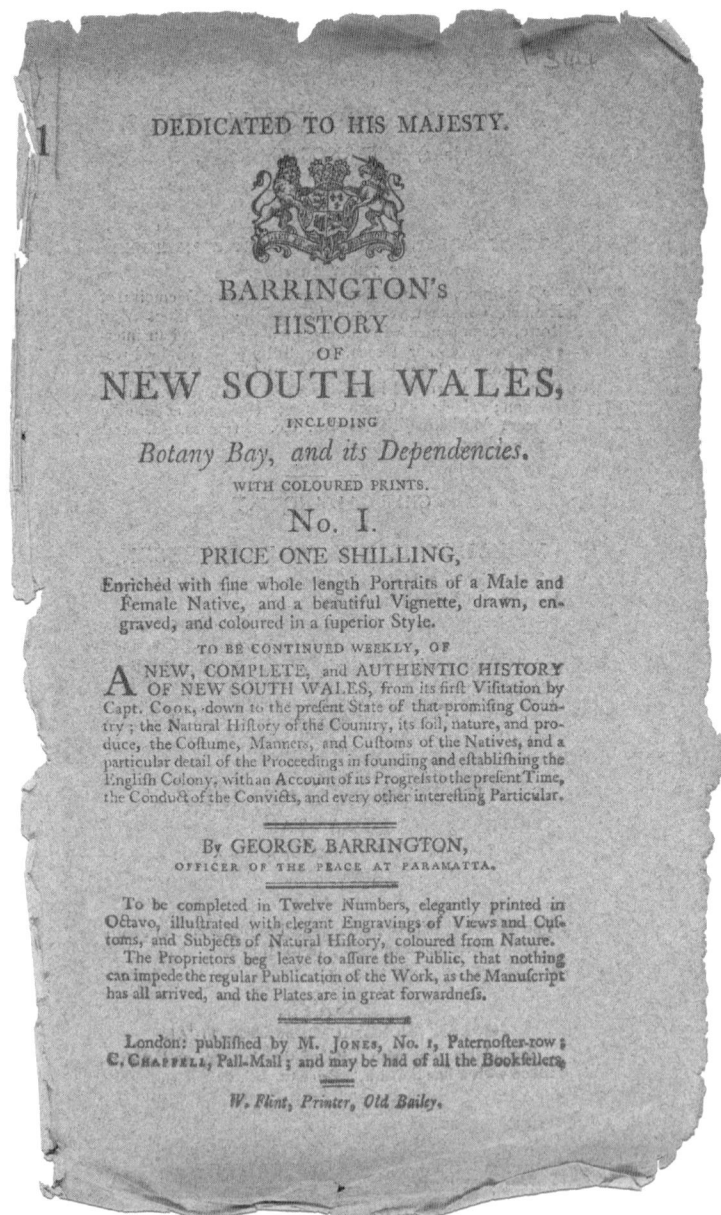

Front paper wrapper from the first number of the part-issued 'Barrington' *History of New South Wales* (1802). Courtesy of National Library of Australia.

circumvent the closer scrutiny of the texts by the London literary establishment.

While Jonathan Wantrup has discerned no link between the Jones 'Barrington' works and the earlier incarnations of the *Voyage*[167], it does appear likely that Jones had reached some sort of accommodation with the original publisher, H. D. Symonds, regarding the use of the Barrington allonym. While the *Voyage to New South Wales* had never been copyrighted[168], and Jones was technically free to use both the Barrington name and the earlier *Voyage* text(s) as he wished, it would have been a bold move for a recently established Paternoster Row bookseller to have taken over the popular work of another in this way. Jones and Symonds, moreover, were partners in at least one other publication at about the same time the *History* was published.[169] Symonds himself published no further 'Barrington' works after Jones began the publication of the *History* and *Barrington's Voyage* in the winter of 1802–1803, but when Jones published second editions of these works in 1810, he did so in partnership with the firm of Sherwood, Neely and Jones – successors to the business of the recently retired Symonds.[170] Under these circumstances, it seems likely that Jones had negotiated the use of the Barrington name and texts with Symonds, and perhaps that the latter had retained some option on future publications.

The elaborate nature of Jones' 'Barrington' works made them unique among the books published under the celebrity convict's name and, remarkably, their high price placed the volumes in a similar market to the authentic narratives from which they had been plagiarised.[171] Whether the literary establishment and the genteel readership of voyage and travel narratives ever really accepted Barrington as a credible colonial authority remains to be seen, however. Neither the *History* nor the *Account* were reviewed in any of the major reviewing journals of the period, a silence which would seem to suggest that they were not regarded as new publications – possibly because of the earlier Symonds *Voyage* editions, or possibly because the plagiaristic origins of the texts were now more easily recognised. Certainly there was recognition among the literary cognoscenti that the book trade abounded with such dubious practices, yet no literary gentleman seems to have been concerned enough to expose these revamped 'Barrington' works as a fraud at the time of their publication. In 1808, however, the use of Barrington as learned editor of pretentious volumes was lampooned in a piece in *The Satirist*, which clearly had the publishing style of Maurice Jones and those like him in mind when it suggested that 'the Celebrated G. Barrington' could now produce an authoritative work on the 'Art of Swindling':

> For since swindling is practiced by all ranks of the community, from those, who, by a false show of patriotism and boast of talent, would swindle the people out of their good opinion and support, down to the trickling book-vamper, who, by a catching title affixed to some stale trash, swindles them out of their money, there can be little doubt but that all would be ready to refine and methodize by a luminous and well digested theory.[172]

If Jones was aware of this attack, it did little to curb his enthusiasm for the 'Barrington' works he had at his disposal. Swindling or not, the 'deceptious mask' remained potentially profitable, even some twenty years on from the peak of Barrington's fame. In 1810, Jones arranged new editions of the *History* and *Account*, which he published, now in conjunction with Sherwood, Neely and Jones, from the start of 1811. Just how far these works should be considered new editions is open to question. There was new preliminary material, including a 'Preface to the Second Edition', and the *History* appended a thirty-nine page 'Supplement', which digested a number of travel accounts published in the British press in the first decade of the nineteenth century.[173] However,

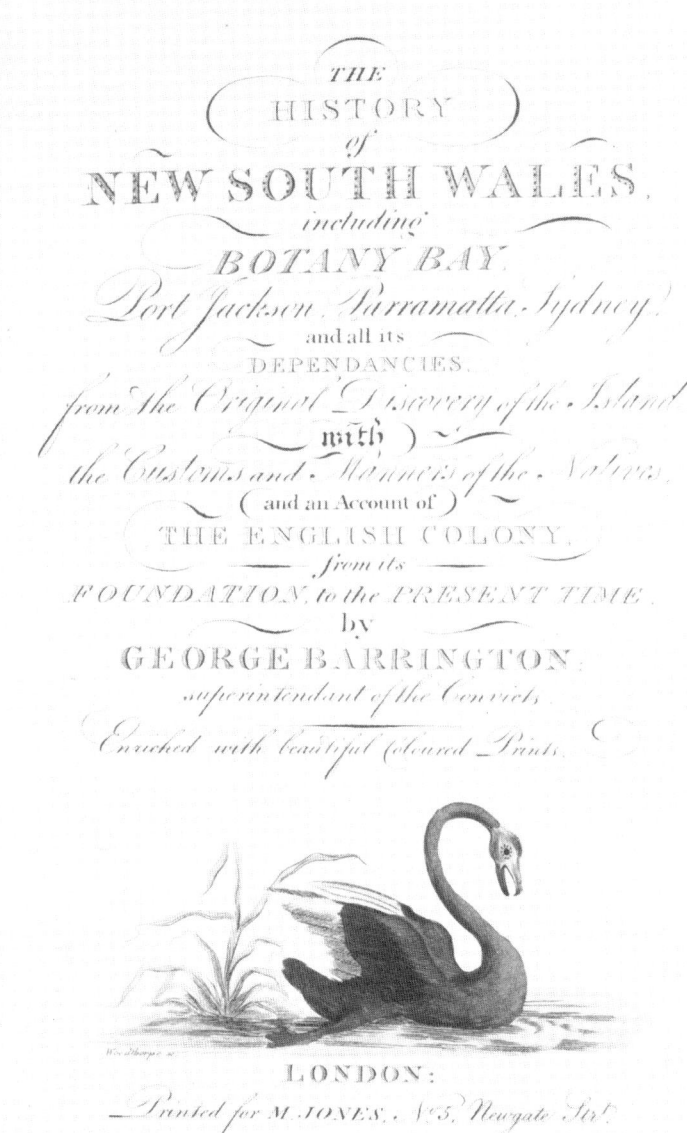

THE

HISTORY

of

NEW SOUTH WALES,

including

BOTANY BAY,

Port Jackson, Parramatta, Sydney,

and all its

DEPENDANCIES,

from the Original Discovery of the Island:

with

the Customs and Manners of the Natives,

(and an Account of)

THE ENGLISH COLONY,

from its

FOUNDATION, to the PRESENT TIME,

by

GEORGE BARRINGTON,

superintendant of the Convicts,

Enriched with beautiful Coloured Prints,

LONDON:

Printed for M. JONES, N.º 5, Newgate Str.ᵗ

& Sherwood, Neely, & Jones,

Paternoster row, 1810.

Title page of the second edition of *The History of New South Wales*. Hordern House
Rare Books.

the greater part of the texts remained the same as the earlier editions, and moreover, while the 1810 *History* was a reprint of the 1802 version, the 1810 *Account* was in fact a reissue of the printed sheets of the earlier edition. The publication of the 'Second Edition, improved and continued to the present time', of the *History* and *Account* was advertised at the start of January 1811, with the works said to form

> two handsome volumes in octavo, and may be had complete, price
> 1l. 7s. [£1 7s.] boards: or in 26 Numbers, each Number embellished
> with one or more prints, finely coloured, illustrative of Views,
> Manners and Customs of the Natives, and Subjects of Natural History,
> coloured from Nature, with a Map of the Country.[174]

Once again, the work did not sell out on its original publication, and advertisements announcing the recommencement of the twenty-six part numbered series, now described as 'Barrington's Botany Bay', appeared in the English press in December 1811, November 1812, July 1813 and January 1815.[175] Evidence from extant copies suggest that the *History* printed in 1810 was still being sold as late as 1824, by which time Maurice Jones had left the trade and the remaining publishers, Sherwood and Jones, were also winding up their affairs – and presumably would have been eager to extract whatever money they could from their remaining stock.[176]

At the same time as the revamped and extended *Voyage* and its companion work appeared courtesy of Maurice Jones, the Barrington allonym was being taken in different directions by an even more enterprising young publisher. This was Thomas Tegg, the redoubtable London bookseller who would rise from runaway apprentice to become one of the great success stories of the early nineteenth-century book trade. In his autobiography, Tegg would claim his success was based on cheap reprints of works on which copyright had lapsed – in his own words, he was 'the broom that swept the booksellers' warehouses'.[177] One reprint Tegg evidently had some success with early in his career was the *Frauds of London Detected*. As we have seen, Tegg was not the first bookseller to republish this text under Barrington's name, but after taking over the publication from J. Lee about 1803[178], Tegg was particularly assiduous in marketing the revived *Frauds* under the brand of the celebrity convict, reprinting the work, as *Barrington's New London Spy*, on numerous occasions over a ten-year period.[179]

While each successive edition of *Barrington's New London Spy* was said to be 'Considerably Enlarged', the changes Tegg actually made in his different editions of the work were somewhat more subtle. The earliest known Tegg version (the 'Third Edition') was a reprint of the Lee *Frauds of London Detected*, adding only a brief 'Treatise on Boxing' attributed to the famous English prizefighter James 'Jem' Belcher.[180] From the 'Fourth Edition', *Barrington's New London Spy for 1805*[181], the work included 'An Appendix, Containing a Sketch of Night Scenes and notorious Characters, in a Ramble through the Metropolis'. This 'Appendix' was in fact a digest of the text of another dated underworld 'guide-book', *The Modern London Spy*[182], in which a young countryman is guided through a tableau of the 'low' scenes of the metropolis by a local savant[183] – in Tegg's version 'Barrington' is cast as the guide, replacing the 'Mr. Ambler' of the original. After the 'Fourth Edition', the text of *Barrington's New London Spy* remained the same in all further editions, although Tegg did make some effort to repackage the work. The 'Fifth Edition', *Barrington's New London Spy* for 1807, included new illustrations and was issued as a part publication in 'Four weekly Numbers at Six-Pence each'.[184] Subsequent editions do not appear to have been issued in parts, but the work was reprinted at least four more times, reaching a nominal 'Ninth Edition' about 1812.[185] So while Tegg's *Barrington's New London Spy* remained a barely reworked combination of texts from the late 1770s, it apparently sold well enough.

Above and opposite: The frontispiece and pictorial title page from Thomas Tegg's *Barrington's New London Spy for 1807*. Courtesy of Mitchell Library, State Library of New South Wales.

BARRINGTON'S

NEW

London Spy

or

THE FRAUDS OF LONDON DETECTED,

1807.

LONDON.

Printed for Thomas Tegg,
N.º III Cheapside.

67343

A further indication of the success of Tegg's revivification of these texts under the Barrington brand can be seen in the interest shown by smaller publishers. Chapbook redactions of 'Barrington's' *London Spy* were produced by Thomas Johnston in Falkirk in 1809[186], and 'at the Office of R. Parker' in Blackburn in 1812[187], and in 1832, some twenty years after the last known Tegg edition, an American reprint entitled *The London Spy; or, the Frauds of London Detected ... by G. Barrington*, was published in Boston.[188]

Thomas Tegg was also responsible for another, more curious addition to the corpus of 'Barrington' books. This was a work published in 1803 as *Barrington's Annals of Suicide, or Horrors of Self-Murder*[189], a collection of short gothic tales on the theme of suicide, of which Barrington was the supposed editor. An introductory 'Advertisement' to the work, which like the preface to the *Voyage* was styled as a letter from Barrington to a friend in England, provided an exposition of the fiction of Barrington's involvement in the work, its opening line echoing the beginning of the *Voyage*:

> It is with the greatest satisfaction, that I inform you of my having arranged and completed the materials which I have been so long collecting; you will recollect, that I was compelled to leave my native country before I could receive some valuable and interesting memoirs from Spain and Italy; part of them have been transmitted to me by a faithful friend ...[190]

The *Annals of Suicide* also included a significant new addition to the 'Barrington' literature in the form of an original New South Wales themed tale, entitled 'Dreadful History of Anaboo, a Native of New Holland, Who Killed Herself Through Love'.[191] The piece, of which 'Barrington' is the narrator, purports to tell the story of Anaboo, the daughter of an Aboriginal 'inferior chief', who falls in love with an English convict. When the convict spurns her advances, the lovelorn heroine is driven by her unrequited passion to commit suicide by throwing herself from the cliffs near

Botany Bay. Though an original work in the sense that it was not plagiarised from another source, there was of course little in the way of literary complexity or originality in this tale of misguided and tragic love. But the novelty of the New South Wales setting, and the Anglo–Aboriginal love theme, was enough for the story to be positioned as a selling point for the *Annals of Suicide*. The story is the opening tale in the collection, and is also prominently referred to in 'Barrington's' epistolary introduction:

> Yes, my dear friend, the Demon of *Suicide* has spread its baneful contagion as far as the inhospitable shores of New Holland: the unhappy native, who put an end to her existence, was so interesting, and the circumstances attending her deplorable exit so lamentable, that I am induced to begin this collection with it.[192]

A gruesome illustration of the heroine's death, engraved by Isaac Cruikshank[193], provides the frontispiece to the *Annals of Suicide*.

As formulaic as the 'Dreadful History of Anaboo' is, its author had clearly done some research into the early material on New South Wales. The name of the heroine, for example, seems to have been adapted from the name of the girl called 'Abaroo' by Watkin Tench (or 'Araboo' in the 'Barrington' *Voyage*), while the name of her father ('Parronnan') was presumably developed from 'Paramatta'. To make the 'charming' heroine a figure of interest to European readers, she is said to be attractive ('well proportioned') and to have 'kept herself very clean … her skin had not acquired that horrid colour that distinguishes the New Hollanders from almost all the inhabitants of the islands in the Great South Sea'.[194] This latter detail was certainly derived from the accounts of colonial officers like John Hunter (perhaps via the 'Barrington' *Voyage*), who, lacking an appreciation of local customs, described the Eora as:

> abominably filthy; they never clean their skin, but it is generally smeared with the fat of such animals as they kill, and afterwards

SUICIDE OF ANABOO.

Pub.ª by Tegg & Cº 29 Warwick Lane, June 29 1803.

Frontispiece illustration used in 'Barrington's' *Annals of Suicide*. Courtesy of Mitchell Library, State Library of New South Wales.

covered with every sort of dirt; sand from the sea beach, and the
ashes from their fires, all adhere to their greasy skin, which is never
washed, except when accident, or the want of food, obliges them to
go into the water.[195]

But while some effort towards verisimilitude had been made in
setting the scene and delineating the characters, there are certainly elements of the story that show it was not written by anyone
with a substantial knowledge of the colony. Once again, the role
and responsibilities – and the relative freedom and authority – of
Barrington the 'head-constable' are exaggerated for the sake of
furthering the plot. Barrington comes and goes as he pleases,
wandering between the settlements at '*Sidney-cove*' and '*Paramatta*'
at will, and without much consideration for the distance and difficulties of making this journey.[196] Even more telling is the narrative's creation of a settlement at '*Cape Banks*' (which the narrator
also walks to from Parramatta).[197] The author of the 'Dreadful
History of Anaboo' had presumably chosen the location from
early maps based on Cook's voyages, where Cape Banks and Cape
Solander, at the northern and southern entrances to Botany Bay
respectively, were given relative prominence as two of the few
named places in the Sydney area.[198]

Like the 'Yeariana' episode in the final chapter of the *Voyage to
New South Wales*, the 'Dreadful History of Anaboo' functioned as
a means for the imaginative exploration of cross-cultural erotic
encounters in the novel setting of the New South Wales penal
colony. As we have seen, the sexual mores of the South Pacific
were a subject of particular interest for European readers, and it
seems fitting that one of the earliest fictional works set in the
colony should concern itself with this subject. 'Barrington' the
narrator is the primary conduit for the expression of sexual
curiosity about Aboriginal women, or at least about the 'princess'
Anaboo. When Barrington first encounters Anaboo, he finds her
fluent in English, and 'extremely desirous of rendering [the

English] every service in her power' with regard to the provision of food and other necessities.[199] A further discovery of Anaboo's history of helping the colonists leads to a greater appreciation on the narrator's part of 'that amiable girl', and Barrington arranges further meetings with the 'chief', Paronnan, because 'the charming *Anaboo* interested me very much'. Barrington becomes 'distressed' when he learns that Anaboo is to be married to a 'tall and powerful' young warrior, but when, shortly thereafter, he is attacked by a 'native dog', he is saved by a 'javelin' thrown by Anaboo herself, whom he subsequently finds 'in playful wantonness concealing herself behind a tree'.[200] Anaboo then thrills Barrington (and presumably the tale's readers) by revealing that she has 'no affection' for her Aboriginal fiancé, and that her erotic and filial associations were divided:

> "Except my father and my brothers ... I do not love my countrymen; they are too cruel: be on your guard, for they will murder you. I shall always be the friend of the English, I like white men."[201]

Unfortunately for Anaboo, this predilection for 'white men' leads to her gory demise, and through her death the story would seem to introduce the possibility of cross-cultural erotic encounters only to make a pronouncement as to their unacceptability. It is not Barrington who Anaboo falls in love with, however, but a fictional 'Man of Feeling': one 'F——k W——n', a convict who bears his chains with 'a dignified calmness'; 'a remarkable handsome man: melancholy was impressed on his countenance, yet he appeared perfectly resigned'.[202] The melancholic countenance which so impresses Anaboo is occasioned by W——n's separation from his wife, Anna; a story which W——n narrates to Barrington as a tangent to the main narrative. Anna is clearly an English parallel to Anaboo. She is the daughter of a 'rich tradesman' in London, 'fair, virtuous and lovely', who W——n marries; he later succumbs to gambling and bad company, which results in his transportation.[203] When Anaboo confesses her love for W——n, he rejects her out of his love for his wife: 'Poor Anna! thy guilty husband will not add to his crimes by being unfaithful to thee, thou best of wives!'.[204] This rejection leads to Anaboo's horrific and drawn-out suicide, where she first stabs herself with her 'javelin', then runs to the top of a nearby 'precipice' and jumps from it, finishing as 'the mangled *Anaboo* ... a shapeless bleeding object'.[205] The moral to be drawn here is made explicit in the final paragraph, where 'Barrington' the narrator states 'she might have lived contented and happy, if her adverse fate had not inspired her with a desire of exalting herself above her humble companions, by aspiring to the love of a European'.[206] The ludicrous idea that this appalling tale was the legitimate production of George Barrington's colonial experience was endorsed in a piece on the story published in *The Native Companion* in 1907, which not only regarded Barrington as the author of the tale, but agreed with 'his' conclusion as to the inevitable consequences of cross-cultural 'sinful love'.[207]

The actual author of the 'Dreadful History of Anaboo' and other tales in the *Annals of Suicide* was possibly Thomas Tegg himself. Tegg had a known predilection for literary activities, and the work dates from the period in which he was in partnership with one Castleman, of which Tegg later wrote that he 'wrote all night and worked all day' in an ultimately futile attempt to make the firm prosper.[208] It is certain that the firm of Tegg and Castleman was in financial trouble by the time *Barrington's Annals of Suicide* was published at the end of June 1803.[209] While the title page of the work gave the address of Tegg and Castleman's 'Eccentric Book Warehouse' at 122 St. John's Street, Clerkenwell, advertisements at the time of publication gave Tegg and Castleman's address as 23 Warwick Square – which was the address of the printer of the *Annals of Suicide*, John Harricott Hart.[210] At some point in 1803, a new title page for the work was printed, altering the title to *Biographical Annals of Suicide*, and using Hart's address for the firm of Tegg and Castleman.[211] As with Maurice Jones' 'Barrington' works, the *Annals of Suicide* was originally distributed as a part-issued publication, but unlike Jones' works it seems not to have met with any great interest. No further issues of the work in parts are known after its initial issue in six fortnightly numbers, priced at one shilling each, from June to August 1803[212], and Tegg attempted to recoup his investment in the work by remarketing sections of the *Annals of Suicide* as gothic chapbooks.[213] The *Annals of Suicide* was also included, in its entirety, in Tegg and Castleman's periodical, *The Marvellous Magazine or Compendium of Prodigies*.[214] It is possible that Tegg and Castleman remaindered the publication after the dissolution of the firm; the Edinburgh firm of Denham and Dick was advertising the *Annals of Suicide* in 1806.[215]

In the decade following the first publication of *A Voyage to New South Wales*, then, the 'Barrington' allonym had outgrown its original purpose and was applied to a range of different texts. From 1806, the publishing history of the *Voyage* itself took a new and somewhat unlikely turn, with the inclusion of the work in a French collection of travel narratives adapted for young readers, entitled *Bibliothèque Géographique et Instructive des Jeunes Gens, ou Recueil de Voyages Intéressants dans touts les Parties du Monde, pour L'Instruction et L'Amusement de la Jeunesse*.[216] Published by J. E. Gabriel Dufour in Paris and Amsterdam from 1804 to 1807, and divided into six nominal 'years' containing twelve volumes each, the *Bibliothèque Géographique* was originally attributed to Johann Heinrich Campe, the German pedagogue and children's author best known for his popular adaptation of Daniel Defoe's *Robinson Crusoe* for young readers.[217] However, while the *Bibliothèque Géographique* was clearly modelled on Campe's collections of travel narratives for young readers – *Sammlung Interessanter und Durchgängig Zweckmäßig Abgefaßter Reisebeschreibungen für die Jugend* (1785–1793) and its continuation, *Neue Sammlung Merkwürdiger Reisebeschreibungen für die Jugend* (1801–1806) – the translator of the French edition, Jean-Baptiste-Joseph Breton[218], and possibly other writers working for the publisher, expanded the *Bibliothèque Géographique* beyond translations from Campe's works. The *Bibliothèque Géographique* extended to some seventy-two volumes, while Campe's two collections of travel narratives contained only nineteen books between them[219], and among the works newly added to the French collection was a version of the 'Barrington' *Voyage*. As the *Voyage et Transportation du Fameux Barrington*, this work took its place as the eighth book in the 'Seconde Année' of the *Bibliothèque Géographique* (published in 1806)[220], alongside versions of canonical voyage narratives such as the Pacific voyages of Cook, the Persian travels of Jean Chardin, and the African travelogues of Mungo Park and John Barrow.

The *Voyage et Transportation du Fameux Barrington* was almost certainly adapted from the 1797–1798 French translation, *Voyage a Botany Bay*, rather than being a new translation of an English version of the *Voyage*. It includes the concluding paragraph first introduced in the *Voyage a Botany Bay*, where 'Barrington' expresses his sentiments on his exile from England. Other sections of the *Voyage et Transportation* are also clearly indebted to the earlier translation, for example, the relation of 'Barrington's' first encounter with the fictional 'natives' Yeariana and Palerino:

> [...] a most interesting scene presented itself to my view: a young creature seated on a jut of the rock, mournfully contemplating the extended body of a man, whose expiring groan had just pierced our ears; all her faculties were so absorbed with grief that we were yet unnoticed: a sympathizing sorrow pervaded all my frame; I gave my gun to Tim, and made signs for him to retire, lest the sight should alarm her [...]
>
> *Voyage*, p. 133

> [...] mais dieu! quel touchant spectacle s'offrit à ma vue! une jeunne sauvage, assise sur un morceau de rocher, les yeux mouillés de larmes

et douloureusement fixes sur le corps étendu d'un jeune homme
dont peut-être je venais d'entendre le dernier soupir. Toutes les
facultés de cette femme étaient si entièrement absorbées par sa
douleur, qu'elle ne m'apperçut pas entrer. A cette vue une sym-
pathique compassion s'empara de mon ame; je donnai mon fusil à
Tim, et de peur que la vue de cette arme n'effrayât cette jeune native,
je lui fis signe de sortir.

Voyage a Botany Bay, pp. 179–80

Dieu! quel touchant spectacle s'offrit à ma vue! Une jeune sauvage,
étoit assise sur un quartier de rocher, les mouillés de pleurs, et
douloureusement fixes sur le corps étendu d'un jeune homme, dont
peut-être je venais d'entendre le dernier soupir.

La a douleur avoit anéanti les facultés de cette femme, au point
qu'elle ne vit pas entrer. Touché de compassion, je donnai mon fusil
à Tim, et, de peur que la vue de cette arme redoutée n'effrayât la
jeune sauvage, je fis signe à mon domestique de sortir.

Voyage et Transportation, pp. 171–72

Yet it does seem likely that those behind the *Voyage et
Transportation du Fameux Barrington* had seen at least one of the
editions of the *Voyage* produced by H. D. Symonds. The frontispiece plate used in the *Voyage et Transportation* is a representation of the scene quoted above, and was probably inspired
by the frontispiece illustration of the same event which had
appeared in the 'Fourth Edition' of the Symonds *Voyage* and in
his subsequent *Voyage to Botany Bay* editions.[221] The *Voyage et
Transportation* illustration, entitled 'Barrington sauve la vie à un
jeune sauvage', is decidedly more elegant than the Symonds
plate, however.[222]

The *Voyage et Transportation du Fameux Barrington* is a significantly different text from the *Voyage a Botany Bay*, however, with
the rewriting of the work for young readers changing much of the
style of the earlier translation. There is also new material. The

Barrington sauve la vie à un jeune sauvage

Frontispiece illustration from the *Voyage et Transportation du Fameux Barrington.*
Author's collection.

text is arranged in eight chapters, with the first not drawn from
the *Voyage* but instead consisting of a general description and
brief history of European exploration in 'Nouvelle-Holland',
along with some notes on Barrington and his career as 'King of
the Pickpockets (roi des filoux)'.[223] The footnotes given through
the text are different from the *Voyage a Botany Bay* notes, and
often refer readers to other volumes in the *Bibliothèque
Géographique* series. Significantly, there is also a new conclusion to
the text, which claims that Barrington eventually married
Yeariana, and that further marriages between Europeans and
Aborigines ('les naturels') like this one probably would have
eliminated any animosity between the peoples ('aurorient
vraisemblablement achevé d'anéantir toute defiance réciproque')
had not Barrington died prematurely.[224] This conclusion goes on
to note that the population of 'Botany Bay' included a number of

Irish prisoners transported for their political views, and suggests that the 'compagnie' at Botany Bay was not as bad as might have been expected from a place intended as a receptacle for felons ('qu'il n'eût été permis de s'y attendre dans un lieu destiné à servir d'exilet de châtiment aux criminels').[225]

The French arrangement of the *Voyage* for young readers was a version of the text that enjoyed considerable longevity and exposure. Dufour republished the *Bibliothèque Géographique* on two further occasions, in 1816 and in 1827–1828, with the *Voyage et Transportation du Fameux Barrington* continuing as the eighth book in the 'Seconde Année' in each of these editions.[226] That the *Bibliothèque Géographique* was republished does not necessarily mean that the series was a wild success, however. The 1827 version of the collection was published as a subscription series sent by mail, and the *Voyage et Transportation* volume was in fact a reissue of the printed sheets of the 1806 edition.[227] Despite his repeated reissues, Dufour apparently had not sold all the material from his 1806 printing, and after 1828 he seems to have offloaded at least some of the remaining stock of the *Bibliothèque Géographique*. In 1834, a Lyon bookseller, J. F. Rolland, published the *Voyage et Transportation du Fameux Barrington* along with other volumes from the *Bibliothèque Géographique* collection. When referring to the *Bibliothèque Géographique* in a bibliographic catalogue he compiled, Rolland wrote that, although the works had been arranged by a man knowledgeable in educational theory, he (Rolland) considered that they still contained material unsuitable for young readers, and declared that he had removed this offensive material 'avec le plus grand soin' from the volumes he sold.[228] Evidently there was nothing Rolland found disturbing in the Barrington narrative, however, since his publication was simply another reissue of the sheets of the 1806 Dufour printing, behind a cancel title page.

But if the *Bibliothèque Géographique* did not sell as well as its original publisher would have wanted, the collection enjoyed enough of a profile to inspire translations in other European languages. A Swedish collection, under the title *Geografiskt Bibliotek för Ungdom*[229], was published in sixteen volumes over the period 1804–1816. Like the *Bibliothèque Géographique*, the *Geografiskt Bibliotek* was attributed to Campe, but the Swedish translator, David Krutmejer[230], had clearly based at least some of his translations on the French collection rather than Campe's German books. Among the narratives in the *Geografiskt Bibliotek* which had not featured in Campe's collections was the 'Barrington' *Voyage*, the sixteenth and last volume in the Swedish collection, translated from the French as *Barrington's Resa och Deportation till Botany-Bay, i Nya Holland.*[231] About the early 1830s, a Madrid-based translator, Santiago de Alvarado y de la Peña, produced a Spanish translation of the *Voyage et Transportation* – as *Viaje y Translaccion del Famoso Barrington a Botani-Bai, en la Nueva Hollanda* – again along with other works from the *Bibliothèque Géographique.*[232] The Swedish and Spanish editions closely follow both the text and the format of the *Voyage et Transportation*, replicating the division of the work into eight chapters – with the first consisting of a general introduction to 'New Holland', and the last giving the description of Barrington's supposed marriage to Yeariana – and each was issued with frontispiece illustrations that closely imitate the frontispiece in the French editions.[233]

The 1834 Lyon edition of the *Voyage et Transportation du Fameux Barrington*, along with the 1832 Boston edition of the *London Spy* and the Spanish *Viaje y Translaccion* published at a similar time, are the last known books published under Barrington's name. The real George Barrington had been dead for thirty years by this point, and further publications would probably have seemed ridiculous, even by the generous standards of the 'Barrington' fraud. The 'deceptious mask' of the ex-convict colonial historian, then, finally outlived its currency some forty years after being concocted in Newgate around 1795. In this time, the putative 'Barrington' had undertaken a remarkably varied international journey of his own.

EPILOGUE

*T*he passing of the Georgian era marked the end of the publication of 'Barrington' biographies and allonymous books. The celebrated Barrington was certainly not forgotten by the Victorians, but they preferred to re-envision his story on their own terms; the 'Prince of Pickpockets' metamorphosed into a kind of nostalgic rogue hero, perfect for popular crime fiction and for the mid-Victorian vogue of historical romances. Charles Dickens thought Barrington's story might provide good fundamentals for a serial novel in his literary journal, *All the Year Round*, since it involved

> the representation of a period, a style of manners, an order of dress, certain habits of street life, assembly-room life, and coffee-room life, etc ... there is a very broad distinction between this and mere Newgate calendar.[1]

Dickens neither wrote nor commissioned a Barrington novel, however, and the field was left to less well-remembered writers whose work was closer to the 'Newgate calendar' style he derided. In 1852, the Soho bookseller George Purkess, a specialist in the sensationalist crime fiction known as 'penny dreadfuls', published Thomas Frost's *George Barrington the Gentleman Pickpocket*[2], and a decade later J. Malcolm Rymer's novel, *George Barrington;*

or, Life in London A Hundred Years Ago, appeared in G. W. M. Reynolds' hugely popular monthly, *Reynolds' Miscellany*.[3] Dramatisations of Barrington's life also continued to crop up on the Victorian popular stage. *Barrington the Pickpocket!* was revived and updated by the company of the actor–manager David Webster Osbaldiston in the late 1840s[4], and in the 1860s at least three dramatic works centred on Barrington (all based to some degree on Rymer's serial novel) featured at different minor theatres in London.[5] Popular novels and tales based on Barrington continued to find audiences into the twentieth century, with Tasmanian author Roy Bridges' *Mr. Barrington* appearing in the New South Wales Bookstall Company's series of paperbacks in 1911, and British writer Ernest Dudley's novel, *Picaroon*, being published in 1952.[6]

While the legend of George Barrington continued to find new literary incarnations, by the end of the nineteenth century the original 'Barrington' books began to attract interest from book collectors and scholars of Australiana. Prominent collectors of early Australasian literature such as David Scott Mitchell, Alexander Turnbull, Sir William Dixson, Sir John Ferguson and Sir Rex Nan Kivell assembled significant collections of 'Barringtonia', which were subsequently bequeathed, as part of their larger collections, to the major public libraries of Australia and New Zealand. To a great extent, however, these works have been neglected by recent scholars, and have remained a bibliographic curiosity of apparently little historiographic importance. While at first glance it seems only right that the texts attributed to Barrington should be dismissed by historians as unoriginal and/or inauthentic source material, this would overlook the significance these texts had for reading audiences around the turn of the nineteenth century. In terms of the number of editions and textual states, the *Voyage to New South Wales* was easily the most widely distributed account of the colony published in Europe during its early years, and several further narratives also ran to multiple editions. That Barrington's name was used fraudulently, that the works of other writers were plagiarised, and that the second-hand textual material was spiced up with fictional embellishments, does not diminish the fact that these works helped to shape European views of Australia during the crucial early years of colonisation.

Previous studies in which an interest in the 'Barrington' books has been shown have often been hampered by a reliance on generalisations and guesswork, with a particularly enduring misconception being that the works were all 'chapbooks'.[7] While it is true that the texts were widely distributed in chapbook form, this was not the original or the most prevalent guise in which the narratives appeared. The original 'Barrington' books and pamphlets may have had similar physical characteristics to chapbooks, but there were important distinctions in the way these works were produced and distributed. Published by London booksellers who employed hack writers to compile their texts, and aimed at the burgeoning market for cheap, topical literature among the middle and lower classes, these works were generally noticed, however cursorily, in the reviewing periodicals, and advertised, sometimes heavily, in the newspaper press. The main mode of their distribution was likely to have been wholesale through the book trade, or as part-issued publications sold by subscription, and they were produced in comparatively large print runs. The distribution channels of chapbooks, on the other hand, were far more limited and localised, relying on the traditional face-to-face commerce of travelling hawkers, and the chapbook 'Barrington' works were almost certainly produced in small print runs for retail sale in a confined geographic area by a specific seller or group of sellers. These chapbooks, too, were always secondary versions of the text, which generally abridged the originals without any rewriting to speak of; in fact, it seems very likely that the only editorial input in their production was that provided by their printers. To gloss the whole 'Barrington' corpus as consisting entirely of 'chapbooks' lumps the original works – which though plagiaristic and unreliable were still carefully constructed, *authored* narratives – together with the works that were simply reprints of these texts in a slightly abridged form.

Chapbook abridgements, moreover, were certainly not the only kind of republications spawned by the popularity of the original 'Barrington' productions emanating from London. In Ireland and America, enterprising publishers produced unabridged reprints of the allonymous Barrington books, and in continental Europe, 'Barrington's' best known work was translated into quasi-scholarly editions, and alongside canonical travel literature as educational material for young readers.

The bibliography that accompanies this book shows the extent of the publishing phenomenon that took place around Barrington, illustrating its scope, longevity, and the number of different purposes this famous name was made to serve. An important finding of this book, however, is that the 'Barrington' books, though numerous, were drawn from an extremely limited pool of textual material. Contrary to the usual process of different writers and publishers assembling narratives for publication, in the 'Barrington' case a small number of texts were appropriated by various publishers and reprinted again and again. While a few new 'Barrington' texts appeared after the turn of the nineteenth century, it was much more common for minor printers and publishers to simply republish established successful works, thereby cashing in on the popularity of the 'Barrington' brand without the expense and inconvenience of employing writers.

The history of the Barrington books has generally been seen as an illustration of the questionable ethics of popular publishing in the late Georgian period, and certainly this remains a relevant approach to the works. The original biographies of Barrington, which themselves capitalised on a considerable body of press mythology about the 'Prince of Pickpockets', fleshed out the Barrington story with novelistic invention and apocryphal anecdotes, while the books published under Barrington's name were even more 'deceptious' in their spurious attribution and counterfeit origins. A closer examination of the publishing history of the books, however, reveals the extent to which the 'Barrington' publishing phenomenon was rooted in the changing political and commercial landscape of the book trade in the late eighteenth and early nineteenth centuries. With their biographies of Barrington, publishers like George Kearsley and H. D. Symonds were competing fiercely for the patronage of an expanding popular reading audience. Later, Symonds would find an innovative – if ethically questionable – way to translate the authoritative information of a cumbersome official voyage narrative for the same market. The publishers responsible for concocting the original 'Barrington' texts would then find themselves the victims of the very popularity of these works, as their counterfeit originals were themselves pirated by other printers and publishers. The success of fraud, moreover, would take the 'Barrington' brand into unexpected territory: the spurious author would eventually achieve a unique international literary fame, based in the dubious publishing practices of a host of booksellers and printers from across the Western world.

The publishing history of the Barrington books is best seen not as an homogeneous fraud or act of forgery, but rather as a series of events – a series of acts of fabrication, intellectual transgression and commercial opportunism – intimately connected with the changing nature of print culture in the late Georgian era. Through these books, the figure of 'the celebrated Barrington', renowned master thief and putative authority on colonial affairs, would come to exist quite independently of the man who died in New South Wales in 1804. The story of these books remains a curious tale of how the culture of celebrity, and the dynamics of popular publishing, created a myth sold throughout the world; a 'deceptious mask', which, fraudulent though it was, nonetheless helped shape the way a little known corner of the world was first apprehended by generations of ordinary readers.

REFERENCES

INTRODUCTION

1   Newspaper report annotated '1807', '[Press cuttings, including portraits, maps, music]', Dixson F8/83, Mitchell Library.

2   Edgar Allan Poe, 'Letter to Mr. ——', in *Poems* (New York: Elam Bliss, 1831), p. 26.

3   See Sheila Box, *The Real George Barrington?: The Adventures of a Notorious London Pickpocket, later Head Constable of the Infant Colony of New South Wales* (Melbourne: Australian Scholarly Publishing, 2001), esp. pp. 11–25.

4   For some recent studies on the heroic outlaw tradition in English and Anglophone popular culture, see Graham Seal, *The Outlaw Legend: A Cultural Tradition in Britain, America and Australia* (Cambridge: Cambridge University Press, 1996); and Gillian Spraggs, *Outlaws and Highwaymen: The Cult of the Robber in England from the Middle Ages to the Nineteenth Century* (London: Pimlico, 2001).

5   For detailed discussions on the subject of literary forgeries and fraud in the eighteenth century, see Ian Haywood, 'The Eighteenth Century: A Prolific Age of Literary Forgery', in *Faking It: Art and the Politics of Forgery* (Brighton: Harvester, 1987), pp. 21–70; Haywood, *The Making of History: A Study of the Literary Forgeries of James Macpherson and Thomas Chatterton in Relation to Eighteenth-Century Ideas of History and Fiction* (Rutherford: Fairleigh Dickinson UP, 1986); and Nick Groom, *The Forger's Shadow: How Forgery Changed the Course of Literature* (London: Picador, 2002).

6   D. D. Mann, *The Present Picture of New South Wales* [London: John Booth, 1811], facs. edn (Sydney: Library of Australian History, 1979), p. 31.

7   That is, William Pitt the Younger (1759–1806). As Alan Atkinson has pointed out, few observers at the time of the scheme's conception in 1786 regarded transportation to the colony as an ongoing endeavour, and the plan attracted criticism and ridicule as an expensive and ineffective solution to the perceived crime problem. See Atkinson, *The Europeans in Australia: A History*, vol. 1 (Melbourne: Oxford University Press, 1997), pp. 52–55; also Ged Martin, ed., *The Founding of Australia* (Sydney: Hale and Iremonger, 1981).

8   Like the majority of voyages of discovery embarked on from Britain in the eighteenth century, the Botany Bay expedition was undertaken under the direction of the Admiralty office. The propertied classes that made up the enfranchised section of the nation took a close interest in the costs and benefits of such publicly funded endeavours, and the publication of semi-official narratives relating the course of the voyage and discoveries made therein became an expected part of their outcomes. See John Edwards, *The Story of the Voyage: Sea-Narratives in Eighteenth-Century England* (Cambridge: Cambridge University Press, 1994); also Nathan Garvey, 'Selling a Penal Colony: The Booksellers and Botany Bay', *Script and Print*, vol. 31, no. 1, 2007, pp. 20–38.

9   See William St Clair, *The Reading Nation in the Romantic Period* (Cambridge: Cambridge University Press, 2004), esp. pp. 19–42; see also Jon P. Klancher, *The Making of English Reading Audiences, 1790–1832* (Madison: University of Wisconsin Press, 1987), pp. 18–38; and James Raven, *The Business of Books: Booksellers and the English Book Trade 1450–1850* (New Haven: Yale University Press, 2007), pp. 241–55.

10   *Gentleman's Magazine*, vol. 66, 1795, p. 760.

11   John West, *The History of Tasmania*, vol. 2 (Launceston: Henry Dowling, 1852), p. 145.

12   See E. A. Petherick, 'Bibliography of Australia', *The Torch: and Colonial Book Circular*, vol. 1, no. 3, March 1888, pp. 94, 96–98; 'George Barrington: Waldron', *The Athenaeum*, 12 February 1898, pp. 22–23; also *Notes and Queries*, 9th ser., 2, November 1898, p. 404.

13   J. A. Ferguson's 'A Bibliography of Literature Ascribed to, or relating to, George Barrington' was first published in the *Royal Australian Historical Society Journal and Proceedings*, vol. 16, 1930, pp. 51–80. The content of this bibliography was later updated and used in Ferguson's monumental *Bibliography of Australia*, 7 vols (Sydney: Angus and Robertson, 1941), see esp. vol. 1, pp. 13–17.

14   Jonathan Wantrup, *Australian Rare Books 1788–1900* (Sydney: Hordern House, 1987), p. 87.

15   Suzanne Rickard, ed., *George Barrington's Voyage to Botany Bay: Retelling a Convict's Travel Narrative of the 1790s* (London: Leicester University Press, 2001), p. 5, and *passim*. Rickard has also published a number of articles on Barrington including 'George Barrington: Enigmatic Prince of Pickpockets', *National Library of Australia News*, vol. 2, no. 7, April 1992, pp. 7–10; 'Barrington, George (1755–1804)', in Iain McCalman, ed., *Oxford Companion to the Romantic Age: British Culture 1776–1832* (Oxford: Oxford University Press, 1999), p. 417; and 'Whose Voice Was It Anyway: The Eighteenth-Century Colonial Experience of George Barrington', in *Selves Crossing Cultures: Autobiography and Globalisation* (Melbourne: Australian Scholarly Publishing, 2002), pp. 41–52. Rickard is also the author of the biography of Barrington in the *Oxford Dictionary of National Biography* [hereafter *ODNB*] (Oxford: Oxford University Press, 2004), online, last update October 2005, <www.oxforddnb.com>, accessed 1 December 2007.

16   A notable example was Marcus Clarke's piece for the *Argus*, subsequently published as 'George Barrington, Pickpocket and Historian' in his *Old Tales from a Young Country* (Melbourne: Trustees of the Public Library, 1871), pp. 8–18. For a partial list of the numerous articles published in the later nineteenth and early twentieth centuries, see Ferguson, *Bibliography of Australia*, vol. 1, pp. 15–17. The romanticised accounts of Barrington's life can be traced back to the original biographies of Barrington published from 1790, discussed in Chapter 2 of this work.

17   R. S. Lambert, *The Prince of Pickpockets: A Study of George Barrington Who Left His Country for His Country's Good* (London: Faber & Faber, 1930).

18   Ferguson, *Bibliography of Australia*, vol. 1, p. 14.

19   A recent essay in *Australian Literary Studies* ventures the erroneous assumption that 'it is virtually impossible to determine conclusively what parts of *A Voyage [to New South Wales]* Barrington wrote and what was added by other writers', and a recent publication in the well-worn tradition of excerpt-based histories of early Australian colonisation includes one 'Barrington' book as an 'eyewitness account'. See Toby R. Benis, 'Criminal Transport: George Barrington and the Colonial Cure', *Australian*

Literary Studies, vol. 20, no. 3, May 2002, p. 167n; Jack Egan, *Buried Alive: Sydney 1788–1792: Eyewitness Accounts of the Making of a Nation* (Sydney: Allen & Unwin, 1999), p. 333.

20   A satirical poem apparently written by one Henry Carter, a 'Gentleman of Leicester', the 'Prologue' took as its inspiration the news that a theatre had been established by convicts in Sydney; the verses were framed as a prologue to the opening performance there. As Robert Jordan's excellent recent article on the publishing history of this piece shows, the original incarnation of the 'Prologue' makes no mention of Barrington at all, though later versions were quick to add the claim that the text was 'spoken [at the theatre] by the celebrated Mr. Barrington'. The satire was subsequently incorporated in one of the spurious 'Barrington' books, *The History of New South Wales*, where the performance of the 'Prologue' at the opening of the theatre was given as an actual historical event, and, though Barrington is not explicitly represented as the speaker or author in the *History of New South Wales* version, it was likely to have been this publication in 'his' book that gave rise to the myth that this satire was Barrington's own work. As the 'Barrington Prologue', the work – or at least the couplets quoted – enjoyed considerable celebrity through the nineteenth and early twentieth centuries. In 1887 the *Quarterly Review* had the 'Prologue' in mind when it wrote of Barrington as the author of 'some of the oftenest quoted lines in the English language'. See Robert Jordan, 'The Barrington Prologue', *Script and Print*, vol. 31, no. 1, 2007, pp. 39–57; Jordan, *The Convict Theatres of Early Australia 1788–1840* (Sydney: Currency House, 2002), pp. 108–110; Arthur Jose, 'The "Barrington" Prologue', *Journal of the Royal Australian Historical Society*, vol. 13, no. 5, 1927, pp. 292–94; *Quarterly Review*, vol. 167, 1887, p. 363.

CHAPTER 1

1   For John Barrington (1715–1773) and his family, see Phillip H. Highfill et al., *A Biographical Dictionary of Actors, Actresses, Musicians, Dancers, Managers and Other Stage Personnel in London, 1660–1800*, vol. 1 (Carbondale: Southern Illinois University Press, c. 1973), pp. 309–312.

2   For Jonah Barrington, see W. N. Osborough, 'Barrington, Sir Jonah (1756/7–1834)', *Oxford Dictionary of National Biography* [hereafter *ODNB*] (Oxford: Oxford University Press, 2004), online, <www.oxforddnb.com>, accessed 1 December 2007.

3   The Barrington baronets during this period were Sir Fitzwilliam (1708–1792) and Sir John (1752–1818), the eighth and ninth of the line respectively. Interestingly, this Barrington family was related by marriage to the Fitzwilliam family of which another early colonist of dubious reputation, D'Arcy Wentworth, was a distant member. See George Edward Cokayne, ed., *The Complete Baronetage*, vol. 1 (Gloucester: Alan Sutton Publishing, 1983), pp. 29–30.

4   See Arthur H. Grant [rev. Phillip Carter], 'Barrington, John Shute, first Viscount Barrington (1678–1734)', *ODNB*, online, <www.oxforddnb.com>, accessed 1 December 2007.

5   Respectively, these were William Wildman (second Viscount Barrington) (1717–1793), Shute Barrington (1734–1836), Samuel Barrington (1729–1800) and Daines Barrington (1727/8–1800). A fifth brother, John Barrington (1719–1764), was a Major

General in the Army, but died in poverty in the same year as his wife, leaving three orphaned sons. John Barrington's three sons were brought up by the childless William Wildman, and each of them succeeded to the title in turn. See the *ODNB* entries by Dylan E. Jones (William Wildman), E. A. Varley (Shute Barrington), Alan G. Jamieson (Samuel Barrington), David Phillip Miller (Daines Barrington) and Jonathan Spain (John Barrington). *ODNB*, online, <www.oxforddnb.com>, accessed 1 December 2007.

6   *St James Chronicle*, vol. 1, 3 July 1788, p. 4c.

7   Charles Mackay, *Memoirs of Extraordinary Popular Delusions and the Madness of Crowds*, 2nd edn, vol. 2 (London: Office of the National Illustrated Library, 1852), pp. 123–24.

8   See Christopher Hibbert, *The Roots of Evil: A Social History of Crime and Punishment* (Stroud: Sutton, 2003), pp. 265–70; Gillian Spraggs, *Outlaws and Highwaymen: The Cult of the Robber in England from the Middle Ages to the Nineteenth Century* (London: Pimlico, 2001), *passim*; and Phillip Rawlings, ed., *Drunks, Whores and Idle Apprentices: Criminal Biographies of the Eighteenth Century* (London: Routledge, 1992), pp. 1–2.

9   Hibbert, *The Roots of Evil*, p. 266.

10   Robert Shoemaker, *The London Mob: Violence and Disorder in Eighteenth-Century England* (London: Macmillan, 2004), pp. 170–76.

11   [Jeremiah Whitaker Newman, *attrib*.], *Lounger's Common-place Book*, vol. 1 (London: Printed for the Author, 1792), p. 41.

12   Mackay, *Memoirs of Extraordinary Popular Delusions*, p. 123.

13   Compare the comments of the Abbé Le Blanc relating the reputation of Dick Turpin (qtd in Spraggs, *Outlaws and Highwaymen*, p. 1) with those on Barrington by Johann Willhelm von Archenholz and Jacques-Henri Meister. See von Archenholz, *A Picture of England* [*England und Italien*, 1785], vol. 2 (London: Edward Jeffrey, 1789), p. 85; and Meister, *Letters Written During a Residence in England* (London: Longman and Rees, 1799), p. 28.

14   Daniel Defoe, *History of … John Sheppard*, in Rawlings, ed., *Drunks, Whores and Idle Apprentices*, p. 67.

15   This phrase, which first appeared in *The Times* of 1 April 1788 on p. 3d, was used by R. S. Lambert for the title of his biography of Barrington, itself a work thoroughly indebted to the myth-making of eighteenth-century journalists.

16   Barrington identified himself as a surgeon in at least two of his court appearances, and according to one version of the *Memoirs of George Barrington*, he was apprenticed to an apothecary in Dublin. See the Old Bailey sessions paper, *The Whole Proceedings on the King's Commission of the Peace, Oyer and Terminer, and Gaol Delivery for the City of London; and also the Gaol Delivery for the County of Middlesex, held at Justice Hall in the Old Bailey* [hereafter cited as *The Whole Proceedings* – the *Whole Proceedings* are now available online at <www.oldbaileyonline.org>; references in the text are to the online version; dates refer to trial dates rather than dates of publication], 29 April 1778 and 25 February 1784; see also *Gazetteer and New Daily Advertiser*, 30 October 1775, p. 3a; and *The Memoirs of George Barrington* (London: 'John Bird' and H. D. Symonds, 1790) [hereafter *Memoirs* (Bird and Symonds)], pp. 4–5.

17   Bentham qtd in Wilfrid Oldham, *Britain's Convicts to the Colonies* (Sydney: Library of Australian History, 1990), p. 202. Barrington's identification by a former prisoner on the hulks occurred at a Magistrate's examination in Newcastle in July 1788. See *Public Advertiser*, 8 July 1788, p. 3c.

18 Irvine Loudon, *Medical Care and the General Practitioner 1750–1850* (Oxford: Clarendon, 1986), p. 13; see also pp. 13–22.

19 ibid., p. 14.

20 *Memoirs of George Barrington* (London: 'M. Smith' [i.e. George Kearsley], 1790), p. 91; see also pp. 31, 47, 49. Hereafter this work will be referred to as *Memoirs* (Kearsley).

21 ibid., pp. 7–17.

22 *Morning Post*, 27 October 1775, p. 2d. 'Ducking' – that is, half-drowning – was a traditional punishment for pickpockets, still reported in the late eighteenth century. See, for example, *The Adventurer*, vol. 4 (London: W. Strahan et al., 1777), p. 130; and 'A Letter from a French Gentleman to His Friend at Paris', *The Wit's Magazine; or, Library of Momus*, vol. 2 (London: Harrison and Co., 1784–1785), p. 133.

23 See, for example, *Morning Post*, 30 October 1775, p. 2d; *Middlesex Journal*, 26–28 October 1775, p. 4c-d; and *London Chronicle*, 26–28 October 1775, p. 419c. Grigory Gregoryevich Orlov (1734–1783), also known as Prince Orlow or Orloff, was a former lover of the Russian empress Catherine and was one of the leaders in the coup responsible for enthroning her. See John T. Alexander, *Catherine the Great: Life and Legend* (New York: Oxford University Press, 1989), pp. 5–13, 56–60, 98–100.

24 *Gazetteer*, 30 October 1775, p. 3a. Suzanne Rickard's assertion that the theft occurred 'while the Count was seated in his box at the Covent Garden Theatre' is erroneous, and seems to be based on a later illustration of the event. See Rickard, ed., *George Barrington's Voyage to Botany Bay: Retelling a Convict's Travel Narrative of the 1790s* (London: Leicester University Press, 2001), p. 9.

25 See *London Chronicle*, 28–31 October 1775, p. 423b; *Morning Chronicle*, 30 October 1775, p. 3d; *Middlesex Journal*, 26–28 October 1775, p. 4c-d; *The Craftsman: Or Say's Weekly Journal*, 4 November 1775, p. 1b; *Adam's Weekly Courant*, 5 November 1775, p. 342d.

26 *Gazetteer*, 2 November 1775, p. 3b. This report was reprinted in *Lloyd's Evening Post*, 1–3 November 1775, p. 428b.

27 *London Chronicle*, 31 October – 2 November 1775, p. 430c.

28 For a discussion of the 'man of feeling', see G. J. Barker-Benfield, *The Culture of Sensibility: Sex and Society in Eighteenth-Century Britain* (Chicago: University of Chicago Press, 1992), pp. 247–50; also pp. 37–98; and R. S. Crane, 'Suggestions Towards a Genealogy of the "Man of Feeling"', *English Literary History*, vol. 1, no. 3, 1934, pp. 205–30.

29 *Morning Post*, 2 November 1775, p. 2d.

30 Simon Schama, 'The Cultural Construction of a Citizen', *Citizens: A Chronicle of the French Revolution* (New York: Knopf, 1989), pp. 150–51.

31 *Memoirs* (Bird and Symonds), p. 10.

32 Stanley Morison, *The English Newspaper: Some Account of the Physical Development of Journals Printed in London Between 1622 and the Present Day* (Cambridge: Cambridge University Press, 1932), p. 169. For the career of Henry Bate [later Bate-Dudley], see Hannah Barker, 'Dudley, Sir Henry Bate (1745–1824), newspaper editor', *ODNB*, online, <www.oxforddnb.com>, accessed 1 December 2007.

33 Lucyle Werkmeister, *The London Daily Press, 1772–1792* (Lincoln: University of Nebraska Press, 1963), p. 4; see also pp. 4–8, 19–108.

34   Werkmeister, *London Daily Press*, pp. 4–5 and *passim*. Hannah Barker has recently thrown a note of caution into the debate on the eighteenth-century press, arguing that Werkmeister and others have 'overestimated the importance to a paper's finances of such sources of income as bribes and "puffs"'. This may well be the case, but the demand for scandal, controversy and salacious gossip is clear, and it is also clear that there were constant machinations from interested parties to either reveal or suppress such 'news'. See Barker, *Newspapers Politics, and Public Opinion in Late Eighteenth-Century England* (Oxford: Clarendon, 1998), p. 49.

35   *Morning Post*, 4 December 1776, p. 3c. The *Early English Newspapers* microfilm series, a reproduction of Charles Burney's collection of newspapers (now in the British Library), unfortunately lacks copies of the *Public Ledger* for this period. However, Barrington's subsequent letter to the *Morning Chronicle* notes the offending 'paragraph' in both the *Post* and the *Ledger*. According to Werkmeister, the *Public Ledger* was the first of the old newspapers to be converted to the *Post*'s 'scandal sheet' format (*London Daily Press*, p. 5).

36   For William Jackson, see Hannah Barker, 'Jackson, William (1737?–1795), Journalist and Spy', *ODNB*, online, <www.oxforddnb .com>, accessed 1 December 2007; and Lucyle Werkmeister, 'Notes for a Revised Life of William Jackson, *Notes and Queries*, vol. 8, no. 2, February 1961, pp. 43–47.

37   Shoemaker, *The London Mob*, pp. 241–73.

38   At least three letters were addressed to and printed in the most reputable paper of the day, the *Morning Chronicle*, and another was published in *The Times*. See *Morning Chronicle*, 5 December 1776, p. 1d; 24 November 1788, p. 3a; and 26 November 1788, p. 2d; and *The Times*, 9 August 1788, p. 3d. A further letter on Barrington's plight in 1789, signed 'A Humane Englishman', may also have been written by Barrington himself. See *St. James's Chronicle*, 24–26 November 1789, p. 3c.

39   *Morning Chronicle*, 5 December 1776, p. 1d. According to a subsequent newspaper report, this 'puff' appeared in 'several papers'. See *General Evening Post*, 14–16 January 1777, p. 2d.

40   Werkmeister asserts that at the peak of the *Morning Post*'s success 'there was hardly a "paragraph" in the newspaper that wasn't paid for by someone' (*London Daily Press*, p. 7). The fact that the paragraph exposing Barrington appeared in two different papers on the same day strengthens the possibility that someone was attempting to blackmail him.

41   John Brewer, *Sentimental Murder: Love and Madness in the Eighteenth Century* (London: HarperCollins, 2004), p. 41; see also pp. 37–40.

42   *Morning Chronicle*, 5 December 1776, p. 1d.

43   That is, *Memoirs* (Kearsley); and *Memoirs* (Bird and Symonds). For a full account of the publishing history of the Barrington biographies, see Chapter 2.

44   *Memoirs* (Kearsley), p. 80; *Memoirs* (Bird and Symonds), p. 10. An earlier version of the story, in a brief biography of Barrington dating from 1779, says only that 'a gentleman observed Barrington in the House of Lords, and pointed him out to ... the deputy usher ... who insisted upon his immediately quitting the house'. See *The Malefactor's Register, or New Newgate and Tyburn Calendar*, vol. 5 (London: Alexander Hogg, [1779]), pp. 267–68.

45   Barrington did spend time in Tothill Fields Bridewell in 1776–1777, but only after he was arrested for the Dudman theft. See *Gazetteer and New Daily Advertiser*, 20 December 1776, p. 4c.

46   *Memoirs* (Kearsley), p. 81.

47   The handwritten original of this letter, dated from Tothill Fields Bridewell, 6 January 1777, survives in the collection of the Mitchell Library (Ms. Ab 4912). Barrington attested to his authorship of the letter in court, and the text is replicated in *The Whole Proceedings*, 15 January 1777.

48   This report was published in a variety of papers at the time. See *Gazetteer and New Daily Advertiser*, 17 January 1777, p. 4b; *General Evening Post*, 14–16 January 1777, p. 2d; *London Chronicle*, 16–17 January 1777, p. 3a. It has been quoted by modern historians as a quintessential prose report of Barrington 'in the dock'. See, for example, Richard Lambert, *Prince of Pickpockets: A Study of George Barrington, Who Left His Country For His Country's Good* (London: Faber & Faber, 1930), pp. 69–70; Box, *The Real George Barrington?*, pp. 4, 44; Rickard, ed., *George Barrington's Voyage to Botany Bay*, p. 11.

49   Michèle Cohen notes that 'the anxiety about masculinity [in the eighteenth century] was articulated in the particular way it was because the defining "other" was neither, as is usually assumed, femininity, nor homosexuality, but *effeminacy*'. Cohen, *Fashioning Masculinity: National Identity and Language in the Eighteenth Century* (London: Routledge, 1996), p. 9.

50   By the late 1770s, 'macaroni' was certainly much more of a caricature than an ongoing fashion trend. For a discussion of the phenomenon and the reception of the macaroni generally, see P. K. McNeil, 'Fashion Victims: Class, Gender, Sexuality and the Macaroni, circa 1765–1780', PhD thesis, University of Sydney, 1999; and Amelia Rauser, 'Hair, Authenticity and the Self-Made Macaroni', *Eighteenth Century Studies*, vol. 38, no. 1, 2004, pp. 101–17.

51   *Morning Post*, 4 May 1778, p. 2d.

52   Rauser, 'Hair, Authenticity and the Self-Made Macaroni', pp. 104–05.

53   See McNeil, 'Fashion Victims', p. 5. Both McNeil and Rauser see 'self-fashioning' and the 'self-made man' as central to the figure of the macaroni.

54   Rauser, 'Hair, Authenticity and the Self-Made Macaroni', p. 102.

55   *The Whole Proceedings*, 19 February 1777. For a history of the hulk system, see W. Branch-Johnson, *The English Prison Hulks* (London: Christopher Johnson, 1957), pp. 4–5.

56   For the career of Duncan Campbell (1726–1803), see Dan Byrnes, 'On the Duncan Campbell Letterbooks', *The Blackheath Connection*, online, <www.danbyrnes.com.au/blackheath/letters.htm>, accessed 1 December 2007.

57   Branch-Johnson, *The English Prison Hulks*, p. 4; also pp. 1–25.

58   See John Howard, *Appendix to the State of the Prisons in England ...* (Warrington: J. Eyres, 1780), pp. 112–13.

59   David Brown Dignam (also called Dignum or Dignan) was another genteel convict, who had been convicted of fraud in April 1777. See *The Malefactor's Register*, vol. 5, pp. 235–40.

60   *London Magazine*, vol. 47, May 1777, pp. 225, 227–28, 265. In its efforts to show that these high-profile criminals were getting their just desserts, the *London Magazine* would

seem to preclude the possibility that Barrington, like so many others among the early convicts sent to the hulks, had genuinely become ill from the conditions there.

61   Another remarkably positive article on the infant hulk system, praising it for inspiring a 'revolution in manners' and 'obedience to discipline', was published in another periodical, the *Scots Magazine*, in June 1777. See Box, *The Real George Barrington?*, pp. 56–57.

62   The prison reformers John Howard and Jeremy Bentham, and public-spirited medical men Daniel Solander and James Irwin, were among the visitors to the hulks in 1777 who recorded their opinions on the conditions there. See Howard, *Appendix to the State of the Prisons in England ...*, pp. 112–13; and Oldham, *Britain's Convicts to the Colonies*, pp. 41–43.

63   Oldham, *Britain's Convicts to the Colonies*, p. 45. In 1791, *The Times* called for the abolition of the hulk system altogether, supporting the current ministerial initiative with the declaration that 'Botany Bay is the only place from whose bourne no felon will ever return' (11 October 1791, p. 3a).

64   Bentham, qtd. in Oldham, *Britain's Convicts to the Colonies*, pp. 202–03. The *Censor* had joined the original prison hulk, *Justitia*, in 1777.

65   ibid., p. 202.

66   George Barrington, remission of sentence, 18 February 1778, PRO SP 44/93 ff., pp. 227–28.

67   *Gazetteer and New Daily Advertiser*, 16 March 1778, p. 2d.

68   ibid.

69   *Morning Post*, 16 March 1778, p. 2c.

70   *The Malefactor's Register*, vol. 5, p. 268. One of the earliest 'Newgate calendar' publications, the work was published, '*by Authority*', in five volumes, and probably first issued in weekly numbers through 1778–1779 by Alexander Hogg, one of the early masters of popular publishing. As ever with Hogg, the nature of the '*Authority*' it was supposedly published under is somewhat dubious. See C. H. Timperley, *A Dictionary of Printers and Printing* (London: H. Johnson, 1839), p. 838.

71   *The frauds of London detected; or, a warning-piece against the iniquitous practices of that metropolis* (London: Alexander Hogg, [1778?]); and *The New Cheats of London Exposed, or the frauds and tricks of the town laid open to both sexes ...* (London: Alexander Hogg, [1780?]), both attributed to 'Richard King, Esq.', shared the same text. Needless to say, booksellers like Hogg who reissued old texts with a new title page were not among the detected frauds.

72   James Sambrook sees the *London Spy* as the work which 'established Ward's name and style'. See Sambrook, *ODNB*, online, <www.oxforddnb.com>, accessed 1 December 2007.

73   West, also tried as Mary West and often referred to as 'Miss West', was another favourite subject of newspaper scandal and conjecture in the 1770s. Her biography in *The Malefactor's Register* labelled her 'one of the most notorious and artful pickpockets that modern times have produced', who 'reigned as the principal female pickpocket in London' and had 'long been an atrocious offender'. A newspaper report of 1773 stated that she was already 'an old offender', while the *Public Advertiser* of 19 October 1776 claimed that 'she has escaped twenty times'. West died in early 1783; an obituary in the

Gentleman's Magazine for April 1783 described her as 'the accomplice of Barrington' and claimed 'she has bequeathed to her two children near 3,000*l*'. See *The Malefactor's Register*, vol. 5, p. 291; '[Press cuttings, including portraits, maps, music]', Dixson F8/83, Mitchell Library; and Horace Bleakley, 'Elizabeth West, Thief', *Notes and Queries*, ser. 12, vol. 1, no. 23, 1916, pp. 448–49.

74   *Gazetteer and New Daily Advertiser*, 16 March 1778, p. 2d.

75   *Daily Universal Register*, 1 June 1786, p. 3c.

76   Sir John Fielding, *A Brief Description of London and Westminster* ... (London: Printed for J. Wilkie, 1776), p. 24.

77   *London Magazine*, 47, p. 1777, also p. 227; *The Malefactor's Register*, vol. 5, p. 268.

78   Anon., *The Favourite: A Character from the Life* (London: J. Bew, 1778), p. 24. This work was a verse satire on the death of the former prime minister, William Pitt (the Elder).

79   For more detail on the textual forms and publishing history of the Barrington biographies, see Chapter 2.

80   *Memoirs* (Bird and Symonds), p. 7.

81   Rawlings, ed., *Drunks, Whores and Idle Apprentices*, pp. 22–23, also p. 4.

82   Lambert, *Prince of Pickpockets*, p. 263.

83   See *Daily Universal Register*, 11 November 1785, p. 2b; and *A Fortnights Ramble through London: or a complete Display of all the Cheats and Frauds Practized in that great Metropolis, ...* (London: J. Roach, 1795), p. 17.

84   See, for example, *The Times* of 26 May 1792, which describes a 67-year-old pickpocket named Esther Usher, 'better known by the name of The Female Barrington' (p. 3c).

85   *Daily Universal Register*, 22 January 1787, p. 3b.

86   *The Whole Proceedings*, 9 December 1789.

87   This account comes from a report on evidence tendered at the trial of Richard Blandy, the constable charged with allowing Barrington to escape. See *Morning Chronicle*, 18 November 1788, p. 3a.

88   Michael Harris, 'Trials and Criminal Biographies: A Case Study in Distribution', in Robin Myers and Michael Harris, eds, *Sale and Distribution of Books from 1700* (Oxford: Oxford Polytechnic Press, 1982), p. 1.

89   *Gazetteer and New Daily Advertiser*, 17 March 1778, pp. 2d–3a. Along with the Bow Street Public Office, Mansion-House (the official residence of the Lord Mayor of London) and Guildhall (the site of the city council), were used by London magistrates for the examination of alleged offenders.

90   ibid.

91   Newspaper report, source unknown, pasted into a scrapbook compiled by Sir William Dixson, and annotated in pen '1778' – the report clearly refers to the same event as described in the *Gazetteer* of 17 May 1778: '[Press cuttings]', Dixson F8/83, Mitchell Library.

92   *Gazetteer and New Daily Advertiser*, 17 March 1778, pp. 2d–3a.

93   ibid.

94   ibid.

95   *Morning Post*, 4 May 1778, p. 2d.

96   *The Whole Proceedings*, 29 April 1778.

97   ibid.

98   Barrington, qtd in *The Whole Proceedings*, 29 April 1778.

99   *Morning Post*, 4 May 1778, p. 2d. The *Morning Post* gives this offender's name as 'Burnet', but he was tried and convicted as John Bennet on 29 April 1778. Bennet clearly had powerful friends. He had previously received a free pardon after being sentenced to death at the Old Bailey (as John Bennet alias Eade) for picking pockets at Covent Garden. See *The Whole Proceedings*, 17 April 1776; and Pardon of John Bennet, 10 July 1776, PRO SP 44/94 ff., pp. 10–11.

100   See John Ritchie, *The Wentworths: Father and Son* (Melbourne: Melbourne University Press, 1997), pp. 3–8.

101   Source and date unknown – from a newspaper clipping annotated '1778' by Sir William Dixson. See '[Press cuttings]', Dixson F8 83, Mitchell Library.

102   *Memoirs* (Kearsley), p. 85.

103   *Memoirs* (Bird and Symonds), pp. 20–21. It is characteristic of these *Memoirs* (in contrast to Kearsley's publication) to interpolate large chunks of text from other sources – principally trial reports and letters. The survival of the hand-written original of the Dudman letter reproduced in this work, added to Barrington's known predilection for letters, makes it seem reasonable to accept that the letters included in this work are genuine, even if some anecdotes in the text are not.

104   *Memoirs* (Bird and Symonds), p. 20.

105   According to his subsequent trial for perverting the course of justice, Barrington received the pardon on 30 April 1782. See *The Whole Proceedings*, 15 January 1783.

106   *Memoirs* (Kearsley), pp. 87–94; cf. Box, *The Real George Barrington?*, pp. 79–80; Lambert, *Prince of Pickpockets*, pp. 123–25; and Rickard, ed., *George Barrington's Voyage to Botany Bay*, p. 11.

107   *The Whole Proceedings*, 15 January 1783.

108   ibid.

109   *Morning Herald*, 21 January 1783, qtd. in Box, *The Real George Barrington?*, pp. 80–81.

110   The 'novel of circulation', or 'It-narrative', was a popular early form of novel, plotted around the adventures of 'a non-human protagonist … as it travels through society, encountering diverse characters and incidents'. The 'novel of circulation' was a low-brow literary form, but as Liz Bellamy has argued, the 'random' character of the plotting allowed these works to anatomise society in a way not open to works with more 'structured and cohesive' plots. See Bellamy, 'Novel of Circulation', *The Literary Encylopedia*, online, <www.litercyc.com/php/stopics.php?rec=true&UID=1535>; see also Mark Blackwell, 'The It-Narrative in Eighteenth-Century England: Animals and Objects in Circulation', *Literature Compass*, vol. 1, 2004.

111   [Dorothy Kilner, *attrib.*], *Adventures of a Hackney Coach* (London: George Kearsley, 1781), p. 72.

112   See, for example, the character 'Barrington Newlight' in Robert Bisset's anti-Jacobin novel, *Douglas, or the Highlander* (London: T. Crowder, 1800), where the disreputable associations of Barrington are used to name a character who personifies dangerous newfangled democratic ideals. See also Hugh Kelly, *The Babler*, vol. 2, 1794, pp. 112–13.

113   See, for example, [Robert Bage, *attrib.*], *Man As He Is: A Novel*, vol. 2 (London:

Minerva Press, 1792), p. 208; and Horace Smith, *The Runaway, or The Seat of Benevolence: A Novel*, vol. 2 (London: Crosby and Letterman, 1800), p. 52.

114   I am working from the English translation of von Archenholz, *A Picture of England*, p. 85. The account was probably written about 1783, as it refers to Barrington being in Newgate at the time.

115   *Public Advertiser*, 2 February 1784, p. 4b-c.

116   *The Whole Proceedings*, 25 February 1784.

117   ibid.

118   Barrington, however, denied crucial elements in Webster's testimony, and characterised his prosecutor as 'fiery and hot' (qtd in *The Whole Proceedings*, 25 February 1784). Webster (c. 1749–1800) was in fact known for his fractious nature; his wife, Elizabeth Vassall, wrote of the 'oftimes frantic temper of the man to whom I had the calamity to be united'. See Christopher Whittick, 'Webster family (per. c. 1650–1836), gentry', *ODNB*, online, <www.oxforddnb.com>, accessed 1 December 2007.

119   Webster, qtd. in *The Whole Proceedings*, 25 February 1784.

120   *The Whole Proceedings*, 25 February 1784. On his arrest in 1778, Barrington was said to have been wearing 'three pairs of breeches'. See *The Whole Proceedings*, 29 April 1778.

121   *The Whole Proceedings*, 25 February 1784.

122   *Morning Post*, 1 March 1784, p. 3c.

123   *Morning Post*, 27 March 1784, p. 2d; *Morning Herald*, 27 March 1784, p. 3b.

124   This 'ritual' was kept up by the constable Richard Blandy, who would later allow Barrington to escape from his custody after the riot at the Brown Bear tavern in January 1787. See *The Whole Proceedings*, 9 December 1789.

125   See John O'Keeffe, *Fontainbleau; or our way in France. A comic opera, in three acts As performed at the Theatre-Royal in Covent Garden* (London: Longman and Broderip, 1784), pp. 51, 67.

126   See Charles Beecher Hogan, ed., *The London Stage 1660–1800: A Calendar of Plays, Entertainments and Afterpieces together with Casts, Box-Receipts and Contemporary Comment*, Part 5: 1776–1800, 3 vols (Carbondale, IL: Southern Illinois University Press, 1960–), vol. 2, pp. 731 ff.; vol. 3, pp. 1480 ff.

127   *The Oriental Chronicles of the Times: Being the Translation of a Chinese Manuscript ...* (London: H. D. Symonds and J. Debrett, [1785]), p. 85.

128   The short-lived coalition government of Fox (1749–1806) and Lord North (1732–1792) was removed from power through the influence of the King in December 1783. After defeat in the general elections of 1784, Fox became the leader of the parliamentary opposition. Pitt (1759–1806), son of a former prime minister and often referred to as 'Pitt the Younger' to differentiate him from his father, became the youngest prime minister in British history when he attained that office in 1783. The general elections of 1784 consolidated his ministry, and he remained in power until 1801, serving again as prime minister from 1804 until his death in 1806. The personality clash between the dour and calculating Pitt and the charismatic, high-living Fox became one of the defining features of the political landscape of the late eighteenth century. See Stanley Ayling, *Fox: The Life of Charles James Fox* (London: John Murray, 1991); and Robin Reilly, *Pitt the Younger, 1759–1806* (London: Cassell, 1978).

129   *The Oriental Chronicles of the Times*, p. [i].

130   Erskine May, *The Constitutional History of England Since the Ascension of George III*, 11th edn, vol. 1 (London: Longmans, Green & Co., 1896), p. 351.

131   ibid.

132   For a discussion of the role of Georgiana and the other Whig ladies in 1784, see Renata Lana, 'Women and Foxite Strategy in the Westminster Election of 1784', *Eighteenth-Century Life*, vol. 26, no. 1, 2002, pp. 46–69.

133   Werkmeister, *London Daily Press*, pp. 78–79, see also pp. 61–108.

134   Date of original publication unknown. This squib was included in the pro-Fox *History of the Westminster Election* (London: Debrett, 1784), where it was presented as one of the advertisements published by the Hood and Wray (Pittite) party, and further bore the caveat – 'the LIE of the noted Editor of that noted lying paper, The Morning Post', p. 235.

135   Fox and his set were particularly associated with Brookes' club in St James – 'the scene of the wildest gambling in town'. See Ayling, *Fox*, p. 49, also pp. 86–94.

136   See *The Times*, 9 August 1788, p. 3b.

137   *Public Advertiser*, 28 February 1785, p. 2d. A reporter for the *Public Advertiser* would later deliver the witticism that '[Barrington] is the Gentleman, who excepting the Managers, has of all others made the best estimate of what Mrs. Siddons could draw, and of course what he might draw also' (*Public Advertiser*, 8 July 1788, p. 3c).

138   Qtd in *The Whole Proceedings*, 6 April 1785.

139   *Morning Post*, 28 February 1785, p. 2c. Brief reports of the arrest of 'the notorious Barrington' could also be found in the *General Evening Post*, 26 February – 1 March 1785, p. 1c); and the *London Chronicle*, 26 February – 1 March 1785, p. 2c).

140   *Gazetteer and New Daily Advertiser*, 28 February 1785, p. 2c.

141   *The Whole Proceedings*, 6 April 1785.

142   Barrington qtd in *The Whole Proceedings*, 6 April 1785.

143   *London Chronicle*, 5–7 April 1785, p. 8c.

144   *The Whole Proceedings*, 6 April 1785.

145   Both the *London Chronicle*, 5–7 April 1785, p. 8c, and the *Morning Post*, 9 April 1785, p. 3a-b), carried long excerpts from Barrington's speech at the Old Bailey.

146   *London Chronicle*, 5–7 April 1785, p. 8c.

147   Werkmeister, *London Daily Press*, pp. 82–83, 133.

148   Peter Stuart qtd in Werkmeister, 'Notes for a Revised Life of William Jackson', p. 44.

149   Werkmeister, *London Daily Press*, pp. 79, 88–90.

150   *Morning Post*, 13 April 1785, p. 3d.

151   *Morning Post*, 14 April 1785, p. 2c.

152   The double entendre here being the dual meaning of the word 'trepan' as both a surgical instrument used for operating on the skull and a slang term for deceiving or entrapping a victim. *The Times*, 1 July 1785, p. 3c.

153   See, for example, the 'report' on Barrington at a musical performance at Westminster Abbey in the *Daily Universal Register* of 2 June 1786, p. 3c: 'upon [Barrington] being asked by an old gentleman, whether he was not charmed with music; "Sir, replied he, how can it be otherwise, when I am an old Member of the *catch* club!"' For similarly jocular references to Barrington, see *Daily Universal Register*, 11 November 1785, p. 2b;

13 December 1786, p. 3b; 15 December 1786, p. 3c; 20 December 1786, p. 2d; 22 December 1786, p. 2c; 28 July 1787, p. 3b; *Morning Herald*, 28 July 1787, p. 3b.

154 While both Box and Rickard have accepted this as a portrait of the pickpocket Barrington, I would introduce a note of caution about the attribution. An inquiry to the National Library of Australia revealed that they have no provenance information on the portrait, formerly in the Rex Nan Kivell collection, and the portrait could well be of Reverend George Barrington (1761–1829), a nephew of William Wildman, Lord Barrington, who would ascend to the title himself as the 5th Viscount Barrington in 1814. See George Edward Cokayne et al., *The Complete Peerage of England, Scotland, Ireland, Great Britain, and the United Kingdom, Extant, Extinct or Dormant*, new edn, vol. 1 (Gloucester: Alan Sutton Publishing, 2000), p. 434. For William Beechey, see John Wilson, 'Beechey, Sir William (1753–1839), portrait painter', *ODNB*, online, <www.oxforddnb.com>, accessed 1 December 2007.

155 Havilland Le Mesurier was the youngest son of the hereditary governor of Aldernay, in the Channel Islands. His elder brother, Paul, who would later act as the prosecuting attorney for his brother over the incident, was a London alderman and Pittite MP. See W. R. Meyer, 'Le Mesurier, Havilland (1758–1806), merchant and commissary officer', and 'Le Mesurier, Paul (1755–1805), merchant and politician', *ODNB*, online, <www.oxforddnb.com>, accessed 1 December 2007.

156 *The Whole Proceedings*, 9 December 1789.

157 *Daily Universal Register*, 22 January 1787, p. 3b.

158 *The World*, 22 January 1787, p. 3b; *General Evening Post*, 20–23 January 1787, p. 3c-d.

159 *Daily Universal Register*, 22 January 1787, p. 3b; *The World*, 23 January 1787, p. 3c; *General Evening Post*, 20–23 January, p. 3c-d.

160 *Memoirs* (Kearsley), p. 96.

161 See *Daily Universal Register*, 13 December 1786, p. 3b; *The Times*, 3 July 1788, p. 3c.

162 *Daily Universal Register*, 2 March 1787, p. 3a. The same article appeared in the West Country weekly *Felix Farley's Bristol Journal* for 3 March 1787.

163 The powerful politician Dundas seems to have been included here mainly on the basis of his being a prominent Scot. There is no indication that Dundas actually visited Scotland in 1787, and he was certainly busy in London in his various roles as treasurer of the Navy, commissioner of the India Board and member of the House of Lords. See Michael Fry, 'Dundas, Henry, first Viscount Melville (1742–1811)', *ODNB*, online, <www.oxforddnb.com>, accessed 1 December 2007.

164 Nonetheless, this story has been given some credence by Rickard in her *ODNB* entry on Barrington (<www.oxforddnb.com>, accessed 1 December 2007).

165 *Memoirs* (Bird and Symonds), p. 26. Gambling on unlicensed premises was of course illegal, as well as morally reprehensible.

166 ibid., 26.

167 See *Newcastle Chronicle*, 5 July 1788, qtd in Box, *The Real George Barrington?*, p. 2.

168 *Daily Universal Register*, 13 April 1787, p. 2d.

169 *Daily Universal Register*, 25 May 1787, p. 3c.

170 *Morning Post*, 12 January 1788, p. 3a; *Public Advertiser*, 14 January 1788, p. 4c; *St. James's Chronicle*, 10–12 January 1788, p. 4b.

171 *Morning Chronicle*, 28 March 1788, p. 3d.

172   *The Times*, 1 April 1788, p. 3d. The *Daily Universal Register* changed its name to *The Times* on 1 January 1788.

173   *The Times*, 11 April 1788, p. 4c.

174   Box, *The Real George Barrington?*, p. 105.

175   To cite a few of many examples, see *An Heroic Epistle from Donna Teresa Pinna Y Ruiz, of Murcia, to Richard Twiss, Esq.* (London: George Kearsley, 1777); [William Coombe, *attrib.*], *An Heroic Epistle to the Right Honourable the Lord Craven* (London: John Wheeble, 1776); *The Heroic Epistle Answered … by the R–H— Lord C–* (London: J. Wilkie, 1776); [George Hamilton, *attrib.*], *The Telegraph; a Consolatory Epistle from Thomas Muir, Esq. of Botany Bay, to the Hon. Henry Erskine, late Dean of Faculty* ([Edinburgh]: n.p., [1796]). Allonymous prose satire was also highly popular, with the figure of the King [George III] often appropriated in such works. A leading example was *The Festival of Wit, or the Small Talker... Selected from Voluminous Work in the Possession of G***** K***, Summer Resident at W—. With the Life of the Author and Compiler, Written by Himself*, which was published in numerous editions by several different publishers between 1782 and 1800.

176   James Semple actually escaped being sent to New South Wales at this time, receiving a pardon on condition of leaving the country. The first publication of the 'Heroic Epistle' I have been able to trace is that in the *Attic Miscellany*, though this does not preclude an earlier publication. See *Attic Miscellany*, 1 February 1790, pp. 169–74. For Semple, see J. G. Alger (rev. Heather Shore), 'Semple, James George (b. 1759, d. in or after 1814), adventurer', *ODNB*, online, <www.oxforddnb.com>, accessed 1 December 2007.

177   'An Heroic Epistle', *Attic Miscellany*, vol. 1, 1790, p. 174.

178   Juvenal's Third Satire is based around the imminent departure from Rome of Cumae of Umbricius, who then begins an embittered rant about the corruption and dishonesty in Rome. See J. D. Duff, ed., *Fourteen Satires of Juvenal* (Cambridge: Cambridge University Press, 1970).

179   'An Heroic Epistle', *Attic Miscellany*, vol. 1, 1790, p. 170.

180   See *The Times*, 1 July 1785, p. 3c.

181   The *Attic Miscellany* was published by William Locke, a printer who traded under the false imprint, 'Bentley & co.'. Locke later went bankrupt owing Lemoine £129 'for writing only'. See *The New, Original and Complete Wonderful Museum*, vol. 5 (London: Alex. Hogg & Co., 1807), p. 2230.

182   A protracted search has failed to locate any extant copies of *The World* from this period. Fortunately, some description of the contents of the article can be found in *The Times* (14 May 1788, p. 3a). Box has erroneously claimed that this biography appeared in 'a letter to the *Morning Chronicle* in 1788' (p. 12, also p. 14).

183   The Della Cruscan movement, a school of poetry following an excessively ornamental and sentimental style, developed from a poetic exchange begun in *The World* in 1787 between Robert Merry (1755–1798), who used the pseudonym 'Della Crusca', and Hannah Cowley (1743–1809), who signed as 'Anna Matilda'. On the whole, the paper can be seen as a more sophisticated version of the fashionable West End daily that the *Morning Post* had been in the mid-1770s. It was hugely successful: indeed, according to Werkmeister, the 'immediacy and extent of *The World*'s success

has no precedent in the history of newspapers'. See W. N. Hargreaves-Mawdsley, *The English Della Cruscans and their Time, 1783–1828* (The Hague: Martinus Nijhoff, 1967); Werkmeister, *London Daily Press*, p. 158; and Morison, *The English Newspaper*, pp. 177–81.

184   Morison, *The English Newspaper*, p. 179; Werkmeister, *London Daily Press*, p. 155. For Topham, see John Russell Stephens, 'Topham, Edward (1751–1820), journalist and playwright', *ODNB*, online, <www.oxforddnb.com>, accessed 1 December 2007.

185   See Werkmeister, *London Daily Press*, pp. 159–60.

186   *Morning Chronicle*, 12 January 1788, p. 2a. This letter, dated from Windsor [perhaps the royal residence?], may have something of a subtext; in any case, it is ironic as Sheridan, according to Werkmeister, was secretly involved with *The World*, furnishing its political reports and manipulating its political agenda – thus the paper was not likely to libel him and indeed any biography may have been contributed by Sheridan himself (Werkmeister, *London Daily Press*, pp. 155, 162–66).

187   *The Times*, 14 May 1788, p. 3a. By its repeated use of the epithet 'Reverend Biographer', *The Times* insinuates, or merely assumes, that Este was the author of 'The Schools'. The biography of Topham in the *ODNB*, on the other hand, naturally enough assumes him to be the author of the articles that detail the alumni of Eton, Topham's alma mater. It may be significant, however, that Este was later to say that he brought to *The World* 'some MS. [likely to] make the fortune of a Paper'. See *Gazetteer and New Daily Advertiser*, 21 September 1790, p. 4b.

188   That is, via *The Times*, 14 May 1788, p. 3a.

189   See *Memoirs* (Kearsley); *Memoirs* (Bird and Symonds), p. 1. In the Bird and Symonds version, Waldron is Barrington's mother's name, and his father was a 'Captain Barrington'.

190   *The Times*, 14 May 1788, p. 3a.

191   *Memoirs* (Bird and Symonds), pp. 26–27.

192   The same report appeared in at least three papers on the same day: *The Times*, 3 July 1788, p. 3b; *Morning Chronicle*, 3 July 1788, p. 4b; and *Whitehall Evening Post*, 1–3 July 1788, p. 2c.

193   *St. James's Chronicle*, 1–3 July 1788, p. 4d.

194   *Newcastle Chronicle*, 5 July 1788, qtd in Box, *The Real George Barrington?*, p. 2.

195   The story of Barrington's wife remains largely obscure, but it does not seem to have been a happy one. After Barrington's embarkation for New South Wales in 1791, the *Morning Chronicle* published a letter (possibly genuine) from Barrington to his wife dated from Plymouth, 2 March 1791, in which Barrington claims that his removal from Newgate without seeing her and 'my dear child' had 'given me infinitely more pain and misery than the punishment itself'. By 1794, the 'wife of George Barrington' was reportedly living with a John Jacques, who 'had no other means of supporting himself but by her prostitution, and other undue means'. At the Old Bailey in November 1796, 'Mary Murray, otherwise Barrington' was acquitted of a capital charge of highway robbery. At the trial her servant had testified that Mary had been 'very ill' and 'in the utmost distress through want and illness' for some time. When asked what line of business Mary was in, her servant testified that she 'keeps company', and that being 'very low in pocket and health' she was struggling to support her eight-year-old son. In

August 1800, the *Morning Herald* reported that 'Mary Murray, alias Mary Barrington, (the wife of George Barrington, of noted memory)' was examined on 'a charge of practicing those lessons which her husband was so capable of inculcating'. She seems to have escaped trial on that occasion, but was back before the magistrates again the following year. The subsequent fate of 'the noted Mrs. *Barrington*', and her son, is unclear, but it seems unlikely that they derived any benefit from the colonial respectability of George Barrington, or from the books of the supposed 'convict-historian'. See *Morning Chronicle*, 9 March 1791, p. 4a; *The Times*, 14 February, p. 3a; *The Whole Proceedings*, 30 November 1796; *Morning Herald*, 18 August 1800, p. 3d; *The Times*, 25 September 1801, p. 3b; and Dixson collection, Drawer Item 65, Mitchell Library.

196   *Newcastle Chronicle*, 19 or 26 July 1788, qtd in Box, *The Real George Barrington?*, p. 54.

197   See *Public Advertiser*, 26 July 1788, p. 3d, and 28 July 1788, p. 4b-d. *The Times* of 29 July 1788, p. 3a, combined both these reports in its notice of Barrington's return.

198   Barrington qtd in *Public Advertiser*, 18 July 1788, p. 4d; *The Times*, 29 July 1788, p. 3a.

199   *Public Advertiser*, 28 July 1788, p. 4c. This claim is in all probability untrue – Townsend knew Barrington well and testified against his fellow constable Blandy over the Brown Bear escape – but at least Barrington had evoked a semblance of sympathy from the *Public Advertiser*.

200   *Morning Chronicle*, 30 July 1788, p. 2d; *Public Advertiser*, 28 July 1788, p. 4c.

201   *Morning Chronicle*, 30 July 1788, p. 2d. 'Last dying words' speeches, where criminals repented on their evil ways on the gallows, were often produced as broadsides for popular consumption. See Harris, 'Trials and Criminal Biographies', pp. 3–4.

202   The epithets here were clearly meant to be interchangeable. *The Times*, 5 August 1788, p. 3a.

203   *The Times*, 5 August 1788, p. 3a.

204   *The Times*, 9 August 1788, p. 3b.

205   Barrington, 'To the Editor of the Times', *The Times*, 9 August 1788, p. 3b.

206   ibid.

207   'What a most virtuous man must Mr. Fox be, when *Barrington* calls him one of the *first characters* in the kingdom'. *The Times*, 12 August 1788, p. 2d.

208   Barrington [Old Bailey, 18 September 1788] qtd in the *Morning Chronicle*, 19 September 1788, p. 3c.

209   Among the newspapers which reported Barrington's speech in full were the *Morning Chronicle*, 19 September 1788, p. 3c-d; *The Times*, 19 September 1788, p. 3b-c; *General Evening Post*, 18–20 September 1788, p. 1b-c); and the *Whitehall Evening Post*, 18–20 September 1788, p. 2b-c).

210   *The Times*, 20 September 1788, p. 2c.

211   Since Barrington's appearance at the Old Bailey on 18 September 1788 was a committal proceeding and not a trial per se, there is no account of it in *The Whole Proceedings*. The broadside may have been produced to make up for this lack, although the facetious use of the honorific 'Esq.' after Barrington's name suggests that the broadside came from a less official source, and may have been intended for broader popular consumption. Early that year, the *Whitehall Evening Post* had complained that

'[the] title of Esquire, so absurdly applied in our days to the name of every idle fellow who has neither business, nor money, in or out of prison, received the *coup de grace* last week in a country news-paper, which mentioned the apprehending "of George Barrington, *Esq.* at Newcastle."' (29–31 July, p. 2c).

212 *The Times*, 20 September 1788, p. 2c.

213 *Whitehall Evening Post*, 20–23 September 1788, p. 2c.

214 *The Times*, 11 November 1788, p. 2b.

215 Townsend qtd in *Morning Chronicle*, 18 November 1788, p. 3a.

216 Blandy received sentence at the start of February 1789, and was dead by the time Barrington's trial took place at the Old Bailey in December. See *The Whole Proceedings*, 9 December 1789.

217 'To the Printer of the Morning Chronicle', *Morning Chronicle*, 24 November 1788, p. 3a.

218 *Morning Chronicle*, 24 November 1788, p. 3a.

219 'To the Printer', *Morning Chronicle*, 26 November 1788, p. 2d.

220 Barrington [Old Bailey, 18 September 1788] qtd in *Morning Chronicle*, 19 September 1788, p. 3c.

221 Garrow had assisted Fox in the cause of the Westminster Scrutiny, though he would later defect to the conservative side of politics and be rewarded with an appointment as King's Counsel. For Garrow, see Beattie, *ODNB*, online, <www.oxforddnb.com>, accessed 1 December 2007.

222 As a Pittite Tory, Paul Le Mesurier had won a narrow and bitterly fought by-election for the seat of Southwark in 1784, reportedly defeating the Foxite candidate by only eleven votes. See Meyer, *ODNB*, online, <www.oxforddnb.com>, accessed 1 December 2007.

223 *The Times*, 21 December 1789, p. 2d.

224 See the *Morning Post*, 27 November 1789, p. 3d. One certainly gets the feeling that the general sentiment of the unfairness of depriving a man of a trial helped dictate the outcome, however.

225 *Morning Post*, 16 November 1789, p. 3b.

226 See, for example, *Term Reports in the Court of King's Bench*, vol. 3 (London: J. Butterworth, 1797), pp. 519 ff.; Matthew Bacon, *A New Abridgement of the Law*, 5th edn (London: T. Cadell et. al., 1798); and John Impey, *The Office of Sheriff: Shewing its History, Antiquity, Powers, and Duties*, 2nd edn (London: J. Butterworth, 1800), p. 492.

227 *The Times*, 16 November 1789, p. 3a; *Morning Post*, 16 November 1789, p. 3b, 27 November 1789, p. 2d; *Morning Chronicle*, 26 November 1789, p. 2c-d; *The World*, 16 November 1789, p. 3c, 27 November 1789, p. 3b; *Whitehall Evening Post*, 18–20 November 1789, p. 2b; *Universal Magazine*, vol. 85, November 1789, p. 275.

228 Barrington qtd in *The Whole Proceedings*, 9 December 1789.

229 *Public Advertiser*, 11 December 1789, qtd in Lambert, *Prince of Pickpockets*, p. 163.

230 *Morning Post*, 11 December 1789, p. 3c.

231 ibid.

232 *The Times*, 12 December 1789, p. 3a; *London Chronicle*, 12 December 1789, p. 8c.

233 The *Morning Post*, as Werkmeister has observed, had been on a steady downward spiral

throughout the 1780s, both in terms of character and of circulation, and by 1789 'was so disreputable that the loss [of the paper by the ministry] could almost be counted as a gain'. See *London Daily Press*, p. 317, also pp. 96–97, 61–108.

234   *Morning Post*, 16 November 1789, p. 2c.

235   *Morning Post*, 18 December 1789, p. 3c.

236   *Morning Post*, 24 December 1789, p. 2d; *The Times*, 24 December 1789, p. 3b.

237   *London Chronicle*, 12 December 1789, p. 3b. The same paragraph featured in *The Times* (14 December 1789, p. 2c) and another abridged account of Barrington's inheritance in Hampshire was published in at least one other paper ('[Press cuttings]', Dixson F8/83, Mitchell Library).

238   *The Times*, 4 March 1790, p. 3b; *Lady's Magazine*, vol. 21, March 1790, p. 165.

239   *The Times*, 4 March 1790, p. 3b.

240   *The Times*, 10 March 1790, p. 3e.

241   ibid., p. 3b.

242   *The Times*, 9 April 1790, p. 3a.

243   *The Whole Proceedings*, 15 September 1790.

244   *Morning Chronicle*, 9 March 1791, p. 4a.

CHAPTER 2

1   *The Times*, 7 October 1790, p. 2c.

2   *The Times*, 22 September 1790, p. 3a; 25 September 1790, p. 2c.

3   *The World*, 7 September 1790, p. 3c.

4   See *The World*, 15 September, p. 4a; 18 September, p. 3c; 21 September, p. 2c; 23 September, pp. 2d, 4a; 24 September, p. 2d; 16 October, p. 3b; 20 October, p. 1a.

5   Two broadside ballads – 'A Pad's Advice on the Noted Geo. Barrington Trip to Botany Bay' and 'A New Flash Song Made on the Noted George Barrington ...' – survive in the Bodleian Library's collection of ballads and are reproduced in their online archive, *Bodleian Library Broadside Ballads*, <www.bodley.ox.ac.uk/ballads/ballads.htm>. The use in these ballads of 'flash', otherwise known as thieves' cant, does not mean that their audience was composed exclusively of criminals, as some writers have thought. Writing on the popular literature of the Regency period, Gregory Dart has noted the existence of 'a considerable vogue among the higher orders for the various kinds of cant and slang', and argues that 'flash' language represented a kind of nexus between the fashionable and the criminal worlds. See J. S. Manifold, *Who Wrote the Ballads? Notes on Australian Folksong* (Sydney: Australasian Book Society, 1964), p. 22; and Gregory Dart, '"Flash Style": Pierce Egan and Literary London 1820–28', *History Workshop*, vol. 51, 2001, pp. 190–91. See also Nathan Garvey, '"Where Sydney Cove Her Lucid Bosom Swells": The Songs of an Imagined Nation, 1786–1789', *Literature Compass*, vol. 4, 2007, p. 603.

6   *The World*, 20 November 1790, p. 3d.

7   *The Trial at Large of George Barrington, Before Lord Chief Baron Eyre, at the Sessions House in the Old Bailey, on Friday the 17th instant, for Robbing Henry Townsend, Esq. at Enfield Races, for which he was found Guilty. With the Pleadings of Counsel, the Judge's Charge to the Jury, and the Prisoner's Two Remarkable Speeches, verbatim. By E. Hodgson, Shorthand*

Writer to the Old Bailey (London: Simmonds [i.e. H. D. Symonds]... and R. Butters...,
1790). See *The Times*, 19 September 1790, p. 1d. The work was also advertised the
following day in *The World*, 20 September 1790, p. 1a, and again in *The Times*,
20 September 1790, p. 1b.

8   *The Times*, 20 September 1790, p. 3a-d); *Gazetteer and New Daily Advertiser*,
18 September 1790, p. 3c-d; *St. James's Chronicle*, 18–20 September 1790, p. 3c; *The
World*, 18 September 1790, p. 3c, and 23 September1790, p. 2d; and *Whitehall Evening
Post*, 16–18 September 1790, p. 3a-b, were among the newspapers which offered
readers detailed accounts of the trial, while magazines that carried the story included
the *Gentleman's Magazine*, vol. 60, September 1790, pp. 855–56; *The Wonderful
Magazine*, vol. 4, September 1790, pp. 351–55; and the *New London Magazine*,
September 1790, pp. 428–32.

9   Then published under the title, *The Whole Proceedings on the King's Commission of the
Peace, Oyer and Terminer, and Gaol Delivery for the City of London; and also the Gaol
Delivery for the County of Middlesex, held at Justice Hall in the Old Bailey* [hereafter *Whole
Proceedings*], the Old Bailey sessions paper had been published since 1674 and had
gradually evolved into a legal document reporting, in more or less detail, on all
trials at the Old Bailey. The *Whole Proceedings* are now available online at
<www.oldbaileyonline.org>; references in the text are to the online version; dates refer
to trial dates rather than dates of publication.

10   For H. D. Symonds, see Chapter 3. The other publisher of the *Trial at Large of George
Barrington*, Robert Butters, was a printer who traded in the Fleet Street area from about
1785 to 1808. See Ian Maxted, *The London Book Trades 1775–1800: A Checklist of
Members* (London: William Dawson, 1977), p. 23.

11   See Michael Harris, 'Trials and Criminal Biographies: A Case Study in Distribution', in
Robin Myers and Michael Harris, eds, *Sale and Distribution of Books from 1700* (Oxford:
Oxford Polytechnic Press, 1982), pp. 3–36.

12   *Morning Chronicle*, 30 July 1788, p. 2d.

13   Both these biographies were advertised in *The Times* of 4 October 1790, pp. 1a, 1b.
Advertisements for the Kearsley *Memoirs* also appeared in the *St. James's Chronicle*, 2–5
October 1790, p. 1d, and for the Bird and Symonds *Memoirs*, in *The World*, 4 October
1790, p. 1a, and 16 October 1790, p. 2a.

14   Hereafter *Memoirs* (Bird and Symonds), see also Bibliography, **B1a-d**. H. D. Symonds
appears only as 'Simmonds' on the title page, but from the address given it is clear that
Symonds was the publisher referred to. The identity of 'J. Bird' is uncertain, but this
was in fact likely to have been a false imprint for a bookseller named William Locke,
who was trading at the address listed on the work (22 Fetter Lane) in this period. Locke
generally published at this time under another false imprint – 'Bentley and Co' (or
sometimes 'E. Bentley' or 'W. Bentley') – and many of the works produced under the
'Bentley' imprint were lurid in character. In particular, Locke specialised in publishing
the proceedings of high-profile adultery trials, and in 1791 he published a translation
of one of the more pornographic *libelles* on the French Queen, Marie Antoinette, as
*Memoirs of Antonio, Queen of Abo. Displaying her Private Intrigues, and Uncommon
Passions* (2 vols, 'Bentley', 1791). Locke, who relocated to 12 Red-Lion Court, Holborn,
about 1792, went bankrupt in 1793, owing the writer Henry Lemoine over £100. See

'Memoirs of Henry Lemoine, the well-known Literary Pedestrian and Eccentric Bookseller and Author, of the City of London', *The New, Original and Complete Wonderful Museum and Magazine Extraordinary ...*, vol. 5 (London: Alexander Hogg, 1807), p. 2229; Maxted, *The London Book Trades 1775–1800*, pp. 22, 46.

15   Hereafter *Memoirs* (Kearsley), see Bibliography, **B2**. The imprint 'M. Smith' was used by Kearsley on a number of other works in the 1770s and 1780s, notably when he published the first edition of *Baron Munchausen's Narrative of his Marvellous Travels* in 1786. See Ruth P. Dawson, 'Rudolph Erich Raspe and the Munchausen Tales', *Lessing Yearbook*, vol. 16, 1984, pp. 207–08. For a general account of Kearsley's life and career, see Trevor Ross, 'Kearsley, George (*c.* 1739–1790)', *Oxford Dictionary of National Biography* [hereafter *ODNB*] (Oxford: Oxford University Press, 2004), online, last update October 2005, <www.oxforddnb.com>, accessed 1 December 2007.

16   Price was probably a fictional character. He was supposed to be an Englishman, from Poole, Dorsetshire, and to have been transported from Ireland to America in early 1773. See *Memoirs* (Kearsley), pp. 9, 22–23.

17   *Memoirs* (Bird and Symonds), p. 5.

18   See Phillip Rawlings, ed., *Drunks, Whores and Idle Apprentices: Criminal Biographies of the Eighteenth Century* (London: Routledge, 1992, pp. 4, 22–23.

19   *Memoirs* (Kearsley), pp. 14–20.

20   *Memoirs* (Kearsley), pp. 9–25; *Memoirs* (Bird and Symonds), p. 7. The Kearsley *Memoirs* also make Barrington three years older than the Bird and Symonds narrative, although the latter's dating is derived from Barrington's own statements concerning his age in court.

21   The greater part of pages 10–40 of the Bird and Symonds *Memoirs* is taken up with trial reports, along with some letters written by Barrington. Somewhere between two-thirds and three-quarters of the narrative is thus made up from material already in the public domain. Once again, some accommodation had probably been reached with Edmund Hodgson, the Old Bailey's shorthand reporter, to furnish this copy.

22   *Monthly Review* [new series], vol. 3, November 1790, p. 350.

23   *Memoirs* (Kearsley), pp. 14, 19, 63, 65–67.

24   Kearsley's biography of Semple, published as *Memoirs of the Northern Imposter; or Prince of Swindlers ...* (London: Kearsley, 1786), went through at least eight nominal editions in the first year of its publication. His biographies of Price, also first published in 1786, appeared under a number of titles and in increasingly elaborate editions. See *An Authentic Account of Forgeries and Frauds of Various Kinds committed by that most consummate Adept in Deception, Charles Price ...* (London: Kearsley, 1786); *A New Edition, Being a more minute and particular Account of that consummate Adept in Deception, Charles Price ...* (London: Kearsley, 1786); and *Memoirs of a Social Monster; or, the History of Charles Price ...* (London: Kearsley, 1786). The latter text, the most extensive and novelistic version of Price's 'life', was republished in 1790 in a 'new edition, corrected and improved', possibly to coincide with the publication of Kearsley's Barrington *Memoirs*.

25   *Monthly Review* [new series], vol. 3, November 1790, p. 350.

26   This paragraph appeared in the *Whitehall Evening Post* of 7–9 March 1786 and the

General Evening Advertiser of 9 March 1786, and is quoted in Rawlings' *Drunks, Whores and Idle Apprentices*, p. 2.

27 Barrington was sentenced on Wednesday, 22 September 1790, and Kearsley attended the Stationers' Hall with his published *Memoirs* on Thursday, 30 September 1790. See *Records of the Worshipful Company of Stationers 1554–1923* [hereafter *RWCS*], *Entries of Copies 1786–1792*, Robin Myers, ed., microfilm, reel 7 (Cambridge: Chadwyck-Healey, 1985–). Stationers' Hall, in Stationers' Alley, near St Paul's Cathedral, was the home of the Stationers' Company, the traditional guild organisation of the London book trade. The Stationers' Company managed and monitored a number of activities connected with the trade, including the legal deposit of books, the intake of book trade apprentices, and the granting of 'freedoms' – that is, the right to trade in the city of London. See Robin Myers, *The Stationers' Company Archive: An Account of the Records 1554–1984* (Winchester: St Paul's Bibliographies, 1990); Robin Myers and Michael Harris, eds, *The Stationers' Company and the Book Trade, 1550–1990* (New Castle, Del.: Oak Knoll Press, 1997); and Cyprian Blagden, *The Stationers' Company: A History, 1403–1949* (London: Allen & Unwin, 1960).

28 The anecdote of Cutler appears on pages 8–9 of the *Memoirs* (Bird and Symonds).

29 J. A. Ferguson, *Bibliography of Australia*, vol. 1 (Sydney: Angus and Robertson, 1941), p. 32 [F68].

30 See Mitchell Library, DSM/S923.41/B276.2J1.

31 'James', whose real name is said to be 'William S——r', appears in the section of the Kearsley *Memoirs* narrating Barrington's supposed first years in England (pp. 35–71). 'James' conveniently disappears from the narrative before it arrives at Barrington's period in the public eye.

32 *The Times*, 22 October 1790, p. 1a.

33 *Analytical Review*, no. 8, October 1790, p. 189.

34 Janine Barchas, *Graphic Design, Print Culture and the Eighteenth-Century Novel* (Cambridge: Cambridge University Press, 2003), pp. 22, 27; see also pp. 21–22, 42.

35 *Monthly Review* [new series], vol. 3, November 1790, pp. 335, 350; *Critical Review*, vol. 70, October 1790, pp. 461–62.

36 See Bibliography, **B3**, **B11**, **B13**, **B15a-b**, **B18**, **B19**, **B21**.

37 The *British Book Trade Index* [*BBTI*] lists several engravers with the name of Barlow – who probably had a family connection – working in the London area at this time, including Jonathan Barlow (*fl.* 1789), James Barlow (*fl.* 1790) and Inigo Barlow (*fl.* 1790). See *BBTI*, online, <www.bbti.bham.ac.uk>, accessed 1 December 2007. Suzanne Rickard, who mistakenly calls the engraver 'Barlin', also states that after the Orlov affair in 1775 'illustrators recreated the scene in memorable and lively engravings that appeared all over town'. Rickard gives no evidence to support this assertion, however; the engraving published by Kearsley in 1790 is the only pictorial depiction of this scene that I have traced (see Rickard, ed., *George Barrington's Voyage to Botany Bay: Retelling a Convict's Travel Narrative of the 1790s* (London: Leicester University Press, 2001), pp. 9–10).

38 Photographs of the Barrington mug are held in the collection of the National Library of Australia. See Staffordshire earthenware Barrington mug, c. 1790–1791 [picture], Lady Viola Tate collection, National Library of Australia, reproduced online at <http://nla.gov.au/nla.pic-vn3600940>, accessed 1 December 2007.

39   See William Zachs, *The First John Murray: and the Late Eighteenth-Century Book Trade* (Oxford: Oxford University Press, 1998), pp. 85–86.

40   The pamphlet was *Love in Captivity; or future felicity anticipated. In a series of eccentrical epistles between several celebrated heroes, and amorous British beauties, bound to Botany Bay* (2nd ed., London: T. Massey and H. D. Symonds, 1787). A prose satire imagining Botany Bay as an ironic sexual utopia for some of the figures involved in high-profile sexual and criminal scandals of the 1780s, Kearsley is included in a minor capacity, probably because the writer (or the publishers) held a personal or professional grudge against him (see pp. 30, 33). Kearsley was declared bankrupt on at least two occasions in his bookselling career, in 1764 and again in 1784. See Maxted, *London Book Trades 1775–1800*, p. 73.

41   *The Times*, 22 October 1790, p. 1a.

42   See Bibliography, **B2**, **B4**, **B5**.

43   *The Times*, 17 November 1790, p. 2a.

44   See *Gentleman's Magazine*, vol. 60, December 1790, p. 1150; *European Magazine and London Review*, vol. 18, December 1790, p. 480. Kearsley's will, proved on 20 December 1790, bequeathed his business to his widow, Catherine, and his son, George (Will of George Kearsley, Bookseller of Fleet Street, City of London, PRO PROB 11/1199).

45   See Bibliography, **B3**. There is no record of any 'B. Urquhart' in the main sources on the London book trade.

46   *Memoirs* ('Urquhart'), pp. 3–4. The author of this introduction seems either to have anticipated a capital conviction, or to have equated transportation to Botany Bay with death.

47   *Memoirs* (Kearsley), pp. 85–87. The passage details Barrington's supposed suicide bid, and his release from the hulks in 1782.

48   ML A923.41/B276/2D1. See also Bibliography, **B3**.

49   See Bibliography, **B15a-b**.

50   A copy of this letter held by the National Library of Australia has been cut out from a contemporary newspaper or magazine, and the headline reads 'Taken from the Doncaster Journal of Saturday, November 5, 1791'. See NLA NK2195.

51   *Life of George Barrington* (London: Printed for the Booksellers, 1792), p. 40. Sheila Box mistakes the recipient for an inhabitant of the city of York; the text of the letter, however, makes it clear that the recipient lived in Doncaster, in the 'County of York' [i.e. Yorkshire], and the letter was presumably forwarded by him to the local periodical upon receipt in late 1791. See Box, *The Real George Barrington?: The Adventures of a Notorious London Pickpocket, later Head Constable of the Infant Colony of New South Wales* (Melbourne: Australian Scholarly Publishing, 2001), p. 126.

52   See bibliography, **B16** and **B17**. Andrew Hambleton is an uncertain figure. The *BBTI* lists his career dates as 1760–1793, but this seems to be based on the misdating of one work. All that is really certain is that Hambleton produced a number of chapbooks in the early to mid-1790s, none of which has an address or any other identifying information, such as advertisements. It seems most probable that Andrew Hambleton was an itinerant chapbook seller, perhaps in the mould of Robert Barker (see below).

53   See Bibliography, **AB3**, **AB4**, **AB5**.

54 *Life of George Barrington*, 7th edn (Hambleton, [1792?]), p. 56. The first news of Barrington's new career arrived via the *Gorgon* in late June 1792. See *The Times*, 21 June 1792, p. 3a.

55 See Bibliography, **B10**. A printer, bookseller, stationer and bookbinder, Appleton had been trading in Darlington, in the north-eastern English county of Durham, from about 1779. In common with many regional eighteenth-century traders, Appleton ran a multifaceted business embracing book trade and other retail activities, and he was known for his prolific production of chapbooks and broadsides on matters of local interest. About 1801, Appleton began a concurrent business in the town of Stockton, and from 1806 to 1809 was trading there in partnership with his son John. After Appleton's death about 1813, the Darlington business was taken over by his widow Mary, who, on her own death in 1826, bequeathed her bookbinding and printing tools to her son John – to be for his life and then to be passed on to her grandson Thomas William Appleton. John Appleton carried on the family's traditional business until 1847, producing numerous chapbooks and broadside ballads. See C. J. Hunt, *The Book Trade in Northumberland and Durham to 1860* (Newcastle: Thorn's Students' Bookshop, 1975), p. 4.

56 *The Life and Extraordinary Adventures of George Barrington* (Darlington, W. A., [179–?]), p. 8.

57 See Bibliography, **B7**.

58 See Bibliography, **B6**, **B8**, **B9**, **B10**. Born in 1729, Robert Barker was a native of Wigan in the county of Lancashire. He completed an apprenticeship with a Liverpool shipwright, and in late 1754 enlisted to travel to Africa and the West Indies aboard the Bristol slaving ship, *Thetis*. It proved an ill-fated voyage. According to his own account, Barker was subjected to a campaign of persecution conducted by the officers of the *Thetis*, and as a result of his ill-treatment, 'contracted a very bad distemper in [his] eyes' which resulted in permanent blindness. On returning to England, Barker began printing and selling ballads based on his experience, which was followed by a sensational chapbook – *The Unfortunate Shipwright: or, Cruel Captain ...* – containing various allegations of cruelty and fraud against the captain and doctor of the *Thetis*. In 1771, Barker published a sequel to *The Unfortunate Shipwright*, in which he outlines how publicising his own story had developed into a career as an itinerant chapbook and ballad peddler, and describes the difficult life associated with this marginal profession. Barker continued to publish chapbooks, presumably in small print runs for his own sale, through the 1770s and 1780s; the August 1791 version of his *Genuine Life of George Barrington* is the last Barker publication I have been able to trace. See *The Unfortunate Shipwright: or, Cruel Captain ...* (London: Printed for, and Sold by the Sufferer [Robert Barker], for his own Benefit; and by no one else, [1759?]); and *The Second Part of the Unfortunate Shipwright; or the Blind Man's Travels Through many Parts of England, in Pursuit of his Right* (London: Robert Barker, 1771); see also Garvey, '"Under a Deceptious Mask": A Publishing History of George Barrington', PhD Thesis, vol. 2, University of Sydney, pp. 317–23.

59 See Bibliography, **B11**, **B13**, **B18**, **B19**, **B21**.

60 Protracted searching has failed to uncover any significant details about these booksellers. No address is given on any titles they published, and their books were

always chapbooks, or pirated texts, or both. Their association with the printer Alice Swindells in Manchester permits the suggestion that they were chapbook sellers based in the northern provinces of England, a theory thinly supported by the fact that the illustration in their editions of the *Genuine Life and Trial of George Barrington* was attributed to an engraver ('W. Green') in Knaresborough (North Yorkshire). This group of chapbook sellers also published a number of editions of the abridged 'Barrington' *Voyage* (see Chapter 3).

61   See Bibliography, **B11**.

62   Alice Swindells (née Anderson) had married the printer George Swindells on 15 October 1778, at the Manchester Cathedral. When George Swindells died on 1 March 1796, Alice took over the family printing and bookselling business at Hanging-Bridge, Manchester, and became a prolific producer of chapbooks. Some time in the 1820s, Alice Swindells retired in favour of her son John. See *International Genealogy Index*, online, <www.familysearch.org>, accessed 1 December 2007; *British Book Trade Index*, online, <www.bbti.bham.ac.uk>, accessed 1 December 2007.

63   Although the Swindells-printed *Genuine Life of George Barrington* chapbooks are all undated, watermark dates on the paper of some copies show that editions were being produced in the later 1790s and 1800s. See Bibliography, **B19**, **B21**.

64   Wosencroft was in business at various addresses in Liverpool, conducting a mix of book trade and non-book trade activities from about 1763 to 1796. See *British Book Trade Index*, online, <www.bbti.bham.ac.uk>, accessed 1 December 2007.

65   *The Life of George Barrington (King of the Pickpockets)* ... (Liverpool: Charles Wosencroft, 1791), p. 115.

66   See Bibliography, **AB17** and **AB21a-b**; see also Chapter 3.

67   For Jones and his role in publishing the allonymous 'Barrington' works, see Chapter 3.

68   See Bibliography, **AB30**, also **AB34**, **AB48**.

69   See Bibliography, **B18**.

70   Cundee was born in 1771, the son of a London watchmaker who lived near the Old Bailey, and was apprenticed to a local printer, John Rider, in 1786. By 1799 he had established his own printery (sometimes known as the 'Albion Press') in Ivy Lane, between Newgate Street and Paternoster Row, where he traded until 1817. He died in Buckinghamshire in 1831. See RWCS, *Apprentice Registers 1763–1786*, microfilm, reel 36; *International Genealogy Index*, online, <www.familysearch.org>, accessed 1 December 2007; William B. Todd, *A Directory of Printers and Others in Allied Trades: London and Vicinity 1800–1840* (London: Printing Historical Society, 1972), p. 51; *The Times*, 15 November 1831, p. 4c.

71   'A Student of the Inner Temple', *attrib.*, *The Criminal Recorder; or Biographical Sketches of Notorious Public Characters*, 3 vols (London: James Cundee ... and T. Hurst, and H. D. Symonds, 1804–1809). The Barrington biography summarised from the Kearsley *Memoirs* appears in volume 1, pages 38–40, along with a handsomely engraved portrait. The 'Newgate Calendar' was a broad series of works that bore that phrase as part of their title; they proliferated to the extent that they could be said to define a genre of criminal biography. See 'The Newgate Calendar: Bibliographical Note', online, <www.exclassics.com/newgate/ngbibl.htm>, accessed 1 December 2007.

72   G. H. Wilson, *attrib.*, The *Eccentric Mirror: Reflecting a Faithful and Interesting Delineation of Male and Female Characters, Ancient and Modern*, 4 vols (London: J. Cundee, 1807). The article on Barrington is in volume 4, pages 16–31.

73   Jonah Nuttall (d. 1837), Henry Fisher (1781–1837) and Francis Dixon (1763–1818) were in partnership, trading as printers, publishers, booksellers and newsagents, in Liverpool from 1807 to 1818. From about 1814 the style of the firm changed to Nuttall, Fisher and Co.; Francis Dixon may have retired prior to his death in 1818. In 1821, a fire destroyed the presses and stock in trade of the remaining partners, who relocated to London. See *British Book Trade Index*, online, <www.bbti.bham.ac.uk>, accessed 1 December 2007.

74   This work, attributed to 'Andrew Knapp and William Baldwin, Attornies-at-Law', was republished in 1824–1826 as *The Newgate Calendar*. The work under the latter title is often referred to as an important landmark in the history of the 'Newgate Calendar' as a genre, yet it was clearly an update of the Cundee *Criminal Chronology* of 1809–1810, which itself was plagiarised from earlier sources. The publisher of the 1824–1826 *Newgate Calendar* was James Robins, at the Albion Press in Ivy Lane – this had previously been Cundee's press, and Robins presumably purchased the latter's stock as well as his business when he bought him out about 1818. See *British Book Trade Index*, online, <www.bbti.bham.ac.uk>, accessed 1 December 2007.

75   'William Jackson', *attrib.*, *The New and Complete Newgate Calendar, or, Malefactor's Universal Register* … (London: Alexander Hogg & Co. and G. Offor and Sons, 1818). Hogg had his own putative 'Barrister at Law', one 'William Jackson', to whom he had also attributed his *New and Complete Newgate Calendar; Or, Villainy Displayed* (c. 1795), though much of that work was taken from Hogg's even earlier (and anonymous) *Malefactor's Register; or, the Newgate and Tyburn Calendar*, of 1779.

76   That is, the biography that appears in *The Malefactor's Register; or, the Newgate and Tyburn Calendar*, vol. 5 (London: Alexander Hogg, [1779]), pp. 235–40.

77   See Bibliography, **B22a-b**. William Mason, a noted publisher of bluebooks in the 1820s, traded in the Clerkenwell area from about 1809, with the firm still in existence as late as the 1860s. See Todd, *A Directory of Printers*, p. 128; see also Trevor H. Hall and Percy H. Muir, *Some Printers and Publishers of Conjuring Books and Other Ephemera* (Leeds: Elmete Press, 1976), pp. 69–70.

78   Cf. *Genuine Life of George Barrington* (Barker, 1790), p. 5; *Life, Amours and Wonderful Adventures of George Barrington* (London: W. Mason, [1820]), p. 3.

79   Ferguson, *Bibliography of Australia*, vol. 1, pp. 29–30 [F61].

80   See Bibliography, **B23**. John Fairburn, the son of a map and printseller of the same name, was in business as a bookseller and publisher specialising in bluebooks in the Minories, near the Tower of London, from about 1817 to 1830. See Todd, *A Directory of Printers*, p. 67; also Hall and Muir, *Some Printers and Publishers*, pp. 68–69.

81   Ferguson, *Bibliography of Australia*, vol. 1, pp. 150–51 [F384]. According to Todd, Fairburn was in business at the address given on the title page of this work from 1820 (*A Directory of Printers*, p. 67). A copy of this work in the collection of the National Library of Australia in its original paper wrappers carries an advertisement (on the back wrapper) for *Fairburn's Wonderful Songster for 1829* (see NLA SR 364.162092 B276F).

82   The conclusion of Fairburn's *Life, Amours and Wonderful Adventures of George Barrington* includes some text derived from the preface of the 1810 *Account of a Voyage*. See Bibliography, **B23** and **AB48**.

83   A manuscript copy of this work survives in the Pettingell Collection at Templeman Library and is signed by the apparent author – 'J. Watkin [?], 20 Anderson Buildings, City Road' (Pett MSS.B.19). See *The Popular Stage: Drama in Nineteenth Century England: the Frank Pettingell Collection of Plays in the Library of the University of Kent at Canterbury*, microfilm, series one (Brighton: Harvester, 1985–1987). A number of playbills also survive; besides the playbill in the Ferguson collection (now in the collection of the National Library of Australia: F/Broadside F1626), playbills from various performances at the Surrey appear in the microfilmed collection of the Victoria and Albert Museum. See *Playbills and Programmes from the London Theatres, 1801–1900 in the Theatre Museum, London*, microfilm (Cambridge: Chadwyck-Healy, 1983–).

84   See R. H. Horne and Charles Dickens, 'Shakespeare and Newgate', [*Household Words*, 4 October 1851], Harry Stone, ed., *The Uncollected Writings of Charles Dickens: Household Words 1850–1859*, vol. 1 (London: Allen Lane, 1969), p. 344.

85   Qtd in William G. Knight, *A Major London 'Minor': The Surrey Theatre 1805–1865* (London: Society for Theatre Research, 1997), p. 86. Osbaldiston's fare may have been popular, however: the comment 'overwhelming the bargemen' implies that theatregoers were crossing to the Surrey side from the more fashionable West End theatres. For Osbaldiston (1795–1850), see Dwayne Brenna, 'A Scandalous Affair and a Buried Actor–Manager: Revisionist History and the Life of David Webster Osbaldiston', *Proceedings of Hawaii International Conference on Arts and Humanities*, 2003, online, <www.hichumanities.org/AHproceedings/Dwayne%20Brenna.pdf>, accessed 1 December 2007.

86   See Bibliography, **B24** and **B25**.

87   Edward Duncombe (1802?–1859) had established himself in the London book trade by 1828, and from 1829 to about 1835 was located in Middle Row, Holborn. By 1839 Duncombe was trading from a shop at 78 Long Acre, at the intersection of Long Acre and Drury Lane. This shop bore the sign of 'John Wilson and Co.', and a press was also registered to 'John Wilson' at the same address. However, in late 1839 Duncombe was revealed as the proprietor of this business in court after he began attracting the attention of the Society for the Suppression of Vice, for 'expos[ing] to public view certain disgusting pictures in the window, as frontispieces to works which were equally disgusting and immoral' (*The Times*, 23 November 1839, p. 7b). Over the course of his career Duncombe would have several further legal entanglements over the nature of the works he sold. See Iain McCalman, *Radical Underworld: Prophets, Revolutionaries and Pornographers in London, 1795–1840* (Cambridge: Cambridge University Press, 1988), pp. 42, 58–60; Pisanus Fraxi [Henry Spencer Ashbee], *Bibliography of Prohibited Books [Index Librorum Prohibitoru, 1877]*, vol. 1 (New York: Jack Brussel, 1962), p. 137; Todd, *A Directory of Printers*, pp. 61, 214; see also *The Times*, 14 January 1843, p. 7a.

88   George Stiff (1807–1873) was an engraver who rose to prominence as a newspaper proprietor after establishing the vastly successful illustrated penny paper, the *London Journal*, in 1845. According to Louis James' *ODNB* entry on Stiff, he was first known to

be in London between 1844 and 1845, when he was supervising the engraving department for the *Illustrated London News*. However it is certainly possible that Stiff had been in London working as an engraver earlier than this. If the 'John Wilson' who published the *Life, Times and Adventures of George Barrington* was in fact Edward Duncombe, the most likely time of publication was around 1840. See Louis James, 'Stiff, George (1807–1873), engraver and newspaper proprietor', *ODNB*, online, <www.oxforddnb.com>, accessed 1 December 2007.

89   *The Life, Times and Adventures of George Barrington* (London: 'John Wilson'), pp. 19–20.
90   ibid., pp. 23, 34–36, 41–42.
91   ibid., pp. 50–66.

CHAPTER 3

1   John Turnbull, *A Voyage Round the World*, 2nd edn, vol. 1 (London: A. Maxwell, 1813), pp. 81–82. See also Pierre Bernard Millius's description of Barrington in 1802, qtd in Suzanne Rickard, ed., *George Barrington's Voyage to Botany Bay: Retelling a Convict's Travel Narrative of the 1790s* (London: Leicester University Press, 2001), p. 52; and Pamela Jean Fulton, ed., *The Minerva Journal of John Washington Price: A Voyage from Cork, Ireland, to Sydney, New South Wales, 1798–1800* (Melbourne: Melbourne University Press, 2000), p. 150.

2   *The Sydney Gazette, and New South Wales Advertiser*, 30 December 1804, pp. 1c, 4c, facs. edn, vol. 1 (Sydney: Trustees of the Public Library in assoc. with Angus and Robertson, 1963).

3   See 'Preface to the Reader', *An Account of a Voyage to New South Wales* (London: M. Jones and Sherwood, Neely and Jones, 1810), [n.p.]; see also Bibliography, **AB30**.

4   Barrington, who was appointed a constable by the colony's first governor, Arthur Phillip, received an absolute pardon from Phillip's replacement, John Hunter, in September 1796. See F. M. Bladen, ed., *Historical Records of New South Wales*, vol. 3 (Sydney: Government Printer, 1895), p. 75; and John Cobley, ed., *Sydney Cove 1795–1800* (London: Angus and Robertson, 1986), p. 101.

5   The Marines detachment that had been sent to the colony with the First Fleet was withdrawn in 1792 and replaced by the New South Wales Corps. For a fuller discussion of the founding of the first police force, and the role of convict officials generally, see Nathan Garvey, 'Reviewing Australia's First Performance: *The Recruiting Officer* in Sydney, 1789', *Australasian Drama Studies*, vol. 40, 2002, pp. 30, 38.

6   David Collins, *An Account of the English Colony in New South Wales*, facs. edn, vol. 1 (Adelaide: Libraries Board of South Australia, 1971), p. 244. For Collins (1756–1810), see especially John Currey, *David Collins: A Colonial Life* (Melbourne: Melbourne University Press, 2000).

7   This letter is reprinted in Geoffrey C. Ingleton, ed., *True Patriots All: Or News from Early Australia As Told in a Collection of Broadsides* (Sydney: Angus and Robinson, 1952), pp. 10, 260. It is dated 11 November 1791 – Barrington had only arrived (on the *Active*) on 20 September that year.

8   *The Times*, 22 June 1792, p. 3a.

9   For Phillip (1738–1814), see especially Alan Frost, *Arthur Phillip, 1738–1814: His Voyaging* (Melbourne: Oxford University Press, 1987).

10   *Annual Register*, vol. 35, 1793, p. 28. This paragraph was also printed in *The Sunday Reformer*, 23 June 1793, p. 2c.

11   *Annual Register*, vol. 35, 1793, p. 28.

12   Watkin Tench, *Complete Account of the Settlement at Port Jackson* (London: G. Nicol and J. Sewell, 1793), p. 156, also p. 136 [hereafter *Complete Account*]. Tench had arrived back in England with the Marine detachment on the *Gorgon* in July 1792, and seems to have spent at least part of the remainder of that year revising his colonial journals for publication. See Nathan Garvey, 'Selling a Penal Colony: The Booksellers and Botany Bay', *Script and Print*, vol. 31, no. 1, 2007, pp. 32–33. For Tench (1758/9–1833), see L. F. Fitzhardinge, 'Tench, Watkin (1758?–1833)', *Australian Dictionary of Biography* [hereafter *ADB*], vol. 2 (Melbourne: Melbourne University Press, 1967), pp. 506–07; see also Adrian Mitchell, 'Watkin Tench's Sentimental Enclosures: Original Relations from the First Settlement', *Australian and New Zealand Studies in Canada*, vol. 11, 1994, pp. 23–33.

13   See Bibliography, **AB1**. The earliest reference I have traced is an advertisement for the work in the *Morning Post* of 27 March 1795 (p. 1b).

14   For the 'imaginary voyage' as a genre, see especially Philip Babcock Gove, *The Imaginary Voyage in Prose Fiction: a History of its Criticism and a Guide for its Study* (New York: Columbia Press, 1941). The spurious travelogues of the eighteenth century, of course, themselves stemmed from a speculative tradition of considerable antiquity. See, for example, David Faucett's fascinating account of early 'Austral fiction' in *Writing the New World: Imaginary Voyages and Utopias of the Great Southern Land* (Syracuse, NY: Syracuse University Press, 1993).

15   John Hunter, *An Historical Journal of the Transactions at Port Jackson and Norfolk Island ...* (London: John Stockdale, 1792) [hereafter *Historical Journal* – page numbers refer to the first (quarto) edition]. Although Hunter was credited as the main author of the work, the *Historical Journal* also included a significant amount of material (primarily detailing events at Norfolk Island) written by Phillip Gidley King; both Hunter and King gained some benefit for their reputations through this prestigious publication, and both would go on to become governors of New South Wales. The journals of Hunter and King were edited for publication by George Chalmers, a Scottish lawyer and writer of pro-Pitt pamphlets, and the work was published by John Stockdale, a Piccadilly bookseller with significant connections to the Pitt ministry – in some senses the *Historical Journal* was a sequel to the official account of the Botany Bay expedition, *The Voyage of Governor Phillip to Botany Bay* (London: Stockdale, 1789). For further detail on the publishing history of the *Historical Journal* and other 'Botany Bay' works, see Garvey, 'Selling a Penal Colony', pp. 21–38. For Hunter, see J. J. Auchmuty, 'Hunter, John 1737–1821', *ADB*, vol. 1, pp. 566–72; and for King, see A. G. L. Shaw, 'King, Phillip Gidley (1758–1808)', *ADB*, vol. 2, pp. 55–61.

16   The work of Iain McCalman has been particularly influential in elucidating the milieu of Symonds and other radical booksellers of the late eighteenth century. See especially 'Newgate in Revolution: Radical Enthusiasm and Romantic Counterculture', *Eighteenth Century Life*, vol. 22, no. 1, 1998, pp. 95–110; and 'New Jerusalems: Prophecy, Dissent and Radical Culture in England, 1786–1830', Knud Haakonssen, ed., *Enlightenment and Religion: Rational Dissent in Eighteenth-Century Britain* (Cambridge: Cambridge

University Press, 1995), pp. 312–35. See also McCalman, *Radical Underworld: Prophets, Revolutionaries, and Pornographers in London 1795–1840* (Cambridge: Cambridge University Press, 1988), p. 205; and Michael T. Davis, Iain McCalman and Christina Parolin, eds, *Newgate in Revolution: An Anthology of Radical Prison Literature in the Age of Revolution* (New York: Continuum, 2005).

17   Thomas Paine's *The Rights of Man* was first published by the influential liberal bookseller Joseph Johnson, with Symonds publishing the cheap edition in 1792 (see note 27 below). Pigott's *The Jockey Club: or, A Sketch of the Manners of the Age* was published anonymously in three parts by Symonds through 1792. A scabrous satire on the political and sexual corruption of the Georgian elites in much the same style as the French *libelles*, this work provoked the ire of the Prince of Wales, who considered it 'the most infamous & shocking libellous production yt ever disgraced the pen of man', and urged the prosecution of its producers. See A. Aspinall, ed., *The Correspondence of George, Prince of Wales 1770–1812*, vol. 2 (London: Cassell, 1963–), pp. 285–87, 298, 694n, 704n. See also Nicholas Rogers, 'Pigott's Private Eye: Radicalism and Sexual Scandal in Eighteenth-Century England', *Journal of the Canadian History Association*, vol. 4, 1993, pp. 247–63, see esp. pp. 253–57.

18   A memoir of William Winterbotham published by his grandson described the Newgate of the 1790s as a place where money could obtain 'anything short of liberty'. Winterbotham was said to have paid eight shillings a week for his cell on the State Side, with numerous additional expenses including paying the turnkeys to admit visiting friends and the payment of a female convict servant. See W. H. Winterbotham, *The Rev. William Winterbotham: A Sketch* (London: Pr. for Private Circulation, 1893).

19   See especially Henry Yorke's *These Are the Times That Try Men's Souls!* (London: Ridgway and Symonds, [1793]), title page, and advertisements following the text [6 pp.]; see also *The Times*, 25 October 1793, p. 1d.

20   See W. Longman, *Tokens of the Eighteenth Century Connected With Booksellers & Bookmakers* (London: Longmans, Green and Co., 1916), pp. 40–42.

21   John Lettsom, *Hints Respecting the Prison of Newgate* (London: Printed for the Author, 1794).

22   *The Political Progress of Britain: or, an Impartial History of the Abuses in the Government of the British Empire, in Europe, Asia, and America*, 3rd edn (Philadelphia: Richard Folwell, 1795), p. 40.

23   Symonds began trading in 1783 and was admitted to the freedom of the Stationers' Company on 2 December 1783. In October 1796, while Symonds was still in Newgate, his business suffered a blow with the death of its 'Superintendant', a Mr M. Gilbert, 'distinguished by his strict probity in his general management of business, and by his laudable diligence and fidelity to his employer'. According to C. H. Timperley, another man running the Paternoster Row shop during Symonds' Newgate years was William Sherwood, Symonds' apprentice and eventual successor, who was said to have 'served … with utmost diligence and activity' while Symonds was imprisoned. See *Records of the Worshipful Company of Stationers 1554–1923* [hereafter *RWCS*], *Court Book N, 4 Feb 1777 to 22 Dec 1785*, microfilm, reel 60; *Monthly Magazine*, November 1796, p. 532; and Timperley, *A Dictionary of Printers and Printing* (London: H. Johnson, 1839), p. 941.

24   On the changing nature of the book trade in the late eighteenth century, see William

St Clair, *The Reading Nation in the Romantic Period* (Cambridge: Cambridge University Press, 2004), esp. pp. 19–42; and James Raven, *Judging New Wealth: Popular Publishing and Responses to Commerce in England, 1750–1800* (Oxford: Clarendon Press, 1992), esp. pp. 31–82.

25   Thomas Rees, *Reminiscences of Literary London* [1896] (New York: Garland, 1974), pp. 62–63. Rees asserted that this method of business meant that 'the trade was greatly accommodated, and [Symonds'] own interest promoted' (p. 62).

26   Jonathan Wantrup, *Australian Rare Books 1788–1900* (Sydney: Hordern House, 1987), p. 87.

27   While St Clair is certainly correct in throwing a note of caution on some of the inflated estimates for the number of copies Paine's *Rights of Man* sold, he nonetheless describes the work as 'probably among the most influential of all texts printed in the Romantic period' and estimates that more than 20,000 copies were printed (see St Clair, *The Reading Nation in the Romantic Period*, pp. 256–57). According to Paine, the numerous requests he had received to make cheap reprints of the work led him to '[conclude] that the best method of complying therewith, would be to print a very numerous edition in London, under my own direction ... and the price be reduced lower than it would be by *printing* small editions in the country, of only a few thousands each'. See Moncure D. Conway, ed., *The Writings of Thomas Paine* (New York: G. P. Putnam's Sons, 1896), p. 64. Symonds boldly advertised his publication of the 'cheap Editions' of Part One and Two of the *Rights of Man* (priced at '6d, each Part, or 1l. 10s. per Hundred') in *The Times* of 13 September 1792 (p. 1c), even going so far as to identify himself as the only authorised publisher of this cheaper version of Paine's work.

28   The prosecution of Symonds seems to have generated considerable paperwork for the clerks at the office of the Treasury Solicitor. A draft indictment citing the objectionable passages in Paine's *Rights of Man* shows that a number of these passages had to be scored out and the indictment redrafted, since many were 'not in the small edn.' See 'Brief for Prosecution: The King against Henry Delahaye Symonds for a Libel in the cheap Edition of the Rights of Man', PRO TS 11/944; and 'The King v Symonds: Draft Indictment for a Libel Paine's Right of Man Cheap Ed.n', PRO TS 11/944.

29   Symonds to Attorney General, 22 February 1793, PRO TS 11/944. Symonds had married Jane Glover at Saint Michael's, Cornhill, London, on 5 October 1783, and the couple had at least three children together: Jane (b. 1784), Henry Delahay (b. 1787) and Ann (b. 1792). See *International Genealogy Index* [hereafter *IGI*], <www.familysearch.org>, accessed 1 December 2007.

30   Qtd in George Dyer, *A Dissertation on the Theory and Practice of Benevolence* (London: James Ridgway, 1795), pp. 87–90.

31   Symonds may have had in mind a further 'Barrington' narrative plagiarised from King's descriptions of Norfolk Island in the *Historical Journal*. The introductory letter in *A Voyage to New South Wales* states that 'Barrington' had 'nearly transcribed some letters from my friend, Mr. Wentworth, containing a pleasant narrative of the rise and progress of the settlement at Norfolk Island' (p. [7]).

32   Barrington, attrib., *A Voyage to New South Wales* [hereafter *Voyage*] (H. D. Symonds, 1795), pp. 13–14. Unless otherwise stated, all subsequent references are to this version of the text.

33   *Voyage*, p. 14.

34   *Voyage*, p. 15.

35   *Voyage*, p. 17.

36   See especially John Edwards, *The Story of the Voyage: Sea-Narratives in Eighteenth-Century England* (Cambridge: Cambridge University Press, 1994).

37   James Bruce (c. 1765–1806) was briefly the man of the hour on his return to England from Africa in 1774, but his amazing tales were soon discredited and ridiculed by Samuel Johnson and others. See Nigel Leask, 'Curious Narrative and the Problem of Credit: James Bruce's Travels to Discover the Source of the Nile', in *Curiosity and the Aesthetics of Travel Writing, 1770–1840* (Oxford: Oxford University Press, 2002), pp. 54–101; see also Percy G. Adams, *Travelers and Travel Liars, 1660–1800* (Berkeley: University of California Press, 1962).

38   In the Hunter *Historical Journal*, two sailors, 'both Americans, one [with] a superficial knowledge of navigation' (p. 555), were said to have aided the convicts in their plot; in the Barrington *Voyage* the conspirators were all convicts, but 'Two of them, Americans, who had some knowledge of navigation', led the plot (p. 18). Newspaper reports on the mutiny had also been published in July 1791 (see, for example, *Dublin Chronicle*, 14 July 1791, reproduced in *Historical Records of New South Wales*, vol. 2, p. 781).

39   In the *Historical Journal*, the mutiny is averted when the Master of the ship 'hearing a noise, took up a blunderbuss ... and discharged it at [the ringleader], who finding himself wounded, dropped [his] sword and ran away' (p. 554), while the *Voyage* has Barrington guarding the quarterdeck until 'the discharge of a blunderbuss from behind me among them wounded several, they retreated ...' (p. 19).

40   *Voyage*, p. 20. 'Lobscourse' is defined by the Oxford English Dictionary as 'a sailor's dish consisting of meat stewed with vegetables and ship's biscuit, or the like', while 'salt-junk' was a slang term for the rope-like, heavily salted and notoriously unappetising meat supplied on long sea voyages.

41   *Voyage*, p. 51.

42   *Voyage*, p. 52.

43   *Voyage*, p. 57.

44   Hunter wrote a glowing testimonial of Barrington's 'unremitting attention to duty' on granting him a pardon in 1796 (*HRNSW*, vol. 3, p. 74), while John Turnbull cited Barrington as one of very few examples of a convict who had reformed in the colony. See *HRNSW*, vol. 3, p. 74; Turnbull, *A Voyage Round the World*, vol. 3 (London: Richard Phillips, 1805), p. 42.

45   There is one caveat to this: a single paragraph on page 127 of the *Voyage*, detailing the poor condition of the Third Fleet convicts on landing, is drawn from a source other than the *Historical Journal*, possibly a newspaper report. For further discussion of this point, see my dissertation, '"Under a Deceptious Mask": A Publishing History of George Barrington', (PhD, University of Sydney, 2007), vol. 1, pp. 200–03. In the context of the work, this is a very minor point, however. For a detailed, chapter-by-chapter analysis of the sources of the *Voyage*, see '"Under a Deceptious Mask"', vol. 1, p. 199; see also Rickard, ed., *George Barrington's Voyage to Botany Bay*, pp. 32, 69–156.

46   Peter Rye, *An Excursion to the Peak of Teneriffe in 1791* ... (London: Robert Faulder, 1793). Rye was a naval lieutenant on the *Gorgon*. Rickard notes that the description in

the *Voyage* was 'likely to have been plagiarized' from this source (Rickard, ed., *George Barrington's Voyage to Botany Bay*, p. 126n), but it is possible to be more emphatic: the *Voyage* even preserves the same tour guide from Rye's narrative: 'an old Spanish soldier, who had been some time a prisoner in England' (*Voyage*, pp. 21–22; cf. Rye, p. 12).

47   The English version of Francois Le Vaillant's work was translated by Elizabeth Helme and published as *Travels from the Cape of Good-Hope, into the Interior Parts of Africa ...*, 2 vols (London: William Lane, 1790). Rickard has missed this source, describing the two chapters on the Cape as 'entirely fictional' (Rickard, ed., *George Barrington's Voyage to Botany Bay*, p. 33, also pp. 39, 127–28n). A close reading of the two texts, however, makes it clear where 'Barrington's' adventures at the Cape were drawn from. Compare, for example, the description of the marriage ceremonies of the Khoikhoi or 'Hottentots' (Le Vaillant, trans. Helme, *Travels from the Cape of Good-Hope*, vol. 2, pp. 65, 69–70; cf. *Voyage*, p. 43).

48   For Bennelong (1764?–1813) in particular, and Eora society at the time of the English invasion generally, see Keith Vincent Smith, *Bennelong: The Coming in of the Eora Sydney Cove 1788–1792* (Sydney: Kangaroo Press, 2001).

49   *Voyage*, pp. 129–39. This was perhaps the first occurrence of what would later become a very familiar trope in nineteenth-century Australian literature.

50   *Voyage*, p. 133.

51   *Voyage*, p. 134. Palerino is at first referred to as 'the deceased', though he comes back to life before the end of the same sentence.

52   *Voyage*, p. 135.

53   John Hawkesworth's *An Account of the Voyages Undertaken by the Order of His Present Majesty, for making Discoveries in the Southern Hemisphere ...*, 3 vols (London: W. Strahan and T. Cadell, 1773) caused something of a sensation for its depiction of Tahiti, and the sexual trade between European voyagers and Tahitian women. See especially Neil Rennie, *Far-Fetched Facts: The Literature of Travel and the Idea of the South Seas* (Oxford: Clarendon Press, 1995), pp. 83–108.

54   *Voyage*, p. 136.

55   *Voyage*, p. 139.

56   See Garvey, 'Selling a Penal Colony', pp. 23–29. For Stockdale (c. 1749–1814) see especially Eric Stockdale's recent biography *'Tis Treason My Good Man! Four Revolutionary Presidents and a Piccadilly Bookshop* (New Castle, DE: Oak Knoll; London, The British Library, 2005).

57   'History and Character of Stockdale the Bookseller', *The Intrepid Magazine* (London: Ridgway, 1784), pp. 53–56.

58   Another traveller on the *Gorgon*, Mary Ann Parker, noted that 'on [Rye's] return to England, his excursion was published; and I recommend it to the perusal of my readers'. See Deirdre Coleman, ed., *Maiden Voyages and Infant Colonies: Two Women's Travel Narratives of the 1790s* (London: Leicester University Press, 1998), p. 188.

59   See *Complete Account*, e.g. pp. 61–70; *Historical Journal*, p. 479.

60   Rickard, ed., *George Barrington's Voyage to Botany Bay*, p. 155. In the Tench *Complete Account*, Gooreedeena is portrayed as a similarly unique specimen of Aboriginal womanhood: 'She excelled in beauty all their females I ever saw... [her] countenance

… was distinguished by a softness and sensibility, unequalled in the rest of her countrywomen: and I was willing to believe, that these traits indicated the disposition of her mind' (pp. 180–81).

61   William Winterbotham's plagiarised work on America was published in parts in late 1794, and subsequently collected as *An Historical, Geographical, Commercial and Philosophical View of the American United States …*, 4 vols (London: Printed for the Editor; Ridway … Symonds … and Holt, 1795). In October 1794, Stockdale wrote to Jedidiah Morse, whose *American Geography* (new ed., Stockdale, 1794) was one of the works Winterbotham had plundered, letting him know that 'three persons confined in Newgate are publishing in numbers the *Geography*'. After checking the work, Morse discovered that Winterbotham had also taken material from David Ramsay's *History of the American Revolution* (J. Johnson and Stockdale, 1791), Thomas Jefferson's *Notes on the State of Virginia* (Stockdale, 1787) and Benjamin Franklin's *Two Tracts: Information to Those Who Would Remove to America* (Stockdale, 1784). See Eric Stockdale, *'Tis Treason My Good Man!*, pp. 327–31.

62   In addition to the *Historical, Geographical, Commercial and Philosophical View of the American United States*, Winterbotham also produced in 1795 *An Historical, Geographical and Philosophical View of the Chinese Empire*, published by Ridgway and W. Button.

63   *Letters from Mr. Fletcher Christian, containing a Narrative of the Transactions on board His Majesty's Ship Bounty, before and after the Mutiny, with his subsequent Voyages and Travels in South America* (London: Symonds, 1796) was advertised in *The Times* on 25 August 1796 (p. 2a).

64   See Caroline Alexander, *The Bounty: The True Story of the Mutiny on the Bounty* (London: Harper Perennial, 2003), pp. 343–45.

65   ibid., p. 344.

66   A brief examination reveals at least two of the sources of *Letters from Mr. Fletcher Christian*: John Luffman's *A Brief Account of the Island of Antigua* (London: T. Cadell, 1789) (compare pp. 158–59 with *Letters*, p. 147); and John Adams' translation of Antonio de Ulloa's *A Voyage to South America*, 3rd edn (London: Lockyer Davis, 1772) (cf. vol. 1, pp. 204–05 with *Letters*, pp. 154–55).

67   Wordsworth's letter, dated 23 October 1796, was published in the *Weekly Entertainer* of 7 November. See J. R. MacGillivray, 'An Early Poem and Letter by Wordsworth', *Review of English Studies*, vol. 17, 1954, pp. 62–66.

68   E. A. Petherick, *The Athenaeum*, 12 February 1898, pp. 22–23; also *Notes and Queries*, 9th ser., 2, November 1898), p. 404.

69   The play mentioned by Petherick was *The Man with Two Wives; or, Wigs For Ever!* (London: Printed for the Author … and H. D. Symonds, 1798), a dramatic version of an Aesop fable. Waldron was also the editor, along with Charles Dibdin, of the short-lived theatrical journal, *How Do You Do?*, published by Thomas Longman and Symonds in 1796.

70   See Trevor R. Griffiths, 'Waldron, Francis Godolphin (bap. 1742, d. 1818), actor and playwright', *ODNB*, online, <www.oxforddnb.com>, accessed 1 December 2007.

71   At the time of the publication of the *Voyage*, Waldron was performing as Tubal in *The Merchant of Venice*, to J. P. Kemble's Shylock and Sarah Siddons' Portia. See Charles

Beecher Hogan, ed., *The London Stage 1660–1800*, vol. 2, part 5: 1776–1800, pp. 694–97.

72   Hastings, a hack writer and itinerant bookseller, was described in one publication as among the 'principal literary *fags*, or labourers of the day'. See 'Memoirs of Henry Lemoine, the well-known Literary, Pedestrian and Eccentric Bookseller and Author, of the City of London', *The New, Original and Complete Wonderful Museum and Magazine Extraordinary*, vol. 5 (London: Alexander Hogg & Co., 1807), pp. 2221–22. See also H. R. Tedder [*rev.* Rebecca Mills], 'Hastings, Thomas (1741–1801), pamphleteer', *ODNB*, online, <www.oxforddnb.com>, accessed 1 December 2007; and Garvey, '"Under a Deceptious Mask"', vol. 2, pp. 242, 247.

73   See 'Memoirs of Henry Lemoine', p. 2232. For further information and bibliography of sources on Lemoine, see David Goldthorpe, 'Lemoine, Henry (1756–1812), author and bookseller', *ODNB*, online, <www.oxforddnb.com>, accessed 1 December 2007.

74   The main publisher of the *Conjuror's Magazine* was William Locke, who had also been the publisher of the *Attic Miscellany*, which Lemoine was also involved in editing. See Chapter 2, and 'Memoirs of Henry Lemoine', pp. 2228–29.

75   McCalman points out that besides the *Conjuror's Magazine*, Lemoine also edited 'a series of fugitive periodicals like the *Wonderful Magazine* [1793–1798] … which attempted to publicise the wonders of both occult and rational-empiricist science' ('New Jerusalems', p. 318, also pp. 317–19).

76   The 'Memoirs of Henry Lemoine' claimed that 'of the first numbers … 10000 were sold each month' (p. 2229); see also McCalman, 'New Jerusalems', pp. 317–19.

77   Both these works were entered at the Stationers' Hall. *Le Petit Sorcier* was registered as the property of 'The Author and H. D. Symonds' on 5 December 1791, while the *Oneirocritic* was entered as the property of Symonds alone on 4 November 1795. See *RWCS Entries of Copies, 1786–1792* [reel 7]; *1793–1796* [reel 8].

78   See 'Memoirs of Henry Lemoine', pp. 2218–40.

79   ibid., p. 2230.

80   ibid., p. 2228.

81   ibid., p. 2239.

82   In his recent survey of 'crossing the line' ceremonies through the centuries, Simon J. Bronner indicates that elaborate ceremonies of the kind described in the *Voyage to New South Wales* were a fairly recent development in the late eighteenth century, likening the proceedings to 'a nautical version of an English mumming play'. See Bronner, *Crossing the Line: Violence, Play, and Drama in Naval Equator Traditions* (Amsterdam: Amsterdam University Press, 2006), pp. 41–42.

83   See *Voyage*, pp. 25–27. This was apparently a popular section of the *Voyage* narrative: the 'crossing the line' episode was published as an extract (from 'Barrington's Account of a Voyage to Botany-Bay') in the *Oracle and Public Examiner* of 19 October 1795 (p. 2b), and the *Weekly Entertainer, or Agreeable and Instructive Repository* of 26 October 1795 (p. 321).

84   *Voyage*, pp. 25–27. 'Ducking' meant being attached by a rope to the main yard arm and dunked three times into the sea. See Bronner, *Crossing the Line*, p. 40.

85   The 1820s and 1830s saw the rise to popularity of the *Flying Dutchman* myth in both popular and high culture. See J. Q. Davies, 'Melodramatic Possessions: *The Flying*

Dutchman, South Africa, and the Imperial Stage, ca. 1830', *Opera Quarterly*, vol. 21, no. 3, 2005, pp. 496–514; and Willard Hallam Bonner, 'The Flying Dutchman of the Western World', *Journal of American Folklore*, vol. 59, 1946, pp. 282–88.

86   *Voyage*, pp. 46–47.

87   *New Lights from the World of Darkness; or The Midnight Messenger; with Solemn Signals from the World of the Spirits* (London: Ann Lemoine, 1800). This work has not been previously attributed to Henry Lemoine, but it bears a marked similarity in form and content to other Lemoine works, such as *Visits from the World of Spirits* (London: Levi Wayland, 1791), and was published by Lemoine's estranged wife Ann, a bookseller with whom he retained a trade connection. See also Franz J. Potter, *The History of Gothic Publishing 1800–1835: Exhuming the Trade* (Houndmills, Basingstoke: Palgrave Macmillan, 2005), pp. 44–45.

88   *Voyages and Travels of Fletcher Christian* (London: Printed for H. Lemoine, 1798). At two shillings, Lemoine was selling the work at 1s. 6d. less than the advertised price of Symonds' edition, and his version apparently lacked the frontispiece illustration found in Symonds' edition.

89   *Gentleman's Magazine*, vol. 66, 1795, p. 760

90   *Monthly Review*, vol. 18, [new ser.], December 1795, pp. 474–75.

91   *Monthly Review*, vol. 10 [new ser.], April 1793, p. 426. The allusion is to 'grub street' compilations made by those with no first-hand experience of the subjects of their narratives.

92   William Wales (1734–1798) was a mathematician and astronomer who had been on James Cook's last two Pacific voyages. Wales was writing for the *Monthly Review* from the late 1770s, and reviewed the 'First Fleet' journals of Hunter and Tench, and the *Voyage of Governor Phillip to Botany Bay*. See Benjamin Christie Nangle, ed., *The Monthly Review, Second Series, 1790–1815: Indexes of Contributors and Articles* (Oxford: Clarendon, 1955), pp. 70, 143, 211, 220, 225.

93   See Nangle, ed., *The Monthly Review, Second Series, 1790–1815*, p. 10. Though noted for his rough manners and unconventional views, James Burney (1750–1821), son of the noted musician and author Charles Burney and brother of the novelist Frances Burney, moved in exalted literary and social circles. He was a friend of Samuel Johnson, and later of Charles Lamb, William Hazlitt and Robert Southey, and also maintained a connection with Sir Joseph Banks and the scientific community. After his naval career ended in 1784, Burney turned to literary pursuits. In 1791 he edited for publication the journal of another friend, William Bligh, as *A Voyage to the South Sea ... in HMS Bounty* (London: G. Nicol, 1792), and from 1803 to 1817 he published the five volumes of his major work, *A Chronological History of the Discoveries in the South Sea or Pacific Ocean* (London: G. and W. Nicol), which described the history of Pacific exploration up to Cook's voyages. See Lars Troide, 'Burney, James (1750–1824), naval officer and writer', *ODNB*, online, <www.oxforddnb.com>, accessed 1 December 2007.

94   Lars Troide states that Burney's naval career was curtailed 'in part because of his openly republican political views' (*ODNB*).

95   The review of the *Voyage* is not specifically attributed in Nangle's indexes to the *Monthly Review*.

96   Stockdale had registered his copyrights to the Hunter work at the Stationers' Hall on 18 January 1793 (*RWCS Entries of Copies* 1792–1795, reel 8).

97   This comment was made about the William Winterbotham work which plagiarised Stockdale's books on America, in a letter to Jedidiah Morse of 5 August 1795. See Eric Stockdale, *'Tis Treason My Good Man*, p. 332.

98   See Bibliography, **AB41**.

99   A 'puff' promoting the *Sequel* to Barrington's *Voyage*, which appeared in an untraced British newspaper about 1801, praised the work as 'highly entertaining to every class of readers'. See 'Biographical Cuttings on George Barrington, convict', National Library of Australia.

100   In addition to the advertisement which appeared in the *Morning Post* of 27 March, advertisements for Symonds' first edition of the *Voyage* appeared in *The Times* of 10 April (p. 3a), the *True Briton* of 19 May (p. 2a), and *The Star* of 19 September (p. 1a).

101   As one modern commentator put it: Symonds 'ministered to the half-crown folk'. See Moncure D. Conway, ed., 'Editor's Introduction', *The Age of Reason: Being an Investigation of True and Fabulous Theology* (New York: G. P. Putnam's Sons, 1896), p. 29. See also Garvey, '"Under a Deceptious Mask"', vol. 2, pp. 235–50.

102   See Bibliography, **AB2**.

103   For Thomas Walker (fl. 1791–1800), see Timperley, *A Dictionary of Printers and Printing*, p. 791.

104   *Voyage to New South Wales* ('London: Printed for the Proprietors' [Preston: T. Walker], 1795), p. 32.

105   St Clair, *The Reading Nation in the Romantic Period*, p. 348, see also pp. 339–56.

106   For the editions of the abridged *Voyage*, and a more specific discussion of their individual features and relationships, see the Bibliography, **AB2**, **AB3**, **AB4**, **AB5**, **AB6**, **AB11**, **AB13**, **AB14**, **AB15**, **AB16**, **AB24**, **AB25**, **AB46**.

107   Three different editions of Hambleton's *Voyage to New South Wales* have survived, including nominal fifth and sixth editions. See Bibliography, **AB3**, **AB4**, **AB5**.

108   See Bibliography, **AB6**, **AB11**, **AB13**, **AB15**, **AB16**, **AB46**, and **B11**, **B13**, **B18**, **B19**, **B21**.

109   St Clair, describing the chapbook trade in the earlier eighteenth century, asserts that 'the minimum print run was a ream, or half a ream, equivalent to editions of 1,000 or 2,000 for chapbooks' (p. 340). The *Barrington's Voyage to New South Wales* chapbooks were, however, 48 pages long – about twice as long as a standard early eighteenth-century chapbook – permitting the suggestion that the minimum print runs would have been 500 to 1,000 copies.

110   See Bibliography, **AB24** and **AB25**. Like Alice Swindells in Manchester, Margaret Angus (d. 1821) was a printer's widow who would carry on the family business after her husband's death, and pass it on to her sons. Margaret (née Marshall) married Thomas Angus at the historic St Nicholas's Church in Newcastle-upon-Tyne on 4 August 1773. By the following year, Thomas Angus had established himself as a printer on 'Trinity Corner, St. Nicholas' Church-yard', where he traded until his death in 1788. Thomas and Margaret Angus were of Scottish extraction; their son George (1782–1829) was baptised at the Presbyterian Groat Market Meeting in Newcastle. Their elder son, Thomas (1773–1808), may have begun an apprenticeship under his father, but the latter's early death meant that the greater part of both sons' instruction in the printing and bookselling trades was carried out under the supervision of Margaret Angus. The

firm operated from an address in Drury Lane, Newcastle, in 1790, and by 1795 Margaret Angus had settled as a 'printer and bookseller' in The Side – a location the firm would occupy for thirty years. By 1801 she had taken her elder son, Thomas, into partnership. An advertisement placed in the *Newcastle Chronicle* in late 1808 stated that 'owing to the lamented Death of her son Thomas, [Margaret Angus] has taken her son George (who has had the sole Management for some time past) into Partnership'. The partnership was 'amicably dissolved' at the end of 1812, and George Angus continued the business on his own. The younger Angus son ran into financial trouble in the years of depression following the Napoleonic Wars, and ceased trading about 1825. See *IGI*, online, <www.familysearch.org>, accessed 1 December 2007; *British Book Trade Index*, online, <www.bbti.bham.ac.uk>, accessed 1 December 2007; and Frances M. Thompson, *Newcastle Chapbooks in Newcastle upon Tyne University Library* (Newcastle-upon-Tyne: Oriel Press, 1969), pp. 23–24.

111   See Bibliography, **AB46**.

112   Susan (d. 1810) and John Bailey, mother and son, were members of a family of printers who had been established in the trade in London from the early eighteenth century. Susan (née Hawes) had married William Bailey, printer, at St Katherine's Creechurch in the City of London in 1767. Various sources give an account of the diverse business William and his family ran at the sign of 'the little a' in Bishopsgate Street in the 1780s and 1790s. One of William Bailey's publications, *The Oddest of all Oddities* (1790), carried an advertisement for his firm written in verse in which he advertised his services in the line of jobbing printing – in the production of shop bills and trade cards – and as a music printer, teacher and musical instrument seller. He also offered poetical and musical composition services:

> Your Shop Bills also at any Time,
> You may have put into jingling Rhime ...
> And those fir'd with Poetic Wit,
> May have their Works to Music set.

William Bailey died some time in the mid-1790s, and his widow Susan took over the family business, maintaining much the same diverse range of printing and retail services that William had offered. William and Susan's son, John Norton Bailey, had been accepted into the freedom of the Stationers' Company (as a printer) in 1795, although he does not seem to have established himself in the trade independently until 1799, when he began trading at 55 East Smithfield, the address at which he appears on the imprint for the 'Barrington' *Impartial and Circumstantial Narrative*. John Bailey would later settle at 116 Chancery Lane, where he became a notable publisher of gothic bluebooks and similar cheap works. Susan and John Bailey were not known to have co-published any other works besides the *Impartial and Circumstantial Narrative*. Susan died in 1810 – her will left only '£5 in mourning' to John and her other son Thomas. The rest of her estate, including 'the whole of my Printing Business together with all Implements Staff in Trade Music in the Shop and every thing thereunto belonging', was to be divided equally between her daughters, Mary Ann Dean and Anna Maria Munday, and the will stipulated that her daughters' inheritance was 'for their own sole use and benefit absolutely not to be subject of Controul of any present or future husbands debts'. It was difficult to ensure a female succession in the early nineteenth-century business world, however. While the firm of Dean and Munday prospered, it came to be particularly identified with Susan Bailey's sons-in-law, Thomas Dean and Thomas Munday. See *IGI*, online, <www.familysearch.org>, accessed 1 December 2007; *BBTI* online, <www.bbti.bham.ac.uk>, accessed 1 December 2007; Odicurious, [pseud.], *The Oddest of All Oddities* (W. Bailey, 1790), see also repr. (S. Bailey, 1797); William B. Todd, *A Directory of Printers and Others in Allied Trades: London and Vicinity 1800–1840* (London: Printing Historical Society, 1972), p. 7; Will of Susan Bailey otherwise Baily, Widow of Saint Martin Outwich, City of London, PRO PROB 11/1508. For further detail on the history of the Bailey family, see Garvey, '"Under a Deceptious Mask"', vol. 2, pp. 309–16.

113   Rickard has maintained that the *Impartial and Circumstantial Narrative* was the original 'Barrington' publication in her *ODNB* entry on Barrington, and the introduction to her edited version of the *Voyage* includes a fanciful publishing history of the work to support this claim (Rickard, ed., *George Barrington's Voyage to Botany Bay*, pp. 35–41, also 32–33). Other recent scholars have followed Rickard's apparently authoritative position on this. See, for example, Glynis Ridley, 'Losing America and Finding Australia: Continental Shift in an Enlightenment Paradigm', *Eighteenth-Century Life*, vol. 26, no. 3, 2002, p. 203; and Toby R. Benis, 'Criminal Transport: George Barrington and the Colonial Cure', *Australian Literary Studies*, vol. 20, no. 3, 2002, p. 167.

114   See Bibliography, **AB14**.

115   It is not clear why Rickard has chosen to ignore the work of scholars with some expertise in bibliography and the history of the eighteenth-century book on this point; Jonathan Wantrup, for example, correctly identified the Symonds *Voyage to New South Wales* as the original 'Barrington' work (*Australian Rare Books*, p. 87). Rickard's confusion may be related to the fact that previous bibliographies and catalogues dated the *Impartial and Circumstantial Narrative* between 1790 and 1791; the version of the text in *Eighteenth Century Collections Online* still carries the date '[1791]' (see Rickard, ed., *George Barrington's Voyage to Botany Bay*, p. 66).

116   See Bibliography, **AB7a-b**, **AB8**. Symonds advertised 'Barrington's Voyage and Description of Botany Bay, Third Edition' in the *Morning Chronicle* of 25 February 1796 (p. 3a), while Dobson's *Voyage* was advertised in the *Philadelphia Gazette & Universal Daily Advertiser* on 17 March (p. 4d), 19 March (p. 2e), and 24 March (p. 2d) 1796. For Thomas Dobson (1751–1823), see Robert D. Arner, *Dobson's Encyclopaedia: The Publisher, Text, and Publication of America's First Britannica, 1789–1803* (Philadelphia: University of Pennsylvania Press, 1991).

117   The other was an edition of Watkin Tench's *Narrative of an Expedition*, published in New York in 1789. See J. A. Ferguson, *Bibliography of Australia: Addenda 1784-1850* (Canberra: National Library of Australia, 1986), p. 13 [F48a].

118   See Bibliography, **AB12**. The Revolutionary calendar took the Year I to begin on 22 September 1792 (as the start of the Republican era); thus *An*s VI embraced the period 22 September 1797 – 21 September 1798.

119   This might well have been post-Terror 'propaganda on the concepts of justice and mercy then circulating in France' as Rickard asserts, but it was also a contribution to the debate on the merits of France seeking a penal colony of its own. See Rickard, ed., *George Barrington's Voyage to Botany Bay*, pp. 26–27; also Leslie Marchant, *France*

Australe: a Study of French Explorations and Attempts to Found a Penal Colony and Strategic Base in South Western Australia, 1503–1826 (Perth: Artlook, 1982), pp. 223–27.

120   *Voyage a Botany Bay* (**AB12**), pp. 191–92.

121   See Bibliography, **AB33**, **AB38**, **AB45**, **AB51**, **AB52**, **AB54**, **AB55**, **AB57**.

122   For a more detailed description of the plate, see Bibliography, **AB9**.

123   See Bibliography, **AB10**.

124   See Chapter 2, and Bibliography, **AB17**.

125   In fact, there is evidence to suggest that the actual printer of Symonds' 'Barrington' works was Charles Lowndes' wife, Jane Lowndes (née Garland). Born in London in 1759, Jane was the daughter of Halhed Garland, a printer, who died in 1773 when Jane was only fourteen. In 1778, she was admitted into the Stationers' Company by patrimony (that is, through her father's connections). By this time, Jane Garland, along with her mother of the same name, had struck up an association with the Drury Lane Theatre company, and was trading at 66 Drury Lane, part of the theatre complex, probably working in the production of playbills and other theatrical material. Jane married Charles Lowndes at St Martin's in the Field, Westminster, in September 1783. From this point on, the productions of their press generally appeared under the imprint 'C. Lowndes': but it seems very likely that Jane, who had a background in printing which her husband lacked, remained active in the production side of the family business. This view is supported by a reference in the letters of Richard Brinsley Sheridan, manager of Drury Lane from 1778 to 1809, which instructed one of his underlings to 'see instantly Mrs Lownds and let her have her press ready' for the printing of some theatre business. In the 1790s, Charles and Jane Lowndes began to dabble in bookselling as well as printing, notably publishing elaborate works on the history of France and the French Revolution by the conservative writer, John Gifford. The staple of the Lowndes' press seems to have been the production of playbills, however, and they fulfilled that role for the Drury Lane company until the early 1820s. Charles Lowndes seems to have died about the mid-1820s, and Jane, though in her seventies, continued the press for a time. See *IGI*, online, <www.familysearch.org>, accessed 1 December 2007; *RWCS Court Book N 4 Feb 1777 to 22 Dec 1785*, microfilm, reel 60; Cecil Price, ed., *The Letters of Richard Brinsley Sheridan*, vol. 2 (Oxford: Clarendon, 1966), p. 245; *The Survey of London. Volume XXXV: The Theatre Royal Drury Lane and The Royal Opera House Covent Garden* (London: Athlone Press, 1970), plate 7, see also pp. 34, 33–35. For further details on Charles and Jane Lowndes and their press, see Garvey, '"Under a Deceptious Mask"', vol. 2, pp. 281–92.

126   See Bibliography, **AB18**. The *Sequel* was advertised, under the header of 'Barrington's Memoirs and Anecdotes of Botany Bay', in the *Morning Herald*, 6 November 1800 (p. 1a), the *Morning Chronicle*, 6 January 1801 (p. 2a), and *The Times*, 9 January 1801 (p. 2b). It was priced at 2s. 6d. – the same price as the original *Voyage*.

127   Collins' *Account of the English Colony* was published by the firm of Thomas Cadell (Junior) and William Davies in the Strand, as a large quarto volume of over six hundred pages with fourteen plates, priced at a guinea (1l. 1s.). One advertisement offered for sale 'a few copies ... printed on fine paper, with early impressions of the plates, price 3l. 3s. in boards' (*The Times*, 12 July 1798, p. 2a). Cadell and Davies published a second volume of Collins' work in 1802, and in 1804 they published an

abridged edition (the abridgements made by Collins' wife Maria) of the two volumes in one. See Ferguson, *Bibliography of Australia*, vol. 1, pp. 101, 134–35, 153 [F263, F350, F390].

128   G. B. Worgan, *Journal of a First Fleet Surgeon* (Sydney: Library of Australian History, 1979), pp. 37–38.

129   *A Sequel to Barrington's Voyage to New South Wales...* (Lowndes and Symonds, 1800 [hereafter *Sequel*], pp. 10–14.

130   See, for example, the episode relating to the apprehension of a fugitive convict named John Crow. The Collins *Account* states that 'the watch apprehended him at Parramatta' (p. 323), while the *Sequel* gives that 'A convict of the name of John Crow fell in my way as I was out on patrol; I accordingly apprehended him ...' (p. 26).

131   *Monthly Review* [new ser.], vol. 35, 1801, p. 218.

132   See Bibliography, **AB20**.

133   Source unidentified, 'Biographical Cuttings on George Barrington, convict', National Library of Australia. The clipping is annotated '1801'.

134   D'Arcy Wentworth was in fact living near Barrington in Parramatta at the time this was published. See John Ritchie, *The Wentworths: Father and Son* (Melbourne: Melbourne University Press, 1997), pp. 81–89.

135   See *The Times*, 4 January 1802, p. 2a.

136   That is, **AB17** and **AB20** – see Bibliography, **AB21a**.

137   See Bibliography, **AB21b**.

138   See Bibliography, **AB22**. For the Dublin reprint trade generally, see Richard Cargill Cole, *Irish Booksellers and English Writers, 1740–1800* (London: Mansell, 1986).

139   See Bibliography, **AB23**.

140   See Cole, *Irish Booksellers and English Writers*, pp. 220–37. Irish reprints were also smuggled into Scotland and the north of England. See Warren McDougall, 'Smugglers, Reprinters, and Hot Pursuers: the Irish-Scottish Book Trade, And Copyright Prosecutions in the late 18th Century', in Robin Myers and Michael Davies, eds, *The Stationers' Company and the Book Trade 1550–1990*, (New Castle, Del.: Oak Knoll, 1997), pp. 151–183.

141   The proposal, which appeared in the *South-Carolina State Gazette* on 31 March (p. 3c), 5 April (p. 3c) and 7 April (p. 3c) 1802, stated that 'this work has run through several editions in London, and was brought to this city, a few days ago. It has been particularly taken notice of by the British Reviewers, and not without foundation, for it certainly is as entertaining a work as ever published in this State'. Timothy also published an 'Extract from George Barrington's Description of the Natives of New South Wales' in the *Gazette* of 1 April 1802.

142   Advertisements for Durell's 'Barrington' publication appeared in the *American Citizen and General Advertiser* of 22 July 1802 (p. 4c), the *Commercial Advertiser* of 7 August 1802 (p. 4a), and the *Mercantile Advertiser* for 29 July (p. 2d), 20 August (p. 4a), 2 September (p. 4c), 3 September (p. 4e), 4 September (p. 4e), and 13 September 1802 (p. 4d).

143   See Bibliography, **AB26** and **AB27**.

144   The paragraph appeared in *The Mercury and New England Palladium* of 19 October 1802 (p. 2d), the [New York] *Evening Post* of 26 October (p. 3a), the *New York Herald*

of 27 October (p. 3a), the *Philadelphia Gazette* of 27 October (p. 3d), and the [Baltimore] *Republican, or Anti-Democrat* of 1 November 1802 (p. 3a).

145   For William Duane (1760–1835), see Kim Tousley Phillips, *William Duane, Radical Journalist in the Age of Jefferson* (New York: Taylor and Francis, 1989), and Jeffrey L. Pasley, '*The Tyranny of Printers': Newspaper Politics in the Early American Republic* (Charlottesville: University of Virginia Press, 2001).

146   See Bibliography, **AB33**.

147   For Golitsyn (1754–1824), see Glynn Barratt, *The Russians and Australia* (Vancouver: University of British Columbia Press, 1988), p. 54.

148   ibid., pp. 54–55; see also Bibliography, **AB45**. V. S. Sopikov's *An Essay in Russian Bibliography* does not mention the Moscow edition of 1803, stating instead that in 1803–1805 Golitsyn had published a collection of travel narratives, to which subsequent works were added as separate volumes – one of these being the *Voyage* translation of 1809. See Sopikov, *An Essay in Russian Bibliography, or a Complete Dictionary of Works Printed in the Church Slavonic & Russian Language from the Introduction of Printing to the Year 1813* [English title], 2nd edn, vol. 2 (London: Holland Press, 1962), p. 156 and pp. 292–93 [nos 9164 and 10990]. I am indebted to Eldar Aliev for his kind assistance with translations relating to the Russian editions.

149   See Bibliography, **AB28**. The 1770s version of the *Frauds of London Detected* had been published by Alexander Hogg, who had also published the work as *The New Cheats of London Exposed* (see also Chapter 1).

150   The identity of J. Lee, who was located at 12 King Street, Covent Garden when he published the 'Barrington' *Frauds of London Detected*, remains uncertain. The character of this and other works of the illustrated bluebook variety published by Lee from his Covent Garden address suggests he may have been Joseph Lee, a printer and publisher who specialised in bluebooks and traded from 24 Half Moon Street, Bishopsgate Without from 1804–1824. Richard Austin, a pupil of Thomas Bewick, worked as an engraver in London from about 1788 to 1833. Alexander Macpherson traded as a printer in Russell Court, Covent Garden, from 1796 to 1824. See *BBTI*, online, <www.bbti.bham.ac.uk>; also Hall and Muir, *Some Printers and Publishers*, p. 48.

151   See 'Barrington', *Frauds of London Detected* (London: Lee, 1802), pp. 50–51; cf. *Frauds of London Detected* (London: Hogg, [1778]), pp. 61–62.

152   Hogg had entered his *Frauds of London Detected* at Stationers' Hall on 21 December 1778 (*RWCS Entries of Copies* 1774–1786, reel 7), which technically protected the work for fourteen years. In his autobiography, the publisher Thomas Tegg would boast of his own assiduity in monitoring this fourteen-year period, and rushing to publish his own versions of popular works once it had elapsed (*Memoir of the Late Thomas Tegg*, p. 17).

153   Where the preface to the original *Frauds of London Detected* (Hogg, [1778]) ends with a statement to the effect that the prevention of future crimes 'will sufficiently reward me for the trouble taken in detecting THE FRAUDS OF LONDON' (vi), the 'Barrington' version has '… will sufficiently reward me for the trouble I have taken to expose and detect THE FRAUDS OF LONDON. My well-known experience, I flatter myself, enables me to do justice to such a work' (vi).

154   See Bibliography, **AB29a-b**.

155   Jones is another somewhat elusive figure. Todd lists Maurice Jones, bookseller, trading

at 1 Paternoster Row from 1804 to1808; the publication of the *History* shows he was there from at least 1802, however. This was also the address of a printer, Vaughan Griffiths, who remained at the address until 1812. About 1810, Jones relocated to 5 Newgate Street, where William Naunton Jones, a printer, joined him in 1812. Maurice Jones was trading from Newgate Street until about 1817, after which I have found no trace of him. See Todd, *A Directory of Printers*, p. 109.

156   The publication of books in parts or 'numbers' was a popular form of publishing in the late eighteenth century, and seems to have been a fiercely competitive field. C. H. Timperley cited Alexander Hogg as one of the pioneers of 'Paternoster-row Numbers', noting that the publication of works in this form did much to supply the growing readership among 'mechanics' and the middling classes, and 'greatly contributed to lay the foundation of that literary taste and thirst for knowledge, which now pervades all classes' (*A Dictionary of Printers and Printing*, p. 838n). See also James Raven, *The Business of Books: Booksellers and the English Book Trade 1450–1850* (New Haven: Yale University Press, 2007), pp. 245–50.

157   See Bibliography, **AB30**.

158   Staunton, who had been secretary to Lord George Macartney on the latter's diplomatic mission to China in 1792, published an account of the embassy in 1797. Quarto editions of the work were published in two volumes by George Nicol, while John Stockdale published a single volume octavo abridgement as *An Historical Account of the Embassy to the Emperor of China* ... (Stockdale, 1797) – the latter version of the narrative was the source of the material borrowed for the 'Barrington' *Account of a Voyage*. See 'Barrington' *Account*, pp. 449–50; cf. Staunton, *An Historical Account*, pp. 176–77.

159   For Woodthorpe (d. 1822) see Rickard, ed., *George Barrington's Voyage to Botany Bay*, p. 47; and *Monthly Magazine*, vol. 54, October 1822, p. 274.

160   The 'Dedication to His Majesty' was issued with the prefatory material for the *History* (see Bibliography, **AB29a-b**).

161   According to this advertisement, the first part was due for publication on 30 October 1802 (see *Caledonian Mercury*, 16 October 1803, p. 1c). However, as Robert Jordan points out, an advertisement in *The Times* of 10 November 1802 stated that the part publication was to commence 'next Saturday' [13 November]. The dates given on the plate illustrations issued with the work suggest that publication from mid-November was more likely. See Bibliography, **AB29a-b**; Jordan, 'The Barrington Prologue', *Script and Print*, vol. 31, no. 1, pp. 47–49; *The Times*, 10 November 1802, p. 1d.

162   'Preface to the Reader', *History of New South Wales* (Jones: 1802), [n.p.]. The National Library of Australia has a complete set of the *History* in its original parts. See NLA FRM F344, Part 14.

163   See *Jackson's Oxford Journal*, 12 February 1803 (p. 4d).

164   The (re)commencement of the works in numbers was advertised in November 1803 and again in July 1805. See *Derby Mercury*, 3 November 1803 (p. 1c) and *Derby Mercury*, 25 July 1805 (p. 2d).

165   *Monthly Magazine*, vol. 10, [1803], p. 569. A similar notice appears in the same section of the *Christian Observer*, July 1803, p. 432.

166   See Bibliography, **AB29a-b**, **AB30**.

167   Wantrup, *Australian Rare Books*, p. 97.

168   See *RWCS Entries of Copies* 1792–1795, reel 8; and *Entries of Copies* 1795–1799, reel 8. Rather cheekily, Susan and John Bailey had emblazoned their *Impartial and Circumstantial Narrative* with the false claim: 'Entered at the Stationer's Hall' (p. [2]).

169   In 1802, Jones and Symonds were partners in a one-volume collected edition of *The Miscellaneous Writings of Sir Francis Bacon*, a work Jones advertised on the paper wrappers of his part-issued 'Barrington' *History*.

170   Symonds retired from the trade about 1808, leaving his business to a firm made up of a former apprentice, William Sherwood (1776–1837), his son-in-law Samuel Dunbar Neely (c. 1780–1848) and one Robert Jones (1781?–1842). All three were admitted to the livery of the Stationers' Company by the end of 1808, and clearly intended to continue the extensive trade Symonds had built up over his twenty years in Paternoster Row. Symonds died at his home in Islington in 1816, leaving £500 to his daughter Jane, the wife of Samuel Dunbar Neely, and the remainder of his estate to his other surviving child, Ann. The firm of Sherwood, Neely and Jones continued trading from Symonds' old premises in Paternoster Row until the mid-1820s. See Will of Henry Delahay Symonds, Gent. of Islington, PRO PROB 11/1583. For further information on the firm of Sherwood, Neely and Jones, see Garvey, '"Under a Deceptious Mask"', vol. 2, pp. 326–30.

171   The first part of Collins' *An Account of the English Colony in New South Wales*, published in a quarto volume priced at 2 guineas (42 shillings), was admittedly rather more expensive than the entire 'Barrington' *History* and *Account* in parts (26 shillings) or for the two volumes bound – £1. 7s (27 shillings). However, the Hunter *Historical Journal of the Transactions at Port Jackson and Norfolk Island*, which had provided the basis for the original *Voyage*, could be had in an octavo volume for just 7s. 6d., while Stockdale's *Voyage of Governor Phillip to Botany Bay* was also sold in an octavo edition for the comparatively cheap price of 10s. 6d. See *The Times*, 12 July 1798, p. 2a; *London Chronicle*, 20–22 June 1793, p. 596c; *Monthly Review*, vol. 3 [new ser.], October 1790, p. 208.

172   'Speciman of a Prospectus; or the Art of Swindling', *The Satirist: or Monthly Meteor*, vol. 2, April 1808, pp. 132–37, microfilm, Goldsmiths'-Kress Library of Economic Literature, Unit 80: Serials, reel 3617.

173   For a detailed description of the contents of the 1810–1811 *History* and *Account*, see Bibliography, **AB47** and **AB48**.

174   *Derby Mercury*, 3 January 1811, p. 3d.

175   See *Derby Mercury*, 19 December 1811, p. 1e; *Morning Chronicle*, 25 November 1812, p. 2d; *Derby Mercury*, 29 July 1813, p. 1d.; *Trewman's Exeter Flying Post or Plymouth and Cornish Advertiser*, 29 July 1813, p. 3c; *Derby Mercury*, 19 January 1815, p. 1d; and *Morning Chronicle*, 21 January 1815, p. 2a.

176   See Bibliography, **AB47**. Samuel Dunbar Neely had left the firm by late 1823, and Sherwood and Jones parted ways by August 1825, when Sherwood was trading with new partners as Sherwood, Gilbert and Piper. See Garvey, '"Under a Deceptious Mask"', vol. 2, pp. 328–30.

177   The autobiography of Thomas Tegg (1776–1846) unfortunately has been lost, but an edited version was published some twenty-four years after his death in the London

periodical, *The City Press*. See Aleph [pseud.], ed., *Memoir of the Late Thomas Tegg: Abridged from his autobiography by permission of his son, William Tegg. From the* City Press *of August 6th, 1870* (London: Collingridge, 1870). See also James J. Barnes and Patience P. Barnes, 'Reassessing the Reputation of Thomas Tegg, London Publisher, 1776–1846', *Book History*, vol. 3, 2000, pp. 45–60; and Garvey, '"Under a Deceptious Mask"', vol. 2, pp. 293–305.

178   The earliest known Tegg version of this work uses the same frontispiece plate found in the Lee *Frauds of London Detected*, making it likely that the two booksellers had reached some accommodation over the publication of the work. See Bibliography, **AB36**.

179   See Bibliography, **AB36**, **AB37**, **AB39**, **AB40**, **AB42**, **AB43**, **AB48**.

180   See Bibliography, **AB36**. For Belcher (1781–1811), see *Jem Belcher: Champion Prizefighter and His Historic Belcher Handkerchief. Including Jem Belcher's Treatise on Boxing* (Belcher, Kentucky: Belcher Foundation, 2006).

181   See Bibliography, **AB37**, also **AB39**.

182   Like the *Frauds of London Detected*, the *Modern London Spy* was published by Alexander Hogg; the first example of the work I have traced is Hogg's *The Modern London Spy, for the Present Year, 1781*. The work was republished by Hogg around the turn of the nineteenth century as *The New London Spy* – this latter version may well have remained in print by the time Tegg published his *Barrington's New London Spy for 1805*.

183   The *Modern London Spy* was descended not only from the tradition of *London Spy* works popularised by Ned Ward at the outset of the eighteenth century, but also from a plentiful eighteenth-century genre of 'broadly comic texts' of a more dialogic and novelistic style, organised around the 'ramble' plot device. See Simon Dickie, 'Chapter Eight: The Mid Eighteenth-Century "Ramble" Novels', in 'In the Mid Eighteenth Century: Hilarity, Pitilessness and Narrative Fiction', PhD Thesis, Stanford University, 2000, online, <http://novel.stanford.edu/pdf/dickie.pdf>, accessed 1 December 2007.

184   See *Derby Mercury*, 18 September 1806, p. 2d and *Ipswich Journal*, 20 September 1806, p. 2c.

185   See Bibliography, **AB48**.

186   See Bibliography, **AB44**. A printer, bookseller and newspaper proprietor, Thomas Johnston succeeded to the business of his father-in-law, Patrick Mair, in 1797. He remained in business in Falkirk until his death in 1831, when the business was inherited by his son Archibald. As the *Scottish Book Trade Index* (online, <www.nls.uk/catalogues/resources/sbti/index.html>, accessed 1 December 2007) points out, the production and sale of chapbooks 'must have formed a principal part' of Johnston's business, and they survive in relatively large numbers in library collections today.

187   See Bibliography, **AB50**. The identity of R. Parker is uncertain: the *BBTI* (online, <www.bbti.bham.ac.uk>, accessed 1 December 2007) has no record of any book trade personnel by the name of Parker located in Blackburn.

188   See Bibliography, **AB56**. I have not seen the Boston edition – however, the fact that its contents include the Belcher 'Treatise on Boxing' shows that it is indebted, to some degree at least, to the Tegg work.

189   See Bibliography, **AB31**, also **AB32**.

190   *Annals of Suicide*, p. 3.

191   ibid., pp. 5–15.

192   ibid., pp. 3–4.

193   For Isaac Cruikshank, father of the renowned George Cruikshank, see Robert L. Patten, 'Cruikshank [Crookshanks], Isaac (1764–1811), caricaturist and painter', *ODNB*, online, <www.oxforddnb.com>, accessed 1 December 2007.

194   'Dreadful History of Anaboo', *Annals of Suicide*, p. 5.

195   Hunter, *Historical Journal*, pp. 58–59. The *Voyage to New South Wales* plagiarises this passage as '… they are abominably filthy. They know no such ceremony as washing themselves; and their skin is mostly smeared with the fat of such animals as they kill, and afterwards covered with every sort of dirt; sand from the beach, and ashes from their fires; all adhere to their filthy skin, which never comes off, except when accident, or the want of food obliges them to go into the water' (p. 62).

196   'Dreadful History of Anaboo', pp. 8–9.

197   ibid., pp. 8–9, 12–13. Cape Banks, on the northern headland of Botany Bay, was never used as a convict station as the narrative portrays, and indeed the area remains undeveloped, as part of the Botany Bay National Park, to this day.

198   See, for example, 'Plan of Botany Bay', in *The History of New Holland …* (London: John Stockdale, 1786), p. [36].

199   'Dreadful History of Anaboo', pp. 5–6.

200   ibid., p. 6.

201   ibid., p. 7.

202   ibid., p. 7.

203   ibid., pp. 10–12.

204   ibid., pp. 10–11.

205   ibid., p. 14.

206   ibid., p. 15.

207   J. Payne Smart, 'George Barrington's "Hopeless Love"' [*Native Companion*, 1907], reprinted in *Margin*, vol. 49, 1999, pp. 29–31.

208   See *Memoir of the late Thomas Tegg*, p. 17. Most of Tegg's literary work was editing of the 'cut and paste' variety, and/or revamping old works for republication, but he is also thought to be the author of several reform-oriented works of the early nineteenth century. See Marc Baer, *Theatre and Disorder in Late Georgian England* (Oxford: Clarendon Press, 1992), pp. 247–48, 257–58.

209   The partnership of Tegg and Castleman was short-lived, lasting from about December 1802 to January 1804. In his *Memoir*, Tegg describes the period as an unhappy time when 'all things seemed wrong', and the partners 'met with various troubles, owing to want of capital'. After the firm's demise, Tegg was able to avoid bankruptcy with the help of his 'noble friend, Mr. Plummer' [the printer Thomas Plummer], while Castleman 'soon drank himself into the grave' (*Memoir of the late Thomas Tegg*, pp. 17–18).

210   See *Derby Mercury*, 30 June 1803, p. 1d, and *Trewman's Exeter Flying Post*, 30 June 1803, p. 3d. For J. H. Hart (*fl.* 1801–1816), see Todd, *A Directory of Printers*, p. 92.

211   See Bibliography, **AB32**.

212   See *Derby Mercury*, 30 June 1803, p. 1d, and *Trewman's Exeter Flying Post*, 30 June 1803, p. 3d.

213   In 1804, Tegg issued a part of the *Annals of Suicide* as a chapbook, apparently as part
       of a series, or intended series, entitled 'Tales of Woe' (see Bibliography, **AB35**), and
       the University of Virginia Library and the Library of Congress hold copies of a
       chapbook entitled *Eliza, or the Unhappy Nun*, which was compiled from another section
       (pp. [73]–107) of the *Annals of Suicide* – although this work was issued without any
       reference to Barrington. I am indebted to Gayle Cooper of the Albert and Shirley
       Small Library, University of Virginia, for information on the latter work.

214   The *Marvellous Magazine* was started in 1802, with the first volume published by
       Thomas Hurst, but Tegg and Castleman seem to have soon taken over publishing the
       work, which continued until 1804. See Angela Koch, 'Gothic Bluebooks in the Princely
       Library of Corvey and Beyond', *Cardiff Corvey: Reading the Romantic Text*, vol. 9, 2002,
       online, <www.cf.ac.uk/encap/corvey/articles/cc09_n01.html>, accessed 1 December
       2007.

215   See *Caledonian Mercury*, 7 April 1806, p. 1b.

216   The *Bibliothèque Géographique* had originally been published as a twelve-volume series
       by J. E. Gabriel Dufour in Paris in 1802–1803, but the subsequent 'nouvelle édition', in
       which the 'Barrington' *Voyage* appeared, was a greatly expanded republication
       extending to some seventy-two volumes. For a description of the contents of the
       Bibliothèque Géographique, see Françoise Huguet, *Les Livres pour L'Enfance et la Jeunesse
       de Gutenburg à Guizot: Les Collections de la Bibliothèque de L'Institut National de Recherche
       Pédagogique* (Paris: Éditions Klincksieck, 1997), pp. 81–91. See also André Monglond,
       *La France Révolutionnaire et Impériale: Annals de Bibliographie Méthodique et Description
       des Livres Illustrés*, vol. 5, 1800–1802 (Grenoble: Éditions B. Arthaud, 1938),
       pp. 1211–16.

217   There is comparatively little literature in English on J. H. Campe (1746–1818); see,
       however, Cedric Hentschel, 'Campe and the Discovery of America', *German Life and
       Letters*, vol. 26, 1972, pp. 1–13. For a detailed description of Campe's works, see Heinz
       Wegehaupt, *Alte Deutsche Kinderbüch: Bibliographie 1507–1850: Zugleich
       Bestandsverzeichnis der Kinder- und Jugendbuchabteilung der Deutschen Staatsbibliothek zu
       Berlin* (Hamburg: Dr. Ernst Hauswedell & Co., 1979), pp. 40–55.

218   Jean-Baptiste-Joseph Breton de la Martinière (1777–1852) trained as a shorthand
       reporter, and from 1792 was involved in reporting the debates of the Legislative
       Assembly in Paris. In 1815 he was appointed parliamentary stenographer, and
       thereafter retained a role in the reporting of legislative and judicial proceedings until
       his death. Breton de la Martinière was known to have translated and/or adapted for
       children the works of a number of authors from French, English and German, and was
       most active in this capacity during the Napoleonic period, possibly because of a
       comparative lack of legislative debates to report. See Olivier Loyer, 'Jean-Baptiste-
       Joseph Breton (1777–1852)', *La Chronique de la Sténographie*, vol. 9, April 1904, n.p.,
       and Huguet, *Les Livres pour L'Enfance et la Jeunesse de Gutenburg à Guizot*, p. 376.

219   See Wegehaupt, *Alte Deutsche Kinderbüch*, pp. 45, 50 [nos. 279 and 341].

220   See Bibliography, **AB38**.

221   See above, and Bibliography, **AB9**, **AB10**, **AB17**, **AB21a-b**.

222   For a description of the plate, see Bibliography, **AB38**.

223   *Voyage et Transportation du Fameux Barrington* (**AB38**), pp. 9, [1]–12.

224   ibid., pp. 196, 195–200.

225   ibid., pp. 198–99.

226   See Bibliography, **AB51**, **AB54**.

227   See Bibliography, **AB54**.

228   J. F. Rolland, *Conseils pour Former une Bibliothèque, ou Catalogue Raisonné: de tout les Bons Ouvrages qui Peuvent Enterer dans une Bibliothèque Chrétienne*, vol. 3 (Lyon: J. F. Rolland, 1843), p. 56. I am indebted to Wallace Kirsop for alerting me to this source. See also Bibliography, **AB57**.

229   For the full title and a description of the contents of each volume, see Göte Klingberg, *Svensk Barn- och Ungdomslitteratur 1591–1839: En Pedagogikhistorisk och Bibliografisk Översit* (Stockholm: Natur och Kultur, 1964), pp. 182–183.

230   For Krutmejer (1778–1854), translator of a considerable number of French and German children's texts, see Klingberg, *Svensk Barn- och Ungdomslitteratur*, pp. 78–79, 182–183, 260–267.

231   See Bibliography, **AB52**. Klingberg neglects to observe that several of the volumes in the *Geografiskt Bibliothek* had not appeared in its supposed source, Campe's *Neue Sammlung Merkwürdiger Reisebeschreibungen für die Jugend*, and he misdates the original 'Barrington' *Voyage* as 'ca. 1790' (*Svensk Barn- och Ungdomslitteratur*, pp. 182–183).

232   See bibliography, **AB55**. The *Viaje y Translaccion del Famoso Barrington* is undated; the Mitchell Library catalogue dates the work at 'c.1815', while the NLA states 'between 1798 and 1810'. In fact the work almost certainly dates from the early 1830s. The National Library of Spain lists fifteen works by Santiago Alvarado y de la Peña as author or translator, all published between 1826 and 1835. These include other works translated from the *Bibliothèque Géographique*, such as *Viaje de Pablo Brydone á Sicilia y á Malta Hecho en el Año de 1770*, and *Viage al Polo Austral ódel Sur y Alrededor del Mundo por el Célebre Capitan Santíago Cook*, which formed part of a series entitled 'Nueva biblioteca de viajes modernos, útiles e interesantes a la juventud española', published in Madrid by Tomás Jordan in 1832–1833. Although the *Viaje y Translaccion del Famoso Barrington* was published under a different imprint and apparently not part of the same series, it seems very likely that Alvarado y de la Peña translated the work at around the time he was working on other translations from the *Bibliothèque Géographique*; the 'Advertencia del Traductor' which follows the *Viaje y Translaccion* text promotes other voyage narratives translated by him.

233   See Bibliography, **AB52** and **AB55**. The plate in the Swedish edition is attributed to 'Ruckman' – probably the Swedish engraver, Johan Gustav Ruckman (1780–1862).

EPILOGUE

1   Dickens, qtd in Noel McLachlan, Introduction, *The Memoirs of James Hardy Vaux* (London: Heinemann, 1964), p. 30. In *Household Words*, the predecessor to *All the Year Round*, Dickens had published a short tale on Barrington by the Australian writer John Lang (1816–1864), entitled 'An Illustrious British Exile' (9 April 1859); this story was also published as a genuine anecdote in Lang's *Botany Bay: True Tales of Early Australia* (London: William Tegg, 1859). See Anne Lohli, *Household Words; a Weekly Journal 1850–1859, Conducted by Charles Dickens. Table of contents, List of Contributors and their*

Contributions Based on the Household Words *Office Book in the Morris L. Parrish collection of Victorian novelists, Princeton University Library* (Toronto: University of Toronto Press, 1973), pp. 191–92, 337–38.

2   Frost's novel appeared in twenty-nine penny numbers; the work was still available as late as 1869, when Purkess advertised it along with other stock in the *Penny Illustrated Paper* (25 December 1869, p. 24). For Thomas Frost (1821–1908), see Peter Gurney, 'Working-Class Writers and the Art of Escapology in Victorian England: The Case of Thomas Frost', *Journal of British Studies*, vol. 45, no. 1, 2006, pp. 51–72; see also Frost's *Reminiscences of a Country Journalist* (London: Ward and Downey, 1886).

3   A work blending elements of romance, crime narrative, comedy and farce, Rymer's serial novel was initially published under the author's anagrammatical pseudonym 'Malcolm J. Errym' in *Reynolds' Miscellany* for March and April 1862. A part-issued version of the novel was subsequently published by John Dicks in the mid-1860s, and in 1872 the work was republished, with 'superb coloured engravings', by Henry Clarence. See Nathan Garvey, '"Under a Deceptious Mask": A Publishing History of the George Barrington Books', PhD thesis, vol. 1, University of Sydney, 2007, pp. 182–83; see also Frank Jay, *Peeps into the Past; Being a History of Oldtime Periodicals, Journals and Books*, [1921], online, <http://geocities.com/justingilb/texts/PEEPS.htm>, accessed 1 December 2007.

4   A two-act afterpiece billed as 'an Original, Melo-Dramatic "Tale of the Road"', *Barrington the Pickpocket!, or, Adventures of the Irish "Dick Turpin!"* was performed at the Royal Victoria Theatre, Surrey; a playbill survives for a performance on Monday, 24 July 1848 (see J. A. Ferguson, *Bibliography of Australia*, vol. 4 (Canberra: National Library of Australia, 1977), p. 171 [F4712]). Though Osbaldiston's name does not appear on the playbill, he had been the manager and sole lessee of the 'Old Vic' since 1841; T. H. Higgie, credited on the playbill as the director of the piece, was ordinarily the company's stage manager. A comparison of the playbills suggests that the 1848 *Barrington the Pickpocket!* was a significantly different work from the 'Dramatic Sketch', *Barrington the Pickpocket!, or the Gypsies of Tiverton Glen*, which Osbaldiston's company had performed at the Surrey Theatre fifteen years earlier. See Garvey, '"Under a Deceptious Mask"', vol. 1, pp. 178–81.

5   Theatre historian Jim Davis has pointed out that popular melodrama and the 'penny periodical press' enjoyed a significant exchange of subject matter in the later nineteenth century. This exchange is well illustrated by the two 'Barrington' plays staged in 1862 – respectively, at the Britannia Theatre in London's East End from June, and at the Royal Victoria Theatre, Surrey, in August–September – both of which capitalised on the popularity of Rymer's serial, published in *Reynolds' Miscellany* earlier that year. A playbill for the Royal Victoria Theatre production in the collection of the National Library (F/Broadside F6711) describes the work as a 'New Romantic Drama, written by Mrs. H. Young ... taken from a tale now publishing in Reynold's [*sic*] Miscellany, entitled George Barrington, or Life in London One Hundred Years Ago'. The Britannia Production, a two-act play entitled *Barrington the Pickpocket*, was written – or rather adapted – by Frederick Marchant, identified by Davis and Victor Emeljanow as the Britannia's 'up and coming' house dramatist. The manuscript of Marchant's playscript, which survives in the Pettingell collection of plays at the University of Kent,

contains a healthy proportion of typescript literally cut and pasted from *Reynolds'*
Miscellany, with hand-written stage directions and annotations. The Marchant
adaptation of Rymer's novel seems to have been the only one of the Barrington-
themed dramatic works to have been presented as a mainpiece (all the others being
staged as shorter afterpieces). It was presumably this play, somewhat exaggerated in the
memory, that was the 'sensation drama in five acts, of which [Barrington] was the
intelligent hero', which Marcus Clarke 'came very near to seeing' before he emigrated
to Australia in 1863. A further dramatic work on Barrington was performed in October
1866 at the City of London Theatre, Norton Folgate, by the company of the
actor–manager W. R. Waldron. The cast of characters that appears on the playbill for
this work (Mitchell Library Q792.27/1) suggests that Rymer's novel also influenced
this production. See Jim Davis, 'The Gospel of Rags: Melodrama at the Britannia,
1863–74', *New Theatre Quarterly*, vol. 7, 1991, pp. 372–73; Davis and Emeljanow,
Reflecting the Audience: London Theatregoing, 1840–1880 (Hatfield: University of
Hertfordshire Press, 2001), p. 74; Ferguson, *Bibliography of Australia*, vol. 5, 1977),
p. 251 [F6711]; F. Marchant, 'Barrington the Pickpocket', *The Popular Stage: The Frank
Pettingell Collection of Plays in the Library of the University of Kent at Canterbury*,
microfilm, series 1, reel 6, Bm (15); Marcus Clarke, 'George Barrington: Pickpocket
and Historian', *Old Tales of a Young Country* (Melbourne: Trustees of the Public
Library, 1871), p. 8. See also Garvey, '"Under a Deceptious Mask"', vol. 1, pp. 182–86.

6   Roy Bridges, *Mr. Barrington* (Sydney: N.S.W. Bookstall Co., 1911); and Ernest Dudley,
     *Picaroon: A Novel, Freely Based on the Scandalous Career of George Barrington, Actor, Beau
     and Prince of Pickpockets* (London: Robert Hale, 1952).

7   See Ferguson, *Bibliography of Australia*, vol. 1, 1975, pp. 13–14; Jonathan Wantrup,
     Australian Rare Books 1788–1900 (Sydney: Hordern House, 1987), pp. 86–87.

BIBLIOGRAPHY

NOTE ON THE SCOPE AND ARRANGEMENT OF THE BIBLIOGRAPHY

The following Bibliography provides a description of all known editions of 'Barrington' books published in the period 1790–1840. A 'Barrington' book is defined here as a book-length narrative about or attributed to George Barrington, produced and sold as an independent work. The Bibliography thus omits items such as broadside ballads, playbills, news-sheets and newspaper reports that refer to Barrington; nor does it record the publication of 'Barrington' texts within anthologies of criminal biography or similar books and magazines of the period. While this ephemeral material certainly helped to shape the Barrington legend, it was thought best to leave aside this copious body of material to focus on the books that traded exclusively on the Barrington name.

The Bibliography is divided into two sections: Barrington biographies – the biographical narratives about Barrington published from 1790, and allonymous Barrington books – the works falsely attributed to Barrington which appeared from 1795. Each of these sections is arranged in chronological order by date of publication, and is numbered along with the prefix **B** (Biographies) or **AB** (Allonymous Books). In some cases where variant versions of a particular work have been identified, these variants are distinguished with an additional letter and are discussed within the larger numbered entry (see for example, **B1a-d**, **AB21a-b**).

The bibliographic descriptions of each work are given in a simplified form. In each entry, the title of the work has been transcribed in full, retaining misspellings and printing errors; however, period typo-graphical features such as ligatures, serifs, and obsolete characters such as the long 's' have not been reproduced. Line breaks in the titles are indicated by a vertical rule. All horizontal dashes, decorative rules, and ornaments are uniformly indicated by [*rule*], [*double rule*] or [*ornament*] within square brackets. Square brackets appearing in the titles have been rendered as curly brackets { } to avoid confusion.

The physical descriptions of each work are also presented in a simplified style. Press signatures have not been recorded, though the format (8vo, 12mo, etc.) dimensions of the works (in centimetres) are shown. As many copies surveyed have been trimmed or cropped as part of a modern binding or re-binding process, measurements have been based on the best extant copy, and will be subject to variation. The number of pages in each work is recorded, noting any errors or idiosyncrasies in the pagination.

The annotations given in each entry provide several kinds of information. Most importantly, they specify the text used in the work in question, and clarify the relationship between that publication and other 'Barrington' works. Illustrations, if any, are described here, and subordinate bibliographic data (such as half-titles, colophons, etc.) is recorded. Where possible, information relevant to the date of publication, derived from both external (such as newspaper advertisements) and internal (such as watermark dates on paper) evidence has been included. Occasionally, contemporary owners' signatures and/or marginalia in particular copies have been described – though this information has generally been included only where it may be relevant to dating the publication or where it may serve to clarify the state of the work.

At the conclusion of each entry, three labelled fields have been included: **DOP** (for Date of Publication), **References**, and **Copies**. The 'Date of Publication' field gives the date of the work based on the evidence introduced in the annotations, or the date given on the title page of the work – if the date is derived from the latter source, it is shown in quotation marks. In cases where there is little or no clear evidence about the date of publication, an approximate date range is given, based on the publishing history of the text and/or the trade history of the publishers. The 'References' field notes other bibliographies and modern sources where the particular Barrington work is recorded, and the 'Copies' field provides a census of known copies of the work in libraries around the world. Every effort has been made to ensure that this census is as comprehensive as possible, which has meant that a great deal of it has been compiled from union catalogues and the online catalogues of individual libraries – the worldwide spread of the books precluded verifying every surviving copy. In the few cases where I have been unable to personally sight copies of particular works, I have described the work as 'not seen' and used an existing bibliographic description (with the source given in parentheses).

In compiling the Bibliography, I have had the great fortune to be able to access two libraries with very significant collections of Barrington books – the Mitchell Library (State Library of New South Wales) and the National Library of Australia. Between them, these libraries possess copies of more than 80 per cent of the works described in this Bibliography, and their collections (which often include multiple copies of the same work) account for nearly 40 per cent of the extant copies of these works I have traced in libraries worldwide. Yet while these excellent collections have provided a sound basis for the following detailed bibliographic survey, it is quite likely that further research will reveal still further variations and previously unknown manifestations of the publishing phenomenon conducted under the name of George Barrington.

ABBREVIATIONS

References

Box   Sheila Box, *The Real George Barrington? The Adventures of a Notorious London Pickpocket, Later Head Constable of the Infant Colony of New South Wales* (Melbourne: Arcadia, 2001).

EAI   *Early American Imprints. Series I, Evans (1639–1800)*, online (New Canaan, CT: Readex; Worcester, Mass.: American Antiquarian Society, 2002–), <http://infobank. neweb.com>.

ESTC   *English Short Title Catalogue*, online (London: British Library), <http://estc.bl.uk>.

Ferguson   J. A. Ferguson, *Bibliography of Australia*, vol. 1, 1784–1830, facs. edn (Canberra: National Library of Australia, 1975); 'Addenda to Vols. 1–III', *Bibliography of Australia*, vol. 4, 1846–1850, facs. edn (Canberra: National Library of Australia, 1976); *Bibliography of Australia: Addenda 1784–1850 (Volumes I–IV)* (Canberra: National Library of Australia, 1986). References are to (cumulative) catalogue numbers rather than page numbers.

Huguet	Françoise Huguet, *Les Livres pour L'Enfance et la Jeunesse de Gutenberg à Guizot: Les Collections de la Bibliothèque de L'Institut National de Recherche Pédagogique* (Paris: Institut National de Recherche Pédagogique, 1997). References are to catalogue numbers.
Klingberg	Göte Klingberg, *Svensk Barn- och Ungdomslitteratur 1591–1839: En Pedagogikhistorisk och Bibliografisk Översit* (Stockholm: Natur och Kultur, 1964).
Monglond	Andre Monglond, *La France Révolutionnaire et Impériale: Annals de Bibliographie Méthodique et Description des Livres Illustrés*, vol. 5, 1800–1802 (Grenoble: Éditions B. Arthaud, 1938).
Rickard	Suzanne Rickard, ed., *George Barrington's Voyage to Botany Bay: Retelling a Convict's Travel Narrative of the 1790s* (London: Leicester University Press, 2001).
Rolland	J. F. Rolland, *Conseils pour Former une Bibliothèque, ou Catalogue Raisonné: de tout les Bons Ouvrages qui Peuvent Enterer dans une Bibliothèque Chrétienne*, vol. 3 (Lyon: J. F. Rolland, 1843).
Todd	William B. Todd, *A Directory of Printers and Others in Allied Trades, London and Vicinity, 1800–1840* (London: Printing Historical Society, 1972).

Libraries

AAS	American Antiquarian Society, USA
Adelaide	University of Adelaide, Australia
ADFA	Australian Defence Force Academy
ANU	Australian National University
APS	American Philosophical Society, USA
ATL	Alexander Turnbull Library [National Library], New Zealand
BA	Boston Athenaeum, USA
BCL	Birmingham Central Library, UK
BEC	Buffalo and Eerie County Library, USA
BL	British Library, UK
BNE	Biblioteca Nacional de España
BNF	Bibliothèque National de France
Bowdoin	Bowdoin College, USA

Brown	Brown University, USA
BS	Bayerische Staatsbibliothek, Germany
BYU	Brigham Young University, USA
California	University of California, USA
Cambridge	Cambridge University, UK
Chicago	University of Chicago, USA
CHS	Connecticut Historical Society, USA
Claremont	Claremont Colleges, USA
CLL	Corporation of London Libraries, UK
Connecticut	University of Connecticut, USA
CSL	California State Library, USA
CWM	College of William and Mary, USA
Czartoryski	Czartoryski Library, Poland
Dartmouth	Dartmouth College, USA
DPL	Detroit Public Library, USA
Edinburgh	University of Edinburgh, UK
Flinders	Flinders University, Australia
Harvard	Harvard University, USA
HHT	Historic Houses Trust [New South Wales], Australia
Huntington	Huntington Library, USA
IF	L'Institut de France
JCU	James Cook University, Australia
JJC	John Jay College of Criminal Justice, USA
Kansas	University of Kansas, USA
KB	Kungl. Biblioteket, Sweden
La Trobe	La Trobe University, Australia
LCP	Library Company of Philadelphia, USA
LoC	Library of Congress, USA
London	University of London, UK
McGill	McGill University Library, Canada
MCL	Manchester Central Library, UK
Melbourne	University of Melbourne, Australia
MH	Musee de L'Homme, France
Michigan	University of Michigan, USA
Minnesota	University of Minnesota, USA
ML	Mitchell Library [State Library of New South Wales], Australia
MML	Mariner's Museum Library, USA

Monash	Monash University, Australia
Newberry	Newberry Library, USA
Newcastle	University of Newcastle, Australia
NLA	National Library of Australia
NLI	National Library of Ireland
NLS	National Library of Scotland
Nottingham	University of Nottingham, UK
NRL	Newcastle Region Library, Australia
NWU	North Western University, USA
NYHS	New York Historical Society, USA
NYPL	New York Public Library, USA
Oberlin	Oberlin College, USA
Ohio	Ohio State University, USA
Oxford	Oxford University, UK
PEM	Peabody Essex Museum, USA
Pittsburgh	University of Pittsburgh, USA
PLC	Public Library of Cincinnati and Hamilton County, USA
PLV	Parliamentary Library of Victoria, Australia
Princeton	Princeton University, USA
QM	Queensland Museum, Australia
Queensland	University of Queensland, Australia
RCSL	Royal Commonwealth Society Library, UK
RIA	Royal Irish Academy, Ireland
Rockdale	Rockdale City Council Library, Australia
Rutgers	Rutgers University, USA
SB	Staatsbibliothek zu Berlin, Germany
SLQ	State Library of Queensland, Australia
SLSA	State Library of South Australia, Australia
SLT	State Library of Tasmania, Australia
SLV	State Library of Victoria, Australia
SLWA	State Library of Western Australia, Australia
Stanford	Stanford University, USA
StP	St Paschal Library, Australia
Sydney	University of Sydney, Australia
Syracuse	Syracuse University, USA
Tasmania	University of Tasmania, Australia
Texas	University of Texas, USA
Toronto	University of Toronto, Canada
Trinity	Trinity College, USA

UBC	University of British Columbia, Canada
UCD	UC Davis University of California, USA
UMSL	University of Missouri-St Louis, USA
UNC	University of North Carolina, USA
UNSW	University of New South Wales, Australia
UWM	University of Wisconsin-Madison, USA
Virginia	University of Virginia, USA
Witwatersrand	University of Witwatersrand, South Africa
Yale	Yale University, USA

BIOGRAPHIES

THE | MEMOIRS | OF | GEORGE BARRINGTON, | CONTAINING | **B1a–d**
EVERY REMARKABLE CIRCUMSTANCE, | FROM HIS BIRTH TO THE
PRESENT TIME, | INCLUDING THE FOLLOWING TRIALS– | [*divided
into two columns, separated by a vertical double rule*:] 1. For robbing Mrs.
Dudman 5. Mr. Bagshaw | 2. Elizabeth Ironmonger 6. Mr. Le Mesurier |
3. Returning from Transportation 7. For Outlawry | 4. Robbing Sir G.
Webster 8. For robbing Mr. Townsend. [*columns end*] | WITH THE
WHOLE OF HIS | CELEBRATED SPEECHES, | Taken from the Records
of the King's Bench, Old Bailey, &c. | [*double rule*] | *LONDON,* | Printed
for J. BIRD, No. 22, Fetter Lane, Fleet Street; and | SIMMONDS, No. 20,
Paternoster Row. | [*rule*] | {PRICE ONE SHILLING.}

8vo. 20 x 12.5 cm. [i] blank, [ii] frontispiece, [1] title, [2] blank, [3] + 4–40 text pp.

This work, one of the two biographies of Barrington published immediately after his sentence to transportation in 1790, contains a significant
proportion of material extracted from newspaper reports of Barrington's
court appearances, with the most likely source being the official Old
Bailey Sessions paper, *The Whole Proceedings*. Some letters written by
Barrington are also included. The bulk of the excerpted material is given
in a smaller font, and on the whole the typography of the work is untidy,
suggesting that it was produced rapidly to meet the demand for
Barrington material at the peak of his fame in 1790. The work was
originally published in marbled stiff paper wrappers – the Mitchell
Library copy at Dixson 79/24 is an example of the work in its original
state.

The frontispiece illustration is divided into two sections. The larger top
section depicts Barrington emptying a man's pocket, while in the lower

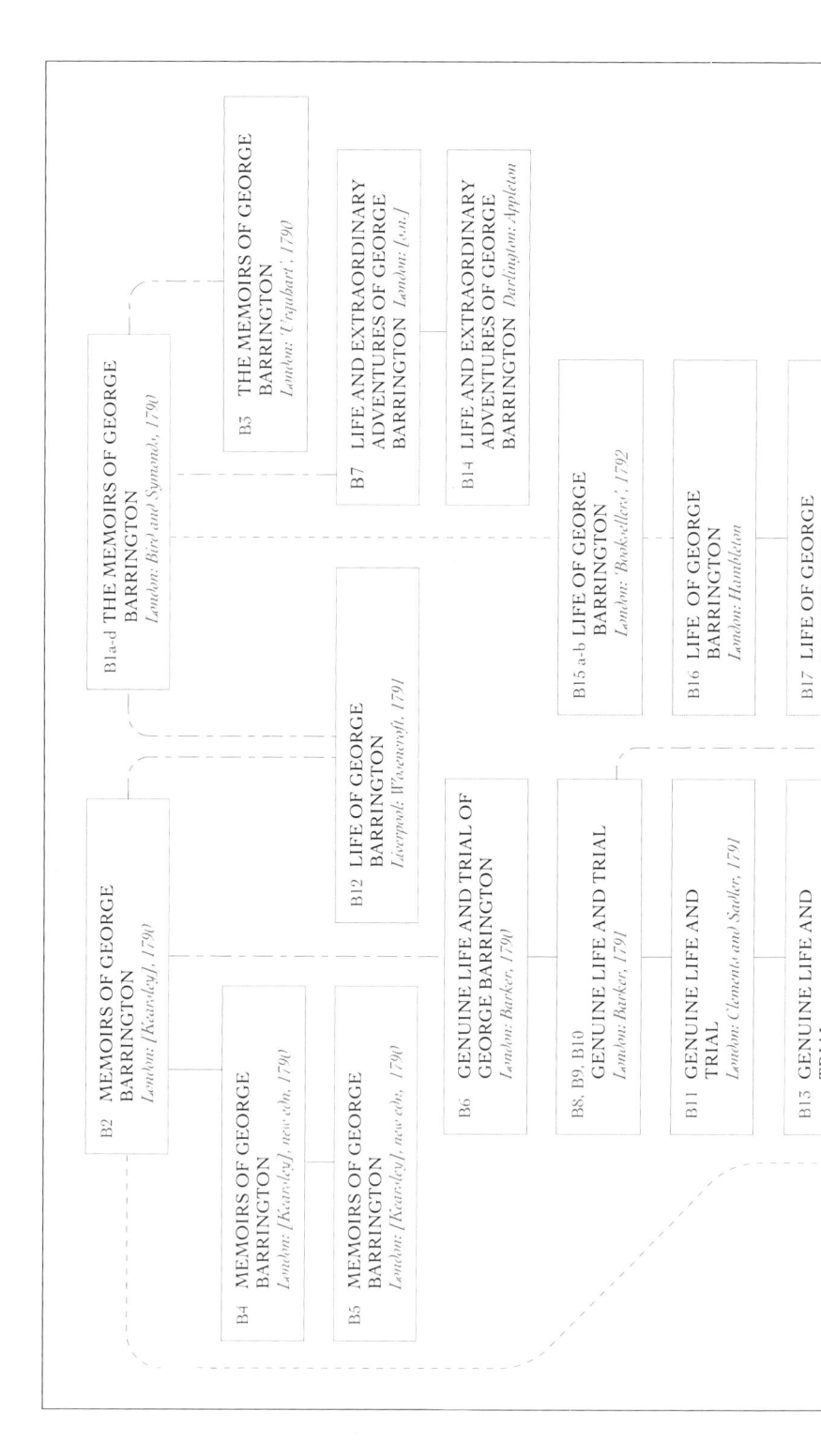

B1a-d THE MEMOIRS OF GEORGE BARRINGTON
London: Bird and Symonds, 1790

B3 THE MEMOIRS OF GEORGE BARRINGTON
London: Urquhart', 1790

B7 LIFE AND EXTRAORDINARY ADVENTURES OF GEORGE BARRINGTON *London: [s.n.]*

B14 LIFE AND EXTRAORDINARY ADVENTURES OF GEORGE BARRINGTON *Darlington: Appleton*

B2 MEMOIRS OF GEORGE BARRINGTON
London: [Kearsley], 1790

B4 MEMOIRS OF GEORGE BARRINGTON
London: [Kearsley], new edn, 1790

B5 MEMOIRS OF GEORGE BARRINGTON
London: [Kearsley], new edn, 1790

B12 LIFE OF GEORGE BARRINGTON
Liverpool: Wosencroft, 1791

B6 GENUINE LIFE AND TRIAL OF GEORGE BARRINGTON
London: Barker, 1790

B8, B9, B10 GENUINE LIFE AND TRIAL
London: Barker, 1791

B11 GENUINE LIFE AND TRIAL
London: Clements and Sadler, 1791

B13 GENUINE LIFE AND TRIAL
London: Clements, Sadler, Estes

B15 a-b LIFE OF GEORGE BARRINGTON
London: 'Booksellers', 1792

B16 LIFE OF GEORGE BARRINGTON
London: Hambleton

B17 LIFE OF GEORGE BARRINGTON
London: Hambleton, 7th edn

Stemma of the
BARRINGTON BIOGRAPHIES

B22 a-b LIFE, AMOURS AND WONDERFUL ADVENTURES OF GEORGE BARRINGTON *London: Mason*

B18 GENUINE LIFE AND TRIAL *J.A.J: Sadler, Eves, Clements*

B19 GENUINE LIFE AND TRIAL *Manchester: Sadler and Clements*

B20 LIFE AND TRIALS OF GEORGE BARRINGTON *London: Jones, 1815*

B21 GENUINE LIFE AND TRIAL *Manchester: Sadler and Thomas*

B23 LIFE, AMOURS AND WONDERFUL ADVENTURES OF GEORGE BARRINGTON *London: Fairburn*

KEY

──────── unabridged from

─ ─ ─ ─ abridged from

· · · · · · expanded from

section various pickpocketing implements are represented, and are labelled in script: '*Key with Hook & Joints*', '*Whalebone Drag*', '*Knife with three Joints*', and '*Ring with Springs*'. Printed above the illustrations is the legend: 'Barrington picking the Pocket of J. Brown, Esq'.'

Though the work was produced in one nominal edition, an examination of the six copies in the collection of the Mitchell Library reveals that a number of different typesettings were made. The distinctive features of these versions are enumerated below.

B1a

Contains a number of printing errors, especially omitted letters and misspellings. For example, 'ag[e]' (p. 4); 'committhted to the Compter' (p. 16); '[*vertical line*] On the 26th of February' (p. 22); 'on the par[t]' (p. 27); [f]orgot (p. 33); 'withstnding' (p. 37); [s]ay' (p. 37).

This version lacks a double line at the top of the first page of text (p. [3]) that other versions have. The final line of this version – 'Mr. Barrington bowed and retired.' (p. 40) – is in plain font, whereas all the other versions give this line in italics. An example of the work in this form is the Mitchell Library's copy at DSM S923.41/B276/2JI.

B1b

Some of the errors of **B1a** are corrected (e.g. pp. 22, 27, 37) though some remain (e.g. pp. 16, 33). There are also new errors in this version – see e.g. 'I was that eveningp' (p. 15); 'Ia am a gentleman' (p. 31). Page 35 is also misnumbered '33'.

Presumably this version was produced in close succession with **B1a**. The changes generally amount to little more than the substitution of a few pieces of type – the layout of the text is identical between the two versions, except for pp. 27–29, where the paragraph arrangement has been reset in a minor way. The last word (other than the catchword) on p. 28 in **B1a** is 'subsisting', while in **B1b** it is 'er-[ror]'. The ML has three copies of this version of the work (DSM C654, SC 549, DSM A923.41/B276/2B).

B1c

Corrects most of the errors of **B1b** (e.g. pp. 15, 31, 33, 35), but retains the spelling error 'committhed' on p. 16, and makes a unique printing error – 'Barringt[on]' on p. 25. The arrangement of the text is identical to **B1b**, until p. 36, from where the type is set differently. The last word at the end of p. 38 (other than the catchword) is 'person' whereas in **B1a** and **B1b** it is 'either'. An example here is ML Dixson 79/25.

B1d

This version corrects the printing errors of **B1a**, **B1b** and **B1c** (e.g. pp. 15, 16, 25, 33, 35). The title page has been reprinted and misspells 'Old Bailey' as 'Old Bailley'; it also omits a full stop in 'Mr[.] Le Mesurier'. The layout of the text is identical to **B1b** and **B1c** up until p. 36, from where the paragraph arrangement is slightly different to **B1c**. In this version the last word at the end of p. 38 is 'no'. The ML copy at Dixson 79/24 is an example of this version.

DOP: September 1790
References: Ferguson 68, ESTC T073567
Copies: ML (6 copies), NLA (2 copies), BL, ATL, NLI, SLV, Flinders, Melbourne, Cambridge, Harvard, Princeton, Cornell, McGill, Newberry, NYPL, BCL (2 copies)

MEMOIRS | OF | GEORGE BARRINGTON; | FROM | HIS BIRTH IN   B2
MDCCLV, | TO | HIS LAST CONVICTION | AT THE | *OLD BAILEY*, |
ON | FRIDAY, THE 17th OF SEPTEMBER, MDCCXC. | [*double rule*] |
LONDON: | PRINTED FOR M. SMITH, | OPPOSITE FETTER-LANE, IN
FLEET-STREET. | MDCCXC.

8vo. 20.5 x 12 cm. [i] half-title, [ii] blank, [iii] blank, [iv] frontispiece, [v] title, [vi] blank,
[1] + 2–115 text, [116] advertisements pp.

The other original biography of Barrington published after his trial in 1790. Published by George Kearsley under the false imprint 'M. Smith', this was a more elaborate, novelised version of the Barrington story. Originally published in marbled stiff paper wrappers – for an example, see the ML copy at Dixson 79/28, where the original covers are preserved within the library binding.

The frontispiece illustration represents Barrington being apprehended by Count Orlov at Covent Garden Theatre. Beneath the illustration in faint script – 'Etch^{d} by Barlow' – and in large script: 'BARRINGTON *detected picking the Pocket* | of PRINCE ORLOW *in the Front Boxes at Covent* | *Garden Theatre, of a Snuff Box set with* | *Diamonds supposed to be worth £30,000.* | Published as the Act directs, Oct.ʳ 6ᵗʰ, 1790, by G. Kearsley Fleet Street.'

Half-title: 'Memoirs | of | George Barrington. | [*rule*] | Price Two Shillings. | (Entered at Stationers Hall.)'

The advertisements following the text are for Kearsley's *Memoirs of Charles Price* ('A New Edition, Corrected and Improved') and *Memoirs of Major James Semple* ('The Ninth Edition, very much enlarged').

DOP: September 1790
References: Ferguson 66, ESTC T116125
Copies: ML (4 copies), NLA (2 copies), BL, SLSA, Glasgow, Harvard, JJC, Trinity

B3   The only Authentic Edition. | [*rule*] | THE | MEMOIRS | OF | GEORGE BARRINGTON, | CONTAINING | EVERY REMARKABLE CIRCUM-STANCE, | FROM HIS BIRTH TO THE PRESENT TIME, | INCLUDING THE FOLLOWING TRIALS– | [*divided into two columns, separated by a vertical rule*:] 1. For robbing Mrs. Dudman 5. Mr. Bagshaw | 2. Elizabeth Ironmonger 6. Mr. Le Mesurier | 3. Returning from Transportation 7. For Outlawry | 4. Robbing Sir G. Webster 8. For robbing Mr. Townsend. [*columns end*] | WITH THE WHOLE OF HIS | CELEBRATED SPEECHES, | Taken from the Records of the King's Bench, Old Bailey, &c. | [*double rule*] | *LONDON:* | Printed for the Author; and sold by B. URQUHART, and all | the Booksellers in Town and Country. | [*rule*] | {Price One Shilling.}

8vo. 22.5 x 13.5 cm. [i] blank, [ii] frontispiece, [1] title, [2] blank, [3] + 4–40 text pp.

This work is largely an abridgement of the Bird and Symonds *Memoirs* (**B1a-d**). It has an original introductory section (lasting three paragraphs), then replicates the text of **B1a-d** until p. 12, where it begins omitting sections. On pp. 17–18, it interpolates three paragraphs from the Kearsley *Memoirs* (**B2**). Unlike **B1a-d**, this work uses a uniform font size throughout, and the typography is substantially neater.

The frontispiece is a loose imitation of the illustration from **B1a-d**, showing Barrington picking the pocket of a gentleman. Above the illustration in copperplate script is the legend 'Barrington picking the pocket of J. Brown, Esqʳ.', and below the main illustration there are depictions of the pickpocketing implements shown in the frontispiece of **B1a-d**.

The Mitchell Library has a variant of this work with an additional advertisement leaf following the text (ML A923.41/B276/2D1). The recto of this leaf advertises the 'seventh edition, much enlarged' of the 'Memoirs of Major Semple', published by George Kearsley, and the verso contains a further 'Advertisement' relevant to the Semple *Memoirs*. The inclusion of a Kearsley advertisement in a work nominally produced by 'B. Urquhart' suggests that 'B. Urquhart', like 'M. Smith', was in fact a false imprint for Kearsley himself. It this was the case, it is of great interest that Kearsley not only produced one of the two original Barrington biographies, but also pirated the text of his main competitor.

DOP: October 1790?
References: Ferguson 69
Copies: ML (2 copies), NLA, Newcastle

A | *NEW EDITION.* | [*rule*] | MEMOIRS | OF | GEORGE BARRINGTON;   **B4** | FROM | HIS BIRTH IN MDCCLV, | TO | HIS LAST CONVICTION | AT THE | *OLD BAILEY,* | ON | FRIDAY, THE 17th OF SEPTEMBER, MDCCXC. | [*double rule*] | London: | PRINTED FOR M. SMITH, | OPPOSITE FETTER-LANE, IN FLEET STREET. | MDCCXC.

8vo. 20.5 x 12.5 cm. [i] half-title, [ii] blank, [iii] title, [iv] blank, [1] + 2–115 text, [116] advertisements pp.

The 'new edition' of the Kearsley *Memoirs* was in fact a reissue of the sheets of the first edition (**B2**), with revised title and half-title leaves.

Half-title: 'A | New Edition | Memoirs | of | George Barrington. | [*rule*] | Price Two Shillings. | {Entered at Stationers Hall.}'

Frontispiece and advertisements page: as for **B2**

DOP: October 1790
References: Ferguson 67a, ESTC N21952
Copies: ML, NLA, Glasgow, MCL, UBC

A NEW EDITION, GREATLY IMPROVED. | [*rule*] | MEMOIRS | OF | **B5** GEORGE BARRINGTON; | FROM | HIS BIRTH IN MDCCLV, | TO | HIS LAST CONVICTION | AT THE | *OLD BAILEY,* | ON | FRIDAY, THE 17th

OF SEPTEMBER, MDCCXC. | [*double rule*] | LONDON: | PRINTED FOR M. SMITH, | OPPOSITE FETTER-LANE, IN FLEET-STREET. | MDCCXC.

8vo. 22 x 13 cm. [i] blank, [ii] frontispiece, [iii] title, [iv] blank, [1] + 2–91 text, [92] advertisements pp.

This 'greatly improved' further edition of the Kearsley *Memoirs* is textually identical to the earlier versions (**B2** and **B4**), though unlike the earlier 'new edition' (**B4**) it was a reprint. The main 'improvement' is the use of a more compact letterpress through pp. [1]–39 of the text, which leads to a reduction in the overall page length of the book. The resetting of the type in this more compact way does not continue after p. 39, and the remainder of the text (pp. 39–91) is identical in layout to the earlier editions.

Frontispiece and advertisements page: as for **B2**.

DOP: October 1790
References: Ferguson 67, ESTC T177089
Copies: ML (3 copies), NLA (3 copies), BL, ATL, SLQ, Oxford, Harvard, Toronto, PLV, Czartoryski

B6   THE GENUINE | LIFE AND TRIAL | OF | George Barrington, | FROM HIS BIRTH, IN JUNE, 1755, | TO THE | Time of his Conviction at the OLD-BAILEY, | In SEPTEMBER, 1790, | For robbing HENRY HARE TOWNSEND, ESQ. | of his gold Watch, Seals, &c. | [*double rule*] | LONDON: | PRINTED FOR ROBERT BARKER, IN NOVEMBER, 1790. | Price Sixpence.

8vo. 17 x 11 cm. [1] blank, [2] frontispiece, [3] title, [4] blank, [5] + 6–48 text pp.

This work was likely to have been the first of the many chapbook redactions of the Kearsley *Memoirs* (**B2, B4, B5**). The abridgement from the Kearsley text was made by simply omitting sections; there was no significant rewriting from the original.

The frontispiece, a crude illustration similar in style to the woodcuts found in earlier eighteenth-century chapbooks, depicts a male figure clasping the hand of a female figure, while another female figure looks on. In the background is a stately house. Below the illustration is the legend: 'George Barrington's first Interview with Miss Egerton.'

DOP: 'November 1790'
References: ESTC T097911
Copies: BL, NLI (2 copies), Oxford, RCSL

The Life and extraordinary adventures of George Barrington, now under **B7** sentence of transportation, in Newgate, for picking the pocket of Mr. Townsend, at Enfield races. Containing, an account of the various robberies he has committed, in England, Ireland, and Scotland. Also, his love exploits, sufferings on board the hulks at Woolwich, various trials, famous speeches, &c. &c... Printed and sold in London. {Price one penny}.

12mo. 12pp. [not seen – ESTC].

A penny chapbook version of the Barrington biography, this has a very similar title to the chapbook printed in Darlington by William Appleton (see **B14**). While **B14** states that Barrington is 'now transported to Botany Bay', this version has 'now under sentence of transportation, in Newgate', and is therefore likely to have been the earlier work.

The ESTC record notes a woodcut on the title page.

DOP: c. 1790–1791
References: ESTC T300606
Copies: Oxford

THE GENUINE | LIFE AND TRIAL | OF | George Barrington, | FROM **B8** HIS BIRTH, IN JUNE, 1755, | TO THE | Time of his Conviction at the OLD-BAILEY, | In SEPTEMBER, 1790, | For robbing HENRY HARE TOWNSEND, ESQ. | of his gold Watch, Seals, &c. | [*double rule*] | LONDON: | PRINTED FOR ROBERT BARKER, IN JANUARY, 1791. | Price Sixpence.

8vo. 17 x 11 cm. [1] blank, [2] frontispiece, [3] title, [4] blank, [5] + 6–48 text pp.

The text is identical to the earlier Barker *Genuine Life* (**B6**), save for a few very minor changes and printing errors – see p. 6 ('entitled' substituted for 'intitled') and p. 23 ('knowledge' for 'knowledg') – which show that the text, along with the title page, has been reprinted.

Frontispiece: as for **B6**.

DOP: 'January 1791'
References: Ferguson 98a
Copies: ML, NLA (2 copies).

B9   THE GENUINE | LIFE AND TRIAL | OF | George Barrington, | FROM HIS BIRTH, IN JUNE, 1755, | TO THE | Time of his Conviction at the OLD-BAILEY, | In SEPTEMBER, 1790, | For robbing HENRY HARE TOWNSEND, ESQ. | of his gold Watch, Seals, &c. | [*double rule*] | LONDON: | PRINTED FOR ROBERT BARKER, IN MARCH, 1791. | Price Sixpence.

8vo. 17 x 11 cm. [1] blank, [2] frontispiece, [3] title, [4] blank, [5] + 6–48 text pp.

Another reprint of Barker's *Genuine Life*, using the same text as **B8**.

Frontispiece: as for **B6**.

DOP: 'March 1791'
References: Ferguson 98aa, ESTC T129321
Copies: NLA, BL, ATL, Monash, Melbourne

B10   THE GENUINE | LIFE AND TRIAL | OF | George Barrington, | FROM HIS BIRTH, IN JUNE, 1755, | TO THE | Time of his Conviction at the OLD-BAILEY, | In SEPTEMBER, 1790, | For robbing HENRY HARE TOWNSEND, ESQ. | of his gold Watch, Seals, &c. | [*double rule*] | LONDON: | PRINTED FOR ROBERT BARKER, IN AUGUST, 1791. | Price Sixpence.

8vo. 17 x 11 cm. [1] blank, [2] frontispiece, [3] title, [4] blank, [5] + 6–48 text pp.

The last known reprint of Barker's *Genuine Life*, with an identical text and layout to **B9**.

Frontispiece: as for **B6**.

DOP: 'August 1791'
References: Ferguson 98, ESTC T222228
Copies: NLA, RIA

B11   THE GENUINE | LIFE AND TRIAL | OF | GEORGE BARRINGTON, | FROM HIS BIRTH, IN JUNE, 1775, | TO THE | TIME OF HIS CON-VICTION | AT THE OLD-BAILEY, | IN SEPTEMBER, 1790, | FOR

ROBBING | *HENRY HARE TOWNSEND, Esq.* | OF HIS GOLD WATCH, SEALS, &c. | [*rule*] | LONDON: | PRINTED FOR, AND SOLD BY W. CLEMENTS, AND | J. SADLER, IN THE YEAR 1791. | PRICE SIX-PENCE.

8vo. 18 x 12 cm. [1] blank, [2] frontispiece, [3] title, [4] blank, [5] + 6–48 text pp.

The text of this work is virtually identical to that of the Robert Barker *Genuine Life* editions (**B6**, **B8**, **B9**, **B10**), making only minor emendations.

While the text replicates Barker's abridgement of the Kearsley *Memoirs* (**B2**, **B4**, **B5**), the frontispiece is an imitation of the illustration from the Bird and Symonds *Memoirs* (**B1a-d**), and much closer to the original than the version found in **B3**. The illustration is framed differently, however: the figures of Barrington and his victim are presented inside an oval frame within a rectangular outer frame, while the pickpocketing implements shown in the illustration of **B1a-d** occupy the spaces in each corner between the oval and the rectangular frames. Inside the oval frame, at the feet of the two figures, is the attribution: 'W. Green sculp'. Knaresbro.', and beneath the outer frame is the legend: 'Barrington picking the Pocket of Henry Hare | Townsend, Esq. of his gold Watch, Seals, &c.'

DOP: '1791'
References: Ferguson 98a, ESTC T217710
Copies: ML, NLA, ATL

THE | LIFE | OF | GEORGE BARRINGTON, | (KING OF THE PICK- **B12** POCKETS) | AS DELIVERED BY HIMSELF, TO A FRIEND, | FROM | HIS BIRTH IN 1755, TO | HIS LAST CONVICTION, | AT THE | *OLD BAILEY*; | ON FRIDAY, THE 17th OF SEPTEMBER, 1790; | ALSO ALL HIS | TRYALS AND ADMIRED SPEECHES, | FAITHFULLY TAKEN FROM THE RECORDS | OF THE | *KING'S BENCH, OLD BAILEY*, &c. &c. | BY A GENTLEMAN OF LINCOLN'S-INN. | [*double rule*] | LIVERPOOL: | PRINTED BY CHARLES WOSENCROFT. | [*rule*] | MDCCXCI.

8vo. 22.5 x 14 cm. [1] title, [2] blank, [3] + 4–140 text pp.

This work blends the Bird and Symonds (**B1a-d**) and Kearsley (**B2**, **B4**, **B5**) texts, without rewriting apart from minor editorial emendations designed to make the two narratives fit together. Barrington's real name is given as 'Waldon' in this text.

Probably originally issued in paste boards – fragments of which survive in the ML copy, which is now disbound. The ML copy lacks several leaves (pp. 11–12, 73–80).

DOP: '1791'
References: None found
Copies: ML

B13 THE GENUINE | LIFE AND TRIAL, | OF | George Barrington, | FROM HIS BIRTH, IN JUNE, 1775, | TO THE | TIME OF HIS CONVICTION | AT THE OLD-BAILEY, | IN SEPTEMBER, 1790, | FOR ROBBING | HENRY HARE TOWNSEND, Esq. | OF HIS GOLD WATCH, SEALS, &c. | [*rule*] | LONDON: | PRINTED FOR AND SOLD BY MRS MARY CLEMENTS, | MR JAMES SADLER, AND MR JOHN EVES. | PRICE SIX-PENCE.

8vo. 19 x 12 cm. [1] blank, [2] frontispiece, [3] title, [4] blank, [5] + 6–48 text pp.

The text of this version of the *Genuine Life* is the same as that of **B11** save for a number of printing errors. In the NLA copy, the only known extant copy of this version, these errors are corrected in ink, and it seems possible that this was a proof copy for another version of the *Genuine Life* produced for the same booksellers (see **B11**, **B18**, **B19**, **B21**). The title page closely follows the typography of **B11**, replicating the error that gives Barrington's date of birth as 'June, 1775'.

Frontispiece: as for **B11**.

DOP: c. 1791–1798?
References: Ferguson 63
Copies: NLA

B14 THE LIFE | AND EXTRAORDINARY ADVENTURES OF | *George Barrington,* | *Now Transported to Botany-Bay, for picking the Pockets of* | *Mr Townsend, at Enfield Races—Containing an Account of* | *the various robberies he has committed in England, Ireland,* | *and Scotland,—Also his Love Exploits, sufferings on board the* | *hulks at Woolwich, various Trials, famous Speeches, &c. &c.* | [*rule*] | *PRICE ONE PENNY.* | [*rule*] | [*text begins*]

12mo [BL – seen only in facsimile]. [1], title [and text begins] – 8 text pp.

This work was a radically abridged redaction of **B1a-d**. The title of this work closely resembles that of another penny chapbook, *Life and Extraordinary Adventures of George Barrington*, said to be 'printed and sold in London' (see **AB7**); the latter work probably served as a model for this.

Colophon (foot of p. 8): 'W. A. *Printer*, DARLINGTON.'

DOP: c. 1791–1800?
References: Ferguson 213, ESTC T040925
Copies: BL, ATL

THE | *LIFE* | OF | GEORGE BARRINGTON | CONTAINING | EVERY **B15a–b** REMARKABLE CIRCUMSTANCE | From his BIRTH to the present TIME. | INCLUDING THE FOLLOWING TRIALS– | [*divided into two columns, separated by a vertical rule*:] 1. For robbing Mrs. Dudman 5. Mr. Bagshaw | 2. Elizabeth Ironmonger 6. Mr. Le Mesurier | 3. Returning from Transportation 7. For Outlawry | 4. Robbing Sir G. Webster 8. For robbing Mr. Townsend. [*columns end*] | WITH THE WHOLE OF HIS | CELEBRATED SPEECHES, | Taken from the Records of the King's Bench, Old Bailey, &c. | [*rule*] | TO WHICH IS ADDED | A Copy of a Letter from him at the Cape of Good-Hope | To a Gentleman in the County of York, dated 1st July 1791 | [*double rule*] | LONDON: | Printed for the BOOKSELLERS, 1792. | {PRICE SIX-PENCE}

8vo. 20.5 x 11.5 cm. [i] blank, [ii] frontispiece, [1] title, [2] blank, 3–42 text pp.

A reprint, without abridgement, of **B1a-d**, with additional material in the form of a letter from Barrington that had appeared in British newspapers in late 1791. The text of the letter runs on from the main text, separated only by a decorative rule (pp. 39–42).

The frontispiece illustration is identical to that found in **B11** and **B13**. It is given a different title, however: above the illustration, in letterpress: 'G. Barrington,' and below it: 'Picking the pocket of J. Brown, Esq. | See Page 11.'.

This work was issued with two different title pages as below.

B15a

The imprint misspells 'Booksellers' as 'Bookselers'. The NLA copy is an example of this variant.

B15b

'Booksellers' is spelled correctly (BL copy).

Apart from the title page there are no other differences; the NLA and BL copies share printing idiosyncrasies which show that the title page only had been reprinted, perhaps merely to correct the error.

DOP: '1792'
References: Ferguson 123
Copies: NLA, BL

B16   The life of George Barrington, containing every remarkable circumstance, from his birth to the present time, including the following trials-1. For robbing Mrs. Dudman ... 8. For robbing Mr. Townsend. With the whole of his celebrated speeches, ... printed and sold by Andrew Hambleton

12mo. 18 cm. 56 pp. front. [not seen – ESTC/Brown]

The description of this work in the ESTC suggests it is very similar to the same publisher's 'Seventh Edition' of the *Life of George Barrington* (see **B17**). **B16** has no edition statement, however.

DOP: c. 1792
References: ESTC N33826
Copies: Brown

B17   *THE LIFE* | OF | GEORGE BARRINGTON, | CONTAINING | EVERY REMARKABLE CIRCUMSTANCE, | *From his BIRTH to the present TIME,* | INCLUDING THE FOLLOWING TRIALS– | [*divided into two columns:*] 1. *For robbing Mrs. Dudman 5. Mr. Bagshaw* | 2. *Elizabeth Ironmonger 6. Mr. Le Mesurier* | 3. *Returning from Transportation 7. For Outlawry* | 4. *Robbing Sir G. Webster 8. For robbing Mr. Townsend.* [*columns end*] | WITH THE WHOLE OF HIS | CELEBRATED SPEECHES, | Taken from the Records of King's Bench, Old Bailey, &c. | [*rule*] | The SEVENTH EDITION. | [*double rule*] | PRINTED AND SOLD | BY ANDREW HAMBLETON. | {PRICE SIX-PENCE.}

12mo. 19 x 12.5 cm. [1] title, [2] blank, 3–56 text pp.

Another unabridged reprint of **B1a-b**, even copying the varying font sizes of the original work. On the final page (p. 56), however, there is a heavily abridged version of the letter from Barrington which had also appeared in **B15a-b**.

DOP: c. 1792
References: Ferguson 123
Copies: ML, NLA

THE GENUINE I LIFE AND TRIAL I OF I G. BARRINGTON, I from his   **B18**
I Birth in June 1755, I to the I *Time of his Conviction in September*, 1790, I
TO THE I OLD BAYLEY, I FOR ROBBING I Henry Hare Townsend, *Esq.*
I OF HIS GOLD WATCH, SEALS, &c. I *[double rule]* I PRINTED I FOR J.
SADLER, J. EVES, AND M. CLEMENTS. I *(Price Sixpence.)*

8vo. 17.5 x 11 cm. [1] blank, [2] frontispiece, [3] title, [4] blank, [5] + 6–48 text pp.

Another reprint using the same text as previous versions of the *Genuine Life*, with a somewhat neater typography than the previous versions.

This work was possibly produced by the Manchester printer Alice Swindells, who printed a number of versions of the *Genuine Life* (**B19**, **B21**) and 'Barrington's' *Voyage* (**AB15**, **AB16**, **AB46**, see also **AB13**) for the same group of booksellers. A printer's ornament (a rose) at the end of the text (p. 48) resembles one used on the title page of **B19**.

The frontispiece is the same illustration as in **B11**, **B13**, and **B15a-b**; the legend here reads: 'BARRINGTON I PICKING THE POCKET OF HENRY HARE I TOWNSEND, ESQ. OF HIS GOLD I WATCH, SEALS, *&c.*'.

DOP: c. 1792–1800?
References: Ferguson 64
Copies: ML, NLA (2 copies)

THE GENUINE I LIFE AND TRIAL, I OF I GEORGE BARRINGTON, I   **B19**
FROM HIS BIRTH, IN JUNE, 1775, I TO THE I Time of his Conviction I
At the OLD BAILEY, I in SEPTEMBER 1790, I For Robbing I HENRY
HARE TOWNSEND, ESQ. I *Of his Gold Watch, Seals, &c.* I *[printer's ornament]* I Printed by A. Swindells, Hanging-bridge. I *Manchester:* I

AND SOLD BY J. SADLER, AND M. CLEMENTS, | [*rule*] | *Price only sixpence.*

8vo. 17 x 10.5 cm. [1] blank, [2] frontispiece, [3] title, [4] blank, [5] + 6–48 text pp.

Again, the text is the same as used in previous incarnations of the *Genuine Life*, and the frontispiece illustration is the same as in **B11**, **B13**, **B15a-b**, and **B18**. The title page of this version replicates the error of **B11** and **B13**, giving Barrington's birth date as '1775'.

This work was the first of the *Genuine Life and Trial* chapbooks to include a printer's name, which in this case was A[lice] Swindells of Manchester.

The ML copy at Dixson 79/1 has a clear watermark date '1798' on its frontispiece leaf (pp. [1]–[2]), making publication in this year or soon after likely. It was originally issued in thin blue paper wrappers – the ML copy at Dixson 79/2 is an example of the work in its original state.

DOP: c. 1798–1800
References: Ferguson 65a, ESTC T183821
Copies: ML (3 copies), ATL, Oxford, Cornell

B20   THE | LIFE AND TRIALS | OF | GEORGE BARRINGTON, | OFFICER OF THE PEACE AT PARAMATTA. | AUTHOR OF | THE VOYAGE TO, | AND | HISTORY | OF | *NEW SOUTH WALES.* | [*rule*] | *LONDON:* | *Printed by W. Flint, Old Bailey,* | FOR M. JONES, NO. 1, PATERNOSTER-ROW. | [*double rule*] | | 1803.

8vo. 22 x 13.5 cm. [i] blank, [ii] frontispiece, [iii] title, [iv] blank, [1] + 2–72 text pp.

A revised version of the text of the Kearsley *Memoirs* (**AB2**, **AB4**, **AB5**).

This work was principally compiled from sheets printed for the same publisher's *Account of a Voyage to New South Wales* (see **AB30**), which included this text as preliminary material. In this separately issued version of the Barrington biography there is a different title page (printed rather than engraved, as in **AB30**), and the final page of the text (p. 72) has been altered; a colophon has been added ('W. Flint, Printer, Old Bailey.'), and the final sentence has been modified: where **AB30** has

... and thus withdrew from public life in Europe, to act a part in the new world; and though in a different sphere, yet not much less distinguished than before, as the following pages will testify (p. 72)

B20 ends:

... and thus withdrew from public life in Europe, to act a part in the new world.

Frontispiece: as for **AB30**.

DOP: 1803
References: Ferguson 364
Copies: ML, NLA, NLI

THE GENUINE | *LIFE AND TRIAL,* | OF | GEORGE BARRINGTON, | **B21**
FROM HIS BIRTH, | TO THE | Time of his Conviction | *AT THE OLD*
BAYLEY, IN SEPTEMBER 1790, | *FOR ROBBING* | Henry Hare
Townsend, Esq. of his Gold Watch, Seals, &c. | *[ornament]* | Printed by A.
Swindells, Hanging-bridge. | *Manchester:* | AND SOLD BY J. SADLER,
AND T. THOMAS. | *[rule]* | *Price ninepence.*

8vo. 17.5 x 11 cm. [1] blank, [2] frontispiece, [3] title, [4] blank, [5] + 6–48 text pp.

A further reprint of the *Genuine Life*, once again using the same text as
found in all previous versions. This was apparently a later version of the
work, printed by Alice Swindells at about the time she produced a version
of the Barrington *Voyage* for the same booksellers (see **AB46**). A water-
mark date on one of the leaves (pp. 17–18) reads '1 , 8 | 0 8' [i.e. 1808?].

Colophon (p. 48): 'Printed by A. Swindells, Hanging-Bridge. | *Manchester:*
| AND SOLD BY J. SADLER, AND T. THOMAS. | *[rule]* | *Price ninepence.*'

Frontispiece: as for **B11**.

DOP: c. 1809
References: Ferguson 65
Copies: ML

THE | LIFE, AMOURS, | AND | Wonderful Adventures | OF THAT   **B22a–b**
MOST | Notorious Pickpocket, | George Barrington, | FROM HIS
BIRTH, | To his | *Conviction at the Old-Bailey,* | FOR ROBBING HENRY
HARE TOWNSEND, ESQ. | *[double rule]* | *Embellished with an Elegant*
Frontispiece, which contains a striking | Likeness of Barrington. | *[double rule]*
| *LONDON:* | PRINTED AND PUBLISHED BY W. MASON, | 21,
CLERKENWELL GREEN. | *[rule]* | *SIXPENCE.*

8vo. 18.5 x 12.5 cm. [i] blank, [ii] [front?], [1] title, [2] blank, [3] + 4–30, [31] + 32–35 text, [36] advertisements pp.

This was a revised version, with the language somewhat updated, of the text of the *Genuine Life* (see **B6, B8, B9, B10, B11, B13, B18, B19, B21**), published as a bluebook pamphlet. At the conclusion of the *Genuine Life* text (p. 35), there is an additional paragraph containing a new 'anecdote of our hero, which may be depended on, [and] appeared in all the newspapers of that period'. The anecdote, an apocryphal tale of Barrington's pickpocketing exploits, was subsequently adapted in later works (see Box, pp. 164–65).

Misdated by Ferguson as '1790', this work appeared in the year 1820 or soon after. The advertisements page at the end of the work advertises a sixpenny pamphlet version of the 'Trial of [Robert] Wedderburn' – the Spencean radical Wedderburn was tried and convicted of 'blasphemous libel' in May 1820. Mason's other advertised works included a 'New Union Spelling Book' and a 'First Book for Children', and he also promoted his wide-ranging trade activities: 'Printing, Bookbinding, and Engraving, in all their Branches, in the first Style of the Art, and on the lowest Terms, by W. Mason, 21, Clerkenwell Green.'

The ML copy at A923.41/B276/2EI preserves the original blue paper wrappers within a library binding. On the outside front cover is the title: 'George Barrington. | [*rule*] | *Published at Mason's Pamphlet Warehouse*. | 21, Clerkenwell Green, | *Where the Trade may be supplied with Pamphlets, Children's | Books, &c. Elegantly Printed on Fine Paper, and Hotpressed*. | *Cheaper than at any other Publishers in London*. | Orders by Post punctually attended to'. The outside back cover contains additional advertisements for the 'New Union Spelling Book' and the 'First Book for Children'.

The 'Elegant Frontispiece' said to embellish the work was possibly an engraving illustrating Barrington's theft of Henry Hare Townsend's watch at the Enfield races in 1790. This plate appears in both ML copies, though it is not bound as a frontispiece in either copy. Both NLA copies lack plates.

One of the NLA copies is a variant (**22b**), in which no price is given on the title page.

DOP: c. 1820
References: Ferguson 61
Copies: ML (2 copies), NLA (2 copies), Connecticut

FAIRBURN'S EDITION | OF THE | LIFE, AMOURS, | AND | **B23**
WONDERFUL ADVENTURES | OF THAT MOST NOTORIOUS |
PICKPOCKET, | *George Barrington,* | GIVING A FULL ACCOUNT OF
HIS | TRIAL, AND CONVICTION, | WITH MANY | CURIOUS
ANECDOTES OF THIS | NOTORIOUS CHARACTER. | [*rule*] |
Embellished with a Coloured Frontispiece. | [*rule*] | *LONDON:* | PRINTED
AND PUBLISHED BY J. FAIRBURN, 110, MINORIES. | *Price Sixpence.*

8vo. 18 x 10.5 cm. [i] blank, [ii] frontispiece, [1] title, [2] blank, [3] + 4–24 text pp.

A later Barrington biography published as a bluebook pamphlet. The
text, derived from the Kearsley *Memoirs* (**B2**, **B4**, **B5**) was likely to have
been abridged from the 'Life of George Barrington' in the 1810 edition
of *An Account of a Voyage to New South Wales*: the final page (p. 24) contains material – such as the refutation that Barrington had died insane –
which had been drawn from that source (see **AB47**, pp. [xi]–[xii]).

The ML copy from the David Scott Mitchell collection preserves the
original blue paper wrappers within a modern binding. On the outside
front cover the title page is reproduced, while the outside back cover is
an advertisements page of 'Books just Published by J. Fairburn, 110,
Minories'. This lists some 37 sixpenny pamphlets, 21 'Childrens' Books'
also priced at sixpence, 3 shilling books, a numbered series of 'Fairburn's
drawing books' (1–23, also sixpence), another numbered series of 'One
Shilling Drawing Books' (1–9), 'a good assortment' of 'School Pieces',
'Valentine Letters, 100 sorts, at 6d and upwards', and 'A fine Engraving
of a Scotchman for Tobacco Shop Windows, 6d'.

The hand-coloured folding frontispiece is divided into two sections, with
the legend below each: 'Barrington robbing a Nobleman at court.' and
'Barrington taken prisoner on the Race Course.' No artist's name is given.

Colophon (p. 24): 'Fairburn, Printer, 110, Minories, London.'

DOP: c. 1820–1830
References: Ferguson 364
Copies: ML (2 copies), NL, ATL

THE | LIFE, TIMES AND ADVENTURES | OF | GEORGE   **B24**
BARRINGTON, | THE CELEBRATED THIEF & PICKPOCKET, |

EMBRACING THE WHOLE OF HIS HISTORY, AND A FULL
ACCOUNT | OF ALL HIS | EXTRAORDINARY FEATS, | WHICH
PROCURED HIM THE NAME OF | "THE PRINCE OF THIEVES;" | HIS
ATTEMPTED MURDER OF O'NEILL, ROBBERY OF | THE DUKE OF
LEINSTER, THE DUKE'S ATTACK | ON BARRINGTON'S WIFE, &c; |
ALSO, | FULL DETAILS OF THE MANY DESPERATE ROBBERIES
COMMITTED | BY BARRINGTON, IN ENGLAND, IRELAND, ETC. |
[rule] | EMBELLISHED WITH MANY BEAUTIFUL ENGRAVINGS. |
[rule] | LONDON: | PUBLISHED BY JOHN WILSON, OXFORD
STREET, | AND SOLD BY ALL BOOKSELLERS.

8vo. 19 x 11 cm. [i] title, [ii] blank, [1] + 2–74 text pp. With 4 additional leaves of plates.

The *Life, Times and Adventures of George Barrington* was probably the
first of the novelisations of the famed pickpocket's life that appeared in
the Victorian era. The work was only distantly related to the earlier
biographies, containing instead a series of entirely fictional adventures.
The first chapter is prefaced by some verses adapted from the so-called
'Barrington Prologue'. The narrative also contrives a happy end to the
Barrington saga; it is stated that after Barrington's trial on 'September
the 1st. 1798', he was transported and appointed constable at
Parramatta:

> Here his conduct was such as to compensate in some measure for his former misdeeds,
> and eventually to raise him in the Office of Chief of the Constabulary Force of the
> Colony—in which he gave great satisfaction, and amassed a very considerable fortune,
> lived to a good old age, and died much respected by all who knew him, at Botany Bay
> (p. 74).

The first edition of the *Life, Times and Adventures of George Barrington*
seems to have been issued as a part publication in four parts of 24 pages
or fewer. The ML copy has stab marks where the original parts had been
sewn, and the text is punctuated by added leaves of thin brown paper.
The recto of each of these is blank, and seems to have served as a cover
for each part, while on the verso of each added leaf is an engraved
illustration. Some of these illustrations carry the imprint of the artist and
engraver, George Stiff.

The illustrations in the ML copy are:

1. Facing the title page: A representation of Barrington in the dock, in
   irons.

2. Facing page 25: Barrington punching a cowering Harlequin figure, while a crowd watches.

3. Facing page 49: Barrington picking a gentleman's pocket. At the foot of the engraving: 'G. Stiff'.

4. Facing page 61: [entitled] '{Barrington and Price encountering the Witch}' At the foot of the engraving: 'G. Stiff Del et Sc'.

Colophon (foot of p. 74): 'Printed by John Wilson, Oxford Street, London.'

DOP: c. 1835–1845
References: Ferguson 774
Copies: ML, BL

SECOND EDITION. | [*rule*] | THE | LIFE, TIMES AND ADVENTURES   **B25**
| OF | GEORGE BARRINGTON, | THE CELEBRATED THIEF &
PICKPOCKET, | EMBRACING THE WHOLE OF HIS HISTORY, AND
A FULL ACCOUNT | OF ALL HIS | EXTRAORDINARY FEATS, |
WHICH PROCURED HIM THE NAME OF | "THE PRINCE OF
THIEVES!" | HIS ATTEMPTED MURDER OF O'NEILL, ROBBERY OF
| THE DUKE OF LEINSTER, THE DUKE'S ATTACK | ON
BARRINGTON'S WIFE, &c.; | ALSO, | FULL DETAILS OF THE MANY
DESPERATE ROBBERIES COMMITTED | BY BARRINGTON, IN
ENGLAND, IRELAND, ETC. | [*rule*] | EMBELLISHED WITH BEAUTI-
FUL ENGRAVINGS. | [*rule*] | LONDON: | PUBLISHED BY JOHN
WILSON, OXFORD STREET, | AND SOLD BY ALL BOOKSELLERS. |
(*Price Half-a-Crown.*)

8vo. 19 x 11 cm. [i] title, [ii] blank, [1] + 2–73 text, [74] blank pp.

The 'Second Edition' of the *Life, Times and Adventures of George Barrington* was for the most part a reissue of the printed sheets of the first (**B24**). Apart from the new title page, the only other alteration was that the final leaf had been reprinted, condensing the text of the last two pages of **B24** into a single page, making textual omissions in the process.

It is uncertain whether the 'Second Edition' of the *Life, Times and Adventures of George Barrington* was also issued in parts (see **B24**). That a price was now given on the title page – 'Half-a-Crown' – may suggest the work was sold as a complete pamphlet. In each of the Mitchell Library's three copies, brown paper leaves with an engraved illustration on one side (see **B24**) appear in only two places in the text – at the beginning (i.e. facing the title page), and in the middle of the work (between pages 36 and 37).

Each of the ML copies is bound with different illustrations, the majority of which had appeared in the first edition; it appears these added leaves were issued with different copies more or less at random.

The following is a list of the illustrations in the different ML copies:

Dixson 82/126:

Facing title: Barrington carousing with a number of ladies. At foot of engraving: 'G. Stiff Sc'.
Between pp. 36–37: As for **B23**, illustration 3.

Dixson 82/127:

Facing title: As for **B23**, illustration 3.
Between pp. 36–37: As for **B23**, illustration 2.

Dixson 82/128:

Facing title: As for **B23**, illustration 1.
Between pp. 36–37: as for **B23**, illustration 2.

DOP: c. 1835–1845
References: Ferguson 775, Ferguson 775a
Copies: ML (3 copies), NLA (3 copies)

ALLONYMOUS BARRINGTON BOOKS

AB1 A | VOYAGE | TO | NEW SOUTH WALES; | WITH | A DESCRIPTION OF THE COUNTRY; | THE | *MANNERS, CUSTOMS, RELIGION*, &c. | OF | THE NATIVES, | In the Vicinity of | BOTANY BAY. | [*rule*] | *BY GEORGE BARRINGTON*, | NOW | SUPERINTENDANT OF THE CONVICTS | AT | PARAMATTA. | [*double rule*] | *London* | PRINTED FOR THE PROPRIETOR; | SOLD BY H. D. SYMONDS, NO. 20, PATERNOSTER-ROW. | [*rule*] | {Price Half-a-Crown.} | [*rule*] | 1795.

8vo. 21 x 12.5 cm. [5] title, [6] blank, [7] dedicatory letter ('1793'), [8] blank, [9]–[12] contents, [13] + 14–140 text pp.

The original form of the 'Barrington' *Voyage*, the first and most significant text spuriously attributed to George Barrington. Substantially plagiarised from John Hunter's *An Historical Journal of the Transactions at Port Jackson and Norfolk Island*, with additional material taken from other 1790s travel narratives, the work also contained original fictional episodes detailing the supposed author's adventures on the voyage and in the colony. Notable among the original sections are a description of a 'crossing the [equatorial] line' ceremony (chapter 3, pp 25–27), a chimerical encounter with the *Flying Dutchman* (chapter 6, pp. 45–47) and a 'first contact' tale involving 'Barrington' and two fictitious 'natives', Yeariana and Palerino (chapter 15, pp. 129–39).

All copies I have surveyed are printed on paper with various watermarks, including the date '1794' (see e.g. pp. [7]–[8], [13]–14). Chapters 10, 11 and 12 are wrongly numbered IX, XIII and XIV in the text.

The text is preceded by a letter from 'Barrington' that serves as a dedication, designed to introduce and validate the narrative as Barrington's work. The text of the letter is as follows:

To Mr: * * * *.

Dear Sir,

I Embrace the earliest opportunity of performing the promise I made you on my quitting England; and should the contents of the accompanying sheets, collected chiefly from personal observation, aided by the best local inquiries, acquit me, in your mind, of a breach of that promise, I shall feel myself more than happy: They had been more ample, but that I was impatient to pay a debt of gratitude that would not brook the loss of an opportunity; consequently you will find the conclusion rather abrupt; but by the next ship I shall, I trust, make amends, having nearly transcribed some letters from my friend, Mr. Wentworth, containing a pleasant narrative of the rise and progress of the settlement at Norfolk Island; together with some farther particulars relative to,

Sir,

Your most obedient,

And obliged,

Humble Servant,

G. Barrington.

Parramatta, November 1793.

The publication of this work was advertised in various English newspapers in late March, April, May and September 1795.

Stemma of the
'BARRINGTON' *VOYAGE*

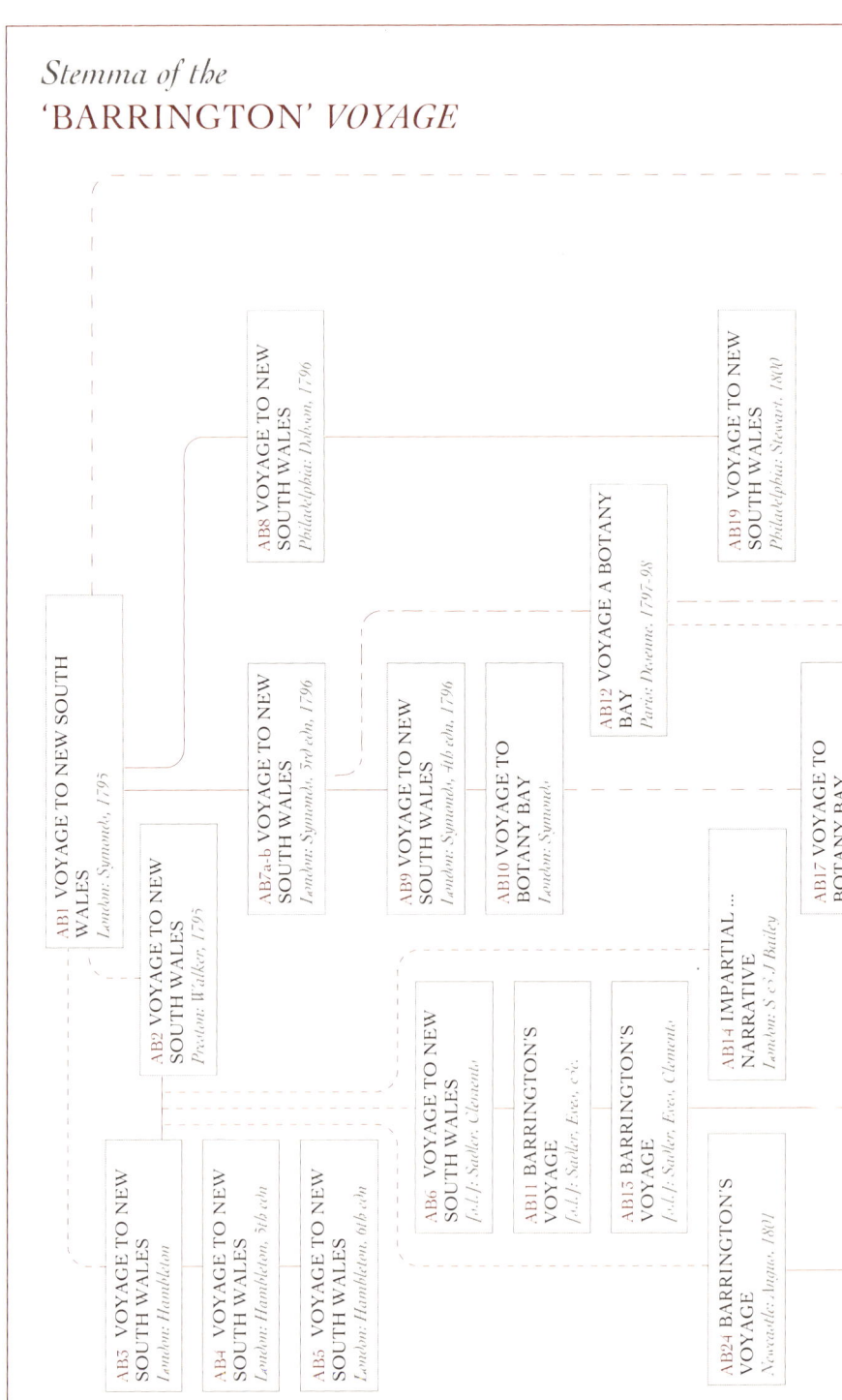

AB1 VOYAGE TO NEW SOUTH WALES
London: Symonds, 1795

AB2 VOYAGE TO NEW SOUTH WALES
Preston: Walker, 1795

AB8 VOYAGE TO NEW SOUTH WALES
Philadelphia: Dobson, 1796

AB7a-b VOYAGE TO NEW SOUTH WALES
London: Symonds, 3rd edn, 1796

AB19 VOYAGE TO NEW SOUTH WALES
Philadelphia: Stewart, 1800

AB9 VOYAGE TO NEW SOUTH WALES
London: Symonds, 4th edn, 1796

AB10 VOYAGE TO BOTANY BAY
London: Symonds

AB12 VOYAGE A BOTANY BAY
Paris: Deterac, 1797-98

AB3 VOYAGE TO NEW SOUTH WALES
London: Hambleton

AB4 VOYAGE TO NEW SOUTH WALES
London: Hambleton, 5th edn

AB5 VOYAGE TO NEW SOUTH WALES
London: Hambleton, 6th edn

AB6 VOYAGE TO NEW SOUTH WALES
J.-J.: Sadler, Clements

AB11 BARRINGTON'S VOYAGE
J.-J.: Sadler, Eves, &c.

AB13 BARRINGTON'S VOYAGE
J.-J.: Sadler, Eves, Clements

AB14 IMPARTIAL... NARRATIVE
London: S & J Bailey

AB17 VOYAGE TO BOTANY BAY

AB24 BARRINGTON'S VOYAGE
Newcastle: Angus, 1801

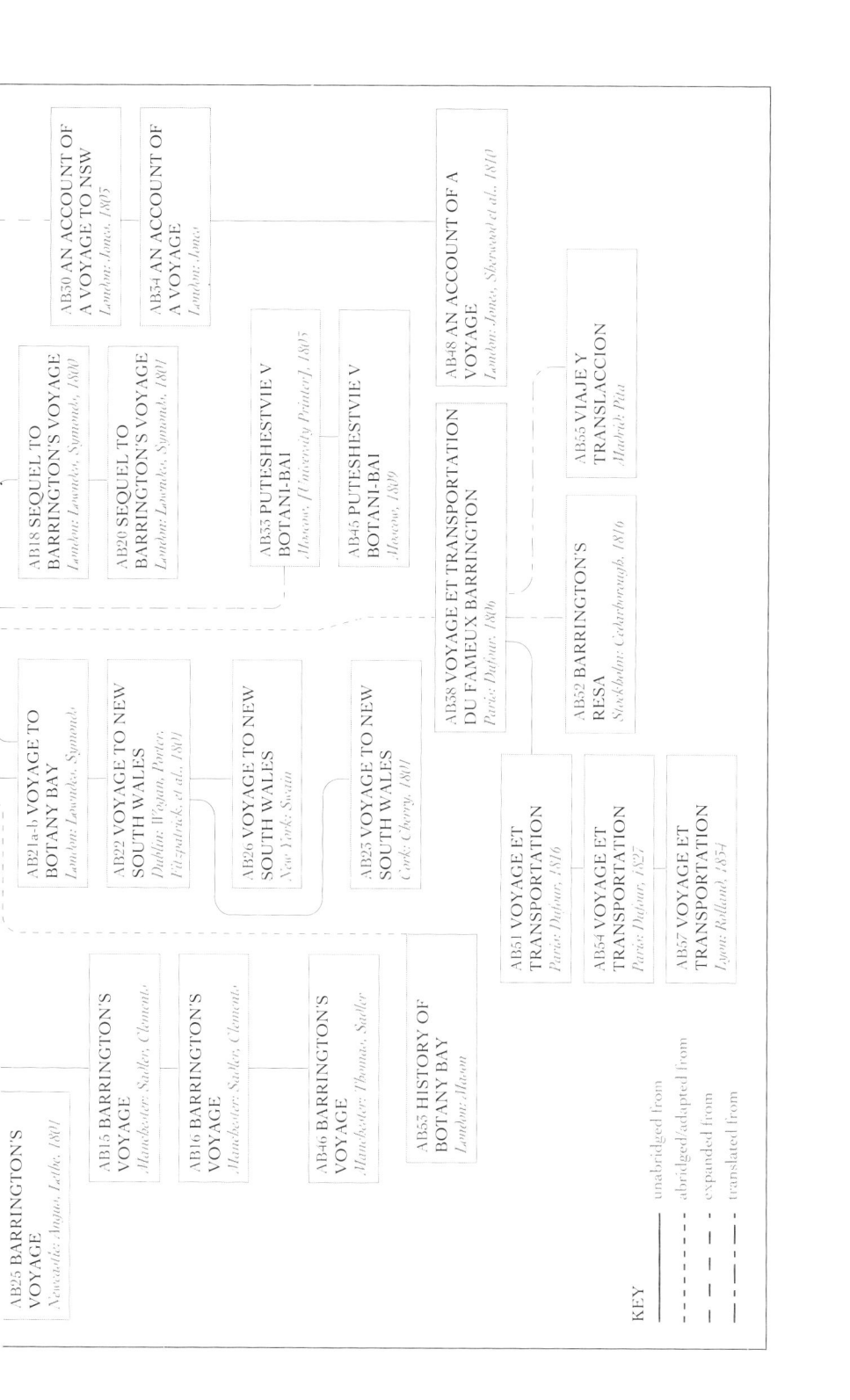

AB25 BARRINGTON'S VOYAGE
Newcastle: Angus, Lothir, 1811

AB15 BARRINGTON'S VOYAGE
Manchester: Sadler, Clements

AB16 BARRINGTON'S VOYAGE
Manchester: Sadler, Clements

AB46 BARRINGTON'S VOYAGE
Manchester: Thomas, Sadler

AB55 HISTORY OF BOTANY BAY
London: Hassan

AB21a-b VOYAGE TO BOTANY BAY
London: Lowndes, Symonds

AB22 VOYAGE TO NEW SOUTH WALES
Dublin: Wogan, Porter, Fitzpatrick, et al., 1801

AB26 VOYAGE TO NEW SOUTH WALES
New York: Swain

AB23 VOYAGE TO NEW SOUTH WALES
Cork: Cherry, 1801

AB18 SEQUEL TO BARRINGTON'S VOYAGE
London: Lowndes, Symonds, 1800

AB20 SEQUEL TO BARRINGTON'S VOYAGE
London: Lowndes, Symonds, 1801

AB33 PUTESHESTVIE V BOTANI-BAI
Moscow: [University Printer], 1803

AB43 PUTESHESTVIE V BOTANI-BAI
Moscow, 1809

AB30 AN ACCOUNT OF A VOYAGE TO NSW
London: Jones, 1805

AB34 AN ACCOUNT OF A VOYAGE
London: Jones

AB48 AN ACCOUNT OF A VOYAGE
London: Jones, Sherwood et al., 1810

AB55 VIAJE Y TRANSLACCION
Madrid: Plta

AB38 VOYAGE ET TRANSPORTATION DU FAMEUX BARRINGTON
Paris: Dufour, 18th

AB52 BARRINGTON'S RESA
Stockholm: Cederborough, 1816

AB51 VOYAGE ET TRANSPORTATION
Paris: Dufour, 1816

AB54 VOYAGE ET TRANSPORTATION
Paris: Dufour, 1827

AB57 VOYAGE ET TRANSPORTATION
Lyon: Rolland, 1854

KEY

—————— unabridged from

– – – – – abridged/adapted from

· – · – · expanded from

· · · · · translated from

DOP: March 1795
References: Ferguson 205, ESTC T149156
Copies: ML (5 copies), NLA (3 copies), BL, Yale, SLQ, QEPA, QM, Cambridge, Glasgow, Manchester, Macgill, Yale, Gottingen

---

AB2   A | VOYAGE | TO | NEW SOUTH WALES; | WITH A | DESCRIPTION OF THE COUNTRY; | THE | *MANNERS, CUSTOMS, RELIGION, &C.* | OF | THE NATIVES, | In the Vicinity of | BOTANY BAY. | [*rule*] | *BY GEORGE BARRINGTON,* | NOW | SUPERINTENDANT OF THE CONVICTS | AT | PARAMATTA. | [*rule*] | To Mr. * * * *. | Dr. Sir. | I EMBRACE THE EARLIEST OPPORTUNITY OF PERFORMING THE PRO- | MISE I MADE YOU ON MY QUITTING ENGLAND; AND SHOULD THE | CONTENTS OF THE ACCOMPANYING SHEETS, COLLECTED CHIEFLY | FROM PERSONAL OBSERVATION, AIDED BY THE BEST LOCAL INQUI- | RIES, ACQUIT ME, IN YOUR MIND, OF A BREACH OF THAT PROMISE, I | SHALL FEEL MYSELF MORE THAN HAPPY:—THEY HAD BEEN MORE | AMPLE, BUT THAT I WAS IMPATIENT TO PAY A DEBT OF GRATITUDE | THAT WOULD NOT BROOK THE LOSS OF AN OPPORTUNITY; CONSE- | QUENTLY YOU WILL FIND THE CONCLUSION RATHER ABRUPT; BUT | BY THE NEXT SHIP I SHALL, I TRUST, MAKE AMENDS, HAVING NEAR- | LY TRANSCRIBED SOME LETTERS FROM MY FRIEND MR. WENT- | WORTH, CONTAINING A PLEASANT NARRATIVE OF THE RISE | AND PROGRESS OF THE SETTLEMENT AT NORFOLK ISLAND; | TOGETHER WITH SOME FARTHER PARTICULARS RELA- | TIVE TO, SIR, YOUR OBEDIENT, AND OBLIGED, | HUMBLE SERVANT, | G. *BARRINGTON.* | *Price Six-pence.* | [*rule*] | LONDON: | PRINTED FOR THE PROPRIETORS. | [*rule*] | 1795.

8vo. 20 x 12 cm. [1] title, [2] blank, [3] + 4–31 text, [32] advertisements pp.

Although nominally produced in London, and published under the anonymous imprint 'Printed for the Proprietors', the advertisements page (on the verso of the last page of text) reveals this as the work of Thomas Walker, a printer, bookseller and newspaper proprietor in Preston, Lancashire. The dedicatory letter from the original Symonds edition (**AB1**) appears on the title page.

This work may well have been the first of the many abridged versions of the 'Barrington' *Voyage*; apart from **AB1**, this was the only work to carry the nominal date '1795' on its title page. It is possible, however, that the undated Hambleton editions of the *Voyage* (**AB3, AB4, AB5**) – which are textually identical to **AB2** – may have been the original redaction(s) of the *Voyage*. It is clear that the first abridged version of the *Voyage* –

whether it was **AB2** or **AB3** – served as the prototype for the other abridged versions published by a number of different printers and booksellers between 1795 and 1810 (see **AB6**, **AB11**, **AB13**, **AB14**, **AB15**, **AB16**, **AB24**, **AB25**, **AB46**).

AB2 condensed **AB1** into a 32-page chapbook. A very small typeface was used, the spacing between letters and lines was very close, and the division into chapters from **AB1** was abandoned in favour of a (mostly) uninterrupted narrative. There were also abridgements from the original text. The abridgement omits the greater part of the descriptions of Tenerife and South Africa that had appeared in **AB1**; thus the actual voyage section of the narrative is considerably shortened. The encounter with the *Flying Dutchman* from **AB1** (chapter 6) is omitted, though the description of the 'crossing the line' ceremony (**AB1**, chapter 3) is left intact. Some minor abridgements from the text of **AB1** are made in the descriptions of New South Wales that occupy pp. 6–24 of **AB2**. After the first paragraph of p. 24, there is a horizontal rule, following which the last two chapters from **AB1** are reprinted in their entirety. At the top of p. 26, the headings from the start of Chapter XV in **AB1** (summarising the contents of the chapter) are also replicated. This idiosyncratic typography, as well as the same abridgements from **AB1**, were replicated to a greater or lesser degree in all subsequent abridged versions of the *Voyage*.

The advertisements page on the verso of the last page of text lists seven works 'lately published by T. Walker… and sold by all the Booksellers who circulate this interesting account of Botany Bay, &c.'. These include a history of the French Revolution, published 'in seventeen weekly numbers, or the whole neatly bound for six shillings', a bound volume of the 'thirteenth edition' of Buchan's *Domestic Medicine*, and several sixpenny tracts, including biographies of Marie Antoinette and Robespierre, *The Witticisms, Anecdotes, Jests and Sayings of Dr. Samuel Johnson*, and an item of local interest, *A copious Abstract of the Lancaster Canal Bill*.

DOP: '1795'
References: Ferguson 203
Copies: NLA, ATL, QM, Yale

A | VOYAGE | TO | NEW SOUTH WALES; | WITH A | Description *of the* AB3
Country; | THE | *MANNERS, CUSTOMS, RELIGION,* &c. | OF | THE
NATIVES, | In the Vicinity of | *BOTANY BAY.* | [*rule*] | By George

Barrington, | NOW | *Superintendant of the Convicts at PARAMATA*, | *and sent to his Friend in England*. | [*rule*] | LONDON: | Printed and Sold by A. HAMBLETON. | Price Six-pence.

8vo. 18.5 x 12.5 cm. [1] title, [2] dedicatory letter, 3–56 text pp.

An abridged version of the 'Barrington' *Voyage*. The text of this version is identical to **AB2**, and it is uncertain as to which of these two is the original redaction (see entry for **AB2**). Like **AB2**, this edition demarcates the start of the unexpurgated text from chapter 14 of the original *Voyage* (**AB1**) with a horizontal line (p. 47), and also retains the chapter summary heads from the final chapter of **AB1** (p. 49).

The printing in this work is untidy – a large font size is used on pp. 3–39 and 42–47, while on pp. 40–41 and 55–56 the font is smaller, and on pp. 47–55 it is considerably smaller again. The section in which this very small font is used (pp. 47–55) corresponds with text taken unexpurgated from **AB1**. There are also sections in which several paragraphs are printed in italics (pp. 15–17, 24–25). A printing error on p. 15 mispells the word 'kangaroo' as 'kanagroo'.

The Mitchell Library copy is in original marbled paper wrappers.

DOP: c. 1795–1800?
References: None found
Copies: ML

AB4   A | VOYAGE | TO | NEW SOUTH WALES; | WITH A | Description of the Country; | THE | *MANNERS, CUSTOMS, RELIGION*, &c. | OF | THE NATIVES, | In the Vicinity of | *BOTANY BAY*. | [*rule*] | By George Barrington, | NOW | *Superintendant of the Convicts at PARRAMATTA*, | *and sent to his Friend in England*. | [*rule*] | The Fifth Edition. | [*rule*] | Printed and Sold by A. HAMBLETON. | Price Six-pence.

8vo. 17.5 x 11.5 cm. [1] title, [2] dedicatory letter, 3–56 text pp.

The 'fifth edition' of Hambleton's abridged version of the *Voyage* is virtually identical to the first (**AB3**), both in textual terms and in the layout. It is certainly a reprint, however. Apart from the new title page, there are minor corrections and printing variations through the text – such as the correction (on p. 15) of 'kangaroo' (**AB4**) for 'kanagroo' (**AB3**). **AB4** also lacks press signatures found in **AB3**.

DOP: c. 1795–1800?
References: Ferguson 260
Copies: ML, NLA

A | VOYAGE | TO | NEW SOUTH WALES; | WITH A | Description of the   **AB5**
Country; | THE | *MANNERS, CUSTOMS, RELIGION, &c.* | OF | THE
NATIVES, | In the Vicinity of | *BOTANY BAY.* | [*rule*] | By George
Barrington, | NOW | *Superintendant of the Convicts at PARRAMATTA,* |
and sent to his Friend in England. | [*rule*] | THE SIXTH EDITION | [*rule*]
| Printed and Sold by A. HAMBLETON. | Price Six-pence.

8vo. 19 x 12.5 cm. [1] title, [2] dedicatory letter, 3–56 text pp.

The 'sixth edition' of Hambleton's *Voyage* is another reprint closely
resembling the previous editions (**AB3, AB4**).

DOP: c. 1795–1800?
References: Ferguson 261
Libraries: NLA

A VOYAGE | TO | New South Wales; | WITH A | DESCRIPTION OF THE   **AB6**
COUNTRY; | THE | MANNERS, CUSTOMS, RELIGION, &c. | OF | The
Natives, | In the Vicinity of | BOTANY BAY. | [*double rule*] | By George
Barrington, | NOW | Superintendant of the Convicts at PARAMATA, |
and sent to his Friend in England. | [*double rule*] | Printed and Sold by J.
Sadler, M. Clements, &c. | PRICE SIX-PENCE.

12mo. 18.5 x 12 cm. [1] title, [2] dedicatory letter, [3] + 4–48 text pp.

A reprint of the abridged version of the *Voyage*. This work uses the text
of **AB2** and **AB3**, also marking the point where the unabridged section
from **AB1** starts with a horizontal rule (p. 39., cf. p. 24 of **AB2**), and
imitating the chapter summary heads used in **AB2** (p. 42, cf. **AB2**, p. 26).
The text here is slightly truncated, however: **AB6** concludes with the
description of Yeariana as being like 'a beautiful Oriental Creole', thus
omitting the last six paragraphs of **AB2** and **AB3**.

It is possible this was in fact a proof copy of the work published for the
same booksellers in a number of editions as *Barrington's Voyage to New
South Wales* (see **AB11, AB13, AB15, AB16, AB46**). In this version, the

start of p. 9 duplicates a section of the text from the previous page. In the ML copy (the only known copy of this edition) the duplicated section is scored out in pencil and ink.

DOP: c. 1795–1800?
References: Ferguson 207
Copies: ML

AB7a–b A | VOYAGE | TO | NEW SOUTH WALES; | WITH | A DESCRIPTION OF THE COUNTRY; | THE | *MANNERS, CUSTOMS, RELIGION*, & | OF | THE NATIVES | In the Vicinity of | BOTANY BAY. | [*rule*] | *BY GEORGE BARRINGTON*, | NOW | SUPERINTENDANT OF THE CONVICT | AT | PARAMATTA. | [*double rule*] | THE THIRD EDITION. | [*double rule*] | *London* | PRINTED FOR THE PROPRIETOR; | SOLD BY H. D. SYMONDS, NO. 20, PATERNOSTER-ROW} | [*rule*] | {PRICE HALF-A-CROWN.} | [*rule*] | 1796.

8vo. 21 x 12.5 cm. [5] title, [6] blank, [7] dedicatory letter, [8]–[11] contents, [12] blank, [13] + 14–140 text pp. With errors in the page numbering (see below).

The text and layout of this edition are identical to the first Symonds edition (**AB1**), and the presence of identical printing flaws indicates either that the bulk of the sheets printed for the first edition were reused in the third (see, for example, the top of p. 57 – '… those that were le[ft] remained at Syndey [*sic*] Cove'), or possibly that, anticipating the popularity of the work, the printer retained standing type from which the third edition was printed. The chapter misnumbering from **AB1** also appears in **AB7a-b**.

Errors in the page numbering show that some reprinting had been done for the production of the third edition, however, and both **AB7a** and **AB7b** have errors and idiosyncrasies on their title page (for example, 'Superintendant of the Convict'). Moreover, variations between copies show that there were different impressions made within the nominal third edition:

AB7a

In this version, p. 105 is misnumbered '97' (ML copies).

AB7b

In this version, p. 105 is numbered correctly, but pp. 106 and 107 are misnumbered '98' and '99' (BL/ESTC).

The Symonds 'Third Edition' was advertised in the *Morning Chronicle* of 25 February 1796.

DOP: February 1796
References: Ferguson 233, ESTC N045485
Copies: ML (3 copies), BL, SLV, ATL, BA, LCP

A | VOYAGE | TO | *NEW SOUTH WALES*; | WITH A | DESCRIPTION OF   **AB8**
THE COUNTRY; | THE | *MANNERS, CUSTOMS, RELIGION, &c.* | OF
THE NATIVES, | *In the Vicinity of* | BOTANY BAY. | [*rule*] | BY GEORGE
BARRINGTON, | *NOW SUPERINTENDENT OF THE CONVICTS AT
PARAMATTA.* | [*double rule*] | *PHILADELPHIA*; | PRINTED BY
THOMAS DOBSON, | AT THE STONE-HOUSE, N° 41, SOUTH
SECOND-STREET. | [*double rule*] | 1796.

12mo. 17 x 10 cm. [i] half-title, [ii] blank, [iii] title, [iv] blank, [v] dedicatory letter, [vi]
blank, [vii] + viii–xi contents, [xii] blank, [1] + 2–150 text, [151]–[152] advertisements pp.

The first American-printed 'Barrington' work, this is a reprint, without abridgement, of the text of the original *Voyage* (**AB1**). Dobson advertised his publication in the *Philadelphia Gazette & Universal Daily Advertiser* in March 1796 – the work was priced at 'half a dollar'.

The advertisements leaf at the conclusion of the text lists some fifty-six works 'published and for sale by' Dobson, ranging in price from 14 cents to 5 dollars.

Half-title: '[*double rule*] A | Voyage | to | New South Wales, &c. [*double rule*]'

DOP: March 1796
References: Ferguson 235, ESTC W029695, EAI
Copies: ML (2 copies), NLA (2 copies), BL, NLI, SLQ, LOC, EAI, Monash, Chicago, CWM, NWU, UNC, Virginia, Yale, PEM, AAS, APS, Huntington, LCP

A | VOYAGE | TO | NEW SOUTH WALES; | WITH | A DESCRIPTION   **AB9**
OF THE COUNTRY; | THE | *MANNERS, CUSTOMS, RELIGION, &c.* |
OF | THE NATIVES | In the Vicinity of | BOTANY BAY. | [*rule*] | *BY
GEORGE BARRINGTON,* | NOW | SUPERINTENDANT OF THE
CONVICTS | AT | PARAMATTA. | [*rule*] | THE FOURTH EDITION. |

[*rule*] | *London* | PRINTED FOR THE PROPRIETOR; | SOLD BY H. D. SYMONDS, NO. 20, PATERNOSTER-ROW. | [*rule*] | {PRICE HALF-A-CROWN.} | [*rule*] | 1796.

8vo. 21 x 12.5 cm. [1] blank, [2] frontispiece, [3] pictorial title page, [4] blank, [5] title, [6] blank, [7] dedicatory letter, [8] blank, [9]–[12] contents, [13] + 14–140 text pp.

The text and layout of Symonds' 'fourth edition' of the *Voyage* are again virtually identical to those of the first and third editions (**AB1**, **AB7a-b**), with the likelihood again being that this edition was formed mainly from leftover sheets from **AB1**, or possibly reprinted from standing type (see **AB7a-b**). The chapter misnumbering remains, but unlike **AB7a** and **AB7b** the pages are all numbered correctly.

This edition was the first to feature the addition of a frontispiece illustration and pictorial title page, parts of the same engraved plate. The frontispiece, in a rectangular frame, depicts an episode from the final chapter of the *Voyage*, where Barrington and his young companion (Tim), who carries a musket, enact expressions of surprise as they encounter a wounded 'native' (Palerino), while a female 'native' (Yeariana) sits nearby with a melancholy expression. Below the plate in script is the caption: 'An interesting discovery | in the Woods.'

The pictorial title page announces the work as:

A | VOYAGE | to | BOTANY BAY | *with a description of the Country,* | *manners, Customs,* *religion, &c. of the* | *NATIVES* | *by the Celebrated* | *GEORGE BARRINGTON.* |

Beneath this title is a vignette illustration, which depicts longboats landing from a ship, while various European and Aboriginal figures interact on shore. In the longboat in the foreground, a soldier with cutlass directs two apprehensive looking female convicts to go ashore, while a 'native' is climbing into the boat and peering up at the oarsman. A flagpole, with no flag attached, rises up from the centre of the illustration, with its top splitting the '*A*' and '*R*' of '*BARRINGTON*' in the title above. Below the illustration is the imprint:

London | *Sold by H. D. Symonds No.20, Paternoster Row.* | *Price Two Shillings and Sixpence*

This was possibly the edition advertised as 'Barrington's Voyage to Botany Bay... Price 2s. 6d.' in the *True Briton* of 23 April 1796.

DOP: '1796'
References: Ferguson 234
Copies: ML, ATL, Claremont, UWM, Witwatersrand

A | *VOYAGE* | to | BOTANY BAY | *with a description of the Country,* | **AB10**
manners, Customs, religion, &c. of the | *NATIVES* | *by the Celebrated* |
GEORGE BARRINGTON. | [*vignette*] | [*double rule*] | *LONDON* | Sold
by H.D. Symonds, No. 20, Paternoster Row. | Price *One Shilling and*
Sixpence

8vo. 18.5 x 11 cm. [i] blank, [ii] frontispiece, [iii] pictorial title, [iv] blank, [v] dedicatory
letter, [vi]–[x] contents, [5] + 6–101, 136 [i.e. 102]–103, 138–139 [i.e. 104–105] text, [106]
blank pp.

A cheaper reprint of the Symonds *Voyage*, using the pictorial title page
that had appeared in the 'Fourth Edition' (**AB9**) as its title. The
engraved plate has been altered to change the stated price from 'Two
Shilling' and Sixpence' to 'One Shilling and Sixpence'; the rest of the
pictorial title and the frontispiece illustration remains the same.

Though the text is unabridged from the earlier Symonds versions of the
Voyage (**AB1**, **AB7a-b**, **A9**), this edition was redesigned to shorten the
page length, thus making the work cheaper to produce. The summaries
of the contents at the start of each chapter found in the earlier editions
have been omitted, and the spacing of the text – both between letters
and between lines – is less generous.

This edition was printed on the same paper as had been used for **AB1**,
AB7a-b, and **A9** – it also shows the watermark date '1794' – making it
likely that it was printed and/or published at a similar time to these
works. The NLA copy from the Ferguson collection has a contemporary
owner's signature on the title page which reads 'H [?]: S: | Hoy[illegible]
| 17 | 96'.

DOP: c. 1796
References: Ferguson 204
Copies: ML, NLA (3 copies), SLT (2 copies), Adelaide, Macquarie,
Melbourne, Monash, California

BARRINGTON's | VOYAGE | TO | NEW SOUTH WALES; | WITH A | **AB11**
DESCRIPTION OF THE COUNTRY; | THE | MANNERS, CUSTOMS,
RELIGION, &c. | OF THE | NATIVES, | In the Vicinity of | BOTANY BAY.
| [*rule*] | A NEW EDITION. | [*rule*] *BY GEORGE BARRINGTON,* | Now

Superintendant to the Convicts at PARAMATA, | and sent to his Friend in ENGLAND. | [*rule*] | PRINTED AND SOLD BY J. SADLER, J. EVES, &c. | [*rule*] | {PRICE SIX PENCE.}

8vo. 19 x 12 cm. [1] title, [2] dedicatory letter, [3] + 4–48 text pp.

A reprint of the abridged version of the *Voyage*, this follows the truncated text and typographical idiosyncrasies of **AB6**, but amends the printing error of a duplicated section in that version.

DOP: c. 1796–1800?
References: Ferguson 207a, ESTC T300799
Copies: NLA, Oxford

AB12 VOYAGE | A | BOTANY-BAY, | AVEC UNE DESCRIPTION | DU PAYS, DES MOEURS, | DES COUTUMES | ET DE LA RELIGION | DES NATIFS. | PAR le célèbre GEORGE BARRINGTON. | *Traduit de l'Anglais, sur la troisième Édition.* | [*rule*] | A PARIS, | Chez DESENNE, Libraire, Palais-Égalité, | N°s 1 et 2. | [*double rule*] | AN VI.

8vo. 20 x 12.5 cm. [i] half-title, [ii] blank, [iii] title, [iv] blank, iij–viij préface du traducteur, [ix] + x–xv contents, [xvi] dedicatory letter, [1] + 2–192 text pp.

French translation of the *Voyage*, nominally made from the third edition (i.e. **AB7a-b**). This edition added various elements to the *Voyage* including a translator's preface, explanatory notes and, more interestingly, an additional paragraph at the conclusion of the work where 'Barrington' laments his exile (pp. 191–92).

The impressive survival rate of copies of this work suggests it was produced in a large print run. Many copies survive bound in original boards. There are slight differences in spine decorations and labels, however, which may suggest that the sheets were bound as required over a period of time.

Half title: 'VOYAGE | A | BOTANY-BAY'

DOP: 'An VI' [22 September 1797 – 21 September 1798].
References: Ferguson 259
Copies: ML (6 copies), NLA, SLV, SLQ, BL, BNF, EPAL, Macquarie, Monash, Melbourne, Leeds, Dartmouth, Brigham, Brown, Harvard, Princeton, Minnesota, IF (2 copies), MH (2 copies)

BARRINGTON'S | VOYAGE | TO | NEW SOUTH WALES; | with a | **AB13**
Description of the Country; | THE | MANNERS, CUSTOMS,
RELIGION, &c. | OF THE | NATIVES, | in the vicinity of | BOTANY
BAY. | [*rule*] | *A New Edition*, *by* GEORGE BARRINGTON, | Now
Superintendant to the Convicts at PARAMATA, and sent to his
FRIEND | in ENGLAND. | [*printer's ornament*] | PRINTED | FOR J.
SADLER, J. EVES, AND M. CLEMENTS, | [*double rule*] | PRICE ONLY
SIXPENCE

8vo. 13.5 x 9 cm. [1] title, [2] dedicatory letter, [3] + 4–48 text pp.

Another reprint of the abridged *Voyage*, using the same text as **AB11**.

No printer is named in this edition, but the ornament on the title page
(a ship in sail) matches that found on the title pages of other *Barrington's
Voyage* chapbooks printed by the Manchester printer Alice Swindells (see
AB15, **AB16**, **AB46**).

This edition appeared around the turn of the nineteenth century: both
copies in the Mitchell Library are printed on paper with a watermark
date: '1798' (see ML 991.14/HI (pp. 9–10) and ML L10/B (pp. 17–18).

DOP: c. 1799
References: Ferguson 208
Copies: ML (2 copies)

AN | IMPARTIAL AND CIRCUMSTANTIAL | NARRATIVE | OF THE   **AB14**
PRESENT STATE OF | BOTANY BAY, | IN NEW SOUTH WALES: | With
a Description of the Country; Treatment of the Convicts on | their
Passage, and after their arrival. | ALSO THE | MANNERS, CUSTOMS,
RELIGION, &c. | OF THE | NATIVES, | TRULY DEPICTED. | [*rule*] |
CONTAINING | AMONG A VARIETY OF ENTERTAINING SUBJECTS |
The Particulars of the Voyage; a description of the Buildings and Soil | at
Sydney Cove; Journey to Paramata; Convict Houses and daily |
Occupations; their Emoluments from Government on the | Expiration of
their Term; Birds; Animals; Vegetables; | manner of taking one of the
Natives, who dies of the | Small-Pox; entrap two others, who escape with
| much Ingenuity; their Retaliation upon the | Governor, who very
narrowly escapes | Death; a reconciliation takes place; | &c. &c. &c. &c. |

BY GEORGE BARRINGTON, | NOW SUPERINTENDANT OF THE CONVICTS AT PARAMATA. | [*double rule*] | LONDON: | Printed by S. and J. Bailey, No. 50, Bishopsgate Street Within, and | No. 55, Upper East-Smithfield. | PRICE SIX-PENCE.

8vo. 18.5 x 12.5 cm. [1] title, [2] dedicatory letter, [3] + 4–44 text pp.

Although claimed by Suzanne Rickard as the original form of the *Voyage*, and 'an outstanding version among many', this was in fact another reprint of the abridged *Voyage*, with little distinguishing it from the other versions apart from the title. The similarity of the text here to previous abridged versions makes it clear that the *Impartial and Circumstantial Narrative* was produced using one of the previous abridgements as the copy text. At the top of p. 36 is a horizontal line distinguishing the start of the unabridged text from **AB1**, familiar from earlier abridgements (see **AB2**, **AB3**, **AB4**, **AB5**, **AB6**, **AB11**, **AB13**). There are, however, some slight differences in this text – as on p. 8, where this version makes some further slight abbreviations to the voyage section of the narrative (see **AB2**). The text taken from an earlier abridgement ends with the description of Yeariana's 'image' as 'the most interesting I ever saw' – omitting the further characterisation of the fictional Aboriginal heroine as a 'beautiful Oriental Creole' (see **AB6**, **AB11**, **AB13**) – and the work concludes with an original paragraph:

> The next day I made a journey to Sydney Cove, and there being a ship lying in the harbour ready for sea, I took the opportunity to remit the foregoing pages, hoping they will meet approbation and by the next conveyance will send a further account of the progress of the settlement etc.

The dedicatory letter in this work is headed by the (specious) assertion: 'Entered at Stationers' Hall.' (p. [2]).

The date of publication of this edition has been incorrectly given as '[1791]' (ESTC), 'c. 1793–1794' (Rickard), and 'c. 1795' (Ferguson). The publishing history of the *Voyage*, and the trade history of the publishers Susan and John Bailey, makes all these estimates too early. There is also internal evidence in both NLA copies that shows that the date of publication of the work was around the turn of the nineteenth century. The NLA copy at FRM F214 survives in its original blue paper wrappers; on the back wrapper is a watermark date: '1797'. On the other NLA copy (NK682), the title page leaf has the watermark date: '1798'. Both these copies are from the same pressing.

DOP: c. 1799–1800
References: Ferguson 214, ESTC T154512
Copies: NLA (2 copies), NLI, JRL

BARRINGTON's VOYAGE | TO | NEW SOUTH WALES; | WITH A | **AB15**
Description of the Country; | THE | MANNERS, CUSTOMS, RELIGION,
&c. | OF | THE NATIVES | IN THE | Vicinity of Botany Bay. | [*rule*] | A
New Edition by GEORGE BARRINGTON, | Now Superintendant to the
Convicts at PARAMATA, and sent to his | FRIEND in England. | [*printer's
ornament*] | Printed by A. Swindells, Hanging-bridge. | *Manchester:* | AND
SOLD BY J. SADLER, AND M. CLEMENTS. | *Price only Ninepence*

8vo. 17.5 x 11.5 cm. [1] title, [2] dedicatory letter, [3] + 4–48 text pp.

Another reprint of *Barrington's Voyage*, using the same text as **AB11** and
AB13.

The ornament on the title page is of a ship in sail, matching that of
AB13, **AB16** and **AB46**.

Colophon: 'Printed by A. Swindells, Hanging-bridge. | Manchester: | and
sold by J. Sadler, and M. Clements. | Price only ninepence'

DOP: c. 1799–1808?
References: Ferguson 211
Copies: ML (2 copies), NLA

BARRINGTON'S VOYAGE | TO | New South Wales; | with a | Description **AB16**
of the Country; | THE | MANNERS, CUSTOMS, RELIGION, &c | OF
THE | NATIVES, | in the vicinity of | BOTANY BAY. | [*rule*] | *A New
Edition*, *by* GEORGE BARRINGTON. | Now Superintendant to the
Convicts at PARAMATA, and sent to his FRIEND | in ENGLAND. | [*rule*]
| [*printer's ornament*] | Printed by A. Swindells, Hanging-bridge. |
Manchester: | AND SOLD BY J. SADLER, AND M. CLEMENTS, | [*rule*] |
Price only sixpence.

8vo. 18 x 10.5 cm. [1] title, [2] dedicatory letter, [3] + 4–48 text pp.

The text and layout of this edition are virtually identical to those of
AB15, with only minor cosmetic changes, suggesting the two versions

were produced around the same time. The price was revised from ninepence to sixpence, however. The ornament on the title page is the same as found in **AB13**, **AB15** and **AB46**.

Colophon at foot of p. 48: 'Printed by A. Swindells, Hanging-bridge. | Manchester: | and sold by J. Sadler, and M. Clements, | [*rule*] | Price only sixpence.'

DOP: c. 1799–1808?
References: Ferguson 212
Copies: ML (2 copies), NLA, SLV

AB17   A | *VOYAGE* | to | BOTANY BAY | *with a description of the Country,* | *manners, Customs, religion, &c. of the* | *NATIVES* | *by the Celebrated* | *GEORGE BARRINGTON.* | [*vignette*] | To which is added his | LIFE and TRIAL | [*double rule*] | LONDON. | *Printed by C. LOWNDES, and* | *Sold by H.D Symonds, No. 20, Paternoster Row.*

8vo. 19 x 11 cm. [i] blank, [ii] frontispiece, [iii] pictorial title, [iv] blank, [1] dedicatory letter, [2] blank, [3] + 4–6 contents, [7] + 8–14 'Life of George Barrington', [15] + 16–18 'Particulars Relating to the Trial and Conviction of George Barrington', [19] + 20–120 text pp. Page 30 is misnumbered '29'.

This was a further Symonds reprint of the *Voyage* using the same text as **AB1**, **AB7a-b**, **AB9** and **AB10** but, like **AB10**, omitting summaries at the start of each chapter and using less generous spacing between letters and lines. This edition also uses the engraved plate (of frontispiece and pictorial title page) that had first appeared in **AB9** and also in **AB10**. The plate has again been modified for this new edition. While the frontispiece, title and vignette illustration remain unaltered, the section beneath the vignette has been modified; the imprint and price from **AB10** has been removed, and in its place appears:

To which is added his | LIFE and TRIAL | [*double rule*] | LONDON. | *Printed by C. Lowndes, and* | *Sold by H D Symonds, No. 20, Paternoster Row.*

As with **AB10**, there is no printed title page in this edition; the modified engraved title page serves as the title for the work.

While the text of the *Voyage* remains the same as previous incarnations, the content of this edition has been expanded by the addition of a brief 'Life of George Barrington'. This biographical sketch was sourced mainly

from the Kearsley *Memoirs* (**B2**, **B4**, **B5**), though it also includes a final
note on Barrington's more recent activities:

> ... Mr. Barrington was found guilty; and sentenced to Botany Bay for seven years, where
> his good and *prudent* conduct has since procured him the office of *Constable*! and it is to
> be hoped, that his sound knowledge will induce him to hold that appointment long, very
> long, after the approaching expiration of his allotted servitude (p. 14).

There is a similarly brief section giving details of Barrington's trial in
1790, entitled 'Particulars relating to the Trial and Conviction of George
Barrington'.

This revamped edition of the *Voyage* seems to have been published to
coincide with the publication of the *Sequel to Barrington's Voyage* (**AB18**,
AB20), and was sold both as a separate work and in a combined issue
with the *Sequel* (see **AB21a**). The paper used for this edition was different
from that of **AB1**, **AB7a-b**, **AB9** and **AB10** – a number of copies have a
watermark date '1798' on the title leaf ([iii–iv] – see ML C655, ML
991/14M3) though some do not (see NLA F206).

This work is sometimes dated '1793', probably on the basis of an erroneous
entry (F146a) in the 1986 Ferguson *Addenda*, which apparently takes the
dedicatory letter dated '1793' literally. The *Addenda* gives no evidence to
support its dating, and the work described is in fact not the 'Barrington'
Voyage at all but the *Sequel* (see **A21a-b**).

This is almost certainly the 'Sixth Edition' of the 'Voyage to New South
Wales...To which is now added, his LIFE and TRIAL', advertised in *The
Star* on 22 August 1800.

Colophon (foot of p. 120): '*Printed by C. Lowndes, Drury-Lane.*'

DOP: 1800
References: Ferguson 206, ESTC T142277
Copies: ML (2 copies), NLA (4 copies), SLV, SLWA, BL, LOC, Adelaide,
Tasmania, Aberdeen, Cornell, Minnesota (2 copies)

A SEQUEL | TO | BARRINGTON'S VOYAGE | TO | NEW SOUTH   **AB18**
WALES, | COMPRISING AN | INTERESTING NARRATIVE | OF THE |
Transactions and Behaviour of the Convicts; | The Progress of the Colony;
| AN OFFICIAL REGISTER | OF THE | CRIMES, TRIALS, SENTENCES,
AND EXECUTIONS | that have taken place: | A Topographical, Physical,

and Moral Account of the | Country, Manners, Customs, &c. of the Natives,— | AS LIKEWISE | AUTHENTIC ANECDOTES | Of the most Distinguished Characters, and | Notorious Convicts that have been Transported to | the Settlement at New South Wales. | By the celebrated | GEORGE BARRINGTON, | Principal Superintendant of the Convicts. | [*rule*] | LONDON | Printed and Published by C. LOWNDES, | No. 66, Drury-Lane; | and sold by H. D. SYMONDS, Paternoster Row. | [*rule*] | 1800.

8vo. 20 x 12 cm. [iii] title, [iv] blank, [v] + vi–viii contents, [5] + 6–36, 39–107 [i.e. 37–105] text, 108–110 [i.e. 106–108] 'Prices of the various Articles of Stock...' [109]–[114] 'An Official Register of the Crimes, Trial and Executions...' pp. Page '39' follows p. 36 with no interruption in the text.

The *Sequel to Barrington's Voyage* was the first new 'Barrington' text to appear after the original publication of the *Voyage* in 1795. The material for this work was almost wholly drawn from the first volume of David Collins' *An Account of the English Colony in New South Wales*, published in London in 1798.

The first page of the main text ([5]) has the drop-head: '[*double rule*] A | Voyage | to | New South Wales. | Part II.' As in the original *Voyage* (**AB1**, also **AB7a-b, AB9**), headings in italics are used at the start of each chapter, summarising the contents. Following the main text there are several pages of tables: 'Prices of the various Articles of Stock, Provisions, European Commodities, &c. in the Colony at New South Wales', and 'An Official Register of the Crimes, Trials, and Executions of the Convicts in New South Wales, From the commencement of the Colony'.

The Mitchell Library holds two copies of this work which are bound with the third edition of the *Voyage to New South Wales* (**AB7a** – see ML 991/14C1, ML 991/14C2). Although neither of these are original bindings, it seems possible that **AB18** was at some stage issued in a combined edition with leftover stock of **AB7a**.

The *Sequel* was advertised under the heading 'Barrington's Memoirs and Anecdotes of Botany Bay... price 2s. 6d.' in the *Morning Herald* of 6 November 1800. Further advertisements appeared in January 1801.

Colophon (p. [116]): 'Printed by C. Lowndes, Drury-Lane.'

DOP: November 1800
References: Ferguson 303

Copies: ML (4 copies), NLA, BL, ATL, SLSA, Queensland, Yale, Gottingen, APS, Newberry.

A | VOYAGE | TO | *NEW SOUTH WALES*; | WITH A | DESCRIPTION   **AB19**
OF THE COUNTRY; | THE | *MANNERS, CUSTOMS, RELIGION, &c.* |
OF THE NATIVES, | *In the Vicinity of* | BOTANY BAY. | [*rule*] | BY
GEORGE BARRINGTON, | SUPERINTENDANT OF THE CONVICTS
AT PARAMATTA | [*double rule*] | PHILADELPHIA: | PUBLISHED BY P.
STEWART | 1800.

12mo [EAI – seen only in facsimile]. Collation as for AB8, omitting pp. [151]–[152].

A reissue of the sheets of the first American edition printed by Thomas
Dobson in 1796 (**AB8**), with a cancel title page, and omitting Dobson's
advertisements at the end of the text.

DOP: '1800'
References: EAI
Copies: AAS, UMSL

A SEQUEL | TO | BARRINGTON'S VOYAGE | TO | NEW SOUTH   **AB20**
WALES, | COMPRISING AN | INTERESTING NARRATIVE | OF THE |
Transactions and Behaviour of the Convicts; | The Progress of the
Colony; | AN OFFICIAL REGISTER | OF THE | CRIMES, TRIALS,
SENTENCES, AND EXECUTIONS | that have taken place: | A Topo-
graphical, Physical, and Moral Account of the | Country, Manners,
Customs &c. of the Natives,— | AS LIKEWISE | AUTHENTIC
ANECDOTES | Of the most Distinguished Characters, and | Notorious
Convicts that have been Transported to | the Settlement at New South
Wales. | By the celebrated | GEORGE BARRINGTON, | Principal
Superintendant of the Convicts. | [*rule*] | LONDON. | Printed and
Published by C. LOWNDES, | No. 66, Drury-Lane; | and sold by H. D.
SYMONDS, Paternoster Row. | [*rule*] | 1801.

8vo. 18.5 x 11.5 cm. [i] title, [ii] blank, [1]–[2] + vii–viii contents, [5] + 6–88 text, [89]–[94]
'An Official Register of the Crimes, Trials and Executions...' pp.

A reprint of **AB18**, intended as a cheaper version. Though the text itself
is unabridged, the spacing between words and lines is closer than in

AB18, the typeface smaller, and the chapter summary heads have been omitted. The table of 'Prices of the various Articles of Stock…' runs on at the end of the text (p. 86), demarcated only by a decorative rule. This version of the *Sequel* was also issued in a combined edition with the *Voyage* (see **AB21a–b**).

DOP: '1801'
References: Ferguson 328
Copies: ML (3 copies), NLA, SLT, ADFA

AB21a–b   A | *VOYAGE* | to | BOTANY BAY | *with a description of the Country,* | *manners, Customs, religion, &c. of the* | *NATIVES* | *by the Celebrated* | *GEORGE BARRINGTON.* | [*vignette*] | To which is added his | LIFE and TRIAL | [*double rule*] | *LONDON.* | *Printed by C. LOWNDES, and* | *Sold by H.D Symonds, No. 20, Paternoster Row.*

8vo. 19 x 11 cm. [i] blank, [ii] frontispiece, [iii] pictorial title, [iv] blank, [1] dedicatory letter, [2] blank, [3] + 4–6 contents, 7 + 8–14 'Life of George Barrington', [15] + 16–18 'Particulars Relating to the Trial and Conviction of George Barrington', [19] + 20–120 *Voyage* text, [I] *Sequel* title, [II] blank, [1]–[2] + vii–viii contents, [5] + 6–88 text, [89]–[94] 'An Official Register of the Crimes, Trials and Executions…', [95]–[96] blank pp.

This combined version of the 'Barrington' *Voyage* and *Sequel* was, initially at least, not a reprint but a simple repackaging of **AB17** and **AB20** in a single bound volume. At least some copies of the combined edition were issued in paste boards. The NLA copy at NK742 has this original binding, along with a spine label which reads '*Barrington's* History of BOTANY BAY / With his Voyage, Life, Trial, &c. / — / 3s. 6d. boards.' The ML copy at 991/14MI is also an example of an original binding, but only a fragment of the spine label survives. The ML copy at 991/14MI has a contemporary owner's signature – 'Ann Heatton - | Lancaster | 1801'. In this copy, the pictorial title page leaf [iii–iv] has the watermark date '1798', while the *Sequel* title leaf [121–22] has the watermark date '1800'.

Two different versions of **AB21** were issued.

AB21a

This version simply combined the works first issued separately as **AB17** and **AB20**.

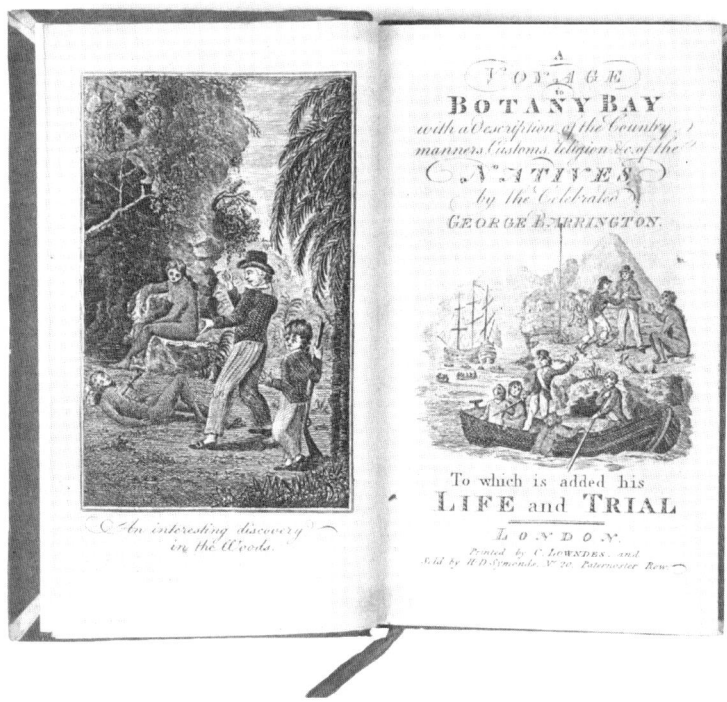

This frontispiece and pictorial title page, parts of a single engraved plate, were used in a number of the Symonds *Voyage* editions. The plate was modified at least twice to reflect changes to the price and additions to the text. The example shown here is from a copy of the combined edition of the *Voyage* and *Sequel* (**AB21a-b**). Hordern House Rare Books.

AB21b

In this version, the *Voyage* section has been reprinted. The text remains the same but there are important changes in the typography, the most obvious being the substitution of a short 's' for the original long 's' throughout the text. The misnumbering of p. 30 is corrected here, and there is no colophon at the end of the *Voyage* section (see **AB17**). The sheets that make up the *Sequel* section of **AB21b**, however, are identical to those of **AB20** (and **AB21a**). This suggests that while the *Voyage* continued to sell well enough to merit reprinting, the *Sequel* was not successful as a separate publication.

The combined edition of the *Voyage* and *Sequel* was advertised in *The Times* of 4 January 1802.

DOP: c. 1801–1802

References: None found (the combined edition has generally been regarded as two separate works)

Copies: ML (8 copies), NLA (4 copies), SLQ, SLWA, BL, BNF, ANU, Melbourne (3 copies), Sydney (2 copies), Oxford, Kansas, Texas, UC, Newberry, NYPL, PEM

AB22   A | VOYAGE | TO | NEW SOUTH WALES, | COMPRISING AN | INTERESTING NARRATIVE | OF THE | TRANSACTIONS AND BEHAVIOUR OF THE CONVICTS; | *THE PROGRESS OF THE COLONY*; | AN OFFICIAL REGISTER | OF THE | Crimes, Trials, Sentences and Executions, | THAT HAVE TAKEN PLACE: | A Topographical, Physical, and Moral Account of the Country, | Manners, Customs, &c. of the Natives. | AS LIKEWISE | *AUTHENTIC ANECDOTES* | OF THE MOST DISTINGUISHED CHARACTERS, | AND | Notorious Convicts that have been Transported to | BOTANY BAY. | [*rule*] | By GEORGE BARRINGTON, | PRINCIPAL SUPERINTENDANT OF THE CONVICTS. | [*rule*] | TO WHICH IS ANNEXED | HIS LIFE AND TRIAL. | [*rule*] | *DUBLIN:* | PRINTED FOR P. WOGAN, W. PORTER, H. FITZ- | PATRICK, N. KELLY, AND J. STOCKDALE. [*rule*] | 1801.

12mo. 16.5 x 10 cm. [i] title, [ii] blank, [iii] dedicatory letter, [iv] blank, [v] + vi–x contents, xi–xvi 'Contents to Second Part.', [1] + 2–9 'Life of George Barrington', 9–13 'Particulars Relating to the Trial and Conviction of George Barrington', [14] blank, [15] + 16–132 *Voyage* text, 133–236 *Sequel* text, 237–240 'Prices of the various articles of Stock…', [241] + 242–244 'An Official Register of the Crimes, Trials, and Executions…' pp.

An 'unauthorised' reprint of the combined *Voyage* and *Sequel* published by Symonds and Lowndes (**AB21a-b**). The contents of this version are virtually identical to **AB21a-b**, with only some minor differences in the setting out of the work. The *Voyage* and *Sequel* sections of the work have drop-head titles 'A Voyage to New South Wales Part I.' and 'A Voyage to New South Wales Part II.' respectively, but the chapter arrangement is continuous, with the *Voyage* covering chapters I–XV, and the *Sequel* chapters XVI–XXVII. The section 'Particulars relating to the Trial and Conviction of George Barrington' runs on from the 'Life of George Barrington', separated only by a rule (p. 9). The 'Official Register of the

Crimes, Trials and Executions…' at the end of the *Sequel* text is here rearranged so that it is set out in normal 'portrait' orientation, as distinct from the Symonds' editions (**AB18**, **AB20**, **AB21a-b**) where this section is unpaginated and printed in 'landscape' orientation (lengthways across the page).

The ML copy at Dixson 80/64 has the signature of a contemporary owner: 'Wallop Brabazon | Dublin Nov 30th | 1801 4/4'.

DOP: 1801
References: Ferguson 325
Copies: ML (4 copies), NLA (2 copies), BS

A | VOYAGE | TO | NEW SOUTH WALES, | COMPRISING AN | AB23
INTERESTING NARRATIVE | OF THE | TRANSACTIONS &
BEHAVIOUR OF THE CONVICTS; | *THE PROGRESS OF THE
COLONY*; | AN OFFICIAL REGISTER | OF THE | Crimes, Trials,
Sentences and Executions, | THAT HAVE TAKEN PLACE: | A
Topographical, Physical, and Moral Account of the Country, | Manners,
Customs, &c. of the Natives. | AS LIKEWISE | *AUTHENTIC ANECDOTES*
| OF THE MOST DISTINGUISHED CHARACTERS, | AND |
NOTORIOUS CONVICTS THAT HAVE BEEN TRANSPORTED TO |
BOTANY BAY. | [*double rule*] | By GEORGE BARRINGTON, | PRINCIPAL
SUPERINTENDANT OF THE CONVICTS. | [*double rule*] | TO WHICH
IS ANNEXED | HIS LIFE AND TRIAL. | [*rule*] | Cork: | PRINTED BY
GEORGE CHERRY, | CIRCULATING LIBRARY, ST. PATRICK' STREET.
| [*rule*] | 1801.

8vo. 17 x 10 cm. [i] title, [ii] blank, [iii] dedicatory letter, [iv] blank, [v] + vi–viii contents,
ix–xii 'Contents to the Second Part', [1] + 2–7 'Life of George Barrington', [8] + 9–10
'Particulars relating to the Trial and Conviction of George Barrington', [11] + 12–102
Voyage text, 103–178 *Sequel* text, 179–181 'Prices of the various articles of Stock…', [182] +
183–185 'An Official Register of the Crimes, Trials and Executions…', [186] blank pp.

Another reprint of the combined *Voyage* and *Sequel* published in Ireland in 1801. The similarities in arrangement of the work – and the almost identical title page – strongly suggest that this work was produced using the Dublin edition (**AB22**) as its copy text (or possibly vice versa). The typeface used in this edition is smaller than that of **AB22**, however, cutting down the length of the book.

DOP: '1801'
References: Ferguson 326
Libraries: ML (2 copies), NLI

AB24   *BARRINGTON's* | VOYAGE | TO | BOTANY BAY | IN | NEW SOUTH
WALES; | WITH A | *Description of the Country, & its Productions;* | THE |
MANNERS, CUSTOMS, RELIGION, &c. | OF THE | NATIVES, | *In the*
Vicinity of the SETTLEMENT, | With the Manner of Treatment, and
present comfortable Situation of | the Convicts: State of Agriculture, &c.
&c. | Written by himself, | SUPERINTENDANT OF THE CONVICTS AT
PARRAMATTA, | AND SENT TO HIS FRIEND IN ENGLAND. | [*rule*] |
NEWCASTLE: | PRINTED BY M. ANGUS AND SON, IN THE SIDE. |
[*rule*] | 1801.

8vo. 17 x 10.5 cm. [1] title, [2] dedicatory letter, [3] + 4–48 text pp.

A reprint of the abridged *Voyage* produced by the Newcastle printing
firm of Margaret Angus and Son. Again, this work has the typographical
idiosyncrasies and uses much the same text as the other abridged
versions (see **AB2**). This version makes some further abridgements to
the text, however, leaving out parts of 'Barrington's' ramble from the last
chapter of the original *Voyage* (i.e. parts of pp. 27–31 of **AB2**) – including
the description of Yeariana as a 'beautiful Oriental Creole'. Since these
omissions remove any suggestion of cross-cultural sexual *frisson* from the
text, it is possible that they were made deliberately as a bowdlerisation.

DOP: '1801'
References: Ferguson 324
Libraries: ML (2 copies), NLA (2 copies)

AB25   *BARRINGTON's* | VOYAGE | TO | BOTANY BAY, | IN | NEW SOUTH
WALES; | WITH A | *Description of the Country, & its Productions;* | THE |
MANNERS, CUSTOMS, RELIGION, &c. | OF THE | NATIVES, | *In the*
Vicinity of the SETTLEMENT; | With the Manner of Treatment, and pre-
sent comfortable Situation of | the Convicts: State of Agriculture, &c. &c.
| Written by himself, | SUPERINTENDANT OF THE CONVICTS AT
PARRAMATTA, | AND SENT TO HIS FRIEND IN ENGLAND. | [*rule*] |
PRINTED FOR J. LETBE, | *By M. Angus & Son, Newcastle.* [*rule*] | 1801.

8vo. 15 x 9.5 cm. [1] title, [2] dedicatory letter, [3] + 4–48 text pp.

The text and layout of **AB25** and **AB24** are all but identical; however, it is clear that the work was reprinted, probably from standing type. Apart from the different title pages, there are a few very minor printing differences: a different decorative rule is used on p. 39, for example, and in the chapter heads on p. 42, **AB24** has 'Conducted to Par- | ramatta' while **AB25** has 'Conducted to | Parramatta'.

DOP: '1801'
References: Ferguson 323
Copies: ML, NLA

A VOYAGE | TO | NEW SOUTH WALES, | COMRISING AN | **AB26**
INTERESTING NARRATIVE | OF THE | TRANSACTIONS AND
BEHAVIOUR OF THE CON-| VICTS: | *THE PROGRESS OF THE*
COLONY; | AN OFFICIAL REGISTER | OF THE | CRIMES, TRIALS,
SENTENCES, AND EXECUTIONS | THAT HAVE TAKEN PLACE: | *A*
Topographical, Physical, and Moral Account of the Country, | *Manners,*
Customs, &c. of the Natives. | AS LIKEWISE | *Authentic Anecdotes* | OF THE
MOST DISTINGUISHED CHARACTERS, | AND | NOTORIOUS
CONVICTS THAT HAVE BEEN TRANSPORTED TO | BOTANY BAY. |
[*rule*] | *By George Barrington,* | PRINCIPAL SUPERINTENDANT OF THE
CONVICTS. | [*rule*] | TO WHICH IS ANNEXED | HIS LIFE AND TRIAL.
| [*rule*] | *New-York:* | PRINTED BY JOHN SWAIN.

8vo. 21 x 13 cm. [i] blank, [ii] title, [iii] blank, [iv] dedicatory letter, [v] blank, [1] + 2–7
'Life of George Barrington', [8] + 9–10 'Particulars relating to the Trial and Conviction of
George Barrington', [11] + 12–102 *Voyage* text, 103–178 *Sequel* text, 179–180 'Prices of the
various Articles of Stock…', 181–184 'An Official Register of the Crimes, Trials and
Executions…', [185]–[186] blank pp.

An American reprint of the combined *Voyage* and *Sequel*. A number of factors suggest that this work was produced using one of the Irish reprints (i.e. **AB22** or **AB23**) – rather than the London original (i.e. **AB21a-b**) – as its model. The title page replicates that of **AB22** and **AB23**, outlining the contents of the work as a whole, rather than following **AB21a-b**, which retain separate title pages for the *Voyage* and *Sequel* sections. As in the Irish reprints, the pagination and chapter organisation are continuous, with the *Voyage* and *Sequel* texts demarcated by dropheads: 'A Voyage to New South Wales' (p. [11]) and 'A Voyage to New South Wales | [*rule*] | Part II.' (p. 103). The 'Official Register of the Crimes, Trials and Executions' following the *Sequel* text is also presented with the same 'portrait' orientation found in **AB22** and **AB23**, rather than the 'landscape' orientation of **AB21a-b**.

A number of estimations of the date of publication of this work have been made, ranging from '[1796?]' to '1803' (see EAI). It is possible that the work was published as early as 1801, though it may have been somewhat later. The ML copy (DSM 991/14Q1) has the date '1805' inked in underneath the imprint at the bottom of the title page, and on the verso of the blank leaf at the end of the work there is a contemporary signature: 'Fra˘ [*illegible*] Jr [?] 15ᵗʰ Feb˘ 1806'. It also seems possible that this work – which bears only the imprint of the printer, John Swain – may have been the combined edition of the 'Barrington' *Voyage* and *Sequel* advertised by the New York bookseller William Durell in mid-1802 (see **AB27**).

DOP: c. 1801–1805
References: Ferguson 327, EAI
Copies: ML, NLA (2 copies), LOC, UNSW, Bowdoin, Dartmouth, Chicago, JJC, Michigan, Minnesota, Rutgers, Yale, BA, CHS, NYHS (2 copies)

AB27   A Voyage to New South Wales… [Published by] William Durell, No. 106 Maiden-lane [New York].

Not seen.

This work was advertised in New York newspapers from July to September 1802. No extant copies under Durell's imprint are known. The description of the work in the advertisement suggests it was an American reprint of the combined *Voyage* and *Sequel*:

> This Day is Published | by William Durell, No. 106 Maiden-lane | (Price 75 cents) | A Voyage to New South Wales— | Comprising an interesting Narrative of the transactions and behaviour of the Convicts, &c. &c. | A topographical, physical and moral account of the country, manners, customs, &c. of the Natives. | Likewise, authentic Anecdotes of the most distinguished Characters that have been | transported to Botany Bay. By George Barrington, Principal Superindant [sic] of the | Convicts. To which is added, his Life and Trial. (*American Citizen and General Advertiser*, 22 July 1802)

It is possible that the work advertised by William Durrell was the combined *Voyage* and *Sequel* edition printed by John Swain (i.e. **AB26**).

DOP: July 1802
References: None found
Copies: None known

THE | FRAUDS | AND | *CHEATS OF LONDON* | DETECTED. | [*double*   **AB28**
rule] | BY THE CELEBRATED | *GEORGE BARRINGTON,* | Principal
Superintendent of the Convicts at Botany Bay. | [*double rule*] | [*vignette*] |
[*double rule*] | EMBELLISHED WITH WOOD CUTS, | Engraved by
R. AUSTIN, PAUL'S ALLEY, BARBICAN. | [*double rule*] | LONDON: |
Printed by A. Macpherson, Russell-court, Drury-lane, | FOR | J. LEE, NO. 12,
KING-STREET, COVENT GARDEN. | 1802. | PRICE ONE SHILLING.

12mo [BL – seen only in facsimile]. [I] blank, [II] frontispiece, [i] title, [ii] blank, [iii] +
iv–vi preface, [vii] + viii–xii index, [13] + 14–80 text pp.

This was a reprint of an earlier work entitled *The Frauds and Cheats of
London Detected* (London: Alexander Hogg, [1778]), republished under
Barrington's name.

There are ten woodcuts in the work, including the title page vignette (of
a woman carrying a bag walking through a forest), and various ornaments and illustrations through the text (at the foot of pages vi, xii, 30,
32, 42, 51, 62, 64 and 74). In addition, there is an engraved frontispiece
plate, depicting the inside of a public house where a shady character
examines an object in his hand, while a well-dressed woman sits at a table
writing on some papers and a man next to her looks on with an expression
of surprise. Another shifty looking character looks in on the scene from
the background. Above the illustration is the title: 'Frontispeice' [*sic*],
while below it is the legend: 'Two Ring Dropers [*sic*] defrauding M^{rs}. R |
in S^t. James' Park of 200 Pounds'.

Originally issued in paper wrappers, preserved in the BL copy. On the
outside front cover is printed:

THE | FRAUDS | AND | CHEATS OF LONDON | *DETECTED.* | [*double rule*] | BY THE
CELEBRATED | GEORGE BARRINGTON, | Principal Superintendent of the Convicts at
Botany Bay. | [*double rule*] | LONDON. | *Printed by A. Macpherson, Russell-court, Drury-lane,*
| FOR | J. LEE, 12, KING-STREET, COVENT-GARDEN. | [*rule*] | Price One Shilling. |

[*double rule*] | *Of whom may be had* | The Valentine Writer, on Love and | Marriage, for 1802 - - 1 0 | Art of Acting; or, a Display of the | Dramatic Passions - - - 0 6 | Original Stories; or, the Ruins of Tusculum - - - 0 6

DOP: '1802'
References: Ferguson 342
Copies: BL, Yale, CLL

AB29a–b   *THE* | HISTORY | *of* | NEW SOUTH WALES, | *including* | *BOTANY BAY,* | *Port Jackson, Pamaratta, Sydney,* | and all its | DEPENDANCIES, | *from the* *Original Discovery of the Island:* | with | *the Customs and Manners of the* *Natives,* | and an Account of | THE ENGLISH COLONY, | *–from its–* | *FOUNDATION to the PRESENT TIME.* | by | GEORGE BARRINGTON: | *superintendant of the Convicts.* | [*rule*] | *Enriched with beautiful Coloured* *Prints.* | [*vignette*] | LONDON: | *Printed for M. JONES, No. 1, Paternoster* *row:* | —1802.—

8vo. 22 x 13.5 cm. [i] half-title, [ii] printer's name, [iii] blank, [iv] frontispiece, [v] title, [vi] blank, [vii]–[viii] 'The Publisher to the Reader', [ix]–[xlvi] contents, [1]–[2] 'Dedication to His Majesty', [3]–[4] preface, [5]–[6] introduction, [7] + 8–505 text, [506] blank, [507] 'A List of the Coloured Prints', [508] blank, [509] 'Particular Directions to the Binder', [510] blank. With 13 additional leaves of plates. Page 447 is misnumbered '477'.

The *History of New South Wales* was an ambitious and elaborate 'new' work, published in tandem with an expanded version of the *Voyage* (**AB30**). The text was for the most part a plagiaristic rewriting of David Collins' *Account of the English Colony in New South Wales* (volume 1, 1798). Along with other preliminary materials ventriloquising 'Barrington's' increasingly grandiose aims as a colonial historian, the work included a dedication to the King (pp. [1–2]).

The *History* was first published in 14 weekly numbers, priced at one shilling each, from November 1802 to February 1803 – a complete copy of the work in parts in their original paper wrappers survives in the collection of the NLA (FRM F344). The fourteenth number contained only one leaf of the text (pp. 505–[506]) and was composed mainly of preliminary and supplementary materials (such as a half-title, table of contents, and list of plates) for binding the work in an octavo volume, along with an advertisement – 'The Publisher to the Reader' – which pro-

Plate illustrating a kangaroo, from *The History of New South Wales* (**AB29a-b** and **AB47**). Hordern House Rare Books.

moted the forthcoming 'Republication, much enlarged, of *Barrington's Voyage to New South Wales, with his Life, Trials, Speeches*, &c. &c.'.

The expanded *Voyage* and the *History* were intended to form a two-volume set, which was advertised as 'Barrington's New South Wales', with the *History* forming the second volume of the set. The two volumes of 'Barrington's New South Wales' were reissued as a 26-part publication, commencing in February 1803, November 1803 and again in July 1805, and bound copies of the two-volume set (priced at 27s.) were available from July 1803. Despite these multiple issues of the work, the uniformity of the printing in all copies I have surveyed indicates that only one impression was made (that is, until a new edition appeared in 1810 – see **AB47**). The engraved title page of the work was however modified and reissued – the original **(AB29a)** has 'Pamaratta', an error the subsequent version **(AB29b)** corrects to 'Parramatta', without making any other changes.

Extant copies of this work exhibit a wide variety of different collations. As the publisher principally distributed the work in parts, individual subscribers – and probably also trade buyers – assembled and bound the work themselves. Since only the text of the *History* is paginated, there is an understandable degree of variation in the placement of the preliminary material in extant copies; it is also common to find parts of the apparatus omitted, or material from the other volume of 'Barrington's New South Wales' (i.e. **AB30**) collated with **AB29a-b** (and vice versa).

The *History* was issued with 15 hand-coloured plates (including the engraved title page). These depicted various flora and fauna of New South Wales, some 'native customs', and the town of Sydney. The illustrations were engraved by Vivian Woodthorpe, whose name is found as 'V. Woodthorpe sc' or 'Woodthorpe sc' below each of the plates. The 'List of the Coloured Prints' named 21 illustrations; some plates, such as 'Botany', featured multiple subjects, and there was an additional woodcut 'View of the New Church at Parramatta' incorporated in the text (p. 503). The following is a list of the plates, with their title and imprint:

1. 'Sydney' | 'Published Dec. 24. 1802, by, M. Jones, Paternoster Row.'
2. [Title page, with vignette of a black swan.]
3. 'A Male and Female Native' | 'Published Nov. 1. 1802, by M. Jones, Paternoster Row.'
4. 'Manhood' | 'Published Dec 17 1802, by M. Jones Paternoster Row'.
5. 'Burning the Dead' | Published, Decr. 3, 1802, by, M. Jones, Paternoster Row'.
6. 'Courtship' | 'Published November 13 by M. Jones, Paternoster Row'
7. 'A Native Dog'. | 'Published Nov. 6. 1802, by M. Jones Paternoster Row'.

8. 'Kangaroo' | 'Published Dec. 13. 1802, by M. Jones Paternoster Row'
9. 'Bird of Paradise' | 'Published, Dec 24, 1802, by M. Jones, Paternoster Row.'
10. 'Black Cockatoo'. | 'Published November 13 1802, by M. Jones Paternoster Row'
11. 'Hornbill' | 'Published Novr. 26, 1802, by M. Jones Paternoster Row.'
12. 'Mountain Eagle' | 'Pub. Novr 7 -1802, by M. Jones, Paternoster Row'.
13. 'Emu'. | 'Published Dec. 31. 1802 by M. Jones Paternoster Row.'
14. 'Blue Snake' and 'Black and White Snake'. | 'Published Dec. 31 1802, by M. Jones Paternoster Row'.
15. 'Botany'. | 'Published Jan. 21-1803, by M. Jones, Paternoster row'.

In the 'Particular Directions to the Binder', the publisher gave specific directions for 'placing the Prints', though as it is common to find plates bound out of order in extant copies it seems these instructions were infrequently followed. The 'Particular Directions to the Binder' page also included a label which could be cut out, 'intended for those which are only boarded'. The label reads: 'BARRINGTON's | HISTORY OF | *New South Wales*. | With 20 Subjects, | beautifully coloured. | *Price* 14s. 6d. *Boards*. | 1803.'

Half-title: 'THE | HISTORY | OF | NEW SOUTH WALES. | [*double rule*] | By GEORGE BARRINGTON, | OFFICER OF THE PEACE AT PARAMATTA. | [*double rule*] | *Price* 14s. 6d. *in Boards*.' On the verso of the half-title page is the printer's statement: '[*double rule*] Printed by W. Flint, Old Bailey, London. [*double rule*]'. A colophon, 'W. Flint, Printer, Old Bailey, London.' appears at the foot of the last page of text (p. 505).

DOP: First issued November 1802 – February 1803
References: Ferguson 344, 345, 345a, 345aa
Copies: ML (8 copies), NLA (8 copies), SLQ (2 copies), SLSA, SLV, LoC, NLI, Adelaide, ANU, La Trobe, Melbourne, Newcastle, Sydney (2 copies), Queensland, Edinburgh, London, Harvard, Kansas, Minnesota, Princeton, Texas, UCD, Virginia, Yale, QM, StP, BA, Newberry, NYHS, NYPL

An | ACCOUNT | —of— | *A VOYAGE* | to | NEW SOUTH WALES, | — **AB30** by— | GEORGE BARRINGTON, | *Superintendant of the Convicts*, | — TO— | which is prefixed a Detail of | HIS LIFE, TRIALS, SPEECHES, &c.

&c. | *Enriched with beautiful Colour'd Prints.* | [*vignette*] | LONDON. | *Printed for M. Jones, No. 1, Paternoster row.* | —1803.—

8vo. 22 x 13.5 cm. [i] blank, [ii] frontispiece, [iii] title, [iv] blank, [v]–[vii] preface, [viii]–[x] introduction, [xi] dedicatory letter ['1793'], [xii] dedicatory letter ['1802'], [1] + 2–72 'Life of George Barrington', [73] + 74–467 text, [468]–[472] index pp. With 11 additional leaves of plates. Page 333 is misnumbered '33'.

An expanded version of the *Voyage*, incorporating a great deal of additional material plagiarised from the first volume of David Collins' *Account of the English Colony in New South Wales* (1798). The extended *Voyage* text is preceded by a 'Life of George Barrington', which was rewritten from the Kearsley *Memoirs* (**B2**, **B4**, **B5**). Along with other prefatory material giving the publishers' motives for bringing the elaborately reworked *Voyage* before the public – and following the text of the '1793' dedicatory letter which had appeared with the original *Voyage* (**AB1**) and all its subsequent manifestations – **AB30** includes a new dedicatory letter, dated 'March 1802', which purports to give the author's reasons for writing the revised edition:

> To Mr. ****
>
> DEAR SIR,
>
> The long silence which I have observed, must have led my friends to conclude that I had relinquished all my European connections,—that from some untoward accident, or the natural visitation of Providence, they would never hear from me more; but that not being the case, after assuring them that it merely proceeded from the multiplicity of business, and the unceasing vigilance my situation demanded. Besides, since my last, I have resolved on writing a regular History of the country, from the first establishment of the Colony to the end of the year 1801, seeing every day since the growing importance of this promising country. I have also corrected and much enlarged the printed copy of my *Voyage*, of the reception of which, in Old England, you gave me such a very flattering account. This was peculiarly gratifying to my heart, and has encouraged me to complete my History, which, with the corrected copy of the Voyage, I herewith transmit to you, for nothing gives me greater happiness than having fulfilled my promise, and added a little to the entertainment of so worthy a friend and patron.
>
> On the morning I left London, on my way down to the ship, I well remember your *
>
> Your grateful
>
> Obliged humble servant,
>
> GEORGE BARRINGTON.
>
> *Parramatta, March, 1802.*

This work was published in tandem with 'Barrington's' *History of New South Wales* (**AB29a-b**), forming a two-volume set advertised as 'Barrington's New South Wales'. The *Account of a Voyage* was originally published in numbers, priced at one shilling each, from February 1803, immediately following the first publication of **AB29a**. The twelve parts of the *Account of a Voyage* were combined with the fourteen of the *History* (reissued) in a single twenty-six part series. This twenty-six part series was recommenced in November 1803 and July 1805, and bound copies of the two-volume set were available from mid-1803 (see also entry for **AB29a-b**). The *Account of a Voyage* was intended as the first volume in the 'Barrington's New South Wales' set; 'Vol. 1' was stamped on every printed sheet, appearing at eight-page intervals through the text.

As 'Barrington's New South Wales' was issued in a single 26-part sequence, it is unsurprising that many extant copies of **AB30** are collated with parts of the preliminary material (and sometimes some of the illustrations) from **AB29a-b**. Since **AB30** was intended as the first volume of the set, it is particularly common to find the table of contents issued with (but referring only to the text of) the *History*, bound with the preliminaries of the *Account* (see e.g. NLA F367, ML Dixson 80/65).

AB30 was published with thirteen hand-coloured plates (including the engraved title page). In a slip of 'Directions to the Binder, For Placing the Prints', the publisher indicated the desired order in which these should be placed in a bound volume. The plates were engraved by Vivian Woodthorpe, who is credited as 'V. Woodthorpe sc' or 'Woodthorpe sc' below the plates (with the exception of no. 5 below, which is unsigned). The following is a list of the illustrations, with the title and imprint as they appear on the plates:

1. [Frontispiece portrait (see below)] 'Pub. March 25 - 1803 by M. Jones Paternoster-row.'
2. [Engraved title page, with vignette of an Aboriginal woman fishing from a canoe.]
3. 'The Cape of Good Hope.' | 'Published by M. Jones Paternoster row. Mar 19. 1803.'
4. 'The Peak of Teneriffe.' | 'Pub. by M. Jones Paternoster Row, Feb^r. 26. 1803.'
5. 'A Plan of New South Wales' [folding map] | 'Pub^d. April 2^d. 1803 by M. Jones Paternoster row.'
6. 'Spotted Hyena' and 'Camelopard' [no imprint].

7. 'Entrance of the Paramatta River.' | 'Pub. March 25. 1803. by M. Jones Paternoster-row.'

8. 'South View of Sydney'. | 'Published by M. Jones, Paternoster-row Mar.1-1803'.

9. 'Town and Cove of Sydney.' | 'Pub. by M. Jones Paternoster-Row March 18. 1803.'

10. 'East View of Sydney.' | 'Published by M. Jones. Paternoster Row. Feb.5.1803.'

11. 'A Native Family.' | 'Publishd by M. Jones, Paternoster-row, Feb'.1-1803'

12. 'Pinchgut Island' | 'Pub. March 11.1803 by M. Jones Paternoster Row.'

13. 'Garden Island.' | 'Pub. March 5 1803 by M. Jones, Paternoster Row.'

The frontispiece portrait of Barrington in this work is clearly designed to further the myth of his authorship. It shows Barrington in half-profile, seated in front of a small table. The long, slender fingers of the former pickpocket are conspicuous: in his right hand he holds a quill, and in the left, he holds a half-opened book. Writing is visible on the last page of the book, as if to suggest that the portrait captures the moment Barrington had just completed his latest work. Beneath the oval frame of the portrait is the legend: 'Engraved from a Miniature Picture in the possession of Mrs. Crane.' Beneath that is the caption: 'GEORGE BARRINGTON, | Late Officer of the Peace, | at Paramatta. | Pub. March 25 - 1803 by M. Jones Paternoster-row.'

DOP: First issued February–April 1803
References: Ferguson 366, 367
Copies: ML (5 copies), NLA (3 copies), SLSA, SLQ, SLT, BL, LOC, NLI, ANU, Adelaide, Melbourne, Newcastle, Sydney, Tasmania, Queensland, UNSW, London, Nottingham, Oxford, Harvard, Kansas, Texas, UCD, Yale, BA, BEC, Newberry, NYPL, StP

AB31 BARRINGTON's | *ANNALS OF SUICIDE,* | OR | HORRORS OF SELF-MURDER; | WHETHER IMPELLED BY | LOVE, | PENURY, | DEPRAVITY, | MELANCHOLY, | BIGOTRY, | REMORSE, OR | JEALOUSY. | [*rule*] | *Calcutated to deter even the most wretched from this horrible Crime,* | AND ENABLE THEM TO BEAR | *WITH FORTITUDE THE ILLS OF THIS LIFE,* | BY A COMPARATIVE VIEW OF THE MISERIES OF SOME | OF

THEIR FELLOW-CREATURES. | [*double rule*] | BY THE CELEBRATED |
GEORGE BARRINGTON, | AUTHOR OF THE NEW LONDON SPY, &c.
| [*double rule*] | London: | PRINTED FOR TEGG AND CASTLEMAN, |
No. 122, St.-John-street, West Smithfield. | [*rule*] | 1803. | J. H. HART, Printer,
23, Warwick-Square.

12mo. 18 x 10.5 cm. [i] blank, [ii] frontispiece, [1] title, [2] blank, 3–4 'Advertisement',
5–107, [108] + 109–179, [180] + 181–215, [216] + 217–239, [240] + 241–251, [252] text pp.
With three additional leaves of plates.

The *Annals of Suicide* contains some 23 tales centred on the theme of
suicide, the first of which, 'Dreadful History of Anaboo, A Native of New
Holland, Who Killed Herself Through Love', is narrated by 'Barrington'.
The work also includes a prefatory 'Advertisement', subtitled 'Extract of
a Letter from the celebrated George Barrington, to his Friend J—, in
London, dated Paramatta, May 22, 1802'. The text of the 'Extract' is as
follows:

"It is with the greatest satisfaction, that I inform you of my having arranged and
completed the materials which I have been so long collecting; you will recollect, that I
was compelled to leave my native country before I could receive some valuable and
interesting memoirs from Spain and Italy; part of them have been transmitted to me by
a faithful friend; and, while I was considering what I should substitute instead of the
remainder, a melancholy instance of *Self-murder* occurred within a few miles of this
place.—Yes, my dear friend, the Demon of *Suicide* has spread its baneful contagion as far
as the inhospitable shores of New Holland: the unhappy native, who put an end [p. 4] to
her existence, was so interesting, and the circumstances attending her deplorable *exit* so
lamentable, that I am induced to begin this collection with it.—The memoirs which I
send you are, I have every reason to suppose, the only complete and authentic *History of
Self-Murder* which has ever been published; they may be well called the *Horrors of Suicide!*
as they describe the agonies of those unhappy wretches, who put an end to their days, in
such glowing colours, that we may indulge the hope that this publication will produce the
most beneficial effects, and deter the unhappy from shortening the days, of which they
must render an account to the Omnipotent. That it may produce this effect is my most
fervent prayer. Adieu, my dear friend; Wheeler and his brother desire their kind
remembrance:— do not forget us.

Barrington's Annals of Suicide was advertised at the end of June 1803 as
being about to be published in six fortnightly parts, priced at one shilling
each. The colophon of the printer, J. H. Hart, appears regularly through
the text of extant copies, and it seems likely that the original parts

corresponded to pages [1]–68, 69–108, 109–144, 145–[180], 181–[216], 217–[252] of the text. There is an additional colophon on p. [240], and it is possible that the initial publication was actually split into seven parts to maximise profit – in which case pp. 217–[240] and 241–[252] would have formed the sixth and seventh parts.

Four engraved plates were included in *Barrington's Annals*, with the artwork and engraving performed by a number of different artists including Isaac Cruickshank, Thomas[?] Vaughan, John[?] Page and James[?] Barlow. The following is a list of the illustrations with titles and imprints:

1. Frontispiece: '*Cruickshank del.* | *Page sc.* | SUICIDE OF ANABOO. | *Pub*^{d}*. by Tegg and Co. 23 Warwick Lane. June 19-1803.*'
2. Facing page 61: 'ELIZA [depicting a woman in a cell, about to cut her wrists with a razor] *Vaughan delin* | *Hollier sc* | *Pub. Aug. 1-1803 by Tegg & Co. 23 Warwick Square*'
3. Facing page 121: 'No. 3. [man, standing over a dead, half-naked woman, stabbing himself in the heart] *Vaughan delin* | *Barlow sculp.*'
4. Facing page 181: 'No. 4. [man and woman aiming pistols at each other] *Vaughan delin* | *Barlow sculp.*'

By the time *Barrington's Annals of Suicide* was published, the firm of Tegg and Castleman was in financial trouble and was giving the printer's address as the address of the firm (see *Derby Mercury*, 30 June 1803). Some time later in the year, a new title page was printed giving this new address and retitling the work *Biographical Annals of Suicide* (see below, **AB32**).

DOP: June 1803
References: Ferguson 365a
Copies: NLA, Syracuse, Huntington

AB32   BIOGRAPHICAL | *ANNALS OF SUICIDE,* | OR | HORRORS OF SELF-MURDER, | WHETHER IMPELLED BY | LOVE, | MELANCHOLY, | PENURY, | BIGOTRY, | DEPRAVITY, | REMORSE, OR | JEALOUSY. | [*rule*] | *Calculated to deter even the most wretched from this horrible Crime,* | AND ENABLE THEM TO BEAR | *WITH FORTITUDE THE ILLS OF THIS LIFE,* | BY A COMPARATIVE VIEW OF THE MISERIES OF SOME | OF THEIR FELLOW-CREATURES. | [*double rule*] | By GEORGE BARRINGTON. | [*double rule*] | London: | PRINTED FOR TEGG AND

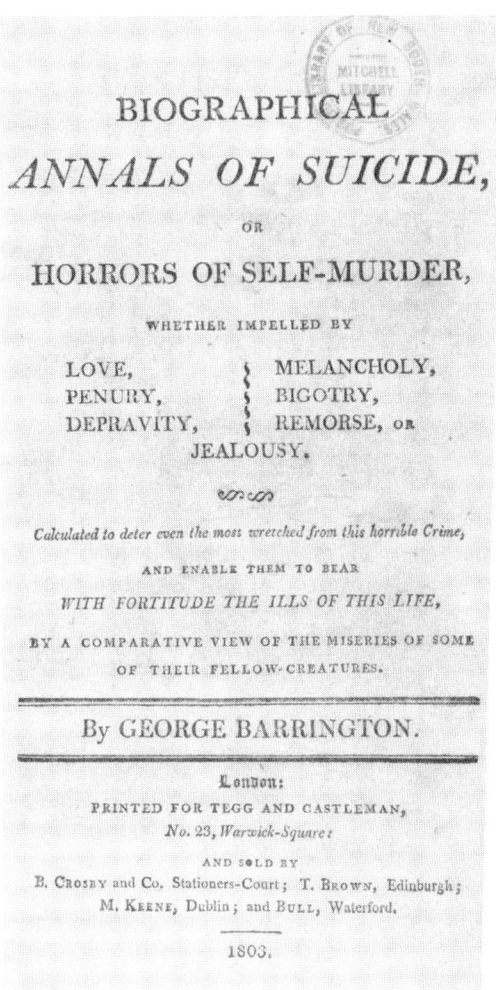

BIOGRAPHICAL
ANNALS OF SUICIDE,

OR

HORRORS OF SELF-MURDER,

WHETHER IMPELLED BY

LOVE,	MELANCHOLY,
PENURY,	BIGOTRY,
DEPRAVITY,	REMORSE, OR
	JEALOUSY.

Calculated to deter even the most wretched from this horrible Crime,

AND ENABLE THEM TO BEAR

WITH FORTITUDE THE ILLS OF THIS LIFE,

BY A COMPARATIVE VIEW OF THE MISERIES OF SOME
OF THEIR FELLOW-CREATURES.

By GEORGE BARRINGTON.

London:
PRINTED FOR TEGG AND CASTLEMAN,
No. 23, Warwick-Square:

AND SOLD BY
B. CROSBY and Co. Stationers-Court; T. BROWN, Edinburgh;
M. KEENE, Dublin; and BULL, Waterford.

1803.

Title page of the *Biographical Annals of Suicide* (**AB32**). Courtesy of Mitchell Library, State Library of New South Wales.

CASTLEMAN, | *No. 23, Warwick-Square:* | AND SOLD BY | B. CROSBY and Co. Stationers-Court; T. BROWN, Edinburgh; | M. KEENE, Dublin; and BULL, Waterford. | [*rule*] | 1803.

Physical description and collation as for **AB31**.

This was a reissue of the sheets of **AB31**, with a new title page giving an altered title and a new address for Tegg and Castleman. There were also new publishers listed in the imprint, who had presumably agreed to take a share in the publication. The University of Virginia's copy of this work, from the Sadleir-Black collection, has an added title page: '*Marvellous Magazine and Compendium of Prodigies* Vol. 4.'

DOP: 1803
References: Ferguson 365
Copies: ML, NLA, LOC, NLI, SLV, Monash, Virginia, LCP

AB33 ПУТЕШЕСТВІЕ | ВЪ | БОТАНИ-БАЙ, | СЪ | ОПИСАНІЕМЪ | *СТРАНЫ, НРАВОВЪ, ОБЫЧАЕВЪ* | и | *РЕЛИГІИ* | ПРИРОДНЫХЪ ЖИТЕЛЕЙ, | *Славнво Георгія Баррингтона,* | *Переведенное съ третъяго Изданія* | Д.С.С.К.А.Г. | [*rule*] | *съ дозволенія Университетскаго Цензора.* | [*rule*] | МОСКВА, 1803. | Въ Университетской Типографіи, | *у Любія, Гарія и Попова.*

8vo. 21 x 13 cm. [1] title, [2] blank, [3]–4 preface, [iii] + iv–vi contents, 5–6 [introduction], [7] + 8–171 text, [172] blank pp.

Russian edition of the *Voyage*, translated by Prince Aleksei Golitsyn, and published in 1803 by the Moscow University Printer. Golitsyn's translation was made from the French edition of 1797–1798 (**AB9**), and is arranged with similar explanatory notes.

A transliterated version of the title appears in the ML catalogue:

Puteshestvie v Botani-Bai : s opisaniem strany, nravov, obychaev i religii prirodnykh zhitelei | Georgïia Barringtona.... Moskva: V Universitetskoi Tipografïi u Liubïia, Garïia i Popova

The title page of this work is reproduced in facsimile in Rickard, p. 42 (plate 10).

DOP: '1803'
References: Ferguson 368
Copies: ML

AB34 AN | ACCOUNT | OF | A VOYAGE | TO | *NEW SOUTH WALES*, | Interspersed with | LIVELY ANECDOTES, | INCLUDING | A Description of the ludicrous Ceremony of | DUCKING and SHAVING, | Which is punctually observed by all Seaman in crossing the | Equinoctial Line; | *And an interesting Narrative of all the Transactions and | Behaviour of the Convicts.* | [*rule*] | BY GEORGE BARRINGTON, | Superintendant of the Convicts. | [*rule*] | TO WHICH IS PREFIXED, | His very interesting and extraordinary | LIFE AND TRIALS, SPEECHES, &c. | [*rule*] | LONDON: | Printed by W. FLINT, Old Bailey, for M. JONES, No. 1, Paternoster-Row. | {Price 14s. in Boards.}

8vo. 22 x 13.5 cm. [i] blank, [ii] extract from a review, [iii] blank, [iv] frontispiece, [v] title, [vi] blank, [vii]–[ix] preface, [x]–[xii] introduction, [xiii] dedicatory letter ('1793'), [xiv] dedicatory letter ('1802'), [1] + 2–72 'Life of George Barrington', [73] + 74–467 text, [468]–[472] index pp.

A reissue of the sheets of **AB30** under a modified title; the title page of this version was printed rather than engraved as in the former work. It is possible that this version was issued with the frontispiece plate as the only illustration – the NLA copy has no plates other than this. This version includes a new preliminary leaf, on the verso of which is an extract from the review of the original *Voyage* (**AB1**) that had appeared in the *Monthly Review* in December 1795.

Frontispiece: as for **AB30**, **B20**.

DOP: c. 1803–1810?
References: Ferguson 367a
Copies: NLA, SLSA

TALES OF WOE. | [*double rule*] | LOVE & CONSTANCY, | OR THE | **AB35**
FATAL DENIAL, | A TRUE STORY; | LEONORA, | OR THE | *EFFECTS OF TREACHERY;* | AND THE | LOVER'S LEAP, | OR THE | SINGULAR EFFECTS | OF | *JEALOUSY AND HONOR,* | A PATHETIC TALE. | [*double rule*] | And running furiously to the brow of the cliff, he precipitated | himself from that amazing height, and was dashed to pieces. | BARRINGTON. | [*double rule*] | London: | PRINTED FOR TEGG AND CASTLEMAN, | *No.* 111, *Cheapside;* | Champante and Whitrow, Aldgate; T. Hughes, Stationer's-Court; | J. Belcher, Birmingham; B. Sellick, Bristol: T. Troughton, Liver- | pool; T. Brown, North-Street, Edinburgh; Wilson and Spence; | York; T. Binns, Leeds; J. Dingle, Bury St. Edmunds; T, Brown; | Bath; B. Dugdale, Dublin; M. Swindels, Manchester; J. Booth; | Norwich; and G. Wilkins, Derby. | [*double rule*] | *T. Plummer, printer, Seething-lane.*

8vo. 18 x 10.5 cm. [i] blank, [ii] frontispiece, [iii] title, [iv] blank, 181–215 + [216] text pp.

This work is a repackaged part of the *Annals of Suicide* (**AB31**, **AB32**), nominally in a new series: 'Tales of Woe'. 'Barrington' still appears on the title page, though the name is not prominently displayed. Apart from the new title page and frontispiece, the work simply reused the sheets from the *Annals*; though 'T[homas] Plummer' appears on the title page as the printer, the bulk of the printing was that previously done by J. H. Hart, whose colophon appears on p. [216].

It is possible that other parts of the *Annals of Suicide* were republished in the same 'Tales of Woe' series, though no other manifestations are known. The University of Virginia's Sadleir-Black collection contains another chapbook, *Eliza, or the Unhappy Nun...*, formed from the printed sheets of another section of the *Annals of Suicide* (pp. [73]–107) – although the new title page to this publication does not include Barrington's name.

The frontispiece illustration shows a woman seated at a desk, with quill in hand and paper before her. Beneath the illustration is the legend: 'The Fatal Denial', and underneath the frame is the imprint: 'London. Published 2nd. Jan.' 1804.'

DOP: '1804'
References: Ferguson 365a
Copies: NLA

AB36 BARRINGTON'S | NEW LONDON SPY, | OR THE | Frauds of London | DETECTED; | BEING A COMPLETE DISCLOSURE OF ALL THE DARK TRANSAC- | TIONS IN AND ABOUT THE CITIES OF | LONDON AND WESTMINSTER: | TO WHICH IS PREFIXED, | BELCHER's | TREATISE ON THE ART OF BOXING. | [*vignette*] | BY THE CELEBRATED | GEORGE BARRINGTON, | *Principal Super-intendant of the Convicts at Botany-bay, and Author of the* | Annals of Suicide. | [*rule*] | THE THIRD EDITION. | [*rule*] | London: | PRINTED for THOMAS TEGG, No. 111, *Cheapside*, | By J. H. HART, 23, Warwick-Square. | [*rule*] | Price *One Shilling and Sixpence.*

8vo. 18 x 11 cm. [I] blank, [II] frontispiece, [i] title, [ii] blank, [iii] + iv 'Preface to the Third Edition', [vi] + vii–x contents, [9] + 10–80 text, [81] + 82–84 'A Treatise on Boxing' pp.

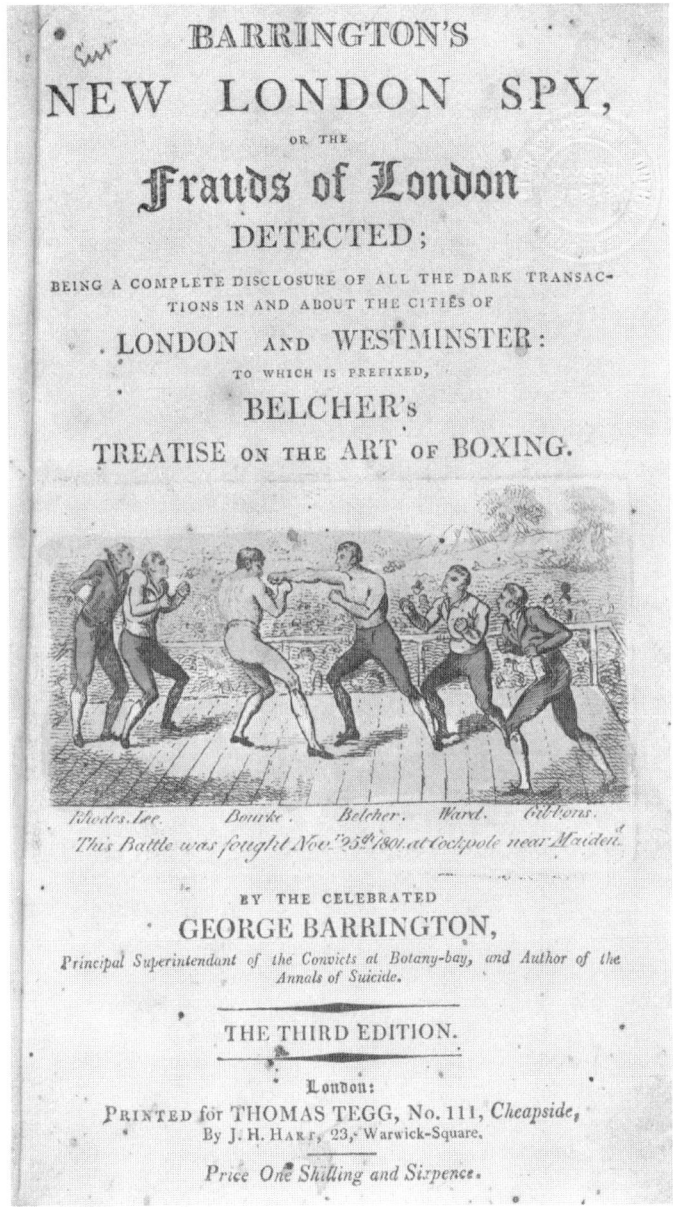

Barrington's New London Spy was another republication of the *Frauds of London Detected*, again using Barrington's name (see **AB28**). The 'Third Edition' is the earliest known extant copy of the work under Thomas Tegg's imprint, though as 'Barrington' was promoted as 'Author of the London Spy, &c.' on the title page of *Barrington's Annals of Suicide* (**AB31**), it does seem likely that Tegg published an earlier edition(s). The text of this edition is the same as that of **AB27**, but for the addition of a 'Treatise on Boxing' attributed to the prizefighter Jem Belcher, which, though said to be 'prefixed' to the work, actually follows the main text.

The frontispiece in this edition was produced from the same plate used in **AB28**, with the same misspelling 'Frontispeice' appearing above the illustration, and the same legend below it. The vignette on the engraved title page depicts a boxing match. Beneath the vignette the characters' names are given, from left to right: '*Rhodes. Lee. Bourke. Belcher. Ward. Gibbons. | This Battle was fought Nov..ʳ 25..ᵗʰ 1801. at Cockpole near Maidenᵈ.*'

The ML catalogue (based on a bookseller's description) gives the date of this publication as [c. 1801]; however, advertisements suggest that Tegg left the firm 'Tegg and Castleman' and moved to 111 Cheapside at the start of 1804.

Colophon (foot of p. 84): 'Printed by J. H. Hart, 23, Warwick-Square.'

DOP: c. 1804
References: Ferguson 385
Copies: ML

AB37   Barrington's New London Spy for 1805, or the Frauds of London detected; to which is added, An Appendix, containing A Sketch of Scenes, and Characters, in a ramble through the Metropolis: Being a complete disclosure of all the dark Transactions in and about the Cities of London and Westminster. By the celebrated George Barrington, Principal Superintendent of the Convicts at Botany Bay, and Author of the Annals of Suicide. Also, A Treatise on the Art of Boxing By Mr. Belcher. The Fourth Edition, considerable enlarged. London: Printed for Thomas Tegg, at his Circulating Library, No. 111, Cheapside. Price One Shilling and Sixpence.

12mo. [ii, frontispiece and pictorial title page], xii, 140pp [not seen – Ferguson].

The 'Fourth Edition' of *Barrington's New London Spy for 1805* was the first to add the 'Appendix' which appeared in all subsequent editions (see **AB39**, also **AB40**, **AB42**, **AB43**, **AB49**). Ferguson's description of the frontispiece and pictorial title page match those that appear in **AB39**.

Pictorial title: 'Barrington's New London Spy for 1805. [Coloured cut of a boxing match.] London: Printed for Thomas Tegg, No.111 Cheapside. Price One Shilling and Sixpence.' (Ferguson)

DOP: '1805'
References: Ferguson 400
Copies: BL

BIBLIOTHÈQUE | GÉOGRAPHIQUE ET INSTRUCTIVE | DES | **AB38**
JEUNES GENS, | OU | RECUEIL | DE VOYAGES INTÉRESSANTS, |
Dans toutes les parties du monde. | *Pour l'instruction et l'amusement de la jeunesse;* | Traduit de l'allemand et de l'angl. par M. BRETON. | Orné de cartes et figures. | SECOND ANNÉE. | TOME HUITIÈME. | VOYAGE DE BARRINGTON. | A PARIS, | Chez J. E. Gabriel DUFOUR, libraire, rue des | Mathurins, n° 7. | Et à Amsterdam, chez le même. | 1806.

18mo. 13.5 x 8.5 cm. [i] half-title, [ii] printer's name, [iii] blank, [iv] frontispiece, [v] title, [vi] blank, [1] drop-head title [*and text begins*] + 2–200 text, [201] + 202–204 contents pp.

A French version of the Barrington *Voyage* published as part of a collection of voyage narratives arranged for young readers, the *Bibliothèque Géographique et Instructive des Jeunes Gens...*, published in Paris by J. E. Gabriel Dufour. The collection was divided into six 'years' (though actually published over three years, 1804–1807) containing twelve volumes each; the Barrington narrative appeared as the eighth book in the second 'year' of the collection. The full title of the 'Barrington' text was given as a drop-head title on the first page of text (p. [1]):

[*double rule*] VOYAGE | ET | TRANSPORTATION | DU FAMEUX BARRINGTON | A
BOTANY-BAY, | DANS LA NOUVELLE-HOLLANDE. | [*rule*] | [*text begins*]

The collection as a whole is usually attributed to Johann Heinrich Campe, the German pedagogue and author of popular collections of travel narratives adapted to young readers. However, the *Bibliothèque Géographique* significantly expanded the number of voyage narratives that had appeared in Campe's original German publications, with one of the works added to the French collection being the 'Barrington' *Voyage*. It is interesting to note that the title page of this volume does not mention Campe (though earlier volumes in the collection had), and the translations were said to be made both from German and English.

In fact, the *Voyage et Transportation du Fameux Barrington* appears not to have been a translation at all, but rather an adaptation of the earlier French translation of 'Barrington's' *Voyage* (i.e. **AB12**). The text here includes the concluding paragraph introduced in **AB12**, where 'Barrington' laments his exile from England (which did not appear in any English versions), and other sections of the *Voyage et Transportation du Fameux Barrington* are very similar to the earlier French edition. However, the language and style of the earlier translation was significantly altered in adapting the work for children, and new material was also added. The text is arranged in eight chapters, with the first not drawn from the 'Barrington' *Voyage* but instead consisting of a brief history of European exploration in 'Nouvelle-Holland' (pp. [1]–12). There is also a new conclusion to the text (pp. 195–200), which claims that Barrington had married his fictional love-interest in the *Voyage*, Yeariana, going on to note that the penal colony included a number of Irish prisoners transported for their political views, and to suggest that the 'compagnie' at Botany Bay was not so bad as might be expected from a place intended as a receptacle for criminals. The text concludes with some verses on Botany Bay by the French poet Jacques Delille (pp. 199–200).

The frontispiece illustration to this work depicts the initial encounter between 'Barrington' and his young companion Tim and the 'natives', Yeariana and Palerino – this is the same scene depicted in the frontispiece plate in Symonds' 'Fourth Edition' and *Voyage to Botany Bay* editions, and was presumably inspired by that illustration (see **AB9**, **AB10**, **AB17**, **AB21a-b**). The *Voyage et Transportation du Fameux Barrington* version is a more elegant engraving than the Symonds version, however, and shows 'Barrington' cradling the wounded Palerino in his arms, while a concerned Yeariana emerges from a nearby cave. As in the Symonds illustration, Palerino is shown with a protruding arrow, rather than the 'spear' mentioned in the text, and Tim carries a musket. Both 'natives' here are wearing loin-cloths, probably because of their more active poses; in the Symonds illustration both were naked. At the top left of the illustration is printed '*Barrington*' and at top right '*Page 174*'. Below the illustration is the legend: 'Barrington sauve la vie à un jeune sauvage'.

The printer's statement 'DE L'IMPRIMERIE DE CRAPELET.' appears on the verso of the half-title leaf (p. [ii]).

DOP: '1806'
References: Monglond, p. 1212, Huguet 175
Copies: BNF, INRP

BARRINGTON's | NEW LONDON SPY | FOR 1807; | OR, | The Frauds of   **AB39** London Detected: | To which is now added, | AN APPENDIX, | Containing | A *Sketch of Night Scenes and notorious* | *Characters*, | IN A | RAMBLE THROUGH THE METROPOLIS; | *Being a complete Disclosure of all the dark Trans-* | *actions in and about the Cities of* | LONDON AND WESTMINSTER. | [*rule*] | BY THE CELEBRATED | GEORGE BARRINGTON, | Principal Superintendant of the Convicts at Botany-bay, and | Author of the Annals of Suicide. | [*double rule*] | Also, | *A TREATISE ON THE ART OF BOXING*, | BY MR. BELCHER. | [*double rule*] | FIFTH EDITION, CONSIDERABLY ENLARGED. | [*double rule*] | London: | Printed for THOMAS TEGG, Apollo Library, No. 111, | Cheapside; WILSON and SPENCE, York; and | DENHAM and DICK, Edinburgh.

12mo. 14 x 9 cm. [I] blank, [II] frontispiece, [III] pictorial title page, [IV] blank, [i] title, [ii] printer's name, [iii] + iv–vi preface, [vii] + viii–xii contents, [13] + 14–134 text, [135] + 136–140 'Treatise on Boxing' pp. With three additional leaves of plates.

While labelled as 'considerably enlarged', the 'Fifth Edition' of Tegg's *Barrington's New London Spy* apparently contained identical material to the 'Fourth Edition' (see **AB37**). The only textual difference between this work and the 'Third Edition' (**AB36**) is the 'Appendix' described in the title, the text of which was plagiarised from *The Modern London Spy* (Alexander Hogg, c. 1781) – presumably the same 'Appendix' used in **AB37**. In the 'Fifth Edition', the 'Appendix' is actually incorporated into the 'Barrington' narrative (pp. 103–34) distinguished only by a heading on p. 103. The 'Preface to the Fifth Edition' is identical to the preface of the 'Third Edition', except that, at its conclusion, 'Barrington' gives a puff for a new Tegg publication:

> I would also advise all young women attentively to read my little volume, they will learn from it many good lessons. If they wish to peruse the true History of an Unfortunate Girl, they will immediately give orders for "*Dr. Pratt's Life of a Lady of Pleasure*, price only 1s. by which they will see that Virtue is its best reward, and all her paths are peace.

Like **AB37**, **AB39** includes an engraved frontispiece illustration depicting a seated man being threatened by a top-hatted figure carrying a club, while two female figures in the background look on. Beneath the illustration is the artists' imprint 'Designed by Craig. / Engraved by Freeman', and beneath that is the title: 'The Bully and the Countryman'. Facing the frontispiece is an engraved pictorial title page, giving the title:

> Barrington's | New | London Spy | or | The Frauds of London Detected, | 1807. | [*vignette*] | London. | Printed for Thomas Tegg, | No. 111 Cheapside.

The vignette illustration depicts two men engaged in a boxing match.

There are also three further coloured engravings interleaved through the text, providing pictorial depictions of various nefarious activities:

1. Facing p. 37, the illustration depicts a large woman, seated inside a house, conversing with a young woman who stands in the doorway. A male figure looks in from a window. Beneath the illustration is the legend 'Mrs Matthews decoying the Innocent Lucy'. Below this is the imprint 'London, Published by Thos. Tegg No. 111, Cheapside.'
2. The illustration which had featured as the frontispiece to **AB27** and **AB36**. Although clearly the same design, the illustration has been re-engraved to fit the smaller format of this edition. The heading 'Frontispeice' has been excised, but the legend – 'Two Ring Dropers [sic] defrauding M^{rs}. R | in S^t. James' Park of 200 Pounds' – has been preserved.
3. Facing p. 105, the illustration of a boxing match which had previously featured as the vignette on the pictorial title page of **AB36**.

Though the 'Fifth Edition' was entitled *Barrington's New London Spy for 1807*, it was actually issued in parts in September–October 1806: the publication of the first number was advertised in the *Derby Mercury* of

18 September 1806. The advertisement stated that the work was to be completed in four weekly numbers at sixpence each; the three extra leaves of illustrations listed above were presumably issued with each part. It is possible that this work was later issued without the extra plates: the ML copy at 364/B has only the frontispiece and pictorial title page.

The printer's name – 'W. Lewis, Printer, Paternoster-Row' is given on the otherwise blank verso of the title page, and appears as 'Printed by W. Lewis, Paternoster-Row' as a colophon at the foot of the last page of text.

DOP: September–October 1806
References: Ferguson 438
Copies: ML, NLA (2 copies), LOC, Princeton

BARRINGTON's | NEW LONDON SPY | FOR 1808; | OR, | The Frauds of **AB40** London Detected: | To which is now added, | AN APPENDIX, | Containing | *A Sketch of Night Scenes and notorious* | *Characters,* | IN A | RAMBLE THROUGH THE METROPOLIS; | *Being a complete Disclosure* *of all the dark Transactions* | *in and about the Cities of* | LONDON AND WESTMINSTER, | [*rule*] | BY THE CELEBRATED | GEORGE BARRINGTON, | Principal Superintendant of the Convicts at Botany-Bay, and | Author of the Annals of Suicide. | [*double rule*] | ALSO, | *A* *TREATISE ON THE ART OF BOXING,* | BY MR. BELCHER. | [*rule*] | SEVENTH EDITION, CONSIDERABLY ENLARGED. | [*double rule*] London: | Printed for THOMAS TEGG, No. 111, Cheapside; | WILSON AND SPENCE, York; and DENHAM | and DICK, Edinburgh.

12mo. 15 x 9.5 cm. [I] blank, [II] frontispiece, [i] title, [ii] blank, [iii] + iv–vi 'Preface to the Seventh Edition', [vii] + viii–xii contents, [13] + 14–130, 127 [i.e. 131], 132, 129–134 [i.e. 133–138] text, [139] + 136–140 [i.e., 140–144] 'A Treatise on Boxing' pp.

A further reprint of *Barrington's New London Spy*, the 'Seventh Edition' was textually identical to the 'Fifth Edition' (**AB39**). The printing and design is less elegant than in **AB39**, however, and there are errors in the pagination. The 'Preface to the Seventh Edition' omits reference to Tegg's *An Unfortunate Girl* (see **AB39**), concluding with: 'I would also advise all young women attentively to read my little volume, they will learn from it many good lessons'.

The frontispiece used in this edition is 'Mrs Matthews decoying the Innocent Lucy' (see **AB39**, illustration 1).

Once again, it is possible that this work was issued in different forms. The ML copy lacks the frontispiece, and the title page has been pasted onto other sheets of paper, to serve as a paper board cover for the work.

Colophon (foot of p. 140): 'T. Plummer, Printer, Seething-lane.'

DOP: '1808'
References: Ferguson 459
Copies: ML, Melbourne, UWM, CLL

AB41   THE | HISTORY | OF | NEW HOLLAND, | FROM ITS | FIRST DISCOVERY IN 1616, TO THE PRESENT TIME. | WITH A | Particular Account | OF ITS | *PRODUCE AND INHABITANTS*; | AND A | DESCRIPTION OF BOTANY BAY. | ALSO, | *A List of the Naval, Marine, Military and Civil Establishment*. | TO WHICH IS PREFIXED, | AN INTRODUCTORY DISCOURSE | *ON BANISHMENT*, | BY THE | RIGHT HONOURABLE WILLIAM EDEN. | [*rule*] | BY GEO. BARRINGTON. | *The Second Edition, illustrated with MAPS*. | [*double rule*] | London: | PRINTED FOR JOHN STOCKDALE, PICCADILLY. | *Price Six Shillings*. | 1808. | [*rule*] | {Entered at Stationer's Hall.}

8vo. 21 x 13 cm. [I] folding map, [i] title, [ii] blank, [iii] + iv–xxvi preface, [xxvii] + xxviii–xxxii 'Discourse on Banishment', [xxxiii] + xxxiv–xxxv contents, [xxxvi] blank, [xxxvii] folding map, [1] + 2–254 text pp.

This work was a reissue of the second edition of the publisher Stockdale's *History of New Holland*, a compilation from the journals of Cook and other sources published in 1787, soon after the decision to found the colony. The only newly printed material in the so-called 'second edition' of 1808 was the cancel title page attributing the work to Barrington. This spurious attribution has seen the 1787 edition also attributed to Barrington in some modern sources.

The map preceding the title page is an incomplete world map entitled 'A General Chart of the Passage from England to Botany Bay in New Holland. 1787.', showing the proposed route of the First Fleet. Under the map in script is the imprint: 'London: Publish'd as the Act directs Jany. 1st 1787. by John Stockdale Piccadilly.', and to the right, 'Drawn and

Engrav'd by J. Andrews'. The map on p. [xxxvii] is divided into two sections. The larger section on the right is a map of the South Pacific and South-East Asia with 'New Holland' and 'New Zeeland' prominent, entitled 'A General Chart of New Holland, including New South Wales & Botany Bay. with The Adjacent Countries, And New Discovered Island'. To its left is a closer survey of part of the New South Wales coastline, entitled 'Chart of Botany Bay, with its Adjacent Harbours in New South Wales'. Beneath the map is the imprint: 'Published Novr. 4, 1786, by J. Fielding, Pater-Noster Row, London.', and to the right the imprint of the artist 'Hatcett sc.' Fielding had published a version of the *History of New Holland* before selling his copyright and stock of the work to Stockdale.

Issued in paste boards, with a spine label reading: 'Barrington's | History | of | New Holland | [*double rule*] | Price 6s. | [*double rule*]'. The NLA copy is an example of the work in this state.

DOP: '1808'
References: Ferguson 458
Copies: ML (3 copies), NLA, BL, BNF, Harvard

Barrington's New London Spy for 1809... Also, A Treatise on the Art of Boxing, by Mr. Belcher. Seventh edition ... enlarged. **AB42**

12mo. 140 pp. [not seen – BL].

DOP: c. 1808–1809
References: None found
Copies: BL, CLL

BARRINGTON's | NEW LONDON SPY; | OR, | The Frauds of London Detected: | To which is now added, | AN APPENDIX, | Containing | *A Sketch of Night Scenes and notorious* | *Characters*, | IN A | RAMBLE THROUGH THE METROPOLIS; | *Being a complete Disclosure of all the dark Transactions* | *in and about the Cities of* | LONDON AND WESTMINSTER, | [*rule*] | BY THE CELEBRATED | GEORGE BARRINGTON, | Principal Superintendant of the Convicts at Botany-bay, and | Author of the Annals of Suicide. | [*double rule*] | ALSO, | *A TREATISE ON THE ART OF BOXING,* | BY MR. BELCHER. | [*double rule*] | EIGHTH EDITION, CONSIDERABLY ENLARGED. | [*double* **AB43** *rule*] | LONDON: | PRINTED FOR THOMAS TEGG, | NO. 111, CHEAPSIDE.

12mo. 15.5 x 9 cm. [I] blank, [II] frontispiece, [i] title, [ii] printer's name, [iii] + iv–vi 'Preface to the Present Edition', [vii] + viii–xii contents, [13] + 14–138 text, [139] + 140–144 'Treatise on Boxing' pp.

Another reprinting of Tegg's *Barrington's New London Spy*, with the same text as the 'Fifth' and 'Seventh' editions (**AB39**, **AB40**). The 'Preface to the Present Edition' is the same as the 'Preface to the Seventh Edition' in **AB40**. Like **AB40**, this edition lacks a pictorial title page, and the frontispiece is still 'Mrs Matthews Decoying the Innocent Lucy' (see **AB39**, illustration 1; **AB40**)

As in previous editions, the printer's name – in this case, 'H. Lemoine, Printer, | Chiswell-street, London.' – appears on the otherwise blank verso of the title page, and as the colophon at the foot of the last page of text as 'H. Lemoine, Printer, 38, Chiswell-street, London.'.

DOP: c. 1808–1811
References: Ferguson 487a
Copies: NLA, NLS, CLL

AB44   THE | LONDON SPY: | OR, THE | Frauds of London | DESCRIBED: | BEING | A COMPLETE DISCLOSURE | OF ALL THE | *DARK TRANSACTIONS* | In and about that great City. | [*rule*] | BY THE CELEBRATED | GEORGE BARRINGTON, | Superintendant of the Convicts at BOTANY BAY. | [*rule*] | [*woodcut*] | FALKIRK: | PRINTED BY T. JOHNSTON. | 1809.

8vo. 16.5 x 9.5 cm. [1] title, [2] + 3–24 text pp.

A much abridged chapbook version of the 'Barrington' *London Spy*. The preface has been reduced to three paragraphs, and the whole text radically cut down: here only the sections on 'Gamblers', 'Sharpers', 'Swindlers', 'Pickpockets', 'Money-Droppers' and 'Ring-Doppers' are included.

Besides the woodcut on the title page, a small woodcut illustration appears at the foot of p. 20. These illustrations are the crude variety of woodcut reminiscent of those found in early eighteenth-century chapbooks. The illustration on the title page shows what appears to be a gallows scene, with a male figure at the centre flanked by a distressed woman to his left and a soldier at arms to his right. The cut on p. 20 shows a man with his arms outstretched, carrying indistinguishable objects in each hand.

DOP: '1809'
Copies: NLA, BL
References: Ferguson 479

ПУТЕШЕСТВІЕ Георгія *Барингтона* въ Ботани-Бай, съ описаніемъ   **AB45**
страны, нравовъ, обычаевъ и религіи природныхъ жителей; перев. съ
Франц. Князь Алексей Голицынъ; M. 1809.

8vo [not seen – Sopikov].

A further Russian edition of the 'Barrington' *Voyage*, published in Moscow in 1809. This was presumably the same translation as the 1803 Moscow edition; the translation here is also attributed to Prince Aleksei Golitsyn, and stated to be from the French [edition of the *Voyage*] (see **AB33**). The title as recorded by Sopikov is different from that of the earlier work, however; Sopikov also asserts that this work was intended to form part of a collection of voyage narratives Golitsyn had translated in 1803–1805.

DOP: '1809'
References: Sopikov 9164
Copies: None found

BARRINGTON's VOYAGE | TO | NEW SOUTH WALES; | WITH A | **AB46**
Description of the Country; | THE | MANNERS, CUSTOMS, RELIGION,
&c. | OF | *The Natives* | in the | Vicinity of Botany Bay. | [*rule*] | A New
Edition, by GEORGE BARRINGTON, | Now Superintendant of the
Convicts at PARAMATA, and sent to his | FRIEND in England. | [*printer's
ornament*] | Printed by A. Swindells, Hanging-Bridge. | *Manchester*. | AND
SOLD BY T. THOMAS, AND J. SADLER. | [*rule*] | *Price only Nine-pence*.

12mo. 19 x 13 cm. [1] title, [2] dedicatory letter, [3] + 4–48 text pp.

A later reprint of the *Barrington's Voyage* produced in Manchester by Alice Swindells. Both of the ML copies have a watermark date '1809' on one of their leaves (see pp. 41–42). This is the same text as previously used in **AB11**, **AB13**, **AB15** and **AB16**. The ornament on the title page is the same as found in **AB13**, **AB15** and **AB16**.

Colophon (foot of p. 48): 'Printed by A. Swindells, Hanging-bridge.'

DOP: c. 1810
References: Ferguson 209, 363b
Copies: ML (2 copies), NLA, SLV (2 copies)

AB47   *THE* | HISTORY | *of* | NEW SOUTH WALES, | *including* | *BOTANY BAY*, | *Port Jackson, Parramatta, Sydney,* | and all its | DEPENDANCIES, | *from the Original Discovery of the Island:* | with | *the Customs and Manners of the Natives,* | and an Account of | THE ENGLISH COLONY, | *–from its–* | *FOUNDATION to the PRESENT TIME.* | by | GEORGE BARRINGTON: | *superintendant of the Convicts.* | — | *Enriched with beautiful Coloured Prints.* | [*vignette*] | LONDON: | *Printed for M. JONES, No. 5, Newgate Str*^t. | & Sherwood, Neely, & Jones, | *Paternoster row*, 1810.

8vo. 20.5 x 12.5 cm. [i] blank, [ii] frontispiece, [iii] title, [iv] blank, [v]–[vi] 'Preface to the Second Edition', [1]–[2] 'Dedication to His Majesty', [3]–[4] 'Preface to the First Edition', [5]–[6] introduction, [7] + 8–503 text, [504] + 505–544 'Supplement', [545]–[548] index pp. With 15 additional leaves of plates.

The reprinted 1810 edition of the 'Barrington' *History* slightly enlarged the content of the work without revising the text of the first edition. The whole of the textual material of the first edition was retained unaltered, aside from the excision of two pages at the conclusion of the original text (i.e. **AB29a-b**, pp. 504–505), which were replaced by a 39-page 'Supplement'. The supplement, which is not claimed to be Barrington's work, rehashed a number of travel accounts that had appeared in the press in the first decade of the nineteenth century, along with sketches of 'Remarkable Persons' in the antipodes, including William Bligh, the 'Scottish Martyrs', and one George Bruce, 'an Englishman, married to a Princess of New Zealand'. The preface (as 'Preface to the First Edition') and introduction from **AB29a-b** were included with the preliminaries for the 1810 *History*, along with an additional 'Preface to the Second Edition of Barrington's *History of New South Wales*, &c. &c. &c.', which gives the publishers' ostensible reasons for republishing the work:

> The rapid sale of the first Edition of this entertaining Work, and the frequent demands and enquiries made relative to the same... having induced the publishers to reprint the present Edition, it has been thought proper to extend and enlarge the original plan by a Supplement, bringing down the History of the Settlement to the present Period of 1811.

This printing has no pagination errors, but some sections (see pp. 49–56 and 169–76) are printed in a smaller type and closer spaced than the rest of the text. The 'Supplement' (pp. [504]–544) is also printed in a very small typeface.

Like the first edition, **AB47** was published in tandem with the reissued *Account of a Voyage* (**AB48**) in a twenty-six part series of weekly numbers; advertisements for the 1810 edition(s) referred to the two-volume set as 'Barrington's Botany Bay'. It seems likely that the first issue of this edition was at the outset of 1811. A notice in the *Derby Mercury* for 3 January 1811 advertised the publication of the first number of the twenty-six part series, noting also that 'two handsome volumes in octavo... may be had complete, price 1l. 7s. boards'. As with the 1802–1803 editions of the *History* and *Account*, the 1810 editions were reissued on several occasions. Advertisements announcing the recommencement of publication of the twenty-six weekly numbers appeared in English newspapers in December 1811, July 1813 and January 1815. All these reissues were clearly of the single edition: that is, the printed sheets of 1810. The 1810 edition of the *History* was never reprinted, as is claimed in the 1986 *Addenda* to Ferguson (see Ferguson 999a). Press markings indicating the place of the sheets within the original part publication can be found in all copies (see, for example, foot of p. 97: 'No.3 Hist', p. 185: 'No. VI.', etc.).

However, it is clear that the 1810 *History* was still being sold as late as the mid-1820s. A copy in the collection of the University of Sydney library includes an additional advertisements section bound after the conclusion of the work, advertising the publications of 'Sherwood, Jones & Co.' The advertised works include a magazine, *The Annals of Sporting*, which includes 'A fine portrait of Jerry, the winner of the Doncaster St. Ledger, 1824', along with *The Turf Herald; or Annual Racing Calendar for 1824*, and *The Turf Guide... containing the nominations for 1825*.

As with **AB29a-b**, collations of **AB47** often vary, as subscribers to the publication in parts and bookbinders assembled the preliminary materials in a variety of different ways, often, again, mixing up elements of the *History* with its companion *Account* (**AB48**). There are also anomalies among extant copies, which mix the 1802 and 1810 editions – see for example ML 991/B/c.1, which is a copy of the 1802 printing with the title page of the 1810 edition, and NLA NK5568, which, conversely, is a copy of the 1810 printing with the title page from 1802.

The majority of the illustrations from **AB29a-b** were reused in **AB47**; a 'Directions to the Binder' section printed after the end of the index (p. [548]), gives the desired placement of the plates. Three plates that had originally appeared in the first edition of the *Account of a Voyage* (**AB30**), however, were now placed in the second edition of the *History*. The view of 'Town and Cove of Sydney' was now the intended frontispiece of the *History*, and the plates illustrating 'A Native Family', and the 'Spotted Hyena' and 'Cameleopard', were now also issued as part of **AB47** (see **AB30**, illustrations 6, 9 and 11). The frontispiece from the first edition of the *History* was now issued with the 1810 edition of the *Account* (see **AB29a-b**, illustration 1; see also **AB48**). Some versions of the 1810 *History* have uncoloured plates (see e.g. NLA FC 999a), and the later issued copies also seem to have substituted the frontispiece portrait of Barrington-the-author found in the *Account* editions (**AB30**, **AB34**, **AB48**, also **B18**) for the 'Town and Cove of Sydney' plate found in earlier copies (see e.g. NLA FC 999a, Sydney F487 c.3).

Colophon (p. 544): 'J. Compton, Printer, Middle Street, | Cloth Fair, London.'

DOP: First issued January 1811
References: Ferguson 487, 345aa, 487aaa, 487aa, 999a, 1001a
Copies: ML (5 copies), NLA (6 copies), SLSA, SLV, BL, LOC, Adelaide, ADFA, Flinders, JCU, La Trobe, Melbourne, Monash, Sydney (3 copies), Tasmania, UNSW, Cambridge, Edinburgh, Oxford, Harvard, Kansas, Michigan, Oberlin, Ohio, Pittsburgh, Stanford, Texas, UC, HHT, Rockdale, StP, CSL, DPL, Newberry, PLC

AB48   *An* | ACCOUNT | —of— | *A VOYAGE* | to | NEW SOUTH WALES, | — by— | GEORGE BARRINGTON, | *Superintendant of the Convicts*, | — TO— | which is prefixed a Detail of | HIS LIFE, TRIALS, SPEECHES, &c. &c. | *Enriched with beautiful Colour'd Prints*. | [*vignette*] | LONDON. | *Printed for M. Jones, No. 5, Newgate Street*. | *and* Sherwood, Neely, & Jones, *Paternoster Row*, 1810.

8vo. 21 x 12 cm. [i] blank, [ii] frontispiece, [iii] title, [iv] blank, [v]–[vii] preface, [viii]–[x] introduction, [xi]–[xii] 'Preface to the Reader', [xiii] dedicatory letter ('1793'), [xiv] dedicatory letter ('1802'), [1] + 2–72 'Life of George Barrington', [73] + 74–472 text, [473]–[476] index. With 10 additional leaves of plates. Page 333 is misnumbered '33'.

Like its companion **AB47**, the 1810 edition of the *Account* added a small amount of material without revising the text of the first edition. Unlike **AB47**, however, the second edition of the *Account* was not reprinted, but principally compiled from the printed sheets of the earlier edition (**AB30**). The only newly printed elements in the 1810 edition of the *Account* are a new 'Preface to the Reader', a new index, and a brief additional section at the conclusion of the text (pp. 467–72), which summarises the French explorer François Péron's description of Sydney. The new preface notes Barrington's death 'within a few months after the publication of the first Edition of this Work', but claims that the publishers of the 'new' edition had 'been assisted by a person resident in the colony to whom Barrington bequeathed his papers' ([vii]). The preface goes on to refute the 'reports' that Barrington 'died *insane!*':

> This was so far from being founded on fact, that there was not the least appearance of any thing that might be supposed to have led to such a catastrophe in the conduct of Barrington (p. [viii]).

Like the 1803 *Account*, **AB48** was issued in parts intended to form a two-volume set with the *History* (for notes on the publication of the 1810 *Account* and *History*, see the entry for **AB47**).

The illustrations issued with the 1810 edition of the *Account* were slightly different from those of the first. Three plates which had been issued with **AB30** were now issued as part of the *History* (see **AB47**). Conversely, the view of Sydney (plate title: 'Sydney') which had been used as the frontispiece for the first edition of the *History* now appeared in the 1810 *Account* (see **AB29a-b**, illustration 1). One new plate, illustrating the 'crossing the line' ceremony described in the text of the *Voyage*, appears in the second edition of the *Account*. This is entitled: 'Ceremony of Ducking and Shaving', with the imprint: 'Published May 1-1810, by M. Jones.' Apart from these substitutions and the new plate, all other plates from **AB30** appear with their original titles and imprints. The 'Directions to the Binder' section, which follows the end of the index (p. [476]), includes the engraved title page as one of the plates; making in total twelve plates, one of which was issued with each part of the publication.

DOP: First issued 1811
References: Ferguson 486
Copies: ML (5 copies), NLA (6 copies), SLSA, SLT, SLV, SLQ, BL, LOC,

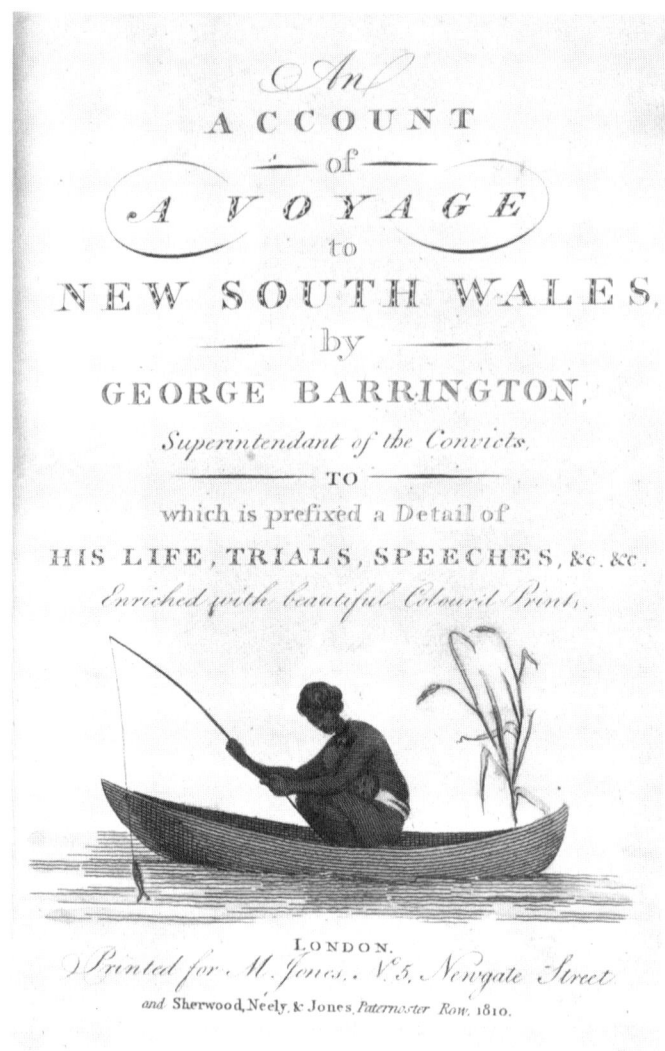

An
A C C O U N T
of
A VOYAGE
to
NEW SOUTH WALES,
by
GEORGE BARRINGTON,
Superintendant of the Convicts,
TO
which is prefixed a Detail of
HIS LIFE, TRIALS, SPEECHES, &c. &c.
Enriched with beautiful Colour'd Prints,

LONDON,
Printed for M. Jones, N°.5, Newgate Street
and Sherwood, Neely, & Jones, *Paternoster Row,* 1810.

Title page of the 1811 edition of *An Account of a Voyage to New South Wales* (**AB48**). Hordern House Rare Books.

Adelaide, ADFA, JCU, Melbourne, Queensland, Sydney (2 copies), Tasmania, UNSW, Oxford, Cambridge, Harvard, Kansas, Michigan, Oberlin, Pittsburgh, Stanford, Texas, UC, Yale, IF, MH, HHT, Rockdale, CSL, DPL, MML, PLC, Newberry, NYPL

BARRINGTON'S | NEW LONDON SPY; | OR, THE | FRAUDS OF **AB49**
LONDON DETECTED: | To which is now added, | AN APPENDIX, |
CONTAINING | *A SKETCH OF NIGHT SCENES AND | NOTORIOUS
CHARACTERS*, | IN A | RAMBLE THROUGH THE METROPOLIS: |
BEING | *A complete Disclosure of all the dark Transactions | in and about the
Cities of* | LONDON AND WESTMINSTER. | [*double rule*] | BY THE
CELEBRATED | GEORGE BARRINGTON, | Principal Superintendant of
the Convicts at Botany- | Bay, and Author of the Annals of Suicide. |
[*double rule*] | ALSO, A | *TREATISE ON THE ART OF BOXING*, | BY MR.
BELCHER. | [*rule*] | NINTH EDITION, CONSIDERABLY ENLARGED. |
[*rule*] | LONDON: | PRINTED FOR THOMAS TEGG, | NO. 111,
CHEAPSIDE.

8vo. 14.5 x 8.5 cm. [I] blank, [II] frontispiece, [i] title, [ii] printer's name, [iii] + iv–vi
preface, [vii] + viii–xii contents, [13] + 14–138 text, [139] + 140–144 'Treatise on
Boxing' pp.

This is the last known version of *Barrington's New London Spy* produced
by Thomas Tegg. Once again, the textual contents are the same as in the
'Fifth Edition' (**AB39**), and the 'Preface to the Present Edition' is
identical to that found in the 'Seventh' and 'Eighth' editions (**AB40** and
AB43). The frontispiece is also the same as in **AB40** and **AB43**, and there
is no pictorial title page.

Although the layout very closely matches that of **AB43**, the work had
once again been reprinted by a different printer. The printer's name – 'J.
Haddon, Printer, Finsbury' appears on the verso of the title page.

Two advertisements for other Tegg publications are included in the text.
At the end of the contents (p. xii) is an advertisement for a new edition
of 'Dr. Johnson's Dictionary of the English Language', claimed to be
edited by Tegg himself and to be published in twenty weekly numbers. At
the foot of the last page of text (p. 144) is an advertisement for the first
number of an edition of 'Shakespeare's Dramatic Works' illustrated by
the artists J. Thurston and R. Rhodes. These works were published in
1812, which was presumably also the date of the 'Ninth Edition' of
Barrington's New London Spy.

DOP: c. 1812–1813
References: Ferguson 530
Copies: NLA, CLL

AB50   THE | London Spy: | OR, THE | *Frauds of London* | DESCRIBED; | BEING | *A COMPLETE DISCLOSURE* | OF ALL THE | Dark Transactions | IN AND ABOUT THAT GREAT CITY. | [*rule*] | BY THE CELEBRATED | *GEORGE BARRINGTON*, | Superintendant of the Convicts at BOTANY BAY. | [*rule*] | BLACKBURN: | *PRINTED AT THE OFFICE OF R. PARKER.* | [*rule*] | 1812. | [*rule*] | *PRICE TWO-PENCE*

16 cm [Melbourne – seen only in facsimile]. [1] title, [2] + 3–12 text pp.

A greatly abridged chapbook redaction of the 'Barrrington' *London Spy*, similar to the version produced in Falkirk by Thomas Johnston (**AB44**), but containing even less textual material. In this version, only truncated versions of the sections on 'Gamblers', 'Sharpers', 'Pickpockets' and 'Money-Droppers' are retained.

Colophon (at foot of p. 12): 'R. Parker, Printer, Blackburn'.

DOP: '1812'
References: None found
Copies: Melbourne

AB51   [*Voyage et Transportation du Fameux Barrington, à Botany-Bay, dans la Nouvelle-Hollande*]

Not seen [bookseller's catalogue – *Librairie du Cardinal*, 2008].

The *Bibliothèque Géographique...*, the French collection of voyage narratives arranged for children in which a version of the 'Barrington' *Voyage* appeared (see **AB38**), was republished by the original publisher J. E. Gabriel Dufour in 1816, with the *Voyage et Transportation du Fameux Barrington* again appearing in the 'Seconde Année of the collection (see **AB38**). Since two later versions of this work exist, reusing the printed sheets of the 1806 edition (see **AB53**, **AB57**), it is reasonable to assume this is also a reissue, rather than a reprinting, of the original work.

DOP: '1816'
References: None found
Copies: None found

GEOGRAFISKT | BIBLIOTEK | FÖR | UNGDOM, | ELLER | *SAMLING* | **AB52**
AF | INTRESSANTA | RESEBESKRIFNINGAR. | TILL | *den uppväxande*
ungdoms nytta och nöje, | af | J. H. CAMPE. | [*rule*] | *ÖFVERSÄTTNING* | af
| D. KRUTMEJER. | [*rule*] | *SEXTONDE DELEN.* | [*rule*] | STOCKHOLM,
1816. | [*rule*] | Tryckt hos *FR. CEDERBORGH & COMP.*

12mo. 15.5 x 9 cm. [i] blank, [ii] frontispiece, [iii] half-title, [iv] blank, [v] title, [vi] blank,
[viii]–[x] contents, [xi] blank, [1] drop-head title [*and text begins*] + 2–148 text pp.

A Swedish translation of the *Voyage et Transportation du Fameux*
Barrington (**AB38**). The Swedish translation closely follows the *Voyage*
et Transportation text, replicating the eight chapter format with the
introductory first chapter on 'New Holland'. The conclusion of the last
chapter is a truncated version of the concluding section of the *Voyage*
et Transportation; however, it does include the claim that Barrington
and Yeariana had married (pp. 147–48). The full title of the 'Barrington'
narrative is given as a drop-head title on the first page of text:

BARRINGTONS | RESA OCH DEPORTATION | TILL | BOTANY-BAY | *i Nya Holland.* |
[*rule*] |

The translator, David Krutmejer, translated sixteen volumes of voyage
narratives for this Swedish collection aimed at young readers, over the
period 1804–1816. While some of these may have been translated from
Campe's German collections of travel narratives adapted for children,
the 'Barrington' narrative, at least, was translated from the French
Bibliothèque Géographique – also attributed to Campe, but in reality a
much expanded collection (see **AB38**). The attribution to Campe of this
work is therefore spurious.

The frontispiece illustration is a remarkably close imitation of the plate
issued with the *Voyage et Transportation du Fameux Barrington* (see **AB38**).
The only differences consist of minor details in the background and the
facial expressions of the characters depicted. Above the Swedish version
of the illustration at top right is 'Pag. 131.', while below at right in faint
script is the attribution 'Grav. af Ruckman.' Below this is the legend:
'*Barrington frälsar en ung Vildes lif.*'

DOP: '1816'
References: Klingberg p. 183
Copies: ML, KB

AB53   THE | HISTORY | OF | *Botany Bay*, | IN | NEW SOUTH WALES; | WITH A | Description of the Country, | *Manners, Customs, Religion,* | *&c. &c.* | OF THE NATIVES; | INCLUDING THE | *PARTICULARS* | OF THE | Treatment of the Convicts, | AND A | *Narrative of a Voyage* | IN A TRANSPORT SHIP THERETO. | [*rule*] | By GEORGE BARRINGTON, | *FORMERLY SUPERINTENDANT OF THE CONVICTS.* | [*rule*] | *LONDON:* | PRINTED AND PUBLISHED BY W. MASON, | 21, CLERKENWELL GREEN. | [*rule*] |

8vo. 17 x 10 cm. [i] blank, [ii] frontispiece, [1] title, [2] blank, [3] + 4–36 text pp.

A later abridged version of the *Voyage*, published as a bluebook pamphlet; the text has no obvious relation to the earlier abridged versions. This version of the work omits the episode of Yeariana and Palerino entirely, concluding with a section from earlier in the final chapter of the original *Voyage* (**AB1**), where 'Governor Phillip' visits Rose Hill (Parramatta) and praises 'Barrington' on the discipline 'manifested in the convicts under my superintendence' (p. 36). The start of the text in this work is introduced by the drop-head title: '*HISTORY* | OF | BOTANY BAY. | [*rule*] | (*In a Letter from George Barrington, a Convict, to* | *his Friend in England.*)' (p. [3]).

The frontispiece illustration shows an Aboriginal warrior aiming a spear at an English officer, while two other English figures behind look on with concern. Beneath the plate is a printed note 'See p. 22.' The passage of the text this refers to describes the incident in which Arthur Phillip was wounded in September 1790 (cf. **AB1**, pp. 85–86).

Dated by Ferguson as '*c.* 1802', this work in fact is likely to have been published in the 1820s; Todd lists William Mason trading at 21 Clerkenwell Green from 1817 to 1829.

Colophon (foot of p. 36): 'W. Mason, Printer, 21, Clerkenwell Green.'

DOP: c. 1817–1829
References: Ferguson 343
Copies: ML, NLA, Monash, Oxford

AB54   BIBLIOTHÈQUE | GÉOGRAPHIQUE | DE LA JEUNESSE, | OU | RECUEIL DE VOYAGES INTÉRESSANS | DANS TOUTES LES PARTIES

DU MONDE, | *Enrichis de Cartes Géographiques coloriées* | ET DE VIGNETTES; | Traduits de l'allemand et de l'anglais, | ET MIS A LA PORTÉE DES JEUNES GENS | PAR M. BRETON. | 1re. SÉRIE.–2e. ANNÉE. | *Tome Huitième*. | A PARIS, | CHEZ G. DUFOUR ET ED. D'OCAGNE, | LIBRAIRES, QUAI VOLTAIRE, N°. 13; | ET A AMSTERDAM, | MÊME MAISON DE COMMERCE. | [*rule*] | 1827.

18mo. 14.5 x 9 cm. [i] half-title, [ii] printer's name, [iii] blank, [iv] frontispiece, [v] title, [vi] blank, [1] drop-head title [*and text begins*] + 2–200 text, [201] + 202–203 contents pp.

The *Voyage et Transportation du Fameux Barrington* again appeared as the eighth book of the second 'year' of the *Bibliothèque Géographique* collection when it was published for a third time in 1826–1828 (see **AB38, AB51**). Identical printing flaws and watermarks on the paper show that this volume was in fact a reissue of the sheets of the 1806 printing (see e.g. **AB54**, p. 15, cf. **AB38**, p. 15); only the title and half-title leaves, and the printed paper wrappers, were newly printed.

The volumes of this later *Bibliothèque Géographique* were issued in blue paper wrappers, with the collection redesigned as a subscription series to be sent by mail. On the front cover of the paper wrappers of the 'Barrington' volume was printed the series title, similar to that above, which also described the publication as a 'nouvelle souscription'. On the back cover was printed the 'Conditions de la Souscription', which stated that, from 15 November 1826, subscribers would receive two volumes sent every 15 days, until the series was complete in May 1828; each delivery of two volumes cost 3 francs with 3 francs for postage.

A printer's statement – 'Imprimerie de Fain, rue Racine, n°.4' – appears on the verso of the half-title leaf, and at the foot of the back cover.

Frontispiece: as for **AB38**.

DOP: '1827'
References: None found
Copies: ML

VIAJE | Y TRANSLACCION DEL FAMOSO | BARRINGTON | A   **AB55**
BOTANI-BAY | EN LA NUEVA-HOLLANDA, | *puesto en español con algunas correcciones* | *y notas* | POR | D. SANTIAGO DE ALVARADO Y DE LA PEÑA, | escribano del ilustre colegio de Madrid, autor y | traducter

de otras muchas obras literarias. | [*rule*] | MADRID: | *Imprenta á cargo de* M. PITA. | *calle de los Remedios n.* 10.

16mo. 11.5 x 8 cm. [1] half-title, [2] blank, [i] blank, [ii] frontispiece, [3] title, [4] blank, [5] + 6–8 Prologo del Traductor, [9] + 10–168 text, [169] + 170–171 'Advertencia del Traductor Alvarado', [172] blank, [173] + 174–188 'Descripcion Geografica de la Nueva-Hloanda', [189] + 190–191 'indice' [actually table of contents], [192] blank pp.

A Spanish translation of the French arrangement of the 'Barrington' *Voyage* for young readers, *Voyage et Transportation du Fameux Barrington* (see **AB38**, also **AB51**, **AB54**, **AB57**). Like the Swedish version (**AB52**), the Spanish translation closely follows the French text, using its eight-chapter format and including the general introduction to 'New Holland' as the first chapter. Almost the whole of the text of the final chapter of the French version is translated here, including the description of Barrington's supposed marriage to Yeariana (pp. 165–66) and the mention of Irish political prisoners (pp. 167–68). Omitted, however, are the verses of Jacques Delille (see **AB38**). The Spanish work does include a few additional elements, such as an advertisement for the translator, an additional section on the geography of 'Nueva-Hloanda' and a history of exploration in the Pacific region.

As with the Swedish edition, the frontispiece illustration in this work is a very close imitation of the plate that appeared in the original French edition (see **AB38**). There is no artist's attribution in the Spanish version; below the illustration is the legend: 'Barrington salva la vida á un joven salvage'.

DOP: c. 1831–1833?
References: None found
Copies: ML, NLA, BNE (2 copies)

AB56   The London spy; or, The frauds of London detected: containing also a sketch of night scenes and notorious characters, in a ramble about the metropolis, being a complete disclosure of all the dark transactions in the cities of London & Westminster. By G. Barrington, ... Also a treatise on boxing... Boston [s.n.], 1832.

16 cm. x, [1], 12–216 pp. front. [not seen – LOC, Harvard catalogues].

An American version of the 'Barrington' *London Spy*, retaining the Belcher 'Treatise on Boxing' from the Tegg editions (see **AB36**, also **AB37**, **AB39**, **AB40**, **AB42**, **AB43**, **AB49**).

DOP: '1832'
References: None found
Copies: LOC, Chicago, Harvard, Minnesota

VOYAGE | ET TRANSPORTATION | DU FAMEUX BARRINGTON | A   AB57
BOTANY-BAY, | Faisant partie séparée de la Bibliothèque | géographique
de la jeunesse, | PAR CAMPE. | [*rule*] | A LYON, | CHEZ J. F. ROLLAND,
LIBRAIRE, | RUE MERCIÈRE, N°39, AU 1er. | 1834.

18mo. 13.5 x 8.5 cm. [i] blank, [ii] frontispiece, [iii] title, [iv] blank, [1] + 2–200 text, [201]
+ 202–203 contents, [204] blank pp.

The Lyon edition of the *Voyage et Transportation du Fameux Barrington*
was a further reissue of the sheets of the 1806 edition printed by Dufour
in Paris (**AB38**, see also **AB51, AB54**). A cancel title page, giving the new
imprint and the statement that the work was taken from the *Bibliothèque
Géographique*, was the only newly printed element.

Frontispiece: as for **AB38**.

DOP: '1834'
References: Rolland
Copies: [Author's collection]

SELECT BIBLIOGRAPHY

ELECTRONIC AND MICROFILM SOURCES

Bodleian Library Broadside Ballads, online (Oxford University), <www. bodley. ox.ac.uk/ballads>.

British Book Trades Index, online (University of Birmingham), <www. bbti.bham.ac.uk>.

British Newspapers 1600–1900, online (British Library and Gale Cengage), <www.gale.cengage.com>.

Early English Newspapers [Burney collection], microfilm (New Haven, Conn.: Research Publications, 1978–2003).

Eighteenth Century Collections Online, online (Gale), <www.infotrac. galegroup.com/galenet/ecco>.

Eighteenth-Century Journals from the Hope Collection at the Bodleian Library, Oxford, microfilm (Marlborough, Wiltshire: Adam Matthew Publications, 2000).

John Johnson Collection of Printed Ephemera, online (Oxford University) <www.bodley.ox.ac.uk/johnson>.

Maxted, Ian, *Exeter Working Papers in British Book Trade History*, online, <http://bookhistory.blogspot.com/2005/12/index.html>.

Oxford Dictionary of National Biography, online (Oxford University), <www.oxforddnb.com>.

Proceedings of the Old Bailey, London 1674 to 1834, online (University of Sheffield), <www.oldbaileyonline.org>.

Records of the Worshipful Company of Stationers 1554–1923, Robin Myers, ed., microfilm (Cambridge: Chadwyck-Healey, 1985–).

The Times Digital Archive 1785–1985, online (Gale), <www.infotrac. galegroup.com/galenet/times>.

PRINTED SOURCES

Atkinson, Alan, *The Europeans in Australia: A History*, vol. 1 (Melbourne: Oxford University Press, 1997).

Box, Sheila, *The Real George Barrington?: The Adventures of a Notorious London Pickpocket, Later Head Constable of the Infant Colony of New South Wales* (Melbourne: Arcadia, 2001).

Branch-Johnson, W., *The English Prison Hulks* (London: Christopher Johnson, 1957).

Clarke, Marcus, *Old Tales of a Young Country* (Melbourne: Trustees of the Public Library, 1871).

Collins, David, *An Account of the English Colony in New South Wales: With Remarks on the Dispositions, Customs, Manners &c. of the Native Inhabitants of that Country. To Which are Added, Some Particulars of New Zealand: Compiled by Permission, From the Mss. of Lieutenant-Governor King* (London: T. Cadell and W. Davies, 1798).

Ferguson, J. A., *Bibliography of* Australia, 7 vols (Sydney: Angus and Robertson, 1941–).

Historical Records of New South Wales, 7 vols (Sydney: Govt. Pr., 1892–1901).

Hunter, John et al., *An Historical Journal of the Transactions at Port Jackson and Norfolk Island: With the Discoveries which have been made in New South Wales and in the Southern Ocean, since the Publication of Phillip's Voyage, Compiled from the Official Papers; including the Journals of Governor Phillip and King, and of Lieut. Ball; and the Voyages from the First Sailing of the Sirius in 1787, to the Return of that Ship's Company to England in 1792* (London: John Stockdale, 1793).

Lambert, R. S., *The Prince of Pickpockets: A Study of George Barrington, Who Left His Country For His Country's Good* (London: Faber, 1930).

Maxted, Ian, *The London Book Trades, 1775–1800: A Preliminary Checklist of Members* (London: Dawson, 1977).

McCalman, Iain, 'Unrespectable radicalism: infidels and pornography in early nineteenth-century London', *Past and Present*, vol. 104, 1984, pp. 74–110.

McCalman, Iain, 'Newgate in revolution: radical enthusiasm and Romantic counterculture', *Eighteenth-Century Life*, vol. 22, no. 1, 1998, pp. 95–110.

Myers, Robin, *The Stationers' Company Archive: An Account of the Records 1554–1984* (Winchester: St Paul's Bibliographies, 1990).

Myers, Robin and Harris, Michael, eds, *Fakes and Frauds: Varieties of Deception in Print & Manuscript* (Winchester: St Paul's Bibliographies, 1989).

Oldham, Wilfrid, *Britain's Convicts to the Colonies* (Sydney: Library of Australian History, 1990).

Petherick, E. A., 'Barrington and the Botany Bay Theatre', *Notes and Queries*, 9th series, vol. 2, 1898, pp. 404–05.

Petherick, E. A., 'George Barrington: Waldron', *The Athenaeum*, 12 February 1898, p. 216.

Rawlings, Phillip, *Drunks, Whores and Idle Apprentices: Criminal Biographies of the Eighteenth Century* (London: Routledge, 1992).

Rickard, Suzanne, ed., *George Barrington's Voyage to Botany Bay: Retelling a Convict's Travel Narrative of the 1790s* (London: Leicester University Press, 2001).

St Clair, William, *The Reading Nation in the Romantic Period* (Cambridge: Cambridge University Press, 2004).

Tench, Watkin, *A Complete Account of the Settlement at Port Jackson, in New South Wales, including an accurate description of the situation of the colony; of the natives; and of its natural productions: taken on the spot* (London: G. Nicoll, and J. Sewell, 1793).

Timperley, C. H., *A Dictionary of Printers and Printing* (London: H. Johnson, 1839).

Todd, William B., *A Directory of Printers and Others in Allied Trades, London and Vicintiy 1800–1840* (London: Printing Historical Society, 1972).

Werkmeister, Lucyle, *The London Daily Press, 1772–1792* (Lincoln: University of Nebraska Press, 1963).

INDEX